Corrections in Canada

Policy and Practice

Second Edition

by

John W. Ekstedt
and
Curt T. Griffiths

School of Criminology
Simon Fraser University

HARCOURT
BRACE
CANADA

Harcourt Brace & Company, Canada
Toronto   Montreal   Orlando   Fort Worth   San Diego
Philadelphia   London   Sydney   Tokyo

Corrections in Canada

Printed and bound in Canada

Canadian Cataloguing in Publication Data

Ekstedt, John W.
   Corrections in Canada: policy and practice

2nd ed.
Includes bibliographical references and index.
ISBN 0-7747-3431-0

1. Corrections – Canada.   I. Griffiths, Curt T.
(Curt Taylor), 1948–   .   II. Title.

HV9507.E57 1993   364.6'0971   C93-094804-1

To W.F. (Bill) Foster and Donald Martin

J.W.E.

To my mother and father
To Dr. R.G. Murphy

C.T.G.

Preface to the Second Edition

During the early eighties, when we first discussed the development and eventual publication of this textbook, there was a keen awareness of how important the previous decade had been in changing the face of corrections in Canada. Much was done at that time in the way of program development and management restructuring. Trends were initiated which will continue to have implications for corrections practice in the future. The number of internal investigations and inquiries, alone, that were undertaken during the seventies distinguish that decade as a unique period in the history of Canadian corrections. Thus the first edition of this text emphasized those factors and events which were signalling change, as well as presenting examples of the nature of correctional decision-making and the problems associated with it.

As we approached the task of providing a new edition of this material, we were immediately aware that the tone and temper of the correctional ethos had changed since the seventies. Perhaps the main change has been that the system itself has become less change-oriented and more inclined toward operational stability. This has largely resulted from the requirement for increased cost efficiency at all levels of correctional activity, because of economic restraint and the political changes emerging from a more conservative environment. We note, for example, that discussions on jurisdictional reform, which were a highlight of the seventies in federal/provincial negotiations, have lapsed since the end of that decade. The various correctional bureaucracies are committing much less energy to internal investigations and inquiries. There have been relatively few new initiatives in correctional programming, although some of the trends begun during the seventies continue to develop.

This is not to say, however, that nothing is changing in the correctional system of Canada. We are just beginning to see the effects of the Charter of Rights and Freedoms. Some court decisions have already been made with regard to various aspects of correctional practice, and indications are that the Charter will have a continuing effect on correctional policy and practice. It seems clear, as well, that problems of restraint management and demands for cost efficiency will continue to motivate the system.

We have added material to the text to help explain the various ways in which these shifts and changes are evidenced. One corrections investigation, the Carson Committee Report, completed since the first edition of this book was published, concentrated on a review of management practice. The interest in improving management practice for purposes of cost efficiency and operational stability reflects in part the changing mood in corrections since the seventies.

It is interesting, as well, to note the greater interest in recording, assessing, and interpreting the history of Canadian corrections. There has been an increase in literature of this kind, and more attention is being given, especially within the provinces, to capturing correctional history. This situation, again, may reflect the changing mood regarding the importance of a sense of stability and rootedness in correctional matters, after ten or fifteen years of relative instability and innovation.

As is usually the case, we are indebted to those who assisted us to research this edition. We would like particularly to acknowledge Patricia Ratel and Karen Lyons for their extensive work in reviewing the text for updating. We would like to thank Robbie Robidoux for calling to our attention some recent changes in the federal penitentiary system, and Linda Kee at Butterworths for her continuing support and guidance throughout the development of this edition.

Preface to the First Edition

The need for a comprehensive examination of Canadian corrections has become more pressing in recent years with the expansion of criminal justice and corrections courses at the university and college level and the development of staff training programs for correctional personnel. Our experience within the Canadian correctional system and involvement in teaching corrections courses at the university has reinforced the belief that Canadian corrections is a unique and distinctive enterprise — one which cannot be wholly understood through the study of the philosophy and operations of corrections in other countries. While Canadian corrections shares many of the policy perspectives and program emphases evident in other jurisdictions, particularly the United States, the unique social and political milieu within which the correctional system operates exerts a direct and significant influence on both correctional policy and practice.

While presenting itself as a cultural mosaic, Canada is also a political mosaic, with jurisdiction distributed between several levels of government, each of which retains a degree of independence and authority in the administration of public affairs. The political organization of Canada is often referred to as "cooperative federalism" and there are few activities of government that do not require negotiation and agreement between political authorities at more than one level. It is this unique setting that gives Canadian corrections its distinctive attributes, and it is against this backdrop that we examine the major areas of the correctional enterprise.

In addition to utilizing a framework which identifies and illuminates the distinctive characteristics of Canadian corrections, the relationship between policy and practice in the delivery of correctional services is highlighted. It is hoped that this thematic choice will serve both to illustrate the particular nature of Canadian corrections and to offer a perspective on correctional practice. Moreover, every effort has been made to systematically present the manner in which correctional policy is formulated, as well as to examine the results of various policy and program initiatives. What emerges from our consideration of the various areas of policy and practice is that Canadian corrections is an exceedingly complex enterprise, one in which both correctional personnel and the clients of the system often struggle to understand the processes at work as well as the consequences of the decisions which are made.

The complexity of the correctional system, however, should in no way diminish efforts to understand it, to examine the manner in which policy is formulated, and to attempt to assess the consequences of policies and programs. It is hoped that the materials presented in this volume will provide the impetus for the development of conceptual and theoretical frameworks through which the correctional enterprise can be studied, informed, and, where required, changed. The reader will note that the volume does not proceed from a particular ideological perspective, but rather attempts throughout to identify the various competing perspectives and their efficacy in addressing the issues under study. Obviously, it has not been possible in one volume to fully address all of the dimensions of correctional policy and practice. However, it is the authors' hope that the materials and discussions presented will provide the basis for further dialogue and research on the correctional enterprise. Should the volume serve these functions, we will have achieved our objectives.

The authors are indebted to many individuals who participated, directly and indirectly, in the completion of this work. In the first instance are the many persons involved in the correctional enterprise in Canada and the United States with whom the authors have interacted over the years, including correctional administrators, inmates in Canadian federal and provincial and U.S. state and federal institutions, individuals associated with private correctional agencies, politicians responsible for corrections, and correctional line personnel. Substantial contributions to the authors' thinking on corrections have also been made by the many students whom they have taught over the years.

While the book is the product of a collaborative effort, each author would like to acknowledge those individuals who made a significant contribution to both the perspective presented and the materials utilized. John Ekstedt would like to acknowledge the invaluable assistance of Gregg Macdonald, Associate Director of the Simon Fraser University Institute for Studies in Criminal Justice Policy, in editing the chapters on correctional policy, administration, planning and reform, and in providing ongoing advice and assistance. Curt Griffiths would like to express his gratitude and appreciation to his former mentors at the University of Montana — Drs. Gordon Browder, Robert W. Balch, and Richard D. Vandiver — for introducing him to the study of corrections and assisting the development of a "critical eye." A further debt is owed to Frank Mann, Eddy Williams, Stan Williamson, and Al Heide.

Both authors would like to acknowledge the research assistance of Hollis Johnson, Linda Weafer, Alison Hatch, Ron Rea and Linda Graham. In a work of this kind, someone must cope with the seemingly endless drafts of the manuscript. In this regard, a special thanks must go to Mrs. Lynn Hill and to Alison Hatch for the innumerable hours of assistance provided in typing, editing, and computer entry. Throughout the writing of the volume, advice and editorial comments were provided by several of our colleagues in the Department of Criminology at Simon Fraser University — Drs. Raymond R. Corrado, Simon N. Verdun-Jones and F. Douglas Cousineau. Their ongoing support for our efforts was much appreciated. At Butterworths, Janet Turner and Linda Kee were a constant source of encouragement, and Shirley Corriveau contributed valuable editorial expertise.

Finally, but importantly, we were fortunate to have the support, encouragement and understanding of our families, without which the project could not have been completed.

John W. Ekstedt
Curt T. Griffiths

Simon Fraser University
Burnaby, British Columbia, 1984

Contents

Tables

Figures

Chapter 1

Introduction

The purpose of this text is to provide an analysis of Canadian correctional policy and practice. The need for such a work has been made timely by the increase in the number of graduate and undergraduate courses on corrections which are being offered at Canadian universities, the development or expansion of correctional worker programs in community colleges, and the growth in both pre-service and in-service staff development programs that are offered to correctional personnel by their agency employers.

While some available material concentrates on specific aspects of Canadian correctional practice, to date there has been very little written which provides the type of information required to give students and general practitioners a broad impression of the Canadian correctional enterprise. This volume seeks to present such a perspective.

At the outset it should be made clear that it is not always easy to separate adults from juveniles in any overall description of Canadian correctional practice. While the legal distinction between the two groups is reasonably well-defined in Canada, some Canadian jurisdictions locate their services to both categories of offenders within the same organizational structure and, occasionally, within the same field office. Although from time to time it will be important to recognize the overlap between adult and juvenile corrections, this volume specifically addresses adult corrections in Canada.

There are a number of ways in which an overview of this kind can be presented. In this volume, the authors have decided to concentrate on the *dynamics* of the correctional process, rather than to approach the subject from a particular ideological stance or from a description and analysis of specific program components. Accordingly, the *interrelationship* between corrections and other areas of the criminal justice system is examined and the process of correctional policy formulation and implementation is investigated in some detail. The nature of adult corrections as a social and political process is emphasized. Correctional programs are viewed in the context of the problems associated with the management of community, political, and professional interests.

WHAT IS CORRECTIONS?

In order to prepare for a more detailed discussion of the issues surrounding adult corrections in Canada, it is first necessary to define corrections as a topic of inquiry. Normally this is done by considering the various ideological points of view that can be discovered through an historical study of punishment and criminal law. While it is true that the history of corrections generally has been regarded as the application of ideological perspectives to the punishment of offenders, an investigation which concentrates on the correctional process provides a somewhat different interpretation.

For the purpose at hand, corrections is presented as a social, political, and bureaucratic enterprise rather than as a theoretical application. In this context, corrections can be understood in reference to four general areas of definition: as a social concept, as a legal entity, as a range of programs, and as a subsystem within the criminal justice system.

CORRECTIONS AS A SOCIAL CONCEPT

It is important to understand that the term "corrections," used to refer to an operating system which acts upon human beings, is not a word which enjoys general understanding or agreement, either among the public-at-large or among persons involved in the delivery of correctional services. On the contrary, "corrections" is often regarded as a misnomer when applied to the description of a state's system for punishment.

This lack of agreement is understandable given the widely held opinion that correctional systems do not "correct" in the sense of fixing the damage which may have resulted from an offence or by promoting the behavioural change required to keep an offender from offending again. Nevertheless, the activity of developing programs or service systems which are conceived to be "correctional" does reflect a *social concept* that gives evidence of general agreement and support.

To understand the nature of this agreement within a society, it should be recognized that societies are constructed according to rules of law and systems of governance. The making of laws and their enforcement is usually conducted through the organized political community, as is the case in Canada. While in most free and democratic societies it is the responsibility of the courts, rather than the governors[1] of the state, to adjudicate offensiveness in relation to the law, it remains the state's responsibility to provide the penalties for offensiveness both in law and in practice. And it is the assigning of penalties or the provision of sanctions *in practice* that forms the basis of corrections as a social concept.

In short, while considerable public, political, and theoretical debate has surrounded the emphasis within, or the character of, the state's sanctioning practices, the social necessity of the correctional enterprise itself is not usually disputed. It is most often the *form* which correctional practice takes in reflecting the social concept that attracts controversy.

Seen in this light, the historical development of criminological theory and correctional practice is centred on the manner by which the state sanctions offenders, as well as on its declared purpose when doing so. As shown in Chapter 2, correctional history can be described in terms of the changing opinions regarding the nature and purpose of the state's sanctioning practices.

The questions generated by adopting this point of view are many and varied: Should the state provide capital or corporal punishment as sanctioning practices? To what degree should the state imprison or institutionalize persons convicted of crimes? Should programs accent punishment or some form of rehabilitation? To what degree should the state's programs of correction emphasize the protection of the community or the community's moral indignation related to the offence in question?

It is crucial when pursuing an inquiry into these issues to separate the idea of corrections as a social concept from the form correctional practice has taken at any one point in history. The most germane question then becomes: How can the correctional enterprise, as an accepted social concept, reflect through its policy and practice the social aspirations and moral principles of society at any moment in history?

CORRECTIONS AS A LEGAL ENTITY

There are two ways to examine corrections as a legal entity. The first views corrections as an activity of government *provided for in law*. The second regards corrections as an activity of government *subject to the general rule of law and to the accepted principles of*

*justice that often find expression through use of the terms "fairness"
and "equity."* While at first reading the two positions seem similar,
they are distinct and fundamentally different. In order to discriminate between them, it is necessary to review the context within
which the Canadian correctional enterprise functions.

In Canada, the law establishes the ground upon which the
governors exercise their authority to engage in correctional work.
The law also sets forth the division of responsibility between levels
of government where correctional services are at issue and
establishes the rules which regulate the development and use of
correctional programs.

The jurisdictional division of authority is vital to an
understanding of the subject. The *British North America Act*
(1867),[2] now included in the *Constitution Act* (1982), provides the
basis for the distribution of power between the federal government
and the provinces. Under Section 91, the Parliament of Canada has
exclusive jurisdiction to make criminal law "including the
procedure in criminal matters." Section 92 provides that "in each
province the legislature may exclusively make laws in relation to
. . . the administration of justice." Section 92 also commits to the
jurisdiction of the provinces power in respect to "the imposition of
punishment by fine, penalty, or imprisonment for enforcing any
law of the province in relation to any matter coming within any of
the classes of subjects enumerated in this section."

The effect of these sections is to place more serious offences,
such as murder or theft, under the exclusive legislative control of
the federal government and to place the less serious offences, such
as many traffic violations, within the jurisdiction of the provincial
legislatures. Moreover, the power to make law may be delegated by
the provinces to the municipalities with the result that the
municipalities may also pass by-laws containing penalties for
persons who do not observe them. As a matter of constitutional law,
it follows that there are no criminal offences in Canada except
those which are declared to be such by the federal Parliament. All
other offences under provincial or municipal legislation for which
penalties are attached are quasi-criminal.

Given the constitutional division of responsibilities in Canada,
it is not surprising that dialogue related to the definition of
authority and to the problems of service delivery remains ongoing.
However, the most important point to grasp is that each level of
government may make laws which require a correctional response
and which contribute directly to the requirements of correctional
work in legal terms.

When commenting upon the legal identity of the correctional

enterprise, it also must be appreciated that criminal law in Canada is based on the British Common Law tradition. At Common Law, crimes historically were divided into treasons, felonies, and misdemeanors. Treasons included offences against the security of the state; felonies included most other serious crimes, usually involving the death penalty; and misdemeanors included less serious offences.

Common Law crimes no longer exist in Canada. In the late nineteenth century a review of all criminal law principles embodied in case law was undertaken for the purpose of reducing them to a logical and organized system.[3] In 1892, this work resulted in the adoption of the *Criminal Code* by the federal Parliament. While the terms "felonies" and "misdemeanors" are still used in the United States, in order to distinguish between serious and less serious offences, they have been eliminated from Canadian law. Crimes in Canada now are divided into *summary* and *indictable* offences.

Indictable offences refer to the more serious crimes such as murder, rape, or robbery, and the maximum sentence for any indictable offence is never less than two years imprisonment in a federal penitentiary. Indictable offences can only be defined by the Parliament of Canada.

Summary offences refer to less serious crimes and are punishable by imprisonment for up to six months in a provincial institution and by a fine of up to $2000. Summary offences are defined by all three levels of government. Examples of summary offences include creating a disturbance, and many of the offences committed in the operation of a motor vehicle.

Taken together, the *Constitution Act* and the Canadian *Criminal Code* establish the parameters within which corrections in Canada must function. They set forth the nature of correctional services required in law and divide responsibility for service delivery between the levels of government.

Additionally, there are other pieces of federal enabling legislation that apply to the provision of correctional programs. These include: the *Prisons and Reformatories Act* (1970), the *Penitentiary Act* (1970), and the *Parole Act* (1958). Each province is also empowered to create enabling legislation directly related to the provision of correctional services and has its own corrections act or an equivalent statute.

While it is clear that corrections in Canada operates within a legal framework, it remains necessary to address the question of the relationship between the practice of corrections and the general rule of law. Much discussion in North America, particularly in the United States, has been directed towards this matter. The issue centres on the rights of persons who have been placed in correctional programs by order of the court. Goldfarb and Singer (1970, 175-320) have organized the rights that correctional clients have attempted to establish into four categories:

1. The right to be free from cruel and unusual punishment and the right to the minimal conditions necessary to sustain life.
2. The right of access to the courts and to others outside of the corrections system.
3. The right of freedom of religion, freedom of expression, voting privileges, and freedom from racial discrimination. This category of rights is usually referred to as "civil rights" when applied to persons who are not under court sanction.
4. The right to the benefits of reasonable standards and procedural protection when decisions are made that have a significant impact on the offender.

There has been a notable increase in the amount of civil and criminal litigation with regard to these issues (see Price 1974; Reid 1981, 413 ff). This increase can be attributed, in part, to the growing willingness of courts in the United States to assume jurisdiction for purposes of reviewing administrative decisions affecting the lives of persons in custody. A similar trend has more recently begun to appear in the deliberations of Canadian courts. More particularly, in Canada, the patriation of the constitution and the accompanying Charter of Rights and Freedoms have strengthened the possibility of judicial review of correctional practices and of the legislation and regulations governing them.

While there is no doubt that the Canadian correctional enterprise operates as a "legal entity," the degree to which corrections functions consistently within the "rule of law" is less obvious. As is revealed in subsequent chapters, this lack of clarity presents problems which are not easily resolved.

CORRECTIONS AS A RANGE OF PROGRAMS

Within the present scope of law, the options available to the court in sentencing range across three fundamental categories of disposition: imprisonment, probation, and fines. It is in providing programs which are available to the court when these sentencing options are exercised that the primary purpose of corrections can be ascertained. Morever, correctional systems in Canada are responsible for bringing forward information to the court concerning offenders awaiting sentence (pre-sentence reports) and for the containment or supervision of persons who are not released by the courts on their own recognizance while awaiting trial. It follows, therefore, that the programs of corrections in Canada can be placed into three further categories: pre-trial, pre-sentence and post-sentence services. Specific programs in each of these categories are discussed in greater detail in subsequent chapters.

When viewing corrections as a range of programs, there are several issues which must be addressed. The first of these has to do with correctional programs as activities of both the private and pubic sectors of society. In Canada today, correctional programs are generally viewed as an undertaking of the public sector. As an activity of government, program responsibility is exercised through line ministries[4] or departments. Accordingly, the location of authority upon which correctional programs proceed is considered to be centred in the executive rather than the legislative or judicial arenas of government.

The locus of authority is not always clear. This is illustrated by the question of whether or not a probation officer reports to the sentencing judge or to a minister of government (Attorney General, Solicitor General, Minister of Corrections, etc) in the preparation of a pre-sentence report. As well, there is sometimes confusion as to whether the accountability for corrections is located at the political or bureaucratic level of government. Be this as it may, correctional programs are usually viewed as a responsibility of government that is exercised through the bureaucracy of the civil service. The widespread acceptance of this view has produced one significant, yet predictable, effect — it has become increasingly difficult for private sector agencies, such as volunteer organizations and non-profit societies, to provide correctional services without first entering into some formal relationship with those government bureaucracies responsible for the administration of correctional programs.[5]

As is discussed in Chapter 2, public sector control over private sector participation in the provision of correctional services has not always existed in Canadian corrections. Indeed, the development of Canadian correctional programs in the past was greatly influenced by agencies outside of government that identified service to offenders as a legitimate responsibility of the community-at-large. As with other areas of government service, the public sector's assumption of increasing responsibility for programs in response to perceived social needs has very much influenced the appearance of correctional initiatives.

Furthermore, it seems evident that the shift toward exclusive government control over the correctional enterprise has caused the public perception to change from one of citizen responsibility for offenders to an increased reliance on government as the primary source for the care and control of such persons. It cannot be stressed enough that the balance between citizen responsibility and government control is extremely important in understanding the nature of correctional programs.

A second, yet related, issue concerns the style of management and organization within correctional programs. As government expands its control over the provision of correctional services, the private sector agencies and the public-at-large are forced to rely on correctional management[6] in order to become involved in the correctional enterprise.

However, as a later chapter points out, the movement toward a "closed" correctional system, which operates for the most part within the public sector, is now being matched by a countervailing force — correctional authorities in Canada are laying ever greater emphasis upon programs that identify the reintegration of offenders into the society as their goal. The reintegration model seeks to encourage increased community participation in correctional programs and must rely upon community acceptance if the model is to be implemented successfully. Correctional managers, therefore, are now charged with a new and difficult task. They must attempt to manage their programs with an "open" style that encourages community inquiry and involvement. At the same time, the programs which they manage are increasingly contained within a "closed" system. Without doubt, the resulting tension directly affects the substance and structure of Canadian correctional programs.

Mention should also be made of the relationship between correctional personnel and correctional programs. While there are legislative and regulatory limits applying to the practices of correctional personnel, it is the nature of the correctional enterprise that the exercise of individual discretion in the day-to-day handling of offenders is not only allowed, it is required. As the number and scope of correctional programs increases, so does the latitude of individual discretion which is possible. In Canada, as elsewhere, this situation has reached the point where efforts are being made to limit and define discretion through the creation of uniform standards of program practice.[7] More is said on this subject in later chapters, but for the present it should be recognized that, regardless of the rules that may be made to apply to correctional practice, it remains axiomatic that the success of correctional programs is directly related to the quality of correctional personnel.

By and large, correctional personnel engage in extremely difficult work. They are responsible for the control and custody of persons who are considered offensive to the community and from whom the community requires some degree of protection. Additionally, correctional personnel are charged with administering the conditions upon which an offender is returned to the community. They do so under the general expectation that their duties will be dispatched in such a way that the protection of the community is maintained, while proper regard for the welfare and rights of offenders continues to be supported. The way in which correctional personnel carry out this task is central to any understanding of correctional programming.

CORRECTIONS AS A SUBSYSTEM WITHIN THE CRIMINAL JUSTICE SYSTEM

A general discussion on the nature of corrections is not complete without some reference to the relationship of corrections to the activities of other government agencies and to the private bar concerned with criminal justice. It is becoming increasingly popular to organize and describe the separate activities that interact in order to dispense justice as components or *subsystems* of a larger criminal justice system.

The criminal justice subsystems are regarded as being the police, those who provide legal services (prosecution and legal defence), the courts, and corrections. The purpose of viewing criminal justice activities as a "system" is usually to increase management efficiency, particularly in those areas where the subsystems directly interrelate and where the policy of one subsystem may have direct influence on the operations of another.

Related to management efficiency and policy development are the questions of cost efficiency and the requirement, faced by governments, to continually evaluate and constrain resource commitments in all areas of public service. Additionally, the systems-based analysis of criminal justice activities serves to clarify individual subsystem responsibilities and to increase the possibility of effecting required reform through the development of a comprehensive criminal justice policy. One obvious way to regulate the impact of one criminal justice system component on another is to have greater coordination of activities. This can only be accomplished through some type of joint systems management.[8]

Corrections is especially affected by the policy and procedures of the other criminal justice subsystems. In essence, the correctional enterprise is the gathering place for those persons who have been screened through one or more of the system's other components. Once a warrant or an order of the court has been issued directing a person into a correctional program, the correctional system must receive and accommodate that person. Therefore, it is not possible for corrections to control or to reform its own practices. It is not independent from the effects of other components within the criminal justice system. Accordingly, some form of joint management initiative is required in order to establish common goals and to allocate resources effectively when resources are limited and crime is increasing.

Clearly, the issue of resource allocation cannot be overlooked. The criminal justice system in Canada is a multi-billion dollar business. In 1977-78, the total expenditure for criminal justice activities was approximately $2.6 billion. The largest percentage of these funds, 64 percent or $1.63 billion, was spent for police activities, with adult corrections receiving 21 percent or $552 million. Table 1.1 provides a summary of manpower commitments and expenditures for criminal justice services by subsystem. (Total criminal justice costs calculated by collating *all* criminal justice services in federal *and* provincial jurisdictions have not been updated since the National Task Force on the Administration of Justice was disbanded in 1980. Further in the text, portions of these costs are updated to 1986.

While corrections cannot be completely understood apart from its relationship to other activities in the criminal justice system, it is important not to carry the concept of criminal justice as a system too far. Within the broad spectrum of the services represented, Canadian criminal justice traditions require that certain activities not be subject to direct control either by another justice subsystem or by some central management authority of the state.

The Canadian criminal justice system may also be viewed as a *process* involving a series of checks and balances which are intended to achieve a fair dispensation of justice by preventing the arbitrary application of group power. The courts must be able to decide, impartially, the matters placed before them and must not be subject to control or to undue influence by the executive arm of government. Similarly, the police must not be used by the state to serve purposes outside their legal mandate nor must they be fettered by improper constraint in their investigation and arrest of persons suspected of breaking the law. Correctional programs must not be used to incarcerate or control persons who have not been

TABLE 1.1 Justice Services: Percent of Total Expenditures 1977-78

In the fiscal year 1977/78 the total expenditure for justice services by all governments in Canada was approximately $2.6 billion and 100,000 persons were employed by municipalities and 23 ministries responsible for justice services. These figures do not include juvenile corrections service expenditure and manpower. It is estimated that 95% of the expenditure was for criminal justice activities.

The overall expenditures and manpower in the five justice sectors were as follows:

	Manpower	Expenditure ($ million)
Police**	63,000	1,631
Crown Counsel	1,600*	51
Legal Aid	1,900*	84
Courts	10,400	248
Adult Corrections	21,900	552
Total	98,800	$2,566

*Excludes use of private practice legal professional services equivalent to 2,380 additional staff.
**Excludes $70 million spent and 2,500 persons employed in police related services.

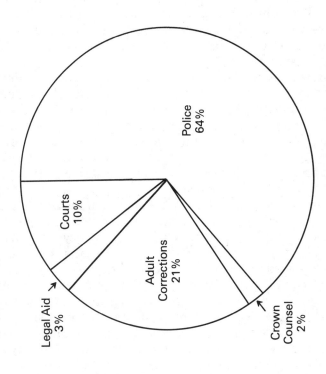

Police 64%
Courts 10%
Legal Aid 3%
Adult Corrections 21%
Crown Counsel 2%

SOURCE: National Task Force on the Administration of Justice, 1979. *Justice Services in Canada, 1977/78*, p. 4.

found guilty of an offence in law or who are improperly confined for any reason. Those authorities which have been established to review the status of incarcerated persons and to effect their release, under appropriate circumstances, must not be subject to undue political and bureaucratic pressure.

As a process established for the protection of society and for the fair dispensation of justice, criminal justice must not be distorted by the simplistic view that it is primarily a system exhibiting common goals, resource constraints, and management efficiency needs. Clearly, the pressures which force a management review based on the systems approach must be balanced by a desire to guarantee a process which assures fair and equitable justice.

"Law is not an exact science nor is justice a simple thing" (*Piche vs. The Queen,* 1970). This sentiment summarizes many of the points which have been made in the Introduction, concerning the difficult and complex subject of correctional policy and practice in Canada. While the search for simple answers is tempting, it should be acknowledged that correctional reform is subject to the same level of complexity that exists in the justice system as a whole. This statement takes on greater significance when it is recognized that a fundamental requirement of the correctional enterprise is to protect the public and to control inappropriate behaviour on the one hand, while assuring individual liberty and the rights of the offender on the other. Hopefully, the present review of correctional policy and practice in Canada will achieve some clarity with regard to major issues of concern and will promote an increased understanding of the options available in the development, operation, and reform of the correctional enterprise.

Notes

1. The term "governors" here refers, in a general sense, to all the elected representatives of the people responsible for the legislative function of government and, more particularly, to the members of the party in power responsible for the executive function of government.

2. There are, in fact, fifteen British North American Acts. The *Act of 1867* spawned fourteen more between 1871 and 1965.

3. Credit for the authorship of the Canadian *Criminal Code* has been ascribed to the English lawyer and judge, Sir James Fitz-James Stephen. In 1877, Stephen published his "Digest of the Criminal Law," and in the next year his "Draft Criminal Code." In 1892, Sir John Thompson, then Minister of Justice and subsequently Prime Minister of Canada, introduced as a government bill a draft code, based on the Stephen code and earlier efforts at reform of the law of criminal procedure.

4. "Line ministry" is a term used to refer to the divisions of responsibility in the bureaucratic organization of government. Governments are charged with the responsibility of providing services which are directed both internally (e.g., Finance and Personnel) and externally (e.g., Welfare, Highways, Parks, Health, Economic Development). The federal government and each provincial government have their own particular way of dividing these responsibilities into ministries or departments but all governments are required to provide the same types of services. Each ministry is headed by an elected member of the party in power who, by virtue of this appointment, becomes a member of cabinet. Cabinet ministers, together with the leader of the party in power (premier or prime minister) comprise the "executive" of government. The responsibility of each cabinet minister is exercised through a "line" extending from the minister to the deputy minister who is the senior civil servant responsible for the management and administration of the ministry or department in question.

5. In 1976, the Continuing Committee of Deputy Ministers Responsible for Corrections, established a "Task Force on the Role of the Private Sector in Criminal Justice." The report of this Task Force was submitted in three volumes in 1977. The Task Force (1977, 27) commented that ". . . it is true that some governments in Canada have involved the 'voluntary agencies' in major direct service responsibilities, such as residential, court, and parole supervisory services. The federal policy of dividing responsibility equally between the National Parole Service and other agencies, public and private, seemed to reflect a genuine desire for partnership. But the concept of 'partnership' has not been more broadly explored or developed. The 'formulation of a policy' on a mutual basis has nowhere begun as a process to be taken seriously." Additionally, the National Work Group on Justice Information and Statistics (1981, 24) reports that "over the past two fiscal years, the CSC has sought greater community involvement in the process of reintegrating offenders into the community. During 1978/79 a task force was established to set national standards for community centres and to facilitate agreements between federal and provincial governments on the use and support of these centres. In 1978/79 a total of one hundred and nine (109) contracts between CSC and community residential centres were in effect to provide accommodation and other services. There is a standard contract fee per inmate per bed day for all facilities utilized by CSC, although the use of such facilities is regionally monitored and controlled."

6. "Correctional management" is used here as a general term applying to persons regarded as having decision-making authority for major programs. They include the senior managers responsible for the full range of corrections programs (such as Directors of Corrections or Deputy Ministers of Corrections) and persons responsible for major programs within corrections (such as the warden or director of a prison or the director of a probation service).

7. On May 13, 1985 the Canadian Criminal Justice Association announced the long-awaited publication of a Manual of Standards for Corrections. Development of the standards required five years of effort. However, the development of these standards establishes Canada as the second country in the world (after the United States) to have developed, through an independent organization, standards which encompass the entire field of adult corrections.

8. While the term "systems management" is often used in reference to

specific technological applications (e.g., communication systems, information systems, etc.), in this case we are using the term more generally, to refer to any formal mechanisms established to coordinate management interests across the entire spectrum of criminal justice services.

References

Goldfarb, R.L. and L.R. Singer. (December) 1970. "Redressing Prisoners' Grievances." 39 *George Washington Law Review.* 175-320.
Greenspan, E. 1981. *Martin's Annual Criminal Code.* Aurora, Ontario: Canada Law Book Limited.
National Task Force on the Administration of Justice. 1979. *Justice Services in Canada, 1977/78.* Victoria: Ministry of Attorney General.
National Work Group on Justice Information and Statistics. 1981. *Justice information Report—Correctional Services in Canada, 1978/79, 1979/80.* Ottawa.
Price, R.R. 1974. "Bringing the Rule of Law to Corrections." 16 *Canadian Journal of Corrections.* 209-55.
Reid, S.T. 1981. *The Correctional System: An Introduction.* New York: Holt, Rinehart, and Winston.
Task Force on the role of the Private Sector in Criminal Justice. 1977. *Report. Community Involvement in Criminal Justice, Vol. 1.* Ottawa: Supply and Services Canada.

Legislation
  British North America Act, 1867.
  Canada *Parole Act,* R.S.C. 1970, c. P-2, s.1.
  Canada *Penitentiary Act,* R.S.C. 1970, c. P-6.
  Canada *Prisons and Reformatories Act,* R.S.C. 1970, c. P-21.

Chapter 2

History of Canadian Corrections

INTRODUCTION

Canadians have traditionally studied correctional history through an examination of materials from other countries, it often being assumed that the development of corrections in Canada was either uneventful or that it closely mirrored events which occurred in the United States and England. To date, the development of a general picture of the history of Canadian corrections has been hindered by a paucity of published materials and it is only with considerable difficulty that a general overview can be pieced together. What does emerge from the available documents is a correctional history unique to Canada — one determined and influenced by the geography, political history, and governmental arrangements of the country as well as by economics, religion, and philosophical movements. In fact, we will see that many of the issues in corrections which first emerged in the eighteenth and nineteenth centuries, such as the debate over punishment versus reformation of the offender, and the controversy over the use of prison labour, continue to the present.

Throughout this chapter, an attempt is made to highlight the events, personalities, and legislative acts which have had an impact on the development of corrections in Canada. As well, the influence of ideas and events originating in the United States and England is discussed. However, prior to an examination of Canadian correctional history, it is important to consider briefly the societal context of corrections and the dynamic, changing nature of the correctional enterprise.

THE PROCESS OF CORRECTIONAL CHANGE

Pursley (1977, 347) has noted that "correctional systems do not exist apart from the influence of society. Society determines how the correctional process is to be defined and develops the broad policy guidelines it expects corrections to adhere to." In fact, the perceptions of crime and the criminal, as well as the responses to criminal behaviour in a society, are closely tied to its social, political, religious, and philosophical attributes. As such, corrections and the correctional process exist within, rather than apart from, the larger societal context. Table 2.1 illustrates the interrelationships between the nature of the social relationships in society, the sanctions which are utilized to respond to criminal behaviour, and the punishments which are inflicted on offenders. Added to this are the shifts which occur in the explanations of criminal behaviour and the perceptions of crime which, in turn, are closely tied to changes in social relationships in society and to the sanctions and punishments which are employed (see Foucault 1977; Newman 1978). As Skinner et al. (1981, 171) note:

> The correctional system has a complex conceptual base. It reflects the interrelationships of such concepts as the nature of man, society, culture, values, economics and politics. The response to crime is formulated on the basis of these interrelationships ... Punishment; deterrence, both individual and general; retribution; the protection of society; incapacitation; humanitarianism; reform; treatment and rehabilitation have all been evident in the way society has dealt with offenders against the law or social order.

According to Shover (1979, 36), correctional change occurs when there is a shift in either the structure or the ideology relating to criminal offenders which results in one or more of the following: (1) a modification of the severity of punishment administered to convicted offenders, (2) a change in the explanations of criminal behaviour, (3) the creation of new structural arrangements, such as the penitentiary, to confine offenders, and (4) a change in the number or proportions of convicted offenders dealt with by the correctional process. Shover (1979, 36) notes that changes in these four areas may occur simultaneously:

> The development of community programs for offenders may be accompanied by changes in prevailing ideological interpretations of offenders, by changes in the total number of offenders under correctional supervision, and ... by some change in the severity of treatments accorded to offenders.

TABLE 2.1 Historical Development of Law and Punishment

	Period						
	Ca. 500,000-200,000 B.C.: Appearance of Genus Homo	Ca. 200,000-25,000 B.C.: Appearance of Early modern man/woman	Ca. 25,000-3500 B.C.: Development of rudimentary religion	Ca. 3500-400 B.C.: Development of first criminal codes	Ca. 400 B.C.-A.D. 500: Development of Roman law	Ca. 500-1750: Medieval and feudal justice	Ca. 1750 to Present
Nature of Social Relationship	Pretribal	Incipient group and tribal	Intermediate group and tribal	Intermediate group and tribal	Advanced group and tribal; incipient organized state	Feudal and intermediate organized state	Advanced organized state
Sanctions	?	Incipient customs and mores	Intermediate customs and mores	Customs and mores; incipient laws	Customs and rudimentary laws	Customs and common law	Statutory laws
Form of Punishment	Personal retribution	Personal retribution; group and tribal retribution	Personal retribution; group and tribal retribution	Personal retribution; group and tribal retribution; state retribution	State retribution group and tribal retribution; personal retribution	State and ecclesiastical retribution	State retribution reformation, rehabilitation and reintegration
	Injury, torture death			Torture, injury, death, banishment, forfeiture		Torture, forfeiture, injury, death, excommunication, banishment	Fine, supervision, incarceration, death

SOURCE: Adopted from Robert D. Pursley, 1977. *Introduction to Criminal Justice.* Encino, California: Glencoe Press, pg. 348.

From a review of the correctional literature, Shover (1979, 39-54) identifies three major perspectives on correctional change "each of which builds upon an implicit, though rarely articulated set of beliefs about the nature of the political process, and about the locus of political power and how it is wielded." These three perspectives are (1) conservatism, (2) liberal-pluralism, and (3) radical-elitism, and each provides a different explanation of the causal factors which contribute to correctional change.

1. *Conservatism.* Social and political institutions reflect a consensus of public sentiments and morality. Changes in the response to and treatment of offenders reflect gradual changes in public sentiment. Focus on social defence and the repression of offenders. Penal practices viewed as a reflection of moral consensus in society. A predisposition to preserve social arrangements and institutions and a favouring of gradual rather than abrupt change.

2. *Liberal-Pluralism.* Political process viewed as proceeding on the basis of well-defined rules within which groups compete equally for power and privilege. Tendency to ignore the social situation from which organized groups, which influence correctional change, emerge, and tendency to offer *ad hoc, post factum* explanations for historical developments in corrections. Emergence of correctional interest groups and ideas are the consequence of humanitarianism and social progress. Correctional change attributed to the "unfolding of a master trend in history, such as the movement toward greater humanitarianism, rationality, or progress" (Shover 1979, 42). Charismatic and innovative individuals play a critical role in correctional change.

3. *Radical-Elitism.* Importance of the political economy in correctional change. The social class that owns and controls the means of production represents a ruling elite that employs the governmental process and institutions to maintain its supremacy and to pacify and control the other classes. Critical of liberal-pluralism explanations involving humanitarian impulses as explanations of correctional change. Views as incomplete perspectives which do not consider the contradictions and modifications in relations of production as having a major role in correctional change. Correctional change requires a change in the relations and control of production in society (see Quinney 1977; Gosselin 1982).

In this chapter, the development of penitentiaries in the United States and Canada is discussed to provide insight into the nature of the correctional enterprise, as well as to illustrate differing interpretations regarding factors that precipitated the confinement of criminal offenders in prisons in North America.

CRIME AND PUNISHMENT IN EARLY CANADA

In the early eighteenth century, the response to individuals whose behaviour contravened the law was quite severe, and there was no provision for the use of confinement for the punishment of offenders. For the serious offences of murder, grand larceny, sodomy, and rape, capital punishment was employed, while for less serious crimes, a wide variety of sanctions were available, including transportation, banishment, fines, and whipping. Reflecting the practices embodied in the English criminal law, punishment was progressive:

> Murderers were hung while thieves were branded with the letter 'T' on first conviction and hung for a second offence. The lash and stocks served as punishment for less serious crimes . . . (Coles 1979, 1).

Further illustration of the types of punishments inflicted on offenders during the early 1700s is provided by the sentence received by one Robert Nichols in the community of Annapolis in what is now the province of Nova Scotia:

> The punishment therefore inflicted on thee is to sit upon a gallows three days, half an hour each day, with a rope about thy neck and a paper upon your breast whereon shall be writ in capital letters AUDACIOUS VILLAIN and afterwards thou art to be whipped at a carts tail from the prison up to the uppermost house of the cape and from thence back again to the prison house receiving each hundred paces five stripes upon your bare back with a cat of nine tails . . . (cited in Coles 1979, 1).

In Lower Canada, punishment was often inflicted on the offender at the location where the offence had been committed. Morel (1963, 28) relates the case of one offender who was condemned by a Montreal judge in 1692 to have his right hand cut off and his limbs broken before being placed on a rack to die, all of this occurring in front of the house of the merchant he had killed (see Lachance, 1985).

The harshness of the early punishments in Canada was the result of the adoption of the English criminal law in Lower and

Upper Canada. In the late 1700s in England, however, the "Bloody Code," under which over 350 offences were subject to capital punishment, administered to both adults and children, came under increasing criticism. As Beattie (1977, 9) observes:

> It was becoming increasingly apparent . . . that the law and judicial system were not performing their main task — to restrain crime. What reformers argued for in place of the gallows . . . were moderate, certain punishments, graded to the seriousness of the crime and applied with uniformity to every prisoner . . . punishments that . . . would not simply coerce and brutalize offenders, but that would reform them.

Reflecting this concern, the *Act of 1800* was passed in Upper Canada, lessening the severity of punishment for many offences.[1] Baehre (1977, 186) notes, for example that the legislation was modified to provide for a person convicted of a felony to be fined or whipped rather than having his or her hand burned, as had previously been the practice. In fact, Baehre (1977, 186) cautions that, while a wide range of capital and corporal punishments remained available to the courts at this time, "severe penalties were relatively rare. The courts largely asked for fines, 'because the revenue was none too buoyant, and partly because gaol facilities were none too adequate' " (see also Tremblay 1986).

In general, punishments were designed to deter both the individual offender and the general public and involved public shaming and humiliation. The pillory was used in Lower Canada until 1842, and in Upper Canada, offenders were often put into stocks, a practice which continued until 1872.[2] Edmison (1976, 351) notes that the use of banishment began in Upper Canada in 1802: "The banished person was ordered to depart the province at his or her own expense and peril." In Newfoundland, for example, offenders were put on a boat which was set adrift, ultimately landing either in Prince Edward Island or in New York State, a practice which continued until 1902. Beattie (1977, 82) notes that dissatisfaction with banishment as a punishment alternative provided a major impetus for the establishment of a penitentiary in Canada in the 1830s and cites a statement made by the Select Committee on the Expediency of Erecting a Penitentiary in 1831: "It is no punishment to a rogue to order him to live on the right bank of the Niagara river instead of the left and it is cruelly unjust to our neighbours to send among them thieves, robbers, and burglars."

Transportation was also employed under the criminal laws of both Upper and Lower Canada. Gibson (1975, 186) notes that, in Upper Canada, the legal basis for sentences of transportation was provided for in the *Act of Legislation of Upper Canada*, passed in 1838, which allowed judges to grant conditional pardons: "Some of the pardons granted, to persons under sentence of death, were 'upon condition that they be respectively transported as convicts to her Majesty's Colony of Van Diemen's Land' for periods specified as seven years, 14 years, and, more severely, 'for and during the term of their natural lives.' "[3] While some convicts from Canada were transported to England and confined in hulks — abandoned or unusable ships anchored in the rivers and harbors — the majority were sent to Australia and Tasmania, with a smaller number being transported to Bermuda. Transportation as a punishment alternative officially ended in 1853, but was seriously reconsidered in 1871 when an attempt was made to persuade England to establish a penal colony in Hudson's Bay Territory to which convicts could be transported and again in 1887 during the meetings of the American Penal Congress in Toronto when proposals were put forth to establish penal colonies in the Canadian North and in Alaska (Edmison 1976, 352-53).[4]

Despite the fact that the use of incarceration for purposes of punishment of criminal offenders was not widespread, there were initial movements to confine individuals convicted of certain illegal activities. In 1754, for example, the first workhouse in the province of Nova Scotia was constructed and it contained a wide variety of offenders: "Besides criminals, local magistrates sentenced to the workhouse vagrants, beggars, prostitutes and fortune tellers, runaways, gamblers, stubborn children and servants, drunkards, and . . . orphans. By 1764 this list extended to include the sickly, the aged and the insane. . . ." (Kroll, cited in Coles 1979, 1). Workhouses had first been developed in the 1500s in England and were built for the employment and housing of London's riffraff, with the aim of instilling in them the Protestant work ethic. Coles (1979, 2) further notes that by 1818, imprisonment in the workhouse had become the chief method of punishment in Nova Scotia.

When the new workhouse was completed in Halifax in 1818, providing the prisoners with employment cutting granite and laying road bed, the beginning of a controversy which has continued to the present between prison labour and outside "free" labour occurred. While not desiring that the inmates in the workhouses should remain totally idle, there was nevertheless concern that prison labour not compete with free labour on the outside. As a solution to this problem, the province considered building a treadmill or "stepping mill," described as "an 'unproductive dispiriting device' upon which prisoners would walk thereby moving sand back and forth or 'grinding the wind' " (Coles 1979, 2). A legislative bill was proposed to implement the treadmill idea, but was defeated by one vote in the legislature. As we will see in our discussion of the building of the penitentiary at Kingston in the 1830s, the conflict between prison labour and free labour would surface again.

Development of the Local Gaols

It was previously noted that in the eighteenth century, with the exception of the erection of workhouses in some areas, there was no use made of confinement for purposes of punishment. Rather, gaols or local lock-ups held individuals who were either awaiting trial or who had been found guilty and were yet to be punished. Toward the end of the eighteenth century, however, gaols were constructed in Upper and Lower Canada. In 1792, the first Parliament of Upper Canada passed an Act providing for the construction of a court house and a gaol in each district in the province, and additional legislation was enacted in 1810 which established gaols as houses of correction in which were to be confined "all and every idle and disorderly person, and rogues and vagabonds, and incorrigible rogues . . ." (cited in Strong 1969, 24).[5] Similar legislation was enacted in Lower Canada in 1799.[6]

Despite these legislative provisions, there were often long delays in constructing gaols in the various districts of the province, primarily because of the low rates of crime at this time and the consequent lack of concern on the part of the community and public officials. There is considerable evidence to suggest that, despite the enactment of legislation providing for their construction, gaols were not a high priority in Upper and Lower Canada in the 1790s. Splane (1965, 121) notes, "There were numerous . . . instances during the pre-Union period of the magistrates' failing to provide adequately for the proper administration of the gaols and care of the inmates. . ." Splane (1965, 122) observes that when the gaols were constructed, due to the lack of alternative resources and facilities, they "were required to act as houses of correction for any homeless or needy person for whom there was no other place, and . . . they were made to serve as institutions for the insane."[7] The conditions under which individuals were confined are illustrated by Baehre's (1977, 187-88) description of the gaol at York:

> The group of twenty-five prisoners interned at York included three lunatics under restraint, nine debtors, one of whom had cohabiting with

him in the gaol his wife and children, and a motley assortment of criminals. The lunatics were confined in the basement "dungeon" from which incessant howlings groans and "disagreeable" smells were carried to the other floors. Indiscriminate mixing among prisoners convicted of capital crimes and those with misdemeanours was permitted . . . There was little soap, and linen was changed infrequently. One inmate complained that he had not been washed in six to eight months.

Baehre (1977, 187) argues that much of the impetus for the reform of Canadian corrections in these early years came from the recognition by the public that the local gaols were inadequate and no longer served to protect the community. This perception, in conjunction with the changes which occurred in attitudes toward crime and punishment in Canada, set the stage for the era of the penitentiary[8] (see also, Kirkpatrick 1964; Fingard 1984; Baehre 1985).

Corrections on the Frontier

If the communities in the more populated areas of the East were slow to develop gaols and other alternatives for the punishment of convicted offenders, this was even more true of the large land areas in the western portion of the country known as Rupert's Land. In their discussion of the history of corrections in the area that now includes the province of Saskatchewan, Skinner et al. (1981, 15) note that "there existed little evidence of a clear penal philosophy unique to the frontier experience. For the most part the administrators, like the settlers, sought to put in place an affordable facsimile of that which they knew in eastern Canada or under British rule." Until the early 1800s, offenders charged with more serious offences were sent to England for trial. When this became too costly, legislation was enacted by Britain which provided for cases from Rupert's Land to be heard in the courts of Quebec or Ontario, and for sentences to be served in the East.[9] Less serious offences were responded to in a fashion similar to that in the Eastern areas of the country, although, as the following description of the flogging of a convicted thief in pre-Confederation Manitoba in 1836 illustrates, the attempt to publicly humiliate and shame the offender could have unanticipated consequences:

On that occasion the crowd, assembled at Upper Fort Garry to witness the exemplary punishment and thus benefit from the most powerful possible deterrence, in fact turned on the flogger and attempted to stone him. Police had to encircle the flogger and the prisoner and lock them in the Fort until the crowd dispersed (cited in James 1978, 35).

During the settlement of the frontier, the Hudson's Bay Company played a major role in the administration of justice. Skinner et al. (1981, 16) point out that the courts of the Hudson's Bay company operated until the federal government purchased Rupert's Land in 1869 and that as late as 1861, "the Hudson's Bay Company presiding judicial officer held the positions of sheriff, coroner, gaoler and chief medical officer." When the province of Manitoba joined Confederation in 1870, courts there assumed responsibility for administering justice in the Northwest Territories and this arrangement remained in effect until a Lieutenant-Governor for the N.W.T. was appointed in 1876. Following the creation of the North West Mounted Police in 1873, offenders sentenced to jail were normally held in police guardhouses in lieu of being sent to the Manitoba Penitentiary. While beyond the scope of this volume, a more extensive examination of the role played by the Hudson's Bay Company and the North West Mounted Police in early Canadian corrections would provide fascinating insights into the legacy of Canadian corrections (see also Harvey 1953; Anderson 1960).

THE CREATION OF THE PENITENTIARY

The period between 1830 and Confederation, in 1867, is one of the most important chapters in Canadian corrections. During this relatively short period of time, several key personalities and events were to shape the course of correctional history. The major development was the building of the penitentiary at Kingston, Ontario, in 1835, and through a close examination of the circumstances surrounding the construction of the prison and its first years of operation, valuable insights can be gained into the correctional process. Consideration of such events also reveals controversy among Canadian historians as to the nature and extent of the influence which developments in the United States had upon the founders of the Kingston penitentiary, the role which specific individuals who were involved in the prison and its operation played, and the reasons why Canadians in the 1830s felt compelled to erect a penitentiary. In the discussion below, we consider these issues as we trace the building of the Kingston prison and its first years of operation. Prior to this, however, the backdrop against which the initial discussions relating to the construction of the Kingston prison took place must be outlined. This necessitates a brief consideration of the changes which occurred in the United States from 1790 to 1830 leading to the "creation" of the prison in America.

The Penitentiary in America

There is considerable debate as to the factors precipitating the development of penitentiaries in the United States, and differences between observers utilizing a liberal-pluralist interpretation and a radical-elitist perspective of corrections are evident. The liberal-pluralist perspective is most clearly illustrated by David J. Rothman's historical analysis of the creation of the American penitentiary in *The Discovery of the Asylum* (1971), while the works of Currie (1973), Takagi (1975) and Scull (1977a, 1977b) provide an interpretation of history from a radical-elitist position.

During the 1600s and 1700s in colonial America, the response to criminal behaviour was heavily influenced by punishment practices in England and, as in Canada, there was widespread use of capital and corporal punishments which tended to be progressive in their severity. This is evident in Rothman's (1971, 52) description of the Massachusetts criminal code:

> A thief upon first conviction was to be fined or whipped. The next time he would pay treble damages, sit for an hour upon the gallows platform with a rope around his neck, and then be carted to the whipping post for thirty stripes. For the third offense, he would be hung.

As in early Canada, institutionalization was rarely employed and gaols, where they did exist, were utilized to confine offenders awaiting trial or punishment.

Until 1790, Americans held a view of crime and criminal behaviour as being endemic to society, and they felt that the best defence against criminality was the development and maintenance of strong community institutions such as the church and the family. Rothman (1971, 53) points out that little use was made of institutions:

> Given their conception of deviant behavior and institutional organization, they did not believe that a jail could rehabilitate or intimidate or detain the offender. Institutionalization seemed unnecessary when numerous offenders could be marched beyond the town line and not be seen again.

In the colonial period, the community assumed full responsibility for individuals who were identified as dependent and deviant, and an extensive system of workhouses and almshouses, structured on a family model, was developed.

Scull (1977a, 21) notes that a wide variety of individuals were confined in the workhouses which "despite their name and the intentions of their founders, became dumping grounds for the decrepit and dependent of all descriptions." For the colonists, crime was an individual phenomenon, due in large measure to humankind's innate susceptibility to corruption, and thus no attempt was made to either confine or rehabilitate offenders. Between 1790 and 1830, however, profound shifts occurred in the colonists' perceptions of crime and criminal behaviour. This was due to influences from the Enlightenment writers in Europe and to changes in the social and economic structure of colonial society.

Near the end of the 1700s, the ideas of the Enlightenment writers, such as Cesare Beccaria, reached America. Beccaria and others had argued that the certainty of punishment was the most effective deterrent against criminal behaviour and that punishments which were too severe served only to perpetuate criminal behaviour rather than to reduce or eliminate it. Such ideas prompted consideration of the confinement of offenders as a punishment alternative: "Incarceration seemed more humane than hanging and less brutal than whipping. Prisons matched punishment to crime precisely: the more heinous the offense, the longer the sentence" (Rothman 1971, 62). The move toward the confinement of offenders was also influenced by the Quakers, who passed legislation in Pennsylvania in 1786 reducing the number of crimes subject to capital punishment and substituting imprisonment at hard labour for the death penalty for all but the most serious offences. This was followed by legislation in 1794 which abolished the use of capital punishment for all crimes except homicide.

In addition to the influences of the writers of the Enlightenment and the religious views of the Quakers, which were translated into legislation, massive demographic and economic changes occurred in colonial society between 1790 and 1830. These were to significantly influence both the view of criminal behaviour and the response to it, further promoting the use of incarceration as a punishment alternative. During this period, there was a substantial increase in population and a concurrent breakdown of the small, self-contained communities which had previously assumed the responsibility for the care and control of deviant and dependent populations. Confronted with an increasingly mobile populace and growing anonymity in communities, the public perceptions shifted from crime as an endemic and individually situated phenomenon to crime as symptomatic of increasing corruption in the community and the breakdown of traditional methods of social control.

In short, the source of criminal behaviour shifted from the individual to the community, and the criminal offender was viewed as the product of an environment of community disorder and family instability, as the victim of an increasingly corrupt and unstable community life. To combat this, Americans sought to create a setting in which the offender could be made into a useful citizen. The setting was the penitentiary and in 1790, amidst unbridled optimism, the Walnut Street Jail opened in Philadelphia. This was followed by the construction of numerous penitentiaries in the Eastern United States which were operated on either the Pennsylvania or the Auburn model.[10]

The above materials indicate that Rothman (1971) interprets the development of the penitentiary in colonial America from a liberal-pluralist perspective of correctional change. As Shover (1979, 44) argues:

> His analysis of the origins of . . . correctional reform places a heavy emphasis upon humanitarian impulses, a generalized belief among many citizens that the basis of social order was being eroded, and changing conceptions of the nature and causes of crime . . . Rothman assumes the existence of a political process that is responsive to citizen opinion and demand. . . . [G]iven changing public opinion, the inevitable result was the penitentiary movement.

Rothman's (1971) liberal-pluralist interpretation of the events surrounding the construction of the first penitentiary in America is disputed by observers such as Takagi (1975) and Scull (177a, 1977b) who adopt a radical-elitist perspective. Takagi (1975, 18-19) argues, for example, that the building of the Walnut Street Jail, rather than being the consequence of humanitarian ideals, was an attempt on the part of the state to consolidate power. Further, Scull (1977a) presents a radically different interpretation of the factors influencing the development of institutions in America at this time.

Like Rothman (1971), Scull (1977a, 19-20) notes that the response to dependent and deviant behaviour in colonial communities occurred on an informal, local basis:

> Towns expelled their criminals and vagrants, or else made use of the standard penalties of corporal punishment, fines, mutilation, and death. Town jails were places of pretrial detention, receptacles for debtors, and a means of ensuring that those convicted of serious offenses were still around for the infliction of sentence.

Scull (1977a, 21-22) also documents the abandonment of community-based methods of responding to deviance in the late 1700s, and the creation of institutions, including penitentiaries, asylums, workhouses, and juvenile reformatories, to address the problems of deviancy and dependency in communities.

Scull (1977a, 24), however, attributes these developments to more than the rise of an urbanized, industrial society with its consequent breakdown in the effectiveness of extreme localism as a mechanism of social control, arguing that even the most highly "urbanized" regions of colonies were still predominately rural in character when the movement toward institutionalization began. He further (1977b, 338) criticizes Rothman's explanation of the emergence of the asylum as a function of an increased anxiety about social order and the ability of the newly created penitentiary to maintain it: "While Rothman persuasively *describes* this anxiety, he almost entirely neglects to *explain* it — to give us any understanding of why these persons became anxious about these things at this time. The structural sources of the concern with imminent breakdown of the social order remain unexplored and unperceived."

Rather, Scull (1977a, 24) argues, the movement toward the increased use of institutions for the confinement of criminal offenders "can be more plausibly tied to the growth of the capitalist market system and to its impact on economic and social relationships." Scull (1977a, 24) supports his argument by noting that the emergence of the capitalist market system at this time created an economic distinction between the rich and the poor, destroying the traditional patterns of relations which had rested heavily upon "the reciprocal notions of paternalism, deference, and dependence. . . ." According to this author (1977a, 25), these changes resulted in the lessening of the sense of social obligation toward the poor, and strained the family-based system of relief, which had been utilized in the colonies for dependent, neglected, and deviant individuals:

> These changes in structures, perceptions, and outlook which marked the transition from the old paternalistic order to a capitalist social system provided a direct source of bourgeois dissatisfaction with the traditional, noninstitutional response to the indigent.

In short, Scull (1977a, 32-33) argues that the assumption of state responsibility for social control, in place of traditional, community-based mechanisms, corresponded with the transformation of the social structure to a capitalist economic system:

> The growth of a single national market and the rise of allegiance to the central political authority to a position of overriding importance undermined the rationale of a locally based response to deviance. . . .[T]hese factors contributed . . . to the development of a state-sponsored system of segregative control.

While the optimism of rehabilitation proved unfounded, the system continued to develop:

> If prisons, asylums, and "reformatories", and the activities of those running them, did not transform their inmates into upright citizens, they did at least get rid of troublesome people. . . . [T]hey remained a convenient way to get rid of inconvenient people (Scull 1977a, 33).

The work of Scull (1977a) and others provides a constrasting view to that of Rothman (1971) and in the discussion below, it becomes evident that similar differences of interpretation surround the emergence of the penitentiary in Canada.[11]

The Origins of the Penitentiary in Canada

In the preceding discussion, we have briefly documented the social and economic changes, and the attendant shifts in the public's view of crime and criminality, which led to the construction of prisons for the confinement of criminal offenders in America. Examination of the historical materials relating to the construction of the first Canadian penitentiary at Kingston, Ontario, in 1835, reveals that this development was also a response to the attitudes toward crime and punishment which existed in the early 1800s, as well as to the political, economic, and philosophical influences of the time. As with consideration of the discovery of the asylum in colonial America, however, there are conflicting interpretations among historical observers as to the events that precipitated the construction of the first penitentiary, again centring on the alternative explanations of the liberal-pluralist and radical-elitist perspectives of correctional change.

In his discussion of the attitudes of Upper Canadians toward crime and punishment during the period 1832 to 1851, Bellomo (1972, 16) argues that an increase in crime in the 1830s, coupled with overcrowding in the local gaols, precipitated the construction of the penitentiary. Beattie (1977, 1-2), to the contrary, argues that during the 1830s and 1840s, serious crime was not widespread, although many Upper Canadians *perceived* crime to be a serious problem and devoted considerable public discussion to criminal behaviour and its punishment: "Accounts of trials appeared regularly in the newspapers and the contemporary debates in England and the U.S. on the central questions of penal philosophy and practice — capital punishment, for example, and the virtues of imprisonment — were followed and echoed in the Canadian press."

Regardless of the actual extent of criminal behaviour, it is clear that the perceptions of Upper Canadians contributed to a major change in penal practice in this country.

In the 1830s, according to Beattie (1977, 2-3), criminality came to be viewed as "evidence of much deeper and more serious evils — evils that threatened the moral and social fabric of the society, and that called for powerful measures of defence." For Upper Canadians, crime and morality became closely intertwined and criminality was evidence that "some members of society did not accept or had not been taught to accept the essential principles on which the social order rested. . . ." Expanding on this, Bellomo (1972, 16) argues that Upper Canadians felt the major causes of crime were "intemperance, immorality, lack of religious practices, idleness, . . . vices directly contrary to the dominant values of the period." As such, the very foundation of Canadian society was threatened. Further, Bellomo (1972, 12-13) observes that for Upper Canadians "the criminal was everything a 'respectable' person was not" and criminals were "people quite distinct from that great body of law-abiding citizens"[12] (see Duncan 1965).

Chunn (1981, 17-18) also relates the development of the penitentiary to social and political changes in Canadian society in the early 1800s, documenting the economic and demographic developments which altered the class structure of Upper Canada. "Prior to 1820, most settlers owned some land but within thirty years the society was composed of wealthy landowners, small farmers, an emergent mercantile and manufacturing class, and landless labourers, both the skilled and unskilled. Not surprisingly, political and social turmoil ensued."

The primary defence mechanisms against crime and disorder would become penal institutions, which, according to Taylor (1979, 406), would impart "education, obedience, religion and constraint on the individuals who made up society." For Upper Canadians, the prison would become the major weapon in the fight to insure order and stability, and the general principles upon which it would operate were the expiation of crime, the deterrence of potential crime, the protection of society, and the reformation of the convict (Baehre 1977, 190).

Baehre (1977), Beattie (1977) and Taylor (1979) adopted a different perspective on the creation of penal institutions in Canada from that of Rothman (1971). While Rothman argued that the first penitentiaries in the United States were constructed to provide a reformative setting within which criminal offenders, who were the products of an increasingly corrupt and unstable community, could become useful citizens, the focus of Canadian observers is on criminal offenders as a "dangerous class" who constituted a clear threat to the stability of Canadian society of the time. Still, the works of Taylor (1979), Baehre (1977), and Beattie (1977) cannot be characterized as utilizing a radical-elitist perspective of correctional change. Such a view, however, is evident in the works of Gosselin (1982) and Smandych and Verdun-Jones (1982).

Perhaps the most radical perspective on the development of the Canadian penitentiary has been proposed by Gosselin (1982). Proceeding from a radical-elitist perspective similar to that of Scull (1977a, 1977b), Gosselin's (1982, 88) interpretation of the events in the late eighteenth and early nineteenth centuries that precipitated the creation of the penitentiary in Canada is in sharp contrast to the views of other observers:

> The country was racked by deep economic crisis and successive waves of popular unrest (which took the form of land occupations and tax revolts) that posed a serious threat to the new State. A system of incarceration, combined with armed repression, assured bourgeois control of the country as a whole.

Further, Gosselin (1982, 97) argues: "The penitentiary system, along with the police, the courts and the army, are key elements in the web of coercion. The role of the penitentiary is to provide a means by which the established order may maintain physical and psychological control, and/or the threat of such control, over the millions of Canadian workers."

In focusing on the role of economic factors in the rise of the insane asylum in nineteenth-century Ontario, Smandych and Verdun-Jones (1982) consider the analytical utility of the several competing perspectives of correctional change.[13] Dismissing the liberal interpretations which identified "well intentioned benevolence" as the primary precipitating factor in the use of the asylum in Upper Canada, these authors (1982, 17) argue that "the perspective does not adequately deal with the recurrent themes . . . of effectiveness and economy, which seem to be associated with institutional reform in Ontario." Rather, Smandych and Verdun-Jones (1982, 11) find the macro-sociological perspective, offered by Scull (1979), a more useful analytical framework, asserting that the origins of Ontario's earliest penal and welfare institutions can be traced to concerns with effectiveness and economy: "The penitentiary held out the promise of being an economically self-sustaining institution."

Concluding their discussion, Smandych and Verdun-Jones (1982, 19) contend:

It is imperative that economic concerns by considered as one of the possible factors underpinning the rise of governmental systems of social control . . . [O]ne of the central themes which stem from the study of institutional reform in Ontario is the finding that social reformers widely assumed that the establishment of separate institutions for the insane, the criminal, and the indigent, would, at least in the long run be of economic benefit to society.

The Construction of the Kingston Penitentiary

The proposal to construct a penitentiary was first presented to the 1826-27 House of Assembly in Upper Canada by H.C. Thomson, editor of the *Upper Canadian Herald* in Kingston, Ontario. In 1831, Thomson was appointed to chair a select committee to investigate "the expedience of erecting a penitentiary" (cited in Beattie 1977, 16) and in February of that year, he visited Bridewell Prison in Glasgow, Scotland, and examined the Auburn system which was in operation at the state prison in Auburn, New York. Thomson prepared a report severely criticizing the existing penal system in Canada and arguing for the construction of a penitentiary. Among the reasons for his recommendation were that (1) the levying of fines was unjust because of the differential ability of offenders to pay, (2) capital punishment was rarely being used to punish offenders, (3) confinement in the local gaols was no longer a practical alternative due to overcrowding and the lack of proper classification of offenders, (4) corporal punishment was improper and degrading, and (5) the sanction of banishment was unenforceable and ineffective. Thomson's report to the House of Assembly in 1831 stated: "A penitentiary . . . should be a place to lead a man to repent his sins and amend his life." Baehre (1977, 191) notes, however, that for Thomson, "The primary purpose of the penitentiary was to punish, to gain penitence; reform was 'only a secondary intention.' " And, as Taylor (1979, 408) observes:

> The penitentiary responded to particular and general concerns: particular concerns about the punishment of crime; general concerns about the state of disorder in the world, resulting from the industrial revolution, urbanization, and immigration and which led to deviant behaviour. . . .

The House of Assembly accepted in principle Thomson's recommendation that a penitentiary be constructed, and it appointed Thomson and John Macaulay, a Kingston businessman, to visit institutions in the United States and report back to the Assembly as to the best prison system to implement in Canada. In their *Report of Commissioners on Penitentiaries,* issued in 1832, Thomson and Macaulay compared the Pennsylvania and Auburn systems and concluded that "the Auburn system is that which is safer to act on in this province" and, noting that the Pennsylvania system was still largely experimental, described the Auburn model as ". . . 'a beautiful example of what may be done by proper discipline, in a Prison well constructed' " (Baehre 1977, 193).

The two commissioners had been provided with a sketch of the Auburn model, to be used for the construction of the Kingston penitentiary, by William Powers, the deputy warden at the Auburn, New York prison, who was subsequently retained to supervise the construction of the Kingston prison.

In making this recommendation, Thomson and Macaulay had been influenced by the writings of John Howard in *The State of the Prisons in England and Wales* (1777) and by the Boston Prison Discipline Society. Howard had lauded the benefits of the separate confinement of prisoners at night and a highly structured work routine during the day. Similarly, the Boston Prison Discipline Society was a major proponent of the Auburn system and endorsed the construction of the Kingston penitentiary. In addition, Chunn (1981, 14) contends that "Kingston was modelled on the congregate Auburn system rather than the Philadelphia system precisely because of the 'higher degree of profit from the labour of the convict.' " Further, Taylor (1979, 400, 406) notes that, for Thomson and Macaulay, the Auburn system made sense:

> Solitary confinement helped prevent escape, prison labour helped finance the institution and reform the criminal, forced labour and confinement were deterrents to crime . . . The congregate system imposed habits of industry on the disordered elements of society, and virtues such as hard work, sobriety, and obedience were enforced.

The recommendations of Thomson and Macaulay were accepted and formally embodied in the *Penitentiary Act* of 1834, the preamble of which stated:

> Whereas, if many offenders convicted of crimes were ordered to solitary imprisonment, accompanied by well regulated labour and religious instructions, it might be the means under Providence, not only of deterring others from the commission of crimes, but also of reforming the individuals, and inuring [*sic*] them to to [*sic*] habits of industry[14] (cited in Baehre 1977, 194).

In addition, the 1835 legislation provided for the creation of a board of five inspectors with "full power and authority to make all necessary rules and regulations respecting the discipline and Police of the said Penitentiary" (cited in Splane 1965, 132). Legislation was also enacted to provide for the maintenance and government of the institution and for the appointment of a warden, physician, chaplain, and other administrative personnel.[15]

On completion in 1835, the new penitentiary differed considerably from the district gaols, and provision was made for the separation of offenders on the basis of sex and type of offence, as well as for prisoners to have their own bedding, clothing, and food. The Kingston penitentiary was the largest public building in Upper Canada and symbolized what Taylor (1979, 407) has labelled a "moral architecture," which reflected the themes of order and morality: "The penitentiary was an ideal society . . . much more than a system of dealing with transgression of the law, it became a projection of the world as it should be." According to Baehre (1977, 199), the penitentiary "was established not only to serve as a model for its inmates but also as a model for society . . . The penitentiary removed those 'sources of temptation and corruption' which fostered crime — such as idleness, uncleanly habits, intemperance, and the use of obscene and profane language" (see also Curtis et al., 1985).

A major cornerstone of the penitentiary regimen was hard labour:

> The explicit goals of punishment were the deterrence of others and reform of offenders in the cheapest possible manner. Hard labour was the key to achieving these aims . . . Through labour, convicts would acquire skills which could be utilized to acquire gainful employment after release from prison. At the same time, hard work would instill industrious habits and the 'correct' values in offenders (Chunn 1981, 14).

One of the controversies which surrounded the building of the Kingston penitentiary was the opposition of the tradesmen in the Kingston area, in what Palmer (1980, 9) has identified as one of the first organized efforts of Canadian working people. When discussions of the possibility of building a prison first appeared, trades people argued that teaching inmates trades in the institution would not only debase the craft skills but also threaten their economic well being. This opposition was reflected in a letter to a Kingston newspaper which characterized the prison as "a system which instead of punishing evil doers, becomes a scourge for them that do well" (cited in Palmer 1980, 10). Having failed to halt the construction of the prison, the trades people filed a petition with the Upper Canada Parliament in 1836 which called for convict labour to be restricted to "breaking stones, pumping water, and working at efforts that would not injure the interests of tradesmen" (Palmer 1980, 16; for a description and discussion of convict labour in Kingston, see Chunn 1981).

The Early Years of Kingston

Prior to and following the construction of Kingston, there was intense debate in Upper Canada as to the purposes of imprisonment, reflecting the long standing concern over punishment versus reformation of the offender. Among historical observers, there are differing interpretations of the objectives which were assigned to the prison. Bellomo (1972, 18) argues that the purpose of confinement was to punish and deter offenders and that the reformation of the offender was only a secondary consideration: "Punishment was not only to bring about individual repentance, it was also to serve as a warning for other potential criminals." If punishment was to set an example, however, "the prisoner could not be provided with a better life than the most under-privileged of non-criminals or otherwise the deterrent value would be lost . . . Hardship had to be institutionalized in the system" (Bellomo 1972, 18-19). Support for this view of the purpose of the prison is provided by Shoom (1966, 217) in his discussion of the operation of Kingston: "According to the penal philosophy of the time, only through a sentence of stern discipline and religious contemplation would the prisoner renounce his previous life of sin." Beattie (1977, 22, 23), however, includes the reformation of the offender as a goal of incarceration:

> The aim . . . was to create an environment which would remove the convict as far as possible from the evil influences that had led him to crime. A life of "labor, silence and strict obedience" would certainly punish him and would also act as a more effective deterrent than a sentence in one of the local gaols . . . It marked a new departure in penal practice — to eradicate crime, not simply by punishing and deterring offenders, but by reforming them.

While there is disagreement concerning the goals of confinement, the conditions under which prisoners were kept in Kingston have been extensively documented:

> Inmates were kept in absolute seclusion from society and were detained in a state of complete inactivity during the non-working hours. The resultant effect was physical atrophy and mental stagnation. Rules of strict silence prevailed. Prisoners were mixed together young with old, sane with

insane. As cells were too small to allow for free movement, inmates were forced to lie down for twelve to sixteen hours a day (cited in MacGuigan 1977, 11).

Shoom (1966, 215) notes that breaches of prison regulations were responded to by punishment of a "swift and often brutal nature" and involved flogging with the cat-o'-nine-tails and rawhide, as well as the use of irons, solitary confinement, and rations of bread and water. To illustrate his point, Shoom (1966, 216) presents the entries from the *Punishment Book of the Penitentiary* for 1843:

Offence	Punishment
Laughing and talking	6 lashes; cat-o'-nine-tails
Talking in wash-house	6 lashes; rawhide
Threatening to knock convicts' brains out	24 lashes; cat-o'-nine-tails
Talking to Keepers on matters not relating to their work	6 lashes; cat-o'-nine-tails
Finding fault with rations when desired by guard to sit down	6 lashes; rawhide, and bread and water
Staring about and inattentive at breakfast table	bread and water
Leaving work and going to privy when other convict there	36 hours in dark cell, and bread and water

In an attempt to maintain discipline and a strict silent system in the institution, inmates were forbidden to "... 'exchange looks, wink, laugh, nod, or gesticulate,' or to 'make use of any signs, except such as are necessary to explain their wants' ..." (cited in Splane 1965, 134). Prisoners were required to walk in a lock-step march and "the ringing of bells informed the convict when to sleep, lie down, or rise" (Baehre 1977, 199). In describing the environment which existed in Kingston during the early years, Chunn (1981, 19) notes: "The over-riding emphasis on control necessitated the bell system, the silent system, the constant surveillance, the lavish use of corporal punishment, the meaningless unproductive labour ... and the lack of resources allocated to reformative programmes."

Beginning in 1840, there was a growing concern with the effectiveness of the penitentiary in general and with the extensive use of corporal punishment in particular. Questions were raised about the adequacy of the penitentiary facilities and the ability of the institution to carry out the reformation/punishment of offenders. Concern was also voiced about the high rate of recidivism among offenders released from the prison, statistics revealing that "in 1841, nearly 25% of the former prison population had been recommitted at least once (Baehre 1977, 200). Criticism was also heard regarding the use of corporal punishment in the institution. Writing as editor of the *Toronto Globe* in 1846, George Brown (cited in Beattie 1977, 148) expressed the following sentiments:

> The Globe, 4 November 1846
> Kingston Penitentiary
> Lash!—Lash!!—Lash!!!
>
> It appears from statements which are not contradicted, that from 200 to 300 punishments are inflicted on the Prisoners of the Penitentiary every month. Supposing these to average 20 lashes, it follows that 1300 lashes are given in a month, and 50,000 in a year, a far greater amount we are sure than the whole British Army and Navy undergo. A hundred and fifty lashes must be given in this den of brutality every day the sun rises. Who can calculate the amount of pain and agony, that must be imposed in this Pendemonium [*sic*]. Who can tell the amount of evil passions, of revenge, and of malice, that must be engendered by such treatment? A penitentiary is a place where the prisoner should reflect on the past, and be placed under such a system of moral training as may fit him for becoming a better member of society. Will the lash do that? Did it ever do anything but harden the person whose body was torn by its infliction?

Two years later, George Brown would chair a commission of inquiry into the administration of the Kingston penitentiary and the administrative practices of its first warden, Henry Smith.

While such editorials appeared with increasing frequency in the mid-1840s, observers have argued that concern for the reformation of the offender had begun soon after the Kingston penitentiary opened, with a report submitted in 1836 to the House of Assembly by Charles Ducombe. However, there is considerable disagreement over the role which Ducombe played in the movement to reform the penitentiary. Bellomo (1972, 20) contends that, while the system implemented in the Kingston prison was the direct result of the report submitted in 1832 by Thomson and Macaulay, Ducombe's *Report on Prisons* expanded the purposes of incarceration to include the reformation of the convict and was "a milestone in Canadian penological history." According to Bellomo (1972, 20), Ducombe introduced a new philosophy for the prison — the moral reformation of the offender:

> Reform . . . [was] to replace revenge as the principle motive of justice . . . Punishment was to be carried out in the manner "least likely to debase the human mind and most calculated to produce the reformation of the convict" . . . Treatment was to be just and consistent, and as lenient as possible.

Bellomo (1972, 21) further asserts that Ducombe's ideas gave impetus to the reform movement in Canada and to the establishment of the 1848 Commission of Inquiry into the operation of the Kingston prison.

A considerably different view of Ducombe's contribution to prison reform is presented by Baehre (1977, 195-96), who notes that Ducombe supported the Pennsylvania system of total solitary confinement "because it combined seclusion with work, thereby bringing about ' a more subdued tone of mind in the convict, and apparently a greater reform in his disposition and habits.' " Ducombe had also proposed the use of the "tranquillizing chair" which he had seen in use in the United States: "A bizarre device in which the prisoner sat restrained as his entire head became forcibly submerged in water which 'thereby suspends animation as long as may seem necessary to subdue his passions, and on allowing him to breathe he has invariably become a reformed man, with his turbulent passions quite subdued' " (Baehre 1977, 196). While there is disagreement among observers over Ducombe's role, the following decade was to witness an increased concern with the operation of the Kingston penitentiary.

THE BROWN COMMISSION: 1848-1849

Public concern with the treatment of prisoners in the penitentiary culminated in the appointment of a Royal Commission of Inquiry in 1848, chaired by George Brown, editor of the *Globe*. The mandate of the commission was to investigate charges of corruption in the institution: "The warden was charged with mismanagement of the business affairs of the penitentiary, theft, excessive cruelty, conspiracy to defraud the government, and starving the convicts" (Shoom 1966, 218). In their investigation, Brown and his five commissioners uncovered gross mismanagement and the excessive use of corporal punishment to maintain order, including the flogging of men, women, and children: "In 1846 . . . one man had been flogged sixty times in the course of the year" and an eleven-year-old boy was "publicly lashed 57 times in eight and a half months" (cited in Beattie 1977, 27).[16]

In the first of two reports, the Brown Commission condemned the extensive use of corporal punishment, and the warden, Henry Smith, was discharged from his duties (see Adamson 1983). Beattie (1977, 28-29) argues that the inquiry had even more important implications than the removal of a warden who had been charged with the impossible task of enforcing a system of total silence:

> What was really on trial was the system itself, the "silent" or "congregate" system under which Kingston was established in 1835 . . . [T]he most damning charge against [Smith] was that he had failed to fulfill the central purpose of the penitentiary . . . to break the spirits of the inmates . . . to impose order and discipline on their lives . . . to reform them.

The evidence against Smith, coupled with an increase in crime during the 1840s and a threefold increase in the population of the institution between 1842 and 1845, heightened concern over the apparent failure of the prison. As Beattie (1977, 30) observes: "An institution that was supposed to be the key to social order and social discipline seemed actually to be contributing to social disorder . . . what was required was a more humane institution and above all a more effective institution."

The changes which were required in the structure and operation of the penitentiary to achieve these ends were outlined in the second report prepared by the Brown Commission and released in 1849. The extremes to which Smith had been required to go in an attempt to maintain the silent system did not, however, result in the Brown Commission questioning the efficacy of the system: "The commissioners fully agreed that the warden had failed to realize 'the benefits to be derived from the silent system' " (Beattie 1977, 29).

The second report of the Brown Commission, released in 1849, attempted to establish the future direction of Kingston in view of the findings of the 1848 study. Incorporating information gathered on a tour of facilities in the United States, the Commission concluded that, while the Auburn system should be retained, it should be modified to provide for the inclusion of part of the Pennsylvania system — new inmates would be kept in solitary confinement for a period of up to six months. According to Beattie (1977, 31-32), the Commissioners felt that such a mix of the congregate and solitary confinement systems would "bring the best of both penal worlds . . . the submission of the separate system with the work habits and economic benefits of the congregate system." The Commission also recommended that there be separate facilities for juvenile offenders, that an asylum be constructed for the criminally insane, and that improvements be made in the system of local gaols. Within the penitentiary, the Commission recommended that educational programs be established and, to assist prisoners in readjusting to the community upon release, that private prison societies be created.

In this second report, the Commission stated that the purpose of the penitentiary was "simply the prevention of crime and that aim demanded 'the reclamation of prisoners whenever possible through using the minimum amount of force, making every attempt at rehabilitation' " (cited in Bellomo 1972, 22). Beattie (1977, 33) further notes that the Commission "hoped to gain by 'moral suasion' what physical force had failed to achieve . . ." The view underlying the recommendations of the Brown Commission, according to Splane (1965, 141), was that with "a programme strongly directed towards reformation there would be little need for the harsh punishments that had been so much in evidence prior to the inquiry."[17]

While the two reports of the Brown Commission were the first systematic inquiry into the operation of the Kingston prison since its completion thirteen years earlier, there is dispute among correctional observers as to the impact of their recommendations on prison reform in Canada. Bellomo (1972, 22) contends that the Brown reports "comprise the core documents in any study of the Upper Canadian penal reform movement," and Splane (1965, 139) argues that the second report, in particular, had a long-term influence on the development of penal policy and is "one of the more significant documents in the history of social welfare." Baehre (1977, 206-07), again dissenting from Bellomo's interpretation of historical events, argues that such characterizations of the Brown Commission reports are "gross exaggerations" and that the documents did not reflect a shift in penal philosophy in this country either in terms of "attitude or application":

> The Commission of 1849 virtually echoes the recommendations of Thomson, Macaulay, and Ducombe. . . . The minor modifications offered by the Commissioners are . . . regressive in light of the fact that by 1842, a committee of the New York State Assembly had publicly concluded 'silence does not reform anyone'. . . . The Commissioners . . . did not abolish the use of the lash or the contracting of prison labour. . . . [T]he ideology of prison practice which structured the original legislation and

the rules and regulations of the penitentiary were carried intact until Confederation . . . The Royal Commission of 1849 . . . did little to change the existing principles of discipline as carried out at Kingston except to make the system run more smoothly in the years to come.

While there is dispute over the impact of the Brown Commission on correctional reform, legislation was enacted in subsequent years which embodied many of the Commission's concerns. The *Penitentiary Act* of 1851 provided for the construction of cells for the initial period of solitary confinement which the new inmates were to undergo, established specific guidelines for the use of corporal punishment within the institution, and reduced the practice of allowing citizens to buy admittance to the facility to view the prisoners.[18] Further, the legislation provided that mentally ill offenders be removed to the Lunatic Asylum of Upper Canada and provided for the appointment of two inspectors who would oversee the operation of the institution (cited in Splane 1965, 144-45). In 1857, the *Prison Inspection Act* was passed which provided for the construction of a separate facility for insane convicts and the building of the reformatory for young offenders (see Shoom 1972).[19] The *Prison Inspection Act* and subsequent legislation enacted in 1859 also established a system of inspection for the penitentiary, the asylums, and for the district gaols (see Smandych 1981; Smandych and Verdun-Jones 1982).

CONFEDERATION AND THE LATE 1800s

In 1867, there were provincial institutions located in Kingston, Ontario, St. John, New Brunswick, and in Halifax, Nova Scotia. At Confederation, all three institutions came under the legislative authority of the Parliament of Canada. In 1868, under the first *Penitentiary Act*, the structure of the federal penitentiary system was created, including the Department of Justice which was charged with the supervision of "all matters connected with the administration of justice in Canada, not within the jurisdiction of the Governments of the Provinces. . . ."[20] Subsequent amendments to this act in 1878, 1879, and in 1880 included various provisions for the administration of the federal prison system. During the 1870s a major expansion of the federal penitentiary system took place, with prisons being constructed in Montreal, Quebec (1873), Stony Mountain, Manitoba (1876), and in New Westminster, British Columbia (1878). In 1880, a new penitentiary was opened at Dorchester, New Brunswick, and the prisons in St. John and Halifax were closed.[21]

The conditions that existed in the federal penitentiaries at this time are documented in the reports of J. G. Moylan, Inspector of Penitentiaries. Moylan (cited in Edmison 1976, 362) criticized the lack of segregative facilities in the Manitoba and British Columbia prisons, labelling them "schools of corruption" which "tend to the propagation rather than the diminution of criminality." Further, Moylan (in Edmison 1976, 364-65) cited the use of corporal punishment at Stony Mountain and questioned the complaints of the warden of the British Columbia prison about the conduct of the prisoners in his charge: "There must have been some laxity and remissness in enforcing observance of the rules and regulations, some want of administrative ability when it is found necessary to report that *thirty-three* convicts cannot be kept in order by the warden and his staff" (emphasis in original). Edmison (1976, 365) contends that individuals such as Moylan were early pioneers of prison reform in Canada, as exemplified by the Inspector's statement that the guiding principle of corrections should be that "none shall leave a prison a worse member of the community than when entering it."

In the local gaols and provincial institutions, meanwhile, conditions had continued to worsen. In the province of Nova Scotia, the attempt to develop a system of workhouses at the local level had failed. Coles (1979, 7) cites an 1834 grand jury report which found that the workhouses had deteriorated into a "miserable condition totally unfit to give shelter to Human Beings." Further, Kroll (cited in Coles 1979, 8) notes that to keep costs down prisoners had to pay

> for meals and liquor as well as rent for themselves and upon release further handed the jailkeeper a fee for his services. Failure to make this payment could result in a longer detention, though more commonly, a prisoner was allowed to beg in the streets for his jail fees.

In an attempt to improve the conditions of confinement, a provincial penitentiary was opened in 1844 to which the majority of offenders were sent. However, as the following description reveals, conditions in this institution soon deteriorated as well:

> Within five years, prison life had tumbled to the lowest common denominator. Singing, whistling, smoking, cursing, drunkenness, and sloth became the order of the day. Gaol keepers fraternized with prisoners and often came to work drunk and disorderly. The Prison's Governor, Thomas Carpenter, spent weeks at a time drunk in his quarters, and in 1849, in a rum-soaked stupor, Carpenter actually aided prisoners in an escape (Coles 1979, 3-4).

Given these conditions, the institutions which became prisons following Confederation in 1867 "were sub-standard even for that time and were no more than intolerable lock-ups, poorly equipped and managed" (Coles 1979, 4). In the 1870s, as an economic move, the provincial government transferred the responsibility for financing and operating the gaols to the municipalities, yet little was done to improve the worsening conditions.

Similar problems also existed at the local level in Ontario. In an attempt to improve the conditions in the gaols, the Parliament of Upper Canada had passed the *Act of 1838*. This legislation created a board of officials to oversee the construction and operation of the gaols, the classification of offenders and other individuals confined in them, and attempted to provide some employment for the inmates, "in order that the common gaols may really serve for places of correction according to the intention of the law" (cited in Splane 1965, 124-25).[22] This Act was the first attempt to legislate control over the gaols, but there is considerable question as to its effectiveness. In 1850, a grand jury in the York Assizes criticized the arrangements in local gaols: "The unthinking boy, and the young girl, as yet unhackneyed in the ways of vice, untainted by the germ of immorality incarcerated for the first time and perhaps for some reckless freak, or trifling technical offence . . . are associated with the old, the profilgate, the abandoned offender" (cited in Beattie 1977, 78-79). Splane (1965, 155) also cites the findings of an 1860 survey which revealed: ". . . 'defects . . . of every possible kind . . . in superintendence . . . in discipline . . . in construction . . . in the sanitary arrangements and . . . in the means of reforming'. . . ." While the legislation enacted in 1859 had included provisions for monitoring the construction and operation of gaols in Ontario, Splane (1965, 156) notes that in 1866, "The inspectors no longer believed that the existing legislation was capable of achieving its intended purpose. . . ." Following Confederation, the province of Ontario passed the *Prison and Asylum Inspection Act* in 1868, which required inspectors ". . . 'to visit and inspect every Gaol, House of Correction, Reformatory, and Prison . . . at least twice in each year' and to 'make a separate and distinct report in writing to the Lieutenant-Governor'. . . ."[23] This legislation was one of the first attempts by a province, following Confederation, to reform the local goals. However, Splane (1965, 179) observes that the problems of the gaols continued throughout the 1800s and into the 1890s:

> The municipalities continued to be grudging in their support; the quality of administration of the gaols by the sheriff and gaolers remained

mediocre; constructive employment for the prisoners was limited or non-existent; classification was inadequate . . . and persons continued to be committed to the gaols who required a different type of care or treatment.

In 1890, the province of Ontario established a commission of inquiry under the direction of J. W. Langmuir to examine the operation of houses of correction and reformatories. Among the findings of the commission (Langmuir 1891, 145) were: local governments often failed to provide sufficient funds for the operation of gaols; the poor physical condition of many of the gaols prevented the effective classification of offenders; nearly 50% of the admissions to the local gaols were for the offences of vagrancy and drunkenness; and, for a large number of those confined in the gaols, "poverty and infirmity are their only crimes." Among the recommendations of the commission (1891, 214-225) were that the province of Ontario assume responsibility for the local gaols and that alternatives be developed for housing the poor, the insane, and youths.

Attempts to reform the gaols, when made, encountered numerous obstacles. Wetherell (1979, 150-51) documents the conditions in Ontario gaols that made classification nearly impossible. Many of the gaols were old and had been constructed when offenders were kept together without regard to age, sex, or offence. In addition, by 1894, overcrowding was becoming a major problem. Further, in the late 1800s, the system of contract labour, under which prisoners were rented to private contractors at a daily rate to produce goods on prison property, came under increasing criticism. Wetherell (1979, 153) cites the comments of Member of Parliament George Ryerson in the legislative debates over prison labour in 1895. Ryerson asserted that productive prison labour was unjust interference with free labour and it was best "to keep prisoners employed in carrying balls and chains or digging holes in the sand and filling them up again."

As a result of this type of opposition, the system of contract labour was abolished in 1895. The emphasis upon discipline and hard work as the primary correctional techniques, however, continued. This is illustrated by the comments in the 1895 report of the Penitentiary Branch which criticized prison officials for conducting educational classes during work hours, arguing that such classes "afford too frequent opportunity for conversation and plotting" (cited in Dixon 1947, 3).

In the West, the conditions in the Manitoba gaols at the time the province joined Confederation in 1870 were also poor, as revealed in an 1871 report to the Secretary of State for the Provinces concerning the construction of a penitentiary:

> At present the only building available is a small wooden house . . . wholly unfit for the purpose of a Penitentiary. The cells are small and there is no means of heating or ventilating them. In winter, prisoners would perish or at all events suffer from cold; in summer they would suffocate from want of air (cited in James 1978, 36).

In the North West Territories, a portion of which was to become the province of Saskatchewan, gaols were constructed in 1886 in Regina and Prince Albert. However, neither facility admitted its first prisoners until the early 1890s, both being poorly constructed and requiring additional work. Skinner et al. (1981, 29) provide the following description of the early gaols in Saskatchewan:

> The territorial jails were far from Ottawa and probably never defined their purpose other than in custodial terms. The objective . . . was to find some activity for the prisoners whenever possible. Farming commended itself naturally to the prison authorities of the North West Territories. It was productive and at the same time, hopefully, character building.

Generally, the latter part of the nineteenth century saw little change in the conditions of either the federal institutions or in the facilities operated on the local and provincial levels. Edmison (1976, 365) states that:

> Prison reform as we now understand the term was not a continuing major issue. Attempts were made here and there to provide prison after-care, but lack of funds crippled such work, and ambitious projects and associations petered out. A few groups interested in penal reform passed resolutions, but these were seldom acted upon.[24]

While observers have documented the increasing disillusionment with the penitentiary system which occurred toward the end of the 1800s in the United States (see Goldfarb and Singer 1973), there is no evidence of widespread concern with the prisons in Canada. Wetherell (1979, 146), for example, describes the state of corrections in Ontario at this time: "Long after many Americans had become dissatisfied with their institutions as places of reform, many concerned Ontarians still placed substantial faith in penal institutions as the locale of rehabilitation."[25]

In 1886, two of the last major pieces of legislation of the nineteenth century were passed. The *Penitentiary Act* provided for the appointment of federal prison inspectors and outlined their powers and duties, addressed issues relating to the separate confinement of female offenders, insane convicts, and youthful offenders, and provided for the use of solitary confinement in federal penitentiaries.[26] An *Act Respecting Public and Reformatory Prisons* was also enacted in 1886, and it included provisions for the operation of provincial correctional facilities, including:

1. the mandatory separation of youthful and older offenders;
2. procedures for federal-provincial agreements for the transfer of prisoners from federal penitentiaries to provincial institutions;
3. powers under which provincial legislatures could establish regulations for the custody, treatment, discipline, training, and employment of prisoners;
4. authority for the provinces to establish prisons and to identify to which facilities offenders were to be sent;
5. the earning of remission or "good time" by offenders in provincial institutions; and
6. the creation of temporary leaves of absence from provincial institutions for medical, humanitarian, or rehabilitative purposes.[27]

This legislation provided a major portion of the framework for the structure and operation of contemporary Canadian corrections.

During the period 1867-1900, federal correctional policy was designed to establish the dominance of the federal government and to create a system of penitentiaries that would assist in the task of building the nation. There was also some initial movements toward a "scientific penology," which included provisions for the assessment and treatment of offenders, although this idea was not to reach fruition until many decades later (Zubrycki 1980).

The Split in Correctional Jurisdiction

One of the unique attributes of the Canadian correctional system is the "two-year rule" under which offenders sentenced to two years or longer fall under the jurisdiction of the federal government, and those offenders receiving sentences of two years less a day are the responsibility of provincial correctional authorities. At this juncture it is important to examine the historical origins of this jurisdictional arrangement. In later sections of the text, the issues surrounding the split in jurisdiction are discussed in further detail.

Prior to Confederation in 1867, penitentiaries were administered by the provinces and there is little clear evidence as to why they were ultimately placed under federal control. Needham (1980, 298) notes that legislation establishing the split in correctional responsibility appeared as early as 1841, and in 1842, legislation was enacted which provided for the confinement of offenders in the provincial penitentiary if the sentence was more than two years.[28] In their historical review of the origins of the two-year split, a recent Task Force on Corrections (Solicitor General of Canada and Attorney General of British Columbia 1976, 7) notes that in 1864 and 1866, resolutions were passed under which the penitentiaries were to remain under provincial jurisdiction but that a "last minute change, which placed penitentiaries under the federal parliament in the B.N.A. Act . . . appears to be inexplicable." The authors of this report do note, however, that Lord Carnarvon, the Colonial Secretary, was committed to strengthening the powers of the central government and may have viewed the federal involvement in corrections as one mechanism to accomplish this. In addition, the Task Force (1976, 8) argues that practical and economic considerations may also have been involved:

> The federal government may have been considered the only government with the resources available to establish long-term institutions, or there may have been insufficient numbers of long-term offenders in some regions of the country to justify an institution for them in each province.

The two-year split in correctional jurisdiction may also have been established in consideration of the types of offenders that would be confined in the federal and provincial institutions. As the Ouimet (1969, 279) committee states in its consideration of the split in jurisdiction:

> Those prisoners who received a sentence of less than two years were probably regarded as ordinary people who needed a lesson while those who received longer sentences were seen as criminals whom it was necessary to separate from ordinary people. This assumption is supported by the terminology used in the British North America Act where the federal institutions are called "penitentiaries" while the provincial institutions are called "reformatory prisons."

Further, as Skinner et al. (1981, 30-31) assert, the concept of the reformatory implied that "a short sentence would be sufficient to reintegrate young, first offenders into the community through education and vocational training."

While the origins of the two-year rule cannot be firmly established, there have been debates over its political, financial, and administrative implications. Needham (1980, 299) notes that the first attempt to challenge the two-year rule was made in 1887 at a federal-provincial conference that was considering the financial implications of the *B.N.A. Act*, under which the provinces were given responsibility for implementing criminal justice legislation enacted by the federal government. At this conference, the provinces argued that such arrangements caused financial hardships and that the federal government should assist in covering the expenses which were incurred for the administration of justice. To ease the financial burden on the provinces, Quebec proposed that the federal government assume responsibility for all offenders serving sentences of six months or more; however, no changes in the jurisdictional split were made. Needless to say, the present jurisdictional arrangements have a profound impact on the operation of the correctional enterprise.

THE EARLY 1900s

In 1906, the *Penitentiary Act* was passed, repealing all previous federal legislation relating to the penitentiaries and including provisions for the administration of the federal penitentiary system, the conditions under which prisoners could earn remission, the powers and duties of the federal penitentiary inspectors, and the removal of youthful and insane convicts from the general penitentiary population.[29]

Despite this legislation in the early 1900s, there was little change in the philosophy of corrections or in the manner in which prisons at the federal level were operated. As Gosselin (1982, 74) notes, "There were intensive studies made throughout the period 1890-1925 into reorganization of the imprisonment system, although no major changes were in fact made." In many institutions, the punitive practices documented by the Brown Commission over half a century earlier continued well into the 1900s: "Punishments included: hosing of inmates by a powerful stream of cold water (used until 1913); ball and chain worn as they worked (used until 1933); handcuffing to bars from 8 a.m. to noon, and 1 p.m. to 5 p.m. (used in the 1930s); as a 'cure' for mental defectives, dunking in a trough of ice and slush (abolished in the 1930s)" (MacGuigan 1977, 12). In addition, the administrative quality of the institutions continued to be poor, as Edmison (1970, 541) found in reviewing the findings of a 1914 report of the Royal

Commission to Investigate the State and Management of Kingston Penitentiary:

> Many of the guards are not qualified by education or character for the positions they fill . . . When they carry on illicit traffic in tobacco and rob the convicts in doing so, they cannot help to make the prisoners honest men. Their influence must have an evil effect which nothing can overcome.

Similar deficiencies continued to plague institutions at the provincial and local levels, as revealed by a series of reports issued in Nova Scotia. In 1901, The Report of the First Inspector of Penal Institutions concluded:

> In the Province of Nova Scotia, remand and sentenced prisoners continue to be housed together due to improper facilities for the classification of inmates . . . problems continue to exist with respect to security, inmate employment and development/maintenance of standard operation procedures within the seventeen County institutions . . . (cited in Coles 1979, 14).

The Report of the Fourth Inspector of Penal Institutions, released in 1928, identified the following problem areas: *(1)* no attempt at systematic employment of prisoners, *(2)* an absence of, or inadequate provision for, classification of prisoners based on their age and nature of offence, *(3)* no provision for exercise of prisoners in open air, and *(4)* an abuse of per diem expenses provided to jailers. In 1931, as a result of a recommendation made in the Report of the Fifth Inspector of Penal Institutions, A Royal Commission Concerning Jails in the Province of Nova Scotia was appointed. Among the findings of this Commission, published in 1933, were the following:

> The jails in Nova Scotia are inadequate as penal institutions, often subject in their control to petty politics, usually antiquated as to structure of buildings, lacking provision for classification, isolation and employment of prisoners, who spend their time in idleness, the young learning evil from the sophisticated, the women often lacking sufficient privacy and supervision by matrons, the innocent experiencing deprivations of social offenders deprived of social treatment which might prevent permanent delinquency (cited in Coles 1979, 9).

In reflecting on the findings of these and subsequent reports on institutions in the province, Coles (1979, 16) concludes: *"All* of the above concerns which were expressed in 1928 *continue* to exist in 1979" (emphasis in original).

From the materials which are available, it appears that there was little change in the structure and operation of institutions at the provincial and local levels during the first decades of the twentieth century. While the provinces enacted legislation providing for the administration of the gaols under their jurisdiction, no major reform efforts were undertaken. Skinner et al. (1981, 51, 80) note that in Saskatchewan there was little change in the administration of the provincial gaols from 1905, when provincial status was achieved, to 1946, when there was a discernible shift toward the treatment and rehabilitation of offenders: "Retribution and deterrence through punishment were considered all-important . . . The task of prison reform was left to church groups, volunteer caring societies, and the fledgling prisoner welfare groups. . . ."

During the 1930s, there were some signs, particularly at the federal level, that the harsh regimen of the penitentiary was changing, albeit slowly:

> Lighting was provided in cells first for special "good conduct" prisoners, to enable them to read and learn during daylight hours . . . As a reward for good conduct, inmates were permitted to write one letter every three months to their immediate families. They were also allowed half-hour visits by relatives once a month (MacGuigan 1977, 12).

A major change at this time was the modification of the strict rule of silence. Under the new regulations, prisoners were permitted to converse prior to work in the morning, during lunch breaks, and until 7:00 p.m. in the evening. Edmison (1970, 535-36) cites the observations of Superintendent of Penitentiaries, General D.M. Ormond, regarding this change: "This experiment has not indicated that any greater dangers to the security of the institutions have developed than existed before abolition of the silence rule . . . however . . . the average conversation is of no reformative value to those taking part."

There was also increased attention given to the payment of prisoners for work performed in confinement. Several of the provinces had enacted legislation providing for the employment of prisoners outside institutions and, in 1935, provisions were made for federal prisoners to be paid five cents per day for their labour. Further impetus for reform was provided by the first Canadian Penal Congress which met in Toronto in 1935 and produced several resolutions, including a call for the reorganization of the Remission Service, the creation of special facilities for juvenile offenders, and for a Royal Commission to investigate the penitentiary system.

In 1936, prompted by disturbances which had occurred in several of the federal prisons and by the recommendations of the Canadian Penal Congress, a Royal Commission on the Penal System of Canada was appointed under the chairmanship of Mr. Justice Archambault. In their report, issued in 1938, the commissioners (Archambault 1938, 9) argued that "the task of the prison should be, not merely the temporary protection of society through the incarceration of captured offenders, but the transformation of reformable criminals into law-abiding citizens. . . ." In addition, the Commission argued that while the responsibility of the state to reform and rehabilitate the offender had been recognized for nearly 100 years, neither had been effectively carried out, and it sharply criticized the Superintendent of Penitentiaries as "arrogant" and "neglectful" and for utilizing "extreme dictatorial methods" in his management of the penitentiary system (see Adamson 1983). The recommendations of the Archambault report included the improvement of vocational training and education programs, and proper classification of offenders, which, the commissioners (Archambault 1938, 104) noted, had been recognized as essential over fifty years earlier, but was still addressed with "very little intelligence or effectiveness." In concluding, the Archambault report (1938, 355) proposed a complete reform of the rules and regulations of the penitentiary system in Canada with consideration for (*1*) the protection of society, (*2*) the safe custody of inmates, (*3*) strict but humane discipline, and (*4*) the reformation and rehabilitation of the offender.

The Archambault Committee also raised the issue of the split in correctional jurisdiction between the federal and provincial governments. Needham (1980, 300) notes that the Committee recommended that all of Canadian corrections should be brought under the jurisdiction of the federal government, not only for financial reasons, but for the " 'obvious' benefits of a single system of classification, of prison discipline and of correctional philosophy."

The increasing focus on the treatment of offenders during the latter part of the 1930s was to provide the basis for the postwar era in Canadian corrections which witnessed the development of vocational training and education programs in prisons, the introduction of various treatment modalities, and subsequently, the creation of community corrections programs. Particularly revealing were the comments of Professor Frank Scott (cited in Edmison 1970, 537) of McGill University, one of the participants at the 1935 Canadian Penal Congress:

Modern penology is a science, one of the new social sciences. It is not philanthropy. Being a science, it must work by the scientific method . . . Being a science, it should be as completely divorced from politics as it is humanly possible to make it in a democracy.

Not only did Scott's comments portend a shift in correctional thinking in Canada toward the treatment and reformation of the offender, but they also raised a critical issue as to the role of political considerations in the correctional process, a topic which is considered in this volume.

POST–WORLD WAR II CORRECTIONS

Following the Second World War, there was a shift toward a treatment model of corrections in Canada. At the federal level, this was reflected in the 1949 *Annual Report of the Commissioner of Penitentiaries* (1950, 7): "Continued progress has been made in the development of facilities necessary to carry out an effective programme of rehabilitation in the Canadian penitentiaries." This effort, the Commissioner (1950, 7) noted, was being undertaken with "an increasing recognition that the true purpose of the prison is not only to keep in safe custody those committed to its care but to train, uplift and educate its inmates for better and future citizenship." The shift toward a rehabilitation model of corrections was also occurring in the United States:

The intent of the rehabilitation, or medical, model was to turn the prison into a hospital to treat the disease of criminality. The therapist was to help offenders resolve the underlying conflicts that drove them to crime. Criminals then would be cured (Bartollas 1981, 23).

Throughout the federal penitentiary system, vocational training, education, and therapeutic intervention techniques, such as group counselling and individual therapy, were introduced. Critical to the rehabilitation model was the proper classification of offenders, as is noted in the 1949 *Annual Report of the Commissioner of Penitentiaries* (1950, 20): "An adequate programme classification is a primary prerequisite to any programme of segregation or treatment." To achieve the proper classification of offenders, psychiatric evaluations, social histories, and psychological testing were employed.

Concurrent with this development was the growth of psychological and psychiatric treatment staff in the prisons. In

1948, the first prison psychiatric hospital was opened in the Kingston prison and electric shock equipment was installed. The philosophy of corrections during this time is best illustrated by the comments of the Commissioner of Penitentiaries in the 1957 annual report (1958, 47):

> The asocial and antisocial type of individuals who are sentenced by the courts to the penal system have failed through unfortunate circumstances and the vicissitudes of their past life to develop mentally as the average person does . . . Reformation, which is the ultimate aim of incarceration, stands to succeed best when the deficiencies and needs of the inmate are known.

The rehabilitation model of corrections received additional support from a Committee of Inquiry, under the chairmanship of Mr. Justice Fauteux, whose report was released in 1956. The commissioners (Fauteux 1956, 87) argued that the basic principles of Canadian corrections should include:

a. a high degree of integration between all parts of the correctional system;
b. a well developed and extensive system of adult probation;
c. a concentration of effort on treatment by way of training, rather than the mere imposition of punishment . . .;
d. specialization of institutions and . . . methods of treatment, with a concentration of professional staff in the areas where it is most needed;
e. the development of small, open, minimum security institutions;
f. a planned policy of recruitment and training of professional staff, and;
g. a willingness to make full-scale experiments in all phases of the correctional system.

From the perspective of the commissioners, the basic thrust of corrections should be the treatment of the offender and the above criteria were required for the successful implementation of the rehabilitation philosophy. As the report (1956, 71) stated: "In general terms, it may be said that persons who violate the criminal law are persons who have been 'damaged' in the process of growing up." This perspective of criminal behaviour was to form the basis of the "medical" model of corrections:

> The medical model . . . assumed the offender to be "sick" (physically, mentally and/or socially); his offense to be a manifestation or symptom of his illness, a cry for help . . . Early and accurate diagnosis, followed by prompt and effective therapeutic interventions, assured an affirmative prognosis — rehabilitation (MacNamara 1977, 439-40).

The Fauteux report also addressed the issue of correctional jurisdiction. Needham (1980, 301) observes that the commissioners seemed to support the idea of a two-year split, but *"in a single, contradictory paragraph* . . . it abandoned tradition in favour of a six-month split, for reasons similar to those which had been advanced by *Archambault* earlier" (emphasis in original). Needham (1980, 302) summarizes the position assumed by the Fauteux Report:

> Sweeping centralization was to be the approach, with provinces to retain responsibility for offenders serving sentences of less than six months, because such short sentences would offer no scope for rehabilitative programming.

A similar shift toward the medical model of corrections occurred at the provincial level. In Saskatchewan, the 1946 Penal Commission (Laycock 1946, 20) argued for the adoption of a treatment philosophy involving the scientific treatment of offenders in institutions: "While it is true that society must have a place for the safe-keeping of those who are dangerous to itself, the essential function of prisons is one of treatment and re-education." The recommendations of this inquiry were incorporated into the *Corrections Act* of 1950, the first major corrections legislation in the province in over fifty years.[30] In British Columbia, the Commission to Inquire into the State and Management of the Gaols of British Columbia (1951, 27-28) recommended the construction of a new provincial institution oriented to "a complete training program . . . physical, academic, and vocational." Further, several new treatment techniques appeared in the provincial institution of Oakalla, including plastic surgery which was first employed in 1953 to correct "any disability which might have contributed towards delinquency, such as scars, squints, unsightly or obscene tatooes, or even a girl's name when there had been a change of affection" (Richmond 1975, 48). Records from Oakalla also indicate that aversion therapy and behaviour modification or electro-convulsive therapy along with group therapy and other psychological treatment modalities were utilized beginning in the early 1950s.

Adoption of the medical model had a substantive impact on the Canadian correctional system, and throughout the 1950s and 1960s, there was increased involvement of behavioural science professionals in correctional programming. In Chapter 7, we examine the operation and effectiveness of many of these programs. At this point, however, it is important to note that, despite the initial optimism surrounding the development and implementation of treatment programs in the federal and provincial institutions, by the late 1960s, there was a growing concern over their effectiveness. As Griffiths et al. (1980, 239) note: "Disenchantment with the rehabilitative approach and its perceived failure to change the attitudes and behaviours of criminal offenders . . . led many correctional observers to call for a return to a philosophy of punishment." Many observers also raised questions relating to the ethics of treatment and the extensive involvement of "professionals" in the treatment effort. From the radical-elitist perspective, Gosselin (1982, 89) argues:

> The great penitentiary reforms of the 1960s, with their emphasis on the role of the intellectuals (psychologists, criminologists, etc.), are to be understood as the power structure's way of seeking to refine still further repression at every level.

The Shift in Correctional Policy

In 1969, the Canadian Committee on Corrections (Ouimet) directly addressed the problems encountered in attempting to implement the recommendations of the Archambault (1938) and Fauteux (1956) reports, particularly those calling for an increased emphasis on the treatment of the criminal offender. The Ouimet Committee suggested that treatment efforts for many offenders might more profitably be pursued within a community setting rather than inside correctional institutions. This report provided the basis for expansion of community-based correctional facilities and programs in the late 1960s. These initiatives were operated by federal and provincial agencies as well as by private, non-profit organizations such as the John Howard Society and the Elizabeth Fry Society (see Skinner et al. 1981, 129-70). In Chapters 4 and 9, we examine the implementation of the "reintegration" model of corrections in more detail.

One other area addressed by the Ouimet Committee (1969) was the split in correctional jurisdiction. In its recommendations, the Committee (1969, 281-83) concluded that a single, centralized system of corrections under federal jurisdiction, as proposed by the Archambault (1938) and Fauteux (1956) reports, was unworkable, and, as Needham (1980, 303) notes, the Committee "sought to reinforce and rationalize the two-year split."

The movement away from an emphasis on treatment within correctional institutions received further support from the Law Reform Commission in 1975. In their report, the Commission (1975, 11) argued that prisons should not be used for purposes of rehabilitation, noting that "it is difficult to show that prisons rehabilitate offenders or are more effective as a general deterrent than other sanctions." This view was further supported by the MacGuigan Subcommittee (1977, 37) which argued that imprisonment for the purpose of rehabilitation should not be used:

> The concept is objectionable on several grounds. It implies that penal institutions are capable of adjusting an individual as if he were an imperfectly-operating mechanism, and, through acting externally on him, can make him over into a better person . . . We prefer to approach the problem with a new term — "personal reformation" — which emphasizes the personal responsibility of the prisoners interested.

These and other statements by the MacGuigan Subcommittee marked the first clear move away from the medical model of correctional treatment in Canada. Finally, in 1977, a federal government Task Force (1977, 28), which had been created to examine the role and responsibilities of the federal government in corrections, offered the following observations on the difficulties with the rehabilitative approach to criminal offenders: "It is both unrealistic and unreasonable to assume that corrections can work the necessary 'magic' that will return an offender to the community as a socially responsible citizen." In its report, the Task Force (1977, 30-31) proposed a major shift in Canadian correctional policy away from the rehabilitative model:

> In order to meet the reality of today's correctional environment, Federal Corrections must provide correctional opportunities, opportunities designed to assist the offender in the development of daily living skills, confidence to cope with his personal problems and social environment and the capacity to adopt more acceptable conduct norms. The opportunities principle is based on the assumption that the offender is ultimately responsible for his behaviour . . . the offender is convicted and sentenced on the basis of his criminal behaviour, not on the basis of some underlying personality disorder or deprived socio-economic condition.

The introduction of the opportunities model in federal corrections marked a formal shift of correctional philosophy away from the rehabilitative ideal which had been so optimistically pursued beginning in the late 1940s. In Chapter 7 we examine correctional treatment programs and, in particular, the controversy over the effectiveness of correctional treatment. In examining the conclusions of the 1975 report of the Law Reform Commission and the 1977 Task Force, it is interesting to note that, while a major justification for abandoning the rehabilitation model was the inability of such an approach to be implemented within correctional institutions, no consideration was given to modifying the environments of correctional institutions to create a more fertile ground for such initiatives. Rather, the reform initiatives were abandoned. The implications of this approach for correctional treatment are also examined in more detail in our discussion in Chapter 8. Unlike the discarded rehabilitation model, no claims were made under the opportunities model regarding the diagnosis, treatment, and "cure" of criminal offenders, and in the words of the Task Force (1977, 77), "the Program Opportunities Model provides Federal Corrections with a realistic goal rather than an unattainable goal of changing offender behaviour."

THE LEGACY OF COMMUNITY CORRECTIONS: PROBATION AND PAROLE

While the reform of correctional institutions was not being pursued on any systematic basis at the close of the nineteenth century, the foundations were being laid for the increased use of the non-institutional alternatives. In the twentieth century, probation and parole were to become the basis of community corrections in Canada. While both of these correctional techniques are discussed in more detail in Chapter 9, it is important here to briefly discuss the events surrounding their development. Similar to the consideration of the factors that influenced the development of prisons, there are competing interpretations among Canadian correctional observers.

The practice of releasing offenders on their own recognizance rather than imposing a sentence was given legal authority in 1889 by the *Act to Permit the Conditional Release of First Offenders in Certain Cases*.[31] This legislation permitted judges to suspend the imposition of a sentence in the criminal court and instead place the offender on "probation of good conduct." In 1921, one of many amendments made to this legislation, which had been included in the *Criminal Code* in 1892, required the offender to report to an officer of the court, thus, in the words of Sheridan and Konrad (1976, 254), "legally recognizing that there was a value in supervising those released on suspended sentence." Despite this legislation, the development of probation services, which came under provincial jurisdiction, has taken place over a fifty-year period of time. Legislation establishing probation services was first enacted in Ontario in 1921, followed over twenty years later by British Columbia in 1946, Saskatchewan in 1949, Alberta and Nova Scotia in 1954, Manitoba in 1957, New Brunswick in 1959, the Yukon in 1964, Newfoundland in 1965, the Northwest Territories in 1966, Quebec in 1967, and Prince Edward Island in 1972. One of the unique aspects in the development of probation in Quebec was the provision of probation services by private agencies prior to the passage of provincial legislation in 1967.

Sheridan and Konrad (1976, 255) note that the number of personnel involved in providing probation services remained relatively small until the 1960s, when rapid expansion occurred. Figures from British Columbia reveal that there were 6 probation officers for a population of 1.1 million in 1950, 72 probation officers for a population of 1.8 million in 1965, and 266 officers for a provincial population of 2.4 million in 1975.

The intensified use of probation was also evident in Alberta, where in 1961, only seven years after the legislation was implemented, 14 percent of the offenders convicted of indictable offences were on probation (Attorney General of Alberta 1973). A report of the Attorney General of Alberta (1973, 1) posits several explanations for the increased use of probation throughout Canada at this time, including:

1. a change in attitude toward the purposes and effects of punishment;
2. replacement of the traditional correctional goals of expiation, retribution and deterrence by a policy stressing re-adjustment under non-institutional conditions;
3. the reduced costs of probation; and
4. the notion of probation as an effective deterrent to future criminal activity.

The utilization of probation as a correctional technique is discussed later in the volume, but it should be noted that discussions between the federal and provincial governments over the creation of uniform standards for probation services in Canada as well as the possibility of federal/provincial cost-sharing arrangements, have been held in recent years. And, as seen in our discussion in Chapter 9, the use of probation as a sentencing alternative has changed perceptibly since its inception in Canada. Concurrent with this shift has been a growing scrutiny of probation and its effectiveness as a correctional technique.

Parole, which was to become the other major component of community corrections, also had historical antecedents to formal legislative enactments. Prior to 1898 in Canada, incarcerated offenders could be released from prison prior to the expiration of their sentence by order of the Governor-General on the advice of a minister of the Crown. This was accomplished as an expression of the Royal Prerogative of Mercy, and Miller (1976, 379-80) notes that such releases were unconditional and mainly awarded on humanitarian grounds. Parole was formally established in 1899 under the *Act to Provide for the Conditional Liberation of Penitentiary Convicts* or the "Ticket of Leave Act" as it was known for over sixty years.[32] This act provided for the reorganization of executive clemency, authorized the Governor-General to grant a license to any convict in a Canadian gaol, penitentiary, or reformatory to be at large under specified conditions, and provided for the use of police officers to monitor the behaviour and location of offenders released on parole (Strong 1969, 76).

This legislation had its historical roots in the system of graduated release developed in the early 1840s by Alexander Maconochie, director of a penal colony near Australia to which offenders were transported, and Sir Walter Crofton, appointed director of the Irish Prison System in 1854. Maconochie employed a "mark system" under which prisoners earned marks for good behaviour and lost marks for being disciplinary problems. As offenders accumulated marks, they passed through successive stages, each of which provided them with more freedom and autonomy, preparing them for eventual release back into the community. The ticket of leave system utilized by Crofton provided for assistance and supervision of offenders who had been granted release from the prison on the basis of good conduct and industriousness (for an extended discussion of Maconochie and Crofton, see Eriksson 1976).

Following passage of the *Ticket of Leave Act,* the primary role in supervising released offenders was assumed by the Salvation Army's Prison Gates section, establishing early the role of private agencies in this stage of the correctional process. In 1905, a Salvation Army officer became the first Dominion Parole Officer in the Department of Justice and assumed the task of visiting institutions, interviewing inmates who were eligible for release, and assisting offenders re-entering the community with employment and housing. As the use of tickets of leave grew, a Remission Branch (later renamed the Remission Service) was created in the Department of Justice.

In the mid-1920s, in response to increasing criticism that tickets of leave were being granted too liberally, there was a reorganization of the Remission Service which included the formulation of policies for granting release. Miller (1976, 381) notes that, following World War II, there was an expansion of both institutional treatment and after-care services and, in response to the increased emphasis upon treatment and rehabilitation, the Remission Services opened several branch offices throughout the country. During this time, there was also increased participation in the supervision of offenders and the provision of after-care services by private agencies, such as the John Howard Society, the Elizabeth Fry Society, and the Salvation Army, under contract with the federal and provincial governments.

In 1956, the report of the Fauteux Committee recommended the creation of a national parole board and outlined the principles upon which Canada's parole system should operate (see Miller 1976, 384). These recommendations were included in the 1959 *Parole Act* which replaced the *Ticket of Leave Act* and created a five person National Parole Board.[33] Numerous amendments to this original legislation have increased the membership of the board, created the status of mandatory supervision, and set the minimum time periods which offenders convicted of different types of crimes are required to serve in confinement prior to being considered for parole.[34]

In Chapter 9, we examine parole in more depth, considering the issues surrounding its use in corrections. At this juncture, suffice it to say that parole has come under increasing criticism in recent years, critics citing the abolition of parole in fourteen U.S. states as evidence that the process surrounding the granting of parole and its usefulness in assisting offenders to readjust to life on the outside are highly questionable.

A Note on the Emergence of Community-Based Corrections

In the Canadian literature, there is a discernible absence of systematic inquiries into the origins and development of community corrections and the extensive use of probation and parole in the "decarceration" movement (for an exception, see Chan and Ericson 1981). Such a gap in the literature is unfortunate, for recent work by Scull (1977a) on the "decarceration" movement in the United States suggests that there were several causal factors involved in the movement toward community-based corrections, other than the generally ascribed "spirit of humanitarianism."

Scull (1977a, 104) points out that the major rationale offered for decarceration of offenders was the dehumanizing and disruptive influence of the correctional institution:

> A crucial element in the move towards a noninstitutional response to deviance has been the purported "discovery" by social scientists in the

1950s and 1960s of the institutional syndrome — the notion that confinement in any asylum may amplify and even produce disturbance. . . .

However, Scull (1977a, 139) argues that the potential debilitating effects of the institution had been raised by critics and widely publicized in the 1800s: "The arguments had not changed, but the structural context in which they were advanced clearly had. Their contemporary reappearance allowed governments to save money while simultaneously giving their policy a humanitarian gloss."

Rather than viewing the community corrections movement as the consequence of humanitarian ideals, Scull (1977a, 152) argues that the shift to decarceration "must be viewed as dependent upon and a reflection of more extensive and deep-seated changes in the social organization of advanced capitalist societies." For Scull (1977a, 138), the primary reason for the movement toward community corrections was economic — a drive to decentralize the rapidly escalating costs of incarcerating ever larger numbers of the population. Such a trend continued despite the lack of evaluative research which would suggest that such strategies are effective in reducing criminal behaviour.

For our purposes, Scull's arguments are important in that they require us to consider alternative explanations for developments in corrections which may appear to be quite easily explained by factors such as humanitarianism. Further, Scull's analysis of the decarceration movement in the United States provides an excellent illustration of an interpretation of correctional events from the radical-elitist perspective, one which challenges the widely accepted liberal-pluralist explanation.

CANADIAN CORRECTIONAL HISTORY IN RETROSPECT

The preceding discussion has undoubtedly raised numerous questions about the major events in Canadian corrections since the eighteenth century. While an increasing amount of literature on correctional history in Canada has emerged in recent years, there remains a paucity of critical inquiries into the relationship of correctional developments and changes in the political, social, and economic fabric of Canadian society (for a notable exception, see Kellough et al. 1980). In our discussion, we have seen not only that there are competing perspectives regarding correctional change, but also that the liberal-pluralist interpretation which has been widely utilized to explain events in Canada and the United States, fails to consider the influence of political and economic factors, which may play a role in correctional developments as important as the humanitarian spirit and benevolent reform efforts of specific individuals.

In reviewing the historical materials on Canadian corrections presented in this chapter, it is evident that, while there have been numerous "reforms" in the correctional enterprise relating to the handling and confinement of criminal offenders, many of these issues were identified as requiring attention in the early 1800s. These included the need for adequate classification of offenders, proper physical facilities for confinement, the protection of prison inmates against the brutality of prison personnel, and the need for meaningful vocational training and educational programs within the prison.

In the following chapters, we attempt to provide additional insights into the correctional process in Canada both at the policy/planning level and at the institutional and community level.

Notes

1. Upper Canada, *Statutes,* 1800, c. 1.

2. Edmison (1976, 350) describes the pillory as a solid wood frame punctured with holes through which the head and hands of the offender were placed. When it was closed, the openings fit around the neck and wrist, holding the offender secure. The pillory was mounted on a pivot so that the person being punished could be made to face in any desired direction. The punishment was imposed in public and often citizens of the community "showered the culprit with rotten eggs and similar refuse." The stocks were a wooden structure with holes for arms and legs in which offenders were seated. See also Knafla and Chapman 1983.

3. 1 Vic., c. 10.

4. Morel (1975) provides additional insights into crime and punishment in Lower Canada, discussing the response to male and female offenders. Examining historical documents, he notes that men and women were treated equally in the imposition of capital punishment and in less severe sanctions such as public humiliation. However, in cases between the two extremes, there was differential treatment. For example, while men were banished or sent to the galleys, women received terms of confinement in the Hôpital Général. Morel (1975) also provides figures from 1712 to 1745 indicating the percentage of females convicted and the severity of the punishments they received. During this period of time, 38 offenders were sentenced to death and 21 percent of these were women; 39 offenders received the punishment of whipping, 13 percent of whom were women.

5. 32 Geo. III, c. 8.

6. 39 Geo. III, c. 6.

7. Care of the destitute in Canada in the early years was left largely to private philanthropic organizations. In the seventeenth century, the Church assumed a major role in caring for dependent and destitute individuals, in contrast to the community-based poor houses and almshouses operating on a family model which developed during the colonial era in America. Strong (1969, 13) notes that "public welfare was regarded as primarily the field of the church." Particularly in Lower Canada, there was a lack of community organizations to care for the sick and the needy and the Roman Catholic church assumed a major role. Strong (1969, 40) also notes that the care of children in early Canada was accomplished through orphanages supported by private philanthropy. For discussions of the history of the treatment of the insane and mentally ill offender in Canada, see Strong 1969, Chalke 1972, Smandych 1981, and Verdun-Jones and Smandych 1981.

8. Additional insight into the differential response in Upper and Lower Canada to public welfare administration, which included crime and delinquency, is provided by Strong (1969, 29): "Both provinces . . . used houses of correction for the incarceration of 'idle and disorderly persons'; both provinces also followed the policy of subsidizing private charity; but in Lower Canada grants were made from the public treasury only to religious communities organized for philanthropic work, while in Upper Canada the public hospitals and houses of industry receiving government support were managed by independent boards."

9. 43 Geo. III, c. 138 (1803).

10. The Auburn plan allowed prisoners to work and eat together during the day under a strict rule of silence, and at night, they were returned to their individual cells. Under the Pennsylvania system, prisoners were kept in total isolation from one another for the duration of the confinement. While there was intense competition between proponents of each system, the Auburn plan was ultimately adopted as the model for the majority of American institutions, while the Pennsylvania system was adopted in many European countries.

11. Similar differences in the interpretations of correctional history between the liberal-pluralist and radical-elitist perspectives are evident in discussions relating to the Reformatory Movement which occurred in the United States in the late 1800s. While Rothman (1971) contends that this movement, characterized by the introduction of vocational and training programs in some institutions, was the consequence of humanitarianism and progressive reform, Currie (1973, 4-5) argues that the Reformatory Movement "was an authoritarian and conservative movement, created by upper-class reformers and propelled by the central aim of instilling industrial discipline in the 'idle and vicious' masses of post-Civil War industrial cities" (see also Gosselin 1982 and Whittingham 1985).

12. Bellomo (1972, 13) further notes that this view of criminal offenders resulted in the penitentiary becoming a "human zoo" where visitors could see the depraved for the price of an admission ticket. Charging an admission fee was justified for its deterrent value for the general public and to help defray operating expenses of the institution. This practice appears to have been unique to the Canadian correctional experience, with no evidence that it took place in the United States or England.

13. In their discussion of the factors surrounding the emergence of the insane asylum and other institutions in Ontario during the period 1830 to 1875, Smandych and Verdun-Jones (1982, 2) argue that few observers "have sought to investigate the common threads that might have underscored these developments in specific historical settings."

14. 4 Wm. IV, c. 37.

15. Upper Canada, *Statutes*, 1834, c. 37.

16. Smith's son was also faced with a number of charges, including shooting arrows at convicts, selling the provisions of the prison, and thrusting pins into the convicts (Shoom 1966, 218).

17. Chunn (1981, 16) identifies the position assumed by the Brown Commission that hard labour was a major ingredient for the success of the penitentiary, citing the conclusion that there was "no reason why the labour of able-bodied men should not produce sufficient to pay for their sustenance." However, Chunn (1981, 16) concludes that "despite the initial optimism of the Brown Commission, Kingston Penitentiary never functioned as a self-sufficient enterprise."

18. Canada, *Statutes,* 1851, c. 2.

19. Canada, *Statutes,* 1857, c. 28.

20. 31 Vic., c. 75.

21. Gosselin (1982, 74), arguing from the radical-elitist perspective, contends that these institutions "provided the infrastructure for more than a century of experiments in repression by the Canadian Penitentiary Service."

22. Upper Canada, *Statutes,* 1837-38, c. 5.

23. Ontario, *Statutes,* 1867-68, c. 21.

24. Dixon (1947, 3) notes that, prior to the close of the nineteenth century, there was some evidence of concern with improving the administration of the penitentiaries. He cites a regulation implemented in 1899 that "no person shall be employed as an officer of the prison who is not able to read and write with facility, or who cannot readily apply the rules of arithmetic."

25. For a discussion of the Reformatory movement which developed in the United States at the end of the 1800s and continued into the early 1900s, see Rothman 1971 and Orland 1975.

26. 46 Vic., c. 37.

27. 49 Vic., c. 182.

28. 4-5 Vic., 1841, c. 24-26; 6 Vic. 1842, c. 5.

29. 6 Ed. VII, c. 38.

30. Statutes of Saskatchewan, 1950, c. 89.

31. 52 Vic., c. 44.

32. 63-64 Vic., c. 49.

33. 7 Eliz. II, 1958, c. 38.

34. Mandatory supervision is a legislated, administrative arrangement whereby offenders who have not been granted parole may be released from the institution at the conclusion of their sentence (minus earned remission or "good time" which reduces the length of confinement by one-third) and are placed under supervision for a specified period of time in the community.

References

Adamson, C.R. (October) 1983. "The Breakdown of Canadian Prison Administration: Evidence from Three Commissions of Inquiry." 25 *Canadian Journal of Criminology*. 433-47.

Anderson, F.W. (April) 1960. "Prisons and Prison Reforms in the Old Canadian West." 2 *Canadian Journal of Corrections*. 209-15.

Annual Report of the Commissioner of Penitentiaries, 1949. 1950. Ottawa: King's Printer.

Annual Report of the Commissioner of Penitentiaries, 1957. 1958. Ottawa: Queen's Printer.

Archambault, J. (Chairman). 1938. *Report of the Royal Commission to Investigate the Penal System of Canada*. Ottawa: King's Printer.

Attorney General of Alberta. 1973. *Adult Probation Research Study, 1973*. Edmonton: Attorney General.

Baehre, R. (September) 1977. "Origins of the Penitentiary System in Upper Canada." LXIX *Ontario History*. 185-207.

_____. 1985. *The Prison System in Atlantic Canada Before 1880*. Ottawa: Solicitor General of Canada.

Bartollas, C. 1981. *Introduction to Corrections*. New York: Harper and Row.

Beattie, J.M. 1977. *Attitudes Towards Crime and Punishment in Upper Canada, 1830-1850: A Documentary Study*. Toronto Centre of Criminology, University of Toronto.

Bellomo, J.J. (March) 1972. "Upper Canadians' Attitudes Towards Crime and Punishment, 1832-1851." LXIV *Ontario History*. 11-26. Toronto: The Ontario Historical Society.

Chalke, F.C.R. (Chairman). 1972. *The General Program for Development of Psychiatric Services in Federal Correctional Services in Canada*. Ottawa: Advisory Board of Psychiatric Consultants.

Chan, J.B.L. and R.V. Ericson. 1981. *Decarceration and the Economy of Penal Reform*. Toronto: Centre of Criminology, University of Toronto.

Chunn, D.E. (Fall) 1981. "Good Men Work Hard: Convict Labour in Kingston Penitentiary, 1835-1850." 4 *Canadian Criminology Forum*. 13-22.

Coles, D. 1979. *Nova Scotia Corrections-An Historical Perspective*. Halifax: Communications Project in Criminal Justice, Correctional Services Division.

Commission to Inquire into the State and Management of the Gaols of British Columbia. 1951. Victoria: King's Printer.

Currie, E.P. (December) 1973. "Managing the Minds of Men: The Reformatory Movement, 1865-1920." Unpublished Doctoral Dissertation. Berkeley, Calif.: University of California.

Curtis, D., A. Graham, L. Kelly, and A. Patterson. 1985. *Kingston Penitentiary: The First Hundred and Fifty Years, 1835-1985*. Ottawa: Supply and Services Canada.

Dixon, W.G. 1947. *History of the Penitentiaries Branch of the Canadian Department of Justice*. Chicago, Illinois: School of Social Service Administration.

Duncan, K. (February) 1965. "Irish Famine, Immigration and the Social Structure of Canada West." 2 *Canadian Review of Sociology and Anthropology.* 19-40.

Edmison, J.A. (October) 1970. "Perspective in Corrections." 12 *Canadian Journal of Corrections.* 534-48.

————. 1976. "Some Aspects of Nineteenth-Century Canadian Prisons." In W.T. McGrath (ed.) *Crime and Its Treatment in Canada.* 2d ed. Toronto: Copyright © Gage Educational Publishing Limited. 347-69.

Eriksson, T. 1976. *The Reformers: An Historical Survey of Pioneer Experiments in the Treatment of Criminals.* New York: Elsevier.

Fauteux, G. (Chairman). 1956. *Report of the Committee Appointed to Inquire Into the Principles and Procedures Followed in the Remission Service of the Department of Justice of Canada.* Ottawa: Queen's Printer.

Fingard, J. 1984. "Jailbirds in Mid-Victorian Halifax." 8 *Dalhousie Law Journal.* 81-102.

Foucault, M. 1977. *Discipline and Punish: The Birth of the Prison.* New York: Pantheon.

Gibson, J.A. (December) 1975. "Political Prisoners, Transportation for Life, and Responsible Government in Canada." LXVII *Ontario History.* 185-98.

Goldfarb, R.L. and L.R. Singer. 1973. *After Conviction: A Definitive and Compelling Study of the American Correctional System.* New York: Simon and Schuster.

Gosselin, L. 1982. *Prisons in Canada.* Montreal: Black Rose Books.

Griffiths, C.T., J.F. Klein and S.N. Verdun-Jones. 1980. *Criminal Justice in Canada: An Introductory Text.* Vancouver: Butterworths.

Harvey, H. (July) 1953. "Some Notes on the Early Administration of Justice in Canada's Northwest." 1 *Alberta Historical Review.* 5-20.

James, J.T.L. (January) 1978/79. "Gaols and Their Goals in Manitoba, 1870-1970." 20-21 *Canadian Journal of Criminology.* 34-42.

Kellough, D.G., S.L. Brickey and W.K. Greenaway. (Summer) 1980. "The Politics of Incarceration: Manitoba, 1918-1939." 5 *Canadian Journal of Sociology.* 253-271.

Kirkpatrick, A.M. (October) 1964. "Jails in Historical Perspective." 6 *Canadian Journal of Corrections.* 405-18.

Knafla, L.A. and T.L. Chapman (June) 1983. "Criminal Justice in Canada: A Comparative Study of the Maritimes and Lower Canada, 1760-1812." 21 *Osgoode Hall Law Journal.* 245-274.

Lachance, A. 1985. "Le Contrôle social dans la société canadienne du régime français au XVIIIᵉ siècle." XVII *Criminologie.* 7-24.

Langmuir, J.W. (Chair). 1891. *Report of the Commissioners Appointed to Enquire into the Prison and Reformatory System of the Province of Ontario.* Toronto: Warwick and Sons.

Law Reform Commission of Canada. 1975. *Working Paper 11: Imprisonment and Release.* Ottawa: Information Canada.

Laycock, S.R. (Chairman). 1946. *Commission to Investigate the Penal System of Saskatchewan.* Regina: Minister of Public Works.

MacGuigan, M. (Chairman). 1977. *Report to Parliament by the Sub-Committee on the Penitentiary System in Canada.* Ottawa: Supply and Services Canada.

MacNamara, D.J. (February) 1977. "The Medical Model in Corrections: Requiescat in Pace." 14 *Criminology*. 439-48.

Miller, F.P. 1976. "Parole." In W.T. McGrath (ed.) *Crime and Its Treatment in Canada*. 2nd ed. Toronto: Macmillan. 376-442.

Morel, A. (January) 1963. "La Justice criminelle en Nouvelle-France." XIV *Cité Libre*. 26-30.

_____. (September) 1975. "Réflexions sur la justice criminelle canadienne au 18e siècle." XXIX *Revue d'Histoire d'Amérique Française*. 241-53.

Needham, H.G. (July) 1980. "Historical Perspectives on the Federal-Provincial Split in Jurisdiction in Corrections." 22 *Canadian Journal of Criminology*. 298-306.

Newman, G. 1978. *The Punishment Response*. New York: Lippincott.

Orland, L. 1975. *Prisons: Houses of Darkness*. New York: Free Press.

Ouimet, R. (Chairman). 1969. *Report of the Canadian Committee on Corrections — Toward Unity: Criminal Justice and Corrections*. Ottawa: Information Canada.

Palmer, B.D. (May) 1980. "Kingston Mechanics and the Rise of the Penitentiary, 1833-1836." XIII *Social History*. 7-32.

Pursley, R.D. 1977. *Introduction to Criminal Justice*. Encino, Calif.: Glencoe Press.

Quinney, R. 1977. *Class, State and Crime*. New York: David McKay.

Richmond, G. 1975. *Prison Doctor*. Surrey, British Columbia: Nunaga Publishing Co.

Rothman, D.J. 1971. *The Discovery of the Asylum*. Toronto: Little, Brown.

Scull, A.T. 1977a. *Decarceration: Community Treatment and the Deviant — A Radical View*. Englewood Cliffs, N.J.: Prentice-Hall.

_____. (February) 1977b. "Madness and Segregative Control: The Rise of the Insane Asylum." 24 *Social Problems*. 337-51.

_____. 1979. *Museums of Madness: The Social Control of Insanity in Nineteenth Century England*. London: A. Lane.

Sheridan, A.K.B. and J. Konrad. 1976. "Probation." In W.T. McGrath (ed.) *Crime and Its Treatment in Canada*. 2nd ed. Toronto: Macmillan. 249-302.

Shoom, Sydney. (July) 1966. "Kingston Penitentiary: The Early Decades." 8 *Canadian Journal of Corrections*. 215-20.

_____. (July) 1972. "The Upper Canada Reformatory, Penetanguishene: The Dawn of Prison Reform in Canada." 14 *Canadian Journal of Criminology and Corrections*. 260-67.

Shover, N. 1979. *A Sociology of American Corrections*. Homewood, Illinois: The Dorsey Press.

Skinner, S., O. Dreidger and B. Grainger. 1981. *Corrections: An Historical Perspective of the Saskatchewan Experience*. Regina: Canadian Plains Research Centre, University of Regina.

Smandych, R.C. 1981. "The Rise of the Asylum in Upper Canada, 1830-1875: An Analysis of Competing Perspectives in Institutional Development in the 19th Century." Unpublished M.A. Thesis. Burnaby, British Columbia: Department of Criminology, Simon Fraser University.

Smandych, R.C. and S.N. Verdun-Jones. 1982. "The Evolution of Institutional Mechanisms of Social Control in Ontario: An Examination of the Evidence and Interpretations." Unpublished Paper. Burnaby, British Columbia: Department of Criminology, Simon Fraser University.

Solicitor General of Canada and Attorney General of British Columbia. 1976. *Bi-Lateral Discussions on the Division of Correctional Responsibilities between the Federal Government and the Province of British Columbia.* Victoria: Ministry of the Attorney General.

Splane, R.B. 1965. *Social Welfare in Ontario, 1791-1893: A Study of Public Welfare Administration.* Toronto: University of Toronto Press.

Strong, M.K. 1969. *Public Welfare Administration in Canada.* Montclair, New Jersey: Patterson-Smith.

Takagi, P. (December) 1975. "The Walnut Street Jail: A Penal Reform to Centralize the Powers of the State." 39 *Federal Probation.* 18-26.

Task Force on the Creation of an Integrated Canadian Corrections Service. 1977. *The Role of Federal Corrections in Canada.* Ottawa: Supply and Services Canada.

Taylor, C.J. (November) 1979. "The Kingston, Ontario Penitentiary and Moral Architecture." XII *Social History.* 385-408.

Tremblay, P. (January) 1986. "L'évolution de l'emprisonnement pénitentiaire, de son intensité, de sa fermeté et de sa portée: le cas de Montréal de 1845 à 1913." 28 *Canadian Journal of Criminology.* 47-68.

Verdun-Jones, S.N. and R.C. Smandych. 1981. "Catch-22 in the Nineteenth Century: The Evolution of Therapeutic Confinement for the Criminally Insane in Canada, 1840-1900." 2 *Criminal Justice History: An International Annual.* 94-96.

Wetherell, D.G. (May) 1979. "To Discipline and Train: Adult Rehabilitation Programmes in Ontario Prisons, 1874-1900." XXI *Social History.* 145-65.

Whittingham, M.D. 1985. "Crime, Punishment, Correction and the Rise of The Institutional State in England and Upper Canada." 19 *The Law Society Gazette.* 201-209.

Zubrycki, R.M. 1980. *The Establishment of Canada's Penitentiary System: Federal Correctional Policy, 1867-1900.* Toronto: Faculty of Social Work, University of Toronto.

Chapter 3

The Canadian
Correctional Enterprise

The correctional enterprise in Canada is, at least in part, a product of its history. In Chapter 2, many of the factors involved in this historical development were described. In this chapter, the current state of Canadian corrections is outlined with particular attention to the emphasis which is being reflected in both policy and practice. The relationship between current practice and recent historical developments is also addressed.

THE NATURE OF THE CORRECTIONAL ENTERPRISE

To a large extent, correctional history can be portrayed by recounting the methods and devices used by social systems in the disposition of offenders — a function unique to corrections within the criminal justice system. In providing dispositions available to the court in sentencing, correctional systems generally reflect the community values which are expressed in the sentencing process.

Traditionally, sentencing has been viewed as an attempt to address the combined objectives of punishment, deterrence and rehabilitation in the disposition of offenders.[1] However, correctional history suggests that these are often contradictory objectives. Since sentence administration is a primary task of corrections, and since corrections must administer sentences against a contradictory set of objectives, it is not surprising that there has been difficulty in establishing clear and consistent principles for the management of correctional programs. These conflicts become more apparent in our discussion of correctional treatment in Chapters 7, 8, and 9. The conflicting principles that emerge at the point of sentencing were made clear by the Federal-Provincial Task Force on the Long Term Objectives in

Corrections in Canada (1977, iv) when it addressed this problem with the following observations:

> In attempting to address the long-term objectives for corrections, the task force felt it was important to emphasize that both the criminal justice system and in particular the corrections system, are concerned with the vital *trade-off* between *protection of society* and *freedom of the individual.* This particular trade-off is constantly changing, sensitive to political and public pressures as well as other constraints. It is the recognition of this trade-off and the constant reassessment of the directions for change in the administration of corrections that will ensure justice in society. In this context, the law is only one of many tools which can be used to implement justice. The task force feels that it cannot too strongly stress the need for constant *reassessment of strategies, objectives and goals* which are pursued by all agencies involved in the administration of justice, in order to approximate more closely the true equilibrium which will assure justice for all (Emphases in original).

As the observations of the Task Force (1977) suggest, the correctional enterprise is subject to constant change and reassessment in its attempts to address competing objectives and to reflect the social and political realities within which corrections operates. This characteristic of the correctional enterprise is common to all correctional systems which operate in free societies and significantly colours any discussion that bears upon correctional issues.

MODELS OF CORRECTIONAL POLICY AND PRACTICE

Two American authors, Bartollas and Miller (1978, 23-25), illustrate the history of correctional policy and practice by identifying the "models" or emphases in vogue at various points in time. These authors view corrections in the United States as moving through six models from colonial times to the present. These models are identified as: the Family Model, the Punishment and Penitence Model, the Reform Model, the Rehabilitation Model, the Reintegration Model and a return to a Punishment Model. Following their lead, a description of the correctional "models" that have been in vogue in Canada at particular times can serve to illustrate the changing nature of the enterprise. More specifically, when correctional history is set forth in this way, it becomes clear that corrections has continuously attempted to define its objectives in sentence administration such that they reflect the general objectives in sentencing as well as the social and political pressures of each era.

When an historical analysis of correctional models is undertaken, it is interesting to note that the language used to describe objectives in *sentence administration* is not necessarily the same as the language used to describe *general objectives in sentencing*. While the language of the court tends to describe the *intention* (rehabilitation, punishment, deterrence) of sentencing as it is reflected in the social consensus of the day, the language of sentence administration seeks to portray the *manner* (reintegration, imprisonment, restitution) by which the general sentencing objectives of the court are addressed through correctional programs. (For a legal/technical discussion of this topic, see Key 1986.)

Canadian correctional programs have been significantly influenced by the U.S. experience. Consequently there is considerable similarity and overlap between the "models" or approaches to correctional practice used in the United States and those used in Canada. However, there are some differences which are worth noting. Consequently, the models of Canadian correctional history are presented as: Punishment (pre-institution), Punishment and Penitence (pre- and post-Confederation), Rehabilitation, Reintegration, and Reparation.[2] Table 3.1 provides a brief outline of these models which summarize the historical developments detailed in Chapter 2.

The Canadian Milieu

While Canadian corrections shares much in common with other correctional jurisdictions, the previous chapter has illustrated that it does have a novel history of its own. This history can only be understood in relation to the particular social and political influences out of which it has evolved. Corrections in Canada is a service of government and is located within the federal and provincial line ministries. The Canadian correctional enterprise, therefore, is susceptible to the federal/provincial division of responsibility as set forth in the *Constitution Act* and the *Criminal Code* of Canada.

Furthermore, as we discussed in Chapter 2, the responsibility for the administration of penal institutions is largely determined by the "two-year rule," by which the federal government is charged with the custody of those offenders receiving a single sentence or a series of sentences totalling two years or more. Under this same prescription, the provinces are responsible for those offenders who receive a sentence or a set of sentences totalling less than two years. The authority for the "two-year rule" is provided in Section 659 of the *Criminal Code.*[3]

This division of responsibility for corrections reflects, in a general way, the nature of relations between the two senior levels of government in Canada. While the delineation of responsibility for the provision of social services takes different forms depending on the service in question, most government services are party to a continuing jurisdictional dialogue to enable national, provincial, or regional interests to be accommodated in some type of cooperative plan. As subsequent chapters reveal, a number of correctional programs in Canada are administered on the basis of federal/provincial agreements and cost-sharing schemes generated out of bilateral or multilateral discussions between the federal and provincial governments.

Over the past 50 years, a number of important inquiries have been launched into aspects of the Canadian criminal justice system and have included in their observations and recommendations the issue of jurisdictional responsibility regarding the delivery of correctional services. Invariably, changes and modifications have been recommended. The Archambault (1938), Fauteux (1956), and Ouimet (1969) inquiries all commented directly on the subject. More recently, the Federal-Provincial Task Force on Long Term Objectives in Corrections (1977) assessed the division of responsibility in corrections and proposed a number of possible options for consideration by the federal/provincial Attorneys General and ministers responsible for corrections.

In a supplementary report titled *Bilateral Discussions on the Division of Correctional Responsibilities between the Federal Government and the Government of British Columbia* (Solicitor General of Canada and Attorney General of British Columbia 1976, 14), the following observation is made:

> A variety of rather complex issues bears upon the question of the organization of corrections. There is clearly an interplay of political and constitutional issues, matters relating to correctional theory, and administrative or economic issues.
>
> The studies of the past only too clearly proceeded under the assumptions of their times in the selection of issues and the appraisal of arguments. They seemed of more help to us in framing the right questions and warning of pitfalls than pointing to obvious solutions.
>
> Yet it also was apparent to virtually everyone, both within and outside of the correctional system, that the present organization entailed significant problems on many counts. . . .

TABLE 3.1 Canadian Correctional Models

Correctional Model*	Time Period (Approximate)	Major Characteristics
Punishment (pre-Institution)	1700-1830	extensive use of capital and corporal punishment, including fines, whipping, transportation
		heavy influence of the English criminal law
		confinement utilized only for offenders awaiting trial or imposition of punishment
		crime viewed as endemic to society; punishment designed to deter the offender and the public
		system of public welfare at local level to assist the dependent and neglected; involvement of church and private philanthropy
Punishment and Penitence (pre-Confederation)	1830-1867	crime and criminals viewed as threat to the order and stability of Canadian society
		decreased use of capital punishment and increased use of confinement designed to punish and deter
		influence from the "age of the asylum" in U.S.
		construction of penitentiaries based on Auburn system
		institutional regimen maintained by hard labour, silent system, religious discipline, and corporal punishment
		lack of classification of offenders and segregation of men, women, youths, and the insane in penitentiaries and local gaols

TABLE 3.1   continued

Correctional Model*	Time Period (Approximate)	Major Characteristics
Punishment and Penitence (post-Confederation)	1867-1938	despite administrative abuses and operational problems, continued faith in prisons
		legislative enactments outlined structure of federal and provincial corrections
		expansion of the federal prison system
		continuing problems in classification, physical facilities, and treatment of inmates
		worsening conditions in provincial and local gaols
Rehabilitation	1938-1970	task of corrections expanded to include the reformation of the offender
		development of the medical model and deterministic view of criminal behaviour
		increased involvement of behavioural science professionals in correctional institutions and programs
		development and implementation of education and training programs and treatment modalities
		continuing problems with classification, physical facilities, and administration of prisons

Reintegration	1970-1978	concern with effectiveness of correctional treatment programs
		imprisonment to be used only as a last resort rehabilitation efforts best pursued outside the prison in the community
		expansion of community-based corrections, including the use of probation, parole, and diversion programs
		offender convicted and sentenced to prison on the basis of criminal behaviour, not underlying disorder as under medical model
Reparation	1978-present	return to the punishment objective of corrections based on concepts of reparation
		emphasis on offender responsibility for rehabilitation; opportunities model introduced in federal corrections
		increasing emphasis on the victims of crimes
		continuing emphasis on the development of alternatives to incarceration

* While identifiable models of corrections have emerged, some of which have emphasized objectives other than punishment, it could be argued that the punishment of the offender has always been the central objective of corrections. This is particularly evident when relating the evolution of correctional "models" to social and economic cycles. In "hard times," there is a demand on all social institutions to "return to the basics." The "basic" in correctional terms is invariably regarded as the punishment of the offender with due attention to the protection of society.

In later chapters, possible options for the future which have been proposed from time to time by the various task forces and commissions are discussed. Here it is important to note that the correctional enterprise in Canada continues at the centre of a federal/provincial dialogue. In this regard, the manner in which correctional responsibilities are divided is regularly criticized. The dialogue and its ramifications should be kept in mind whenever a general description of the nature of responsibilities within each government jurisdiction is presented.

THE CURRENT MODEL OF
CANADIAN CORRECTIONAL PRACTICE

Using the representation of correctional models presented earlier in this chapter, current Canadian correctional *practice* can be placed under the category of the *reintegration* model. However, as noted in Table 3.1, since approximately 1978 Canadian correctional *policy* has been moving toward a *reparation* model, with an increase in emphasis on the punishment of offenders and attention to the needs of the victims of their crimes. Some emphases in correctional practice are emerging which reflect this shift. This movement is treated in greater detail in the chapter on correctional reform. Here, we address the dominant model in recent Canadian correctional history, from both a policy and practice perspective: the reintegration model explains much of what is transpiring in Canadian correctional practice at the present time, even though a shift toward reparation is occurring.

The fundamental principle of the reintegration model is that the community is considered central in the care of offenders and confinement should be used only as a last resort. Historically, most attempts to "label" the major emphasis within a correctional system have required an assessment of the way in which correctional programs are organized as well as an evaluation of what those programs actually accomplish.

It has been unusual in Canadian correctional practice for the operating systems[4] to communicate their intention or to describe the program emphasis they are adopting as statements of public policy.[5] Recently in Canada, however, deliberate attempts have been made at both the federal and provincial levels to declare and to communicate statements of purpose and objectives. Take, for example, the position set forth in *The Role of Federal Corrections in Canada* (Task Force on the Creation of an Integrated Canadian Corrections Service 1977, 57). In this document, one of the major objectives identified was "to manage and control the reintegration of the offender into the community." Similarly, in 1978 the British Columbia Corrections Branch (British Columbia Ministry of the Attorney General 1978, 14) produced an information document entitled *Statement of Goals, Strategies and Beliefs,* in which it was stated, "since the community is the natural environment to which offenders will eventually return, the effectiveness of Corrections Branch programs is increased by allowing as many programs as possible to operate in the community." Giving impetus to the trend toward the adoption of the reintegration model, the Heads of Corrections[6] in Canada, significantly, have developed a joint statement of principles and objectives emphasizing their intention to provide opportunities through correctional programs for the reintegration of the offender into society.

Before a conclusion on the real nature of the operating model can be made, however, these statements of public policy must be assessed in relation to the operational characteristics that are revealed by an investigation of Canadian correctional practice. Clearly, such a review indicates that reintegration strategies are still an important emphasis within Canadian correctional practice today.

Social, Political and Economic Factors Associated with the Reintegration Model

Before proceeding with a discussion of the general categories of correctional programming, a brief review of factors and influences associated with current social, political, and economic interests is necessary. This will complete the background against which programs can be presented and assessed.

There is an increasing interest in the way in which correctional systems are being influenced by the social and economic circumstances affecting society as a whole. Much of the work in the social and behavioural sciences during this century has demonstrated that social and economic cycles have a direct influence on criminal offence characteristics and, consequently, on offender populations (for an interesting discussion of this subject, see Toby 1967; Rusche 1980; Brantingham and Brantingham 1984). Often these studies associate social and economic change with the pressures that are brought to bear on correctional institutions. This is in keeping with the view that correctional institutions represent the central program ingredient contained within the correctional enterprise. However, the trends connected with the reintegration model have resulted in both an increased requirement and an increased ability to address factors related to social and economic change. This development is evidenced in several ways:

1. *An increase in the ability of most correctional systems to measure the effects of social and economic change.* This advance is largely due to the development of management information systems and the implementation of program evaluation and monitoring techniques related to program planning and budgeting.
2. *Emphasis on the development of short- and long-term planning strategies.* During the past 25 years, it has not been uncommon for governments to commit significant resources to the correctional enterprise at the peak of economic cycles, only to find that the programs resulting from these resource commitments could not be sustained. It has become increasingly important to find ways of reducing the negative effects of abrupt changes in social and economic cycles.
3. *A requirement to address the specific administration and planning problems generated by the emphasis on reintegration strategies.* As with most changes in emphasis throughout correctional history, the general trend toward adopting the reintegration model results in part from a reaction to the perceived failures of previous correctional models. It also results from the perceived cost-efficiency of community-based programs as compared to programs offered in secure institutions. Furthermore, the trend has been given impetus by the increased opportunity for experimentation and expenditure which resulted from recent peaks in economic cycles.

   While the reintegration model may be considered a reaction to the perceived failure of institutional confinement, the desire to develop a wide range of alternatives to secure incarceration has not alleviated the financial commitment necessary to maintain institutional programs. In fact, the need to secure continued resource commitments to correctional institutions proceeds simultaneously with the need to fund the development of institutional alternatives. In times of affluence, money to proceed with both commitments at the same time is more readily available. Similarly, during periods of economic vitality, social attitudes tend to be relaxed and supportive of non-institutional responses to offenders, particularly when they are regarded as being "more humane." Therefore, it is not surprising that the most recent period of high economic viability (approximately 1965-75), accompanied by a prevailing sense of social well-being, gave rise to an era of experimentation in the development of correctional programs involving alternatives to incarceration. History also reveals that the last decade of pronounced economic health was very quickly followed by an economic down-turn and increasing social uncertainty. Clearly, the down-turn has had a direct influence on the character of correctional programs and the ability of the correctional enterprise to maintain its momentum in the development of both institutional alternatives and alternatives to institutions.

4. *The increasing public awareness of the correctional enterprise.* As suggested previously, the adoption of the reintegration model necessarily leads to an "opening up" of the correctional system and to an increased public awareness and public review of correctional activities. As a result, the type and extent of external interventions in correctional affairs have increased over the last two decades. These have taken the form of civil liberties interventions, the organization of Prisoners' Rights groups, the establishment of citizen advisory committees, and other similar developments. Consequently, spokespersons for public concern now have access to a much more formalized process of feed-back into the correctional system.

Taken together, the net result of these factors has rendered the character of the correctional enterprise more "political" than at almost any other point in its history. While the correctional system has always been the target of criticism from within and without, historically these criticisms and the responses to them have been contained within the correctional enterprise itself. More recently, public and political scrutiny of correctional affairs has been intensified. Seen through the lens of history, therefore, it is arguable that the most dramatic current change in the correctional enterprise finds expression in two ways: first, increased public and political awareness concerning correctional operations; and second, the way in which the correctional enterprise has organized itself to communicate its intentions and defend its practices.

CORRECTIONAL INSTITUTIONS

Incarceration in correctional institutions is the feature that most people regard as the essence of corrections, and there is justification for their point of view. It will be recalled from the previous chapter that the history of corrections in Canada can best be portrayed by following the evolution of penal institutions. Most of the literature in the correctional field addresses institutional problems and speculates on the nature of correctional philosophy from the point of view of institutional practice. Confinement in secure institutions creates a situation where the problems associated with the power of the state to regulate, control, and sanction its citizens becomes magnified in the most extreme ways. Equally important, within the range of correctional programs, penal institutions are the least subject to external monitoring and control. In secure institutions, practices which contravene the intentions that are expressed through statements of public policy are less likely to be observed.

In recent correctional history, the trend toward community-based corrections has proceeded with close attention being paid to the effect community-based programs have on institutions. Two questions present themselves. First, what effect has the reintegration model had on secure institutions in Canada? And second, have these institutions changed in character as a result of this trend?

As evidenced in later chapters, "prison reform" registers as the dominant theme pursued by formal inquiries into correctional practice. Jayewardene and Jayasuriya (1981, 127-28) discuss the relationship between public policy and correctional practice, arguing that, historically, correctional institutions were able to operate in relative isolation from the larger society. This was due in large measure to the fact that prisons were constructed in sparsely populated areas. Further, the management and operation of institutions was carried out in an authoritative manner which, in conjunction with the organizational regimen of the prison, reduced interaction and input from the community. These authors (1981, 128) note, however, that in recent decades the isolation of prisons has diminished considerably:

> The history of penology clearly indicates that penal institutions have not been permitted to continue unsullied . . . . even though the management of penal institutions have made a concerted effort to keep their operations free of public interference, they have not been successful.

It seems evident that a review of institutional policy and practice is essential to an understanding of the overall correctional enterprise. But, its importance notwithstanding, institutional practice is the most difficult program option to assess in relation to declared public policy. Nevertheless, there are some general trends evident within Canadian correctional institutions that present a picture of the model of correctional practice they reflect.

As discussed earlier, correctional organizations in Canada have now become more willing than in the past to declare publicly their intentions in the operation of all correctional programs. This trend alone indicates a change in the traditional posture of institutional administrators and has arisen as a matter of necessity, given the overall movement of correctional systems toward the reintegration ideal. The comments of Jayewardene and Jayasuriya (1981, 129) on this trend are particularly instructive:

> In recent times the public contribution to the operation of penal institutions has become more or less a necessity. The rehabilitative orientation, which penal institutions are supposed to have adopted, has placed an emphasis on the desirability of protecting the public through the reintegration of the offender into society rather than through his temporary incapacitation and isolation from society. This emphasis forces the orientation of institutional philosophy towards society. . . .
>
> Public involvement in the operation of penal institutions tends to promote institutional acceptance of community objectives and the community support for institutional activities. Whether the former or latter results, whether the community begins to realize the difficulties that the institution faces and appreciates the efforts that it makes or whether the institution begins to alter its operations to make them more acceptable to a critical public, the end result is institutional philosophy becoming more consonant with that of larger society and the institutional atmosphere reflecting cultural dictates.

The statements of principles and objectives for correctional institutions in Canada depict an adherence to the reintegration model. It should be recalled, however, that the reintegration ideal assumes that persons will only be incarcerated as an option of last resort. This philosophy drives correctional systems to create a wide range of non-institutional alternatives in sentencing. One predictable, yet novel, result of systems that have seriously moved toward the adoption of the reintegration model, is that their institutions of containment are left holding those prisoners least capable of taking advantage of the community-based options. Moreover, if the institutions that are situated within such systems are to keep faith with principles of reintegration, they in turn must restructure their institutional programs to reflect the reintegration model's characteristics.

There is ample evidence that, even with more difficult populations, Canadian correctional institutions have been restructured around reintegration objectives. For example, as we discussed in Chapter 2, federal and provincial institutions have begun to abandon the strategy of enforced institutional rehabilitation based on medical or other means (see Task Force on the Creation of an Integrated Canadian Corrections Service 1977, 25-32). The tendency in Canadian correctional institutions has been to move away from client-centred treatment applications to case-management strategies. Accordingly, a new emphasis is being placed on providing opportunities within institutions for use by inmates in preparation for release. In order to effect gradual release into the community, case-management strategies also include increased use of temporary releases — either through coordination with the National Parole Board federally or through administrative arrangements provincially.

Following in a similar direction, institutions at both the federal and provincial levels are now providing inmates with clear routes in their preparation for return to the community which lead them from greater to lesser security classifications (see National Work Group on Justice Information and Statistics 1981, 40). And even in those cases where long-term incarceration is viewed as necessary, Canadian correctional institutions are gearing up to provide at least some opportunities for offenders to experience a "normalized" lifestyle and to make a contribution toward some of the social costs associated with their imprisonment.[7] Recent experiments to develop and apply prison industries within Canadian correctional institutions provide a current example of this trend (see Macdonald 1982).

While the difficulties of implementing the reintegration model in secure institutions are pronounced, on analysis it would appear that secure institutions are beginning to reflect the trend which now may be observed across the entire spectrum of correctional programs.

COMMUNITY-BASED CORRECTIONS

As already noted, the primary element of the reintegration model is the emphasis on community-based correctional programs. In Chapter 9 we discuss their operation and effectiveness in detail. At this juncture, however, we will outline the basic assumptions that are associated with programs of this type:

1. Programs with direct rehabilitation potential, such as work, education, and counselling programs, are best provided outside of the environment of secure custody by agencies specializing in those services apart from the correctional system.

2. The offender's return to the community from a secure setting should be gradual with de-escalation in levels of control and supervision.
3. The offender should have the opportunity to develop the social and technical skills required in order to maintain a satisfying lifestyle in the community, free from a return to criminal behaviour.
4. Wherever possible, the offender should contribute to the social costs resulting from the offence and subsequent incarceration by participation in constructive work activity.

A variety of programs can be identified under the general heading of community-based corrections. Some of those currently operating in Canada are as follows:

1. *Community-Based Centres* include a wide range of residential or correctional centres which are utilized by sentenced persons, parolees, by persons on post-release status, persons on remand[8] status and, in some cases, by probationers. The general distinction between community-based residential centres and community correctional centres is that the former are operated by agencies in the *private sector* while the latter are programs of *government*. Although the nature of their operations and services vary considerably from one location to another, generally the centres provide supervision and guidance to residents as a way of facilitating their re-entry into the community. Often, residents are working or undergoing some type of training.
2. *Attendance Centre Programs* are government-supervised programs which operate within the community and which require regular attendance at a specified location or in a specified activity. Attendance can be daily, on weekends, or full-time, depending upon the particular program. Entry to attendance centre programs is through probation, either as a condition of a probation order or on the recommendation of the supervising probation officer.
3. *Bail Supervision Programs* provide an alternative to remand in custody through the placement of accused persons under community supervision while awaiting trial.
4. *Pre-Trial Diversion Programs* are those in which alleged offenders,[9] deemed not to require the full and formal court process, are diverted out of the justice system into a more appropriate resource.
5. *Temporary Absence Programs* provide for the conditional release of selected offenders from a correctional facility in

order to pursue employment, training, education, medical treatment, maintenance of family ties, involvement in community service programs, and pre-parole release planning.

6. *Restitution Programs* provide for the repayment by offenders of specific costs to the victim or victims of their crimes.

7. *Fine Option Programs* offer an alternative to offenders by affording them the opportunity to voluntarily work out the payment of their fine through community service activities.

8. *Community Service Order* is a condition imposed by the court through a probation order. A Community Service Order requires the performance by an offender of an assigned task that represents a service to a member of the community or to the community collectively.

9. *Probation* is a sentence of the court providing for supervision within the community. A probation order requires regular reporting to the supervising probation officer and the fulfillment of any other conditions which the court may impose.

10. *Parole* is a program which provides for the release of incarcerated persons under community supervision during a portion of their sentence of imprisonment.

In reference to the program descriptions appearing above, it is clear from an examination of annual reports on Canadian correctional programs that community-based correctional alternatives have increased dramatically during the past two decades.[10]

While community-based correctional programs are offered by both the federal and provincial governments, given the division of responsibilities that exists in Canada, most programs in this category fall under provincial jurisdiction and are made available to those offenders who are serving shorter sentences and who have committed less serious offences. The most significant exception to this general observation concerns the federal government's responsibility for the supervision of persons on parole. For the fiscal year 1985/86, the cost to the federal government of all programs related to the provision of parole services was $30,620,200 out of the total budget for the Correctional Service of Canada of approximately $729,689,100 (Statistics Canada 1986). Table 3.2 presents a breakdown of cost commitments to community-based correctional programs for each province and territory. Although the characteristics of these programs are developed in greater detail later, the special nature of probation and parole requires additional comment here.

TABLE 3.2 Provincial/Territorial Expenditures on Community Supervision Services, 1979/80 and 1985/86[1]

Province/ Territory	1979/80		1985/86		1979/80–1985/86	
	Expenditures ($000's)	% of Total Correctional Expenditures	Expenditures ($000's)	% of Total Correctional Expenditures	Expenditure Increase ($000's)	Expenditure Increase %
Newfoundland[2]	332	5.6	703	6.0	371	112
Prince Edward Island*	188	11.5	332	12	144	76.5
Nova Scotia*[3]	992	11.1	2,601	17	1,609	162
New Brunswick	977	15.4	1,747	15	770	78.8
Quebec	6,174	8.1	9,145	9	2,971	48.1
Ontario	17,288	12.6	30,015	11	12,727	73.6
Manitoba[4]	4,027	27.8	3,956	16	-71	-1.7
Saskatchewan	887	7.1	3,714	10	2,827	319
Alberta	6,129	14.2	9,382	13	3,253	53
British Columbia	9,111	16.0	9,569	14	458	5
Yukon Territory	338	17.7	564	16	226	66.9
Northwest Territories	—	—	371	4	—	—
Total[5]	46,443	12.6		11.9	25,285	82.7

SOURCE: Statistics Canada. 1986. *Adult Correctional Services in Canada, 1985/86.* Ottawa: Canadian Centre for Justice Statistics.

1 Includes expenditures on probation, parole, parole boards, and other non-custodial correctional services
2 Excludes costs of outport jails
3 Includes municipal expenditures
4 Includes costs of juvenile probation services
5 Data on the Northwest Territories unavailable prior to 1983
* Calendar year

Probation

Because in Canada the major sentencing options are fines, imprisonment, and probation, applied either individually or in some combination, then it is appropriate to view probation as the leading correctional service included within the general definition of community-based corrections. Unlike most other programs that may be included under the definition of community-based services, probation exists as a separate sentencing option of the court. Currently, many of the community-based correctional programs are accessed by offenders either as a condition of probation or through administrative arrangements associated with the sentence of imprisonment. However, in 1986, the Canadian Sentencing Commission completed its study and submitted its recommendations to the Ministry of Justice. These recommendations are being considered as part of the current Criminal Law Review in Canada (discussed in Chapters 10 and 11). Amendments to the sentencing provisions of the *Criminal Code* are likely to result.[11] Until such changes are passed by the federal Parliament, probation will remain the only community-based correctional program accessed by direct order of the court.

As suggested, probation's basic purpose is to provide supervision within the community as a sentence of the court. A probation order requires regular reporting to the supervising probation officer and the fulfillment of any other conditions which the court may impose. By definition, probation satisfies many of the criteria associated with community-based corrections. As the most extensive community-based program option within the broad spectrum of correctional services, it follows that probation must be examined closely when any judgements about the philosophy and trends within the correctional system as a whole are made. Such a review needs to address at least two general areas:

1. The extent to which the probation option is used in relation to other options available to the court, and
2. The manner in which probation is organized to provide its services.

It should be kept in mind that probation is a program administered by the provinces as a sanction available for less serious offenders. Consequently, its use by the courts needs to be measured in relation to the use of other options falling under provincial jurisdiction.

In speaking of the first area of interest, it was noted at the conclusion of Chapter 2 that the use of probation has increased in Canada as compared to provincial sentences of imprisonment.[12] With regard to the manner in which probation services are organized, two trends are notable. The first concerns the increasing tendency to attach conditions to probation orders which provide the probationer with access to other, more specialized, community-based correctional programs. The second trend is directly related to the first and involves movement away from the client-centred counselling model in favour of a case-management model for probation supervision.[13] This is compatible with the trend in correctional institutions described previously.

The trends referred to are discussed in subsequent chapters with reference to the specific elements of practice and to the problems that are associated with program evaluation. For the present, it is worth noting that these trends appear to be in harmony with the basic principles of the reintegration model. More particularly, they reveal an attempt to involve non-correctional agencies in the rehabilitation of offenders; they maintain as normal an association as possible between the community and the offender while under sanction; and they reinforce the principle that imprisonment is an option of last resort.

Parole

Parole refers to the supervised release of an offender from a correctional institution after a portion of the sentence has been served. In Canada, the National Parole Board is given authority under the federal *Parole Act* to grant full and day parole to both federal and provincial inmates; to grant temporary absences to federal inmates; and to terminate/revoke parole or mandatory supervision[14] releases. Although federal inmates are considered automatically for parole at their parole eligibility dates, provincial inmates must apply for parole by virtue of Section 8(1) of the *Parole Act*. As a consequence of recent amendments to the *Parole Act,* individual provinces now can assume jurisdiction over inmates detained in provincial institutions. To date, Quebec, Ontario, and British Columbia have established their own parole boards.

The National Parole Board is an independent agency located within the Ministry of the Solicitor General (Canada). The Board forms a part of the criminal justice system in its daily operations and works closely with the police, the judiciary and corrections. In the exercise of its decision-making role, it is completely independent of outside control, although in Chapter 9 we see that there are numerous outside pressures that may influence the decisions of the Board. While the Parole Board maintains its independence, the responsibility for monitoring and supervising parolees (parole services) belongs to the federal Corrections Service and to the provincial corrections services in those provinces where provincial parole boards have been established.

Given the nature of their mandates and the responsibilities which they exercise, the National Parole Board and the federal and provincial parole services are directly related to the overall correctional enterprise. Most investigators include parole as a subsystem within corrections (see Coffey 1975; Bartollas and Miller 1978; Shover 1979; Griffiths et al. 1980). It therefore becomes important to analyze the philosophy and function of parole in any assessment of correctional trends.

In the *Annual Report* of the Solicitor General of Canada (1982, 45) the following comments are made:

> The philosophy and principles underlining correctional programs and parole in particular have changed since the legislation on which these programs were based came into effect more than twenty years ago. These changes need to be reflected in the establishment of new mandates for the future roles of parole and correctional authorities at the federal level in Canada. The Parole Act could need significant amendment in the three to five year time frame. Constitutional concerns expressed by the provinces in the area of the administration of justice, the current readiness of governments to establish interim administrative arrangements and the whole complex of issues related to the existing split in jurisdiction for corrections are major concerns of the National Parole Board.

This statement reflects the view that parole, like corrections generally, has been subject to changes in philosophy and principles. Furthermore, it suggests that constant reassessment is required, given the complexities of jurisdictional authority which exist in Canada. For example, changes in Canadian paroling philosophy have resulted in the National Parole Board's assuming responsibility for the granting of short-term releases to assist in the reintegration of offenders into the community.[15] Similarly, the parole services have expanded their use of community correctional centres for parolees and have extended their coordination with private agencies for the provision of after-care services[16] (for a general discussion of this trend, see National Advisory Commission on Criminal Justice Standards and Goals 1973, 430-32; Coffey 1975, 158-59). Finally, it is clear that general trends within the parole system are similar to the trends evident within the correctional system as a whole.

AN OVERVIEW OF OFFENDER POPULATIONS, PROGRAM DISTRIBUTION AND COSTS

In continuing our description of the Canadian correctional enterprise, it is necessary to provide some general information on the distribution of offender programs and associated costs across Canada. It is only recently that information of this type has been available in an organized way. It was not until the formation of the National Task Force on the Administration of Justice[17] in 1976 that the compiling of operational data on correctional programs across Canada gained impetus. Although the National Task Force is no longer active, its work was continued by the National Work Group on Justice Information and Statistics, established in June, 1980, and continuing today as an activity of the Centre for Justice Statistics, an agency within Statistics Canada (for a discussion of these developments, see the Report of the Implementation Work Group on Justice Statistics 1981).

While the work of the National Task Force and its successors represents a considerable advancement in the collection of national data on corrections, it must be recognized that a great deal of work remains to be done before a standardized, accurate, and consistently updated set of statistics will be available. Nonetheless, a much better statistical picture of the Canadian correctional enterprise is available now than ever before.

However, a few special problems associated with the acquisition of correctional data on a national basis should be mentioned. As noted previously, the responsibility for the provision of adult correctional services in Canada is shared among all federal, provincial, and territorial governments. Until recently, the federal *Juvenile Delinquents Act* (1929) specified the age of criminal majority at 16 years, while allowing for provincial discretion in setting the age higher, at either 17 or 18 years. Consequently, the age of majority was not consistent across all jurisdictions. Clearly, the absence of uniformity presented significant implications for the compatibility of data regarding offender populations and expenditures respecting adult services. Also recently, new legislation was passed by the House of Commons to replace the *Juvenile Delinquents Act* (proclaimed effective April, 1984). Entitled the *Young Offenders Act,* the new legislation establishes 18 years as a consistent age of majority across Canada (proclaimed effective April, 1985). When approaching the data that are described later in this chapter, therefore, it must be realized that much of the information currently available is based on the age distribution resulting from the provisions of the federal *Juvenile Delinquents Act.* Table 3.3 provides the age of majority applicable to each province and territory under the provisions of the *Juvenile Delinquents Act.*

TABLE 3.3   Legal Adult Age by Province (Prior to April 1, 1985)

The age at which persons were legally considered as adults was not uniform across Canada and thus the share of the numbers of persons served by juvenile and adult agencies varied. The age limits within the provinces and territories was as follows:

Province	Adult Age
Newfoundland	17
Prince Edward Island	16
Nova Scotia	16
New Brunswick	16
Quebec	18
Ontario	16
Manitoba	18
Saskatchewan	16
Alberta	16
British Columbia	17
Yukon Territory	16
Northwest Territories	16

SOURCE: National Task Force on the Administration of Justice, 1979a (updated 1987). *Corrections Services in Canada and Comparison of Services 1977/78,* pp. 5-6.

Yet another reason can be cited to account for the problems associated with data compatibility in the Canadian correctional enterprise. Federal adult correctional services are provided by the Correctional Service of Canada (CSC) and the National Parole Board (NPB).[18] Both of these agencies operate under the auspices of the federal Ministry of the Solicitor General. The provincial organization of adult services, both pre-trial and post-trial, varies from jurisdiction to jurisdiction (see National Task Force on the Administration of Justice 1979a, 5).

Table 3.4 lists the departments and ministries providing correctional services for adults in Canada. New Brunswick, Manitoba, Saskatchewan, British Columbia, and the Northwest Territories do not have completely separate administrative or service structures for handling adult and juvenile offenders. As a consequence of these anomalies in the data base, attempts to identify a national adult case-load or the precise expenditures made on adult services presents great difficulty (National Task Force on the Administration of Justice 1979b, 3).

With these provisos in mind, the following general information will serve as an overview of Canadian correctional program costs and related data. The information presented below is based on summary data compiled by the National Work Group on Justice Information and Statistics (1981, 318-20). Some updating of this base information has been possible using data from more recent years. Keep in mind, however, that the primary reason for presenting this information is to increase understanding of the *categories* of expenditures and the approximate relationships (ratios) between them. Detailed information related to specific programs is presented in subsequent chapters and some updating of information is provided in categories where new trends are emerging. The following information establishes a comparative base to assist in understanding the categories of services and related expenditures as provided by the federal and provincial governments.

TABLE 3.4 Ministries and Departments
Responsible for Adult Corrections

Government	Ministry/Department
Newfoundland	Department of Justice, Corrections Division
Prince Edward Island	Department of Justice, Corrections Division
Nova Scotia	Department of Attorney General, Correctional Services Division
New Brunswick	Department of Justice, Correctional Services Division
Quebec	Ministère de la Justice — Direction générale de la Probation et des établissements de détention
Ontario	Ministry of Correctional Services
Manitoba	Department of Community Services, Corrections Division
Saskatchewan	Department of Justice, Corrections Division
Alberta	Department of the Solicitor General, Corrections Division
British Columbia	Ministry of the Attorney General, Corrections Branch
Yukon Territory	Department of Justice, Institutional Services Branch and Community Corrections Branch
Northwest Territories	Department of Social Services, Corrections Service
Federal	Ministry of the Solicitor General

SOURCE: National Task Force on the Administration of Justice, 1979a (updated 1987). *Corrections Services in Canada and Comparison of Services, 1977/78.* p. 8.

Correctional Institutions

1. In 1985/86, the average federal per diem inmate cost was $108.00, while the average provincial per diem inmate cost was $80.03.
2. The total average inmate count for Canada has remained stable from the 1984/85 fiscal year to the 1985/86 fiscal year at approximately 27,600.
3. The majority of offenders admitted to provincial institutions are sentenced to three months or less; in 1979/80, the proportion of admissions with sentences of less than one month ranged from 32 percent to 87 percent among the provinces; the proportion with sentences of three months or less ranged from 57 percent to 96 percent.
4. Among provinces from which data were available, the proportion of total sentenced admissions made up of offenders who were sentenced to custody for defaulting on a fine ranged from 16 percent to 65 percent in 1985/86.
5. Among provinces from which data were available, the proportion of total sentenced admissions made up of offenders who were sentenced to custody for drinking/driving offences ranged from 5 percent to 34 percent in 1985/86.
6. In 1985/86, the average age of federal offenders was 30 years and of provincial offenders 27 years.
7. In 1979/80, the proportion of total remand and sentenced admissions to provincial institutions who were less than 25 years of age ranged from 45 percent to 60 percent (among provinces where data were available and similarly categorized).
8. In 1985/86, over 97 percent of admissions to federal institutions were male.
9. Across all provinces, the vast majority of those admitted to custody or probation supervision were male; in 1979/80, the proportion among provinces of those admitted to custody on remand status who were female ranged from 3 percent to 21 percent; the proportion of those sentenced to custody who were female ranged from 2 percent to 9 percent; the proportion of those admitted to probation supervision who were female ranged from 8 percent to 16 percent. For 1985/86, female admissions to provincial institutions in Canada averaged 7 percent of total admissions.
10. Among provinces from which data were available, the proportion of the total remand and sentenced admissions to institutions made up of natives ranged in 1979/80 from 3

percent to 62 percent. For 1985/86, native persons accounted for 10 percent of federal and 18 percent of provincial institutional admissions.
11. For 1985/86, the total number in all categories of escapes from federal and provincial institutions was 2,127.
12. For 1985/86, 40 inmate deaths occurred in federal institutions — 20 from suicide. Suicide has been the leading cause of death in federal institutions for the four years ending in 1986.

Probation/Parole Services

1. In the fiscal year 1985/86, there were 62 local federal parole offices operating in Canada, with a staff complement of 318 persons; in 1985/86 there were an average of 7,317 individuals on parole or mandatory supervision.
2. During the year 1979/80, there were approximately 1,264 full-time probation officers employed in Canada; of provinces from which data were available, the average supervision case-load per officer ranged from 23 to 29.
3. In 1979/80, the total provincial probation supervision admissions were approximately 57,000; in 1981/82, 66,245; in 1985/86, 54,838. The total number of probation admissions has been declining each year since 1981/82.
4. In 1979/80, the proportion of total admissions to provincial probation supervision who were less than 24 years of age ranged (among provinces where data were available and similarly categorized) from 60 percent to 78 percent.

Expenditures

1. From 1977/78 to 1978/79, total federal expenditures on correctional services increased by 8.9 percent, while total expenditures on provincial correctional services increased by 18 percent; from 1978/79 to 1979/80, total federal expenditures increased by 1.3 percent while total provincial expenditures increased by 10.3 percent. This trend of increasing costs continued through 1984/85. In 1985/86, a 3 percent decrease (19.5 mil.) in costs occurred.
2. The overall expenditure increase on provincial correctional facilities was 9.4 percent from 1978/79 to 1979/80; in 1979/80, expenditures on correctional facilities made up over 81 percent

of all provincial correctional expenditures, with the proportion ranging from 71 percent to 93.3 percent among the provinces. These ratios of expenditures have remained constant through the 1985/86 fiscal year.

3. The overall expenditure increase on community supervision services was 21.4 percent from 1978/79 to 1979/80; in 1979/80, expenditures on community supervision made up 12.6 percent of all provincial correctional expenditures, with the proportion ranging from 5.6 percent to 17.7 percent among the provinces. These ratios of expenditures have remained constant through the 1985/86 fiscal year.

4. The overall increase in provincial correctional personnel expenditures was 7.9 percent from 1978/79 to 1979/80; in 1979/80, personnel expenditures made up 76.8 percent of all correctional expenditures, with the proportion ranging from 64.4 percent to 81.1 percent among the provinces. For 1985/86, personnel expenditures were 73 percent of all correctional expenditures.

5. In 1979/80, the per capita cost of federal correctional services in Canada was $15.56, in 1985/86, $24.07. Among the provinces the per capita cost of provincial correctional services ranged from $9.06 to $22.09 in 1979/80; in 1985/86, from $15.82 to $34.95.

The total expenditures for adult correctional services in Canada (1985/86) were 1.367 billion, of which $744 million were federal expenditures and $622 million were provincial (Statistics Canada 1986, 16).

At the time of this writing, the information presented above is from the most recent reporting years in which information was collated in this form. However, these figures are constantly changing and, with the creation of the Canadian Centre for Justice Statistics (1981) as a division of Statistics Canada, it is now possible to receive yearly updates in most of these information categories. It must be emphasized that the above information is presented for a comparative overview only and to assist the reader in acquiring a sense of the general distribution of correctional services across Canada in selected categories.

Against this background, we will proceed with a more detailed examination of policy and practice in Canadian corrections.

Notes

1. While the terms punishment, deterrence, and rehabilitation are commonly used to describe sentencing objectives, there is no real consensus on how sentencing objectives or justifications for imposing a criminal sanction should be defined (see Griffiths et al. 1980, 179 ff). Despite the importance of sentencing, the *Criminal Code* of Canada is virtually silent on the principles and objectives which should guide and be reflected in sentencing practice. The Law Reform Commission of Canada (1976) has proposed guidelines for sentencing as part of a general criminal law review currently underway in Canada.

2. It is important to note that these distinctions are not necessarily those used by the correctional system or its employees to describe what they currently do or have done in the past. These distinctions result from analyses by observers of policy statements, operational guidelines, and public documents produced by the system or about the system over time.

3. Section 659, subsection 1 of the *Criminal Code* provides that "a person who is sentenced to imprisonment for . . . a term of two years or more, or . . . that, in the aggregate, amount to two years or more, shall be sentenced to imprisonment in a penitentiary." The *Penitentiary Act* defines a penitentiary as "an institution or facility of any description including all lands connected therewith, that is operated by the Service for the custody, treatment, or training of persons sentenced or committed to penitentiary, and includes any place declared to be a penitentiary pursuant to subsection (1.1) or (1.2); Service means the Canadian Penitentiary Service referred to in section 3" (now called the Correctional Service of Canada). Subsection 3 provides that "a person who is sentenced to imprisonment and who is not required to be sentenced as provided in subsection 1 . . . shall, unless a special prison is prescribed by law, be sentenced to imprisonment in a prison or other place of confinement within the province in which he is convicted, other than a penitentiary. . . ."

While the "two-year rule" reflects the basic division of responsibility between the federal and provincial governments in the delivery of correctional services, there are some historical and current exceptions worthy of note. Prior to the passage of the *Criminal Law Amendment Act (1977),* the Provinces of British Columbia and Ontario were responsible for the administration of definite-indeterminate sentences for young offenders. In both instances, the sentence length could extend to four years less two days in duration. Sections providing for repeal of the definite-indeterminate sentence were proclaimed for Ontario in 1978 and for British Columbia in 1980. It also should be made clear that the federal government presently has responsibility for parole supervision of offenders serving definite sentences of any length in those provinces which have not established their own provincial parole boards under Section 5 of the *Parole Act.*

Moreover, all governments in Canada are empowered to operate custodial facilities to the level of maximum security for one purpose or another. For example, the provinces provide long-term custodial facilities for the dangerously insane and municipalities operate lock-up facilities for offenders, prior to court appearance. In most provinces, the prisoners who are remanded in custody awaiting trial are the responsibility of provincial authorities until acquitted, released on other grounds, or sentenced. Provincial authorities also retain custody for the period of time provided for appeal of sentence in Section 16 of the *Penitentiary Act.* Given these exceptions, the "two-year rule" does not accurately portray the division of responsibility in all categories of correctional programming, particularly if the custody of prisoners on pre-trial status is considered.

4. The term "operating systems" is used here to refer to the management, administration, and program structures of government which have been established to provide services directly to the client. In the case of Corrections, this refers to all systems established to provide for the care and custody of offenders.

5. The term "public policy" is used here with reference to any statement, by government agencies, of intention or purpose articulated in a form which is available for public scrutiny.

6. "Heads of Correction" refers to all persons, at both the federal and provincial levels of government, who are bureaucratically responsible, as senior civil servants, for the delivery of correctional services in their jurisdiction. These persons meet regularly in Canada as a continuing committee to discuss correctional issues. This committee is called the Continuing Committee of Heads of Corrections (Canada).

7. While the social costs of imprisonment could be said to include all costs accruing to society related to the incarceration of offenders, for our purposes the costs to society to meet the basic care and custody needs of the offender will not be included. Instead, social costs are taken to mean the cost to the victim (restitution), family maintenance, economic viability upon release, and personal expenditures within the institution over and above basic survival requirements.

8. The term "remand" refers to the status of a person between the time of initial court appearance and final adjudication. If, during this time, a person is placed in custody, he or she is referred to as being on "remand in custody."

9. The term "alleged offenders" is used to refer to those persons concerning whom there is sufficient information to lay a charge but who have not admitted guilt or been found guilty in the legal/technical sense. In Chapter 10, we see that the status of "alleged offenders" who have been placed in diversion programs has been the subject of continuing debate.

10. For example, a review of the *Annual Report* for B.C. Corrections in 1972 shows no reference to community correctional centres or the funding of community-based residential centres, while in 1980 six community correctional centres are identified, with $5,999,335 committed to the funding of community-based programs other than probation (pages 6 and 32 ff). Similarly, the *Annual Report* of the Solicitor General of Canada in 1973 had no description of community-based corrections programs other than parole, while the 1980-1981 *Annual Report* of the Solicitor General (1982, 54) reports an average count of 321 federal inmates in community correctional centres at a total cost of $5,502,653. In addition, the *Justice Information Report — Correctional Services in Canada 1978/79, 1979/80* (National Work Group on Justice Information and Statistics 1981, 24) reports that $3,574,965 was committed by the federal government to maintain a total of 109 contracts between the CSC and community residential centres operated by private agencies.

Also, in March 1979, an "alternative entry project" for the classification of prisoners was approved in British Columbia. The alternative entry project provides for direct admission from the courts of sentenced adults to forest camps and community correctional centre programs (British Columbia Ministry of the Attorney General 1981, 64).

11. The Canadian Sentencing Commission was established in May, 1984. Under the chairmanship of J.R. Omer Archambault, the Commission had a mandate to thoroughly examine sentencing in Canada and to make recommendations on how the process could be improved. The report of the Sentencing Commission was submitted in February, 1987.

12. According to the report of the National Work Group on Justice Information and Statistics (1981, 318-19), the total sentenced admissions to provincial institutions remained stable over the two-year reporting period while the average probation supervision count in Canada increased by 14 percent.

13. The *client-centred counselling model* is based on the principle of one-on-one therapeutic intervention. In this model, the primary responsibility of the probation officer is to supervise each probationer on the case-load with regard to any conditions which may have been imposed by the court. The *case-management model* is based on the assumption that other community agencies can contribute to the supervision of the probationer and the realization of any special conditions imposed by the court in the probation order. The primary responsibility of the probation officer is to "manage" the entire case-load with attention to the involvement of individual probationers with other agencies where appropriate.

14. Section 15 of the *Parole Act* reads, "Where an inmate is released from imprisonment, prior to the expiration of his sentence according to law, solely as a result of remission, including earned remission, and the term of such remission exceeds sixty days, he shall, notwithstanding any other act, be subject to mandatory supervision commencing upon his release and continuing for the duration of such remission." Sections 6 and 7 of the *Prisons and Reformatories Act* makes general provision for remission and establishes the maximum amount of remission that may be earned.

15. The 1985/86 *Annual Report* of the Solicitor General of Canada (1987) divides the short-term release responsibility of the National Parole Board into two categories: day parole and temporary absences. In 1985/86, the total applications (both federal and provincial) for day parole which were considered by the National Parole Board numbered 6,718 of which 3,885 were granted. The Board received 1,613 applications for unescorted temporary absences; 806 of these applications were granted.

16. Regional reports included in the 1980/81 *Annual Report* of the Solicitor General of Canada are consistent in their mention of increased activity related to the coordination between parole services and private agencies in the provision of after-care services. The National Task Force on the Administration of Justice (1979b) reported that both the penitentiary and parole services placed offenders in approximately 100 residential programs operated by private agencies. About 98 percent of the placements were made through the parole service.

17. The National Task Force on the Administration of Justice (1979a) was established by the provincial Ministers of Justice and Attorneys General in 1976

"to examine the existing justice services in Canada; gather data relating to the cost of delivery of these justice services, including both operating and projected capital costs; and recommend minimum standards for justice services and present the cost implications thereof."

18. The Correctional Service of Canada was created in its present form in 1978 through an amalgamation of the National Parole Service and the Canadian Penitentiary Service. It is comprised of five regions: Atlantic region, covering the four Maritime provinces; Quebec region, Ontario region; Prairie region, including Manitoba, Saskatchewan, Alberta, the Northwest Territories and the parole offices in Kenora and Thunder Bay, Ontario; and the Pacific region which includes British Columbia and the Yukon. A Commissioner of Corrections is appointed under the authority of the *Penitentiary Act* and reports to the Solicitor General of Canada. The Commissioner of Corrections is responsible for the control and management of the Service, including custody and programs, and the supervision of offenders in the community. In the years 1980-81, the Correctional Service of Canada operated 59 penitentiaries in all provinces except P.E.I., Newfoundland, the Yukon, and the Northwest Territories, with a total average inmate population of 23,650 (Statistics Canada 1982, 59 ff).

References

Archambault, J. (Chairman). 1938. *Report of the Royal Commission to Investigate the Penal System of Canada.* Ottawa: King's Printer.

Bartollas, C. and S.J. Miller. 1978. *Correctional Administration: Theory and Practice.* New York: McGraw-Hill.

Brantingham, P. and P.L. Brantingham. 1984. *Patterns in Crime.* New York: Macmillan.

British Columbia Ministry of the Attorney General. 1973. *Annual Report, 1972.* Victoria: Corrections Branch.

_____. 1978. *Statement of Goals, Strategies and Beliefs.* Victoria: Corrections Branch.

_____. 1981. *Annual Report, 1979-80.* Victoria: Corrections Branch.

Coffey, A.R. 1975. *Correctional Administration: The Management of Institutions, Probation and Parole.* Englewood Cliffs, New Jersey: Prentice-Hall.

Fauteux, G. (Chairman). 1956. *Report of a Committee Appointed to Inquire into the Principles and Procedures Followed in the Remission Service of the Department of Justice of Canada.* Ottawa: Queen's Printer.

Federal-Provincial Task Force on the Long Term Objectives in Corrections. 1977. *The Long-Term Objectives and Administration of Corrections in Canada.* Ottawa: Solicitor General of Canada.

Greenspan, E. 1981. *Martin's Annual Criminal Code.* Aurora, Ontario: Canada Law Book Limited.

Griffiths, C.T., J.F. Klein and S.N. Verdun-Jones. 1980. *Criminal Justice in Canada: An Introductory Text.* Vancouver: Butterworths.

Jayewardene, C.H.S. and D.J.N. Jayasuriya. 1981. *The Management of Correctional Institutions.* Toronto: Butterworths.

Key, J. 1986. *A Guide to Sentence Administration in Canada.* Vancouver: Best Efforts Ink Ltd.

Law Reform Commission of Canada. 1976. *Report: Dispositions and Sentences in the Criminal Process.* Ottawa: Information Canada.

Macdonald, G. 1982. *Self-Sustaining Prison Industries.* Vancouver: Institute for Studies in Criminal Justice Policy, Simon Fraser University.

National Advisory Commission on Criminal Justice Standards and Goals. 1973. *Corrections.* Washington, D.C.: U.S. Government Printing Office.

National Task Force on the Administration of Justice. 1979a. *Corrections Services in Canada and Comparison of Services, 1977/78.* Victoria: Attorney General of British Columbia.

_____. 1979b. *Justice Services in Canada, 1977/78.* Victoria: Attorney General of British Columbia.

National Work Group on Justice Information and Statistics. 1981. *Justice Information Report-Correctional Services in Canada, 1978/79, 1979/80.* Ottawa.

Ouimet, R. (Chairman). 1969. *Report of the Canadian Committee on Corrections — Toward Unity: Criminal Justice and Corrections.* Ottawa: Information Canada.

Report of the Canadian Sentencing Commission. 1986. *Sentencing Reform: A Canadian Approach.* Ottawa: Supply and Services Canada.

Report of the Implementation Work Group on Justice Statistics. (April) 1981. *Towards the Establishment of the Canadian Centre for Justice Statistics.* Ottawa.

Rusche, G. (Summer) 1980. "Prison Revolts or Social Policy Lessons from America." 13 *Crime and Social Justice.* 41-44.

Shover, N. 1979. *A Sociology of American Corrections.* Homewood, Illinois: The Dorsey Press.

Solicitor General of Canada. *Annual Report, 1973.* Ottawa: Supply and Services Canada.

_____. 1982. *Annual Report, 1980/81.* Ottawa: Supply and Services Canada.

_____. 1987. *Annual Report, 1985/86.* Ottawa: Supply and Services Canada.

Solicitor General of Canada and Attorney General of British Columbia. 1976. *Bilateral Discussions on the Division of Correctional Responsibilities between the Federal Government and the Province of British Columbia.* Victoria: Ministry of the Attorney General.

Statistics Canada. 1982. *Adult Correctional Services in Canada, 1980/81.* Ottawa: Canadian Centre for Justice Statistics.

_____. 1986. *Adult Correctional Services in Canada, 1985/86.* Ottawa: Supply and Services Canada.

Task Force on the Creation of an Integrated Canadian Corrections Service. 1977. *The Role of Federal Corrections in Canada.* Ottawa: Supply and Services Canada.

Toby, J. 1967. "Affluence and Adolescent Crime." In the President's Commission on Law Enforcement and Administration of Justice. *Task Force Report: Juvenile Delinquency and Youth Crime.* Washington, D.C.: U.S. Government Printing Office. 132-44.

Corrections Legislation
    Canada. *Parole Act*. R.S.C. 1970, c. P-2, S.1.
    Canada. *Penitentiary Act*. R.S.C. 1970, c. P-6.
    Canada. *Prisons and Reformatories Act*. R.S.C. 1970, c. P-21.
    Canada. *Criminal Law Amendment Act*. S.C. 1976-77, c. 53.

Chapter 4

Policy Making in Canadian Corrections

In this chapter, some of the major factors involved in the making of correctional policy are identified. Policy is defined both as a *concept* and as an *activity of government*. Since policy making in government is a political responsibility, the motivation and interests of politicians as policy makers are highlighted.

Against this background, the various influences on correctional policy are discussed. While there are many ways in which these influences may be categorized, the authors have chosen to divide them according to those which seem to arise from *within* the correctional system and those which result from initiatives taken *outside* of the system. While somewhat simplistic, this method of organization will reinforce the major point that correctional policy and practice are the products of a constant interaction between the correctional enterprise and the environment within which it exists.

THE NATURE OF POLICY

Before proceeding with the discussion of correctional policy, it is necessary to address the general question of the nature of policy itself. A clear definition of policy is difficult to produce since the word is used in different ways by politicians, senior executives of government, line managers and line staff. It is possible nevertheless to discuss the term in a way which throws some light on its general characteristics.[1]

The term "policy" derives from "polity," which is both a condition and a process of civil order. Policy implies wisdom in statesmanship and prudence in the course of action chosen by government. Criminal justice policy defines the parameters and gives direction to the decisions made in response to behaviour perceived by the governors to be criminal. It also extends to the management of those institutions charged with administering the criminal justice system. Policy is necessary only where decisions are necessary. Policy sets out the way in which judgements can be made between alternative choices and serves as a guide for settling disputes.

But policy is not merely a superior decision that directs other decisions. In a more primary sense, policy is an expression of meaning. A policy statement in the criminal justice system constitutes a declaration of social value, and it is upon the basis of the declared value that subsequent decisions are shaped.

For example, a policy decision to divert alleged offenders out of the criminal justice system at the earliest possible stage reflects the value that social conflict is best resolved in the community or between offender and victim. This would support the principle that the sanctioning power of the State should be reserved for those conflict situations which are beyond the ability of the local community to resolve in a less formal way. Such a policy forces "the system" (particularly police and prosecutorial services) to develop standards for diversion decisions and to work with other non-justice agencies in the development of diversion programs. Thus, this policy decision sets in motion a complex series of further decisions to manage and implement the policy. The social value is declared in specific enough terms to allow operating agencies to develop programs and procedures which can be evaluated to assure they adequately promote a policy intention.

In broad terms, policy is nothing more than deciding what to do about a particular course of action and communicating that decision to those persons and agencies responsible for carrying the decision into practice. As an activity of government, however, the judgement about what is to be done and its subsequent implementation not only establishes the parameters within which specific tasks are to be accomplished but also gives meaning to those tasks. Policies, whether of government as a whole, or of a particular government agency, become expressions of social value either directly or indirectly. The power of policy is that it shapes, reflects and reinforces social values by the way in which it gives meaning to the activities of government; by the emphasis in practice it requires of its agents; and by the tone of the relationship it establishes between government and the citizens who are at once subject to its regulations and recipients of its services.

Policy making should therefore not be taken lightly in any area of government service. Policy which is developed primarily for the purpose of solving an immediate "maintenance" problem,[2] without attention to the social purpose which that policy is intended to support, will often produce a confusing and counter-productive result at the point of its implementation.

In summary, policy may be viewed as a decision which constrains other decisions and gives meaning to the work to be done. As such, policy making is a management task involving both political and bureaucratic interests of government. For the purpose at hand, procedural or administrative decisions are not considered statements of policy in their own right. Instead they are seen to be decisions that are taken within the constraints which policy establishes to reinforce the social purpose which policy statements set forth. For instance, a decision establishing the form and content for a pre-sentence report ought to be described as a procedural decision that arises out of a policy which stipulates that pre-sentence reports will be written and which establishes the purpose such reports are expected to fulfill. Simply stated, the development of policy is a management responsibility, while the creation of forms and procedures to reflect policy is an administrative task. Hartman (1982, 119), in discussing the relationship between management responsibility for the development of policy and the administrative tasks which result, emphasizes the importance that top management decisions be clear and formally stated as policy. If this is not the case, different assumptions will be made at different levels of the organization about what is to be done, thus resulting in confusing or contradictory procedures.

> A statement of assumption is necessary to assure that program planning and control activities, performed at levels below top management, are consistent with the strategic plan. If, for example, different assumptions about the likely environment of the organization are made at different levels in the organization, not only will any apparent consistency between strategic plans and program action plans be purely coincidental, but severe problems will be encountered later when implementing and reviewing these plans. If actual performance deviates from planned [sic], then top management ... and lower levels of management ... will inevitably find themselves at odds about the responsibility and causes for deviation and what, or if any, remedial action to take. It is imperative, therefore, that the key assumption made by top management in defining a Justice mission, objective and strategy be formally stated and communicated throughout the organization.

This distinction between policy and procedure is fundamental and will be developed in detail when the division of responsibilities between the management and administration of correctional operations is described with respect to policy planning.

Finally, the nature of policy is such that it requires reference to a "policy maker" and to a process of "policy making." Both inside and outside government, policy making is not usually characterized as a rational, linear process where each step is either knowable or predictable. Nor is it always easy to identify the "maker" of a particular policy since a number of persons at different levels of authority may be involved in its development and the identity of the "real" decision maker may be obscured in the process. For definitional purposes, however, a policy maker may be defined as the person holding office where the ultimate accountability for the policy is located. In government terms, this is usually a political office (the Minister responsible for ———) although sometimes accountability can be seen to reside with the most senior civil servant in the government agency responsible for the policy's implementation. Against this background, the activity of policy making can be investigated in greater detail.

THE ACTIVITY OF POLICY MAKING

The interaction between politicians and senior civil servants responsible for the delivery of government services can properly be labelled *policy management*. While this concept is developed in greater detail in Chapter 6, it is worth noting here that, regardless of the manner in which government departments are organized to provide information and advice in the development of policy, it is the senior civil servants who ultimately become the chief advisors to the political decision makers. Accordingly, it is important for senior civil servants to be cognizant of the underlying nature of policy when tendering policy advice.

Such an appreciation takes on added force when it is realized that the same senior civil servants also are absorbed with the practical matters of day-to-day administration. It should further be understood that the advice systems that are available to them normally are located in the administrative apparatus of the government departments responsible for the provision of operational services. When the policy "need" is identified out of this milieu, it should not be surprising that it often takes the form of a response to administrative problems related to operational maintenance. When policy need is identified in this way, it becomes an element of what some commentators describe as "crisis-centred management." As Bartollas and Miller (1978, 115) state:

Administrators who have failed to conceptualize the total organization are likely to end up with crisis-centered management. This means that they will spend most of their time "putting out fires". The chances are that the administrator who sees only part of the problem or situation will either underreact or overreact to the problem. Thus, the chief responsibility of the administrator is to think in terms of and to understand the entire organization.

By displaying a tendency to generate policy "advice" out of a sense of administrative urgency, the criminal justice system as a whole and corrections in particular have often been criticized for their propensity for "crisis management." This was suggested by Ekstedt (1979, 40), while he was acting as senior policy advisor for the Ministry of Attorney General in British Columbia:

> Our system has operated on the basis of what I would call crisis management for a very long period of time. Planning efforts have tended to be ad hoc and planning decisions usually made on the basis of either charismatic leadership or political expediency. It became clear to us in this decade that such a state of affairs could not continue to exist.

Similarly, Waller (1979, 200) states:

> In general, policy stems from crisis issues. Policy makers are concerned about avoiding scandals and solving immediate problems. Politicians tend to have at least one eye on the next election, which in Canada is always less than five years away. Permanent public servants can focus on longer-term goals, but they have to be responsive to their political leader and to government budgetary cycles that are not longer than twelve months. The establishment of a research program and a long-term planning group structures a commitment to the long term, but their continued existence is constantly threatened by the pressures to resolve yesterday's crises. (I. Waller, "Organizing Research to Improve Criminal Justice Policy: A Perspective from Canada," *Journal of Research in Crime and Delinquency,* vol. 16 (July 1979), p. 200. Copyright©1979 by the National Council on Crime and Delinquency. Reprinted by permission of Sage Publications, Inc.)

As suggested earlier, policy developed from this perspective seldom gives due regard to the broader questions of social purpose which it must ultimately reflect.

Generally, the policy-making *process* is intended to service the needs of the policy maker, either individually, as in the case of a senior civil servant or politician, or collectively, through a group such as a management team or a cabinet committee. What may be referred to as the policy *process* is clearly distinct from the policy *result* which can be said to serve the organization as a whole; an element within the organization; the clients of the services provided by the organization; or, the public at large.

For example, a political need to take a policy initiative which will result in more efficient strategies to curb drinking-driving intends as a *result* to reduce the incidence of drinking-driving and the negative effects of such behaviour on the community. However, in order to achieve this result, a *process* must first be initiated to give the politician the data needed to make an informed decision in an atmosphere of support from those agencies which will eventually implement the policy (in this case, law enforcement, liquor control, insurance, social welfare, etc.). Thus, the policy *result* serves the larger community, while the policy *process* serves the policy maker.

In order to render the policy-making process competent, therefore, it is essential that both the policy maker and the policy maker's needs can be clearly identified. While the structural elements of management and administration which generate *content* for the purpose of policy planning will be discussed later, for now it is enough to emphasize that the policy maker must have access to reliable information in order to arrive at the best possible policy decision. However, there are other needs experienced by the policy maker that are very nearly as pressing.

Not least among them is the fact that the policy-making process is coloured by the *role* which the policy maker wants to play. This is an extremely important variable and helps cast light upon the difficulty outside observers encounter when they attempt to "rationalize" the policy-making process in relation to any known result.[3] Naturally, the role adopted by the policy maker is as much a result of personality as it is of the way in which the policy maker defines the responsibility of his office; the advantages or disadvantages that may flow from taking a "high profile" or "low profile" stance on the issue at hand; or the sense of personal commitment to the issue being addressed. As Waller (1979, 205) observes:

> The process of policy development is primarily a political process of satisfying a number of different interest groups. The process can be characterized in three alternative ways. There is the action to "neutralize" the symptom of crisis. The "altruistic" politician or policy planner wants to use the crisis to bring about a more lasting improvement in the country, often consistent with his or her personal ideology. There are also those who want to find the most "rational" solution by choosing between alternatives on the basis of reliable information. (I. Waller, "Organizing Research to Improve Criminal Justice Policy: A Perspective from Canada," *Journal of Research in Crime and Delinquency,* vol. 16 (July 1979), p. 205. Copyright © 1979 by the National Council on Crime and Delinquency. Reprinted by permission of Sage Publications, Inc.)

Usually a policy maker exhibits reasonable consistency in the role he/she chooses to play. Contributors to the policy-making process must be aware of these influences if they are to be successful in tendering policy advice. In governments, a change of policy makers or a change in the dynamics of a policy group is regarded by other individuals and agencies in the process as problematic, since attention must be given to "re-learning" the role that the new policy makers wish to play. The election of a new government or change in the political leadership of a department provides ample illustration of this phenomenon. Clearly, successful policy making requires that all participants in the process keep constantly in touch with the dynamics surrounding variations in the role policy makers adopt.[4]

Regardless of the role chosen, there are at least three needs of the policy maker which must be addressed:

1. *The requirement to make the best decision possible.* Policy makers in government are often criticized for not making the most "knowledgeable" decision possible in relation to the issue under consideration. While in many cases this may be a legitimate criticism, an *ideal* decision that follows from a rational analysis of available knowledge in the subject area may not be the *best* decision given other constraints. Accordingly, it is important that the constraints arising from such sources as the political, legislative, and financial environments inhabited by the policy maker can be identified and weighed against the ideal policy decision.

2. *The requirement to make decisions in a context which reduces problems of implementation.* Although a policy decision may represent the best possible choice available, it nonetheless may fail if implementation strategies are not addressed during the policy-making process. While it is generally unimportant whether or not policy makers are conversant with all the issues related to policy implementation, individuals and agencies providing policy advice must consider implementation strategies when constructing their advisory contribution to the policy maker.

3. *The requirement to be accountable for policy decisions which are made.* Part of the stress associated with policy making resides in the knowledge that once a decision is made the policy maker must be accountable for it. The policy process serves the policy maker best when the requirement for accountability is addressed as part of the content of the decision itself. If this is not done, at least two undesirable outcomes are possible. First,

the policy maker may delay a necessary decision due to uncertainty associated with his responsibility to be accountable. Second, once the decision is made, the policy maker may withdraw his support for it under the pressure of criticism or for some other reason. For the policy maker, exercising accountability should be taken to mean "owning" the decision in a way that assures his commitments to its implementation and to its continuing maintenance.

It is common in government service that participants who tender policy advice direct their work to defining the elements of the *best possible* policy without paying proper attention to the other requirements set out above. It is therefore not surprising that policy decisions which appear to have been taken with certainty and dispatch (such as closing an outdated prison) may be subject to interminable delays or outright failure during the process of implementation.

While it is difficult to document this effect, it is interesting to follow the progression of policy statements made by politicians over time concerning the difficult task of closing a major correctional institution. There are numerous examples of this phenomenon in Canada. In the Province of British Columbia, the closure of the B.C. Penitentiary and the promised closure of the Lower Mainland Regional Correctional Centre (Oakalla) provide good illustrations. With regard to Oakalla, the major provincial institution, it is interesting to note that its closure has been "promised" at the political level for a number of years. In recent history, reports of its imminent demise have been fairly constant. The Vancouver *Province* (1973, 29) reported an announcement by the Ministry of Municipal Affairs that the Oakalla Prison was to be phased out and the prison lands transformed into a recreational park. On March 8, 1974 the *Province* reported an announcement by the Attorney General pledging to phase out the provincial prison system, as it then existed, and assuring his commitment to the "critical task" of developing alternatives to imprisonment. The Vancouver *Sun*, on the same date, quoted the Attorney General as pledging to begin the phase-out of Oakalla immediately, with a schedule that would result in complete closure of the Institution by 1979. The *Vancouver Express,* December 22, 1978, reported the Attorney General as announcing "the first step leading to the eventual closure of the Lower Mainland Regional Correctional Center [sic] (Oakalla)". These announcements reflected public commitments on the part of two different governments and, consequently, two different Attorneys General. Recently, further public announcements have been made related to the proposed closure of this particular prison. As of this writing, the prison still stands. Attempts to close or phase out other prisons in Canada also provide illustrations of this phenomenon (for an interesting discussion of issues related to the closure of the Prison for Women in Kingston, Ontario, see Rusk 1980, 8).

In light of these considerations, it seems evident that the activity of policy making in government exists in a context where many competing, and often contradictory, forces are at play. But the demands upon the responsibility of all participants in the policy-making process do not stop here. Policy makers also must recognize their role as stewards of the public purse and in doing so must acknowledge the taxpayers' interests. Because policy makers contribute to the regulation of others and to the imposition of social meaning in public affairs, they are further subject to pressure from public, professional, political, and personal forces.

At yet another level, there is the responsibility placed on government to maintain the "moral obligation"[5] between itself and the electorate; to keep faith with the philosophy and principles which were presented to the citizens and which resulted in their acquisition of power. Without doubt, policies which violate these understandings lead to dissension and political disruption. As a final challenge, therefore, the activity of policy making must somehow be made consonant with the political promises made to the public by the government of the day.

THE ORIGINS OF CORRECTIONAL POLICY

The general principles of policy and policy making apply to all activities of government and, consequently, to the correctional enterprise as well. However, there are specific issues attached to each area of government activity which relate to the nature of work performed; the source of the clientele served; the public, political, and professional expectations that are raised; and the legal mandate which influences policy and the policy-making process. In this section, the factors that affect the formulation and direction of *correctional* policy will be identified and discussed.

Generally, the influences on correctional policy can be organized according to whether or not they emerge from inside or outside of the correctional system. Given the constant interaction between internal and external forces, it is not always clear in practice where such influences originate. However, the distinction can be useful in helping to isolate the probable sources of influence on correctional policy.

Regardless of the origin of the interaction or the direction in which the influence flows, it is important to appreciate that the interaction exists and that policy is generated out of the tension it creates. The Task Force on the Creation of an Integrated Canadian Corrections Service stated, in *The Role of Federal Corrections in Canada* (1977, 109-10):

> Tension, which exists in all organizations, is paramount in Corrections. It underlies the decision making on the offender, beginning with his initial classification and continuing through decisions in respect of segregation, temporary absences, parole, suspensions, and revocations. It is reflected in the organizations of Corrections: almost all committees, boards and the like, derive their existence from this inescapable tension. Management and organization must recognize, reflect, and accommodate this tension.

Generally, the external influences on correctional policy can be organized into four categories, presented in Figure 4.1.

1. The requirements of legislation and the process of law review;
2. Short-term political needs;
3. The policy and procedures of related subsystems within criminal justice; and
4. Academic research.

Internal influences can be organized according to three general categories:

1. Professional interests;
2. Resource capabilities; and
3. Operational maintenance needs.

External Influences on Correctional Policy

The Requirements of Legislation and the Process of Law Review

In our previous discussion on corrections as a legal entity (Chapter 1), the legislation which establishes the mandate for corrections in Canada was identified. In addition, the requirement for the correctional enterprise to conform to the general "rule of law" and to the accepted "principles of justice" was set forth. From the

FIGURE 4.1 Internal and External Influences on the Formulation of Correctional Policy

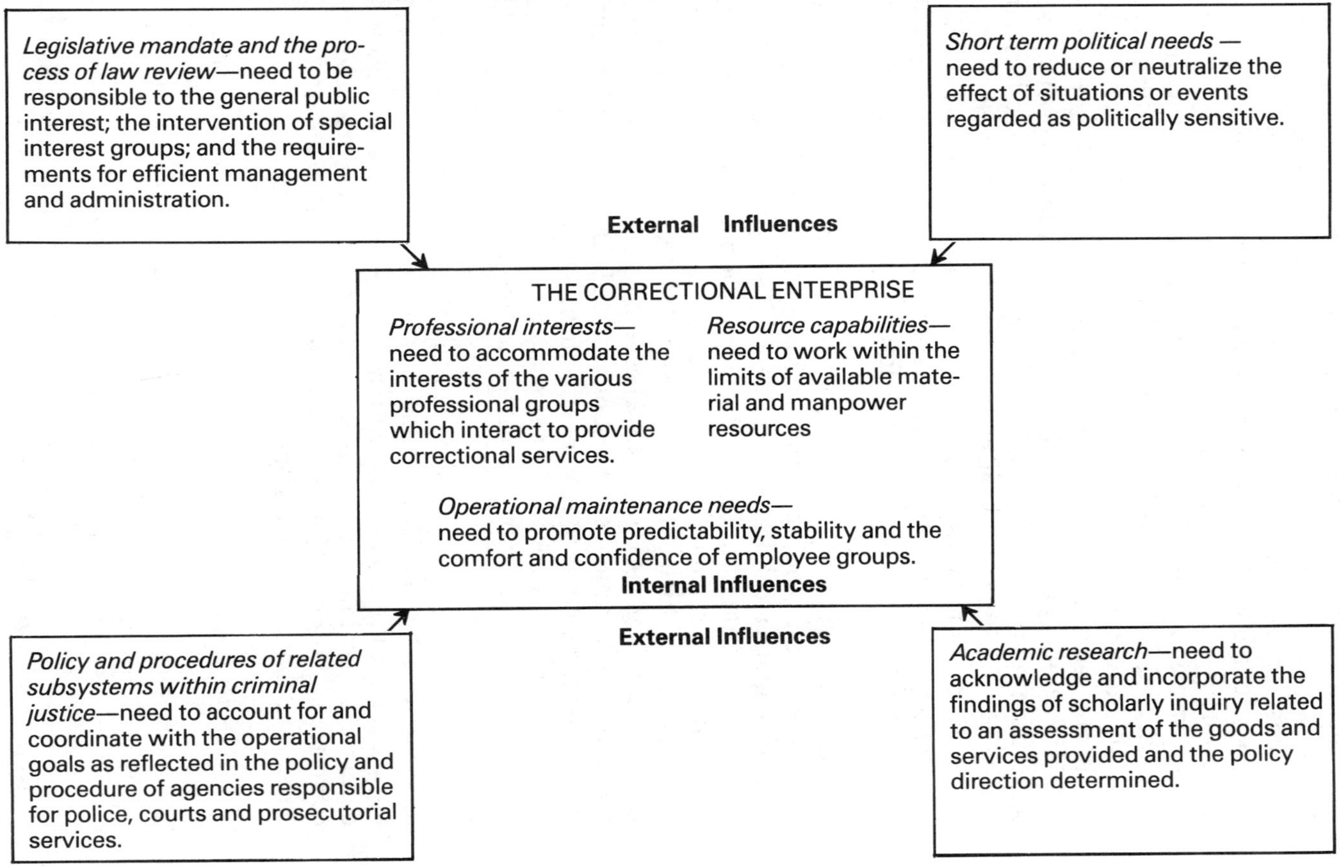

Short term political needs — need to reduce or neutralize the effect of situations or events regarded as politically sensitive.

*Academic research—*needs to acknowledge and incorporate the findings of scholarly inquiry related to an assessment of the goods and services provided and the policy direction determined.

External   Influences

THE CORRECTIONAL ENTERPRISE

Professional interests— need to accommodate the interests of the various professional groups which interact to provide correctional services.

Resource capabilities— need to work within the limits of available material and manpower resources

Operational maintenance needs— need to promote predictability, stability and the comfort and confidence of employee groups.

Internal Influences

External Influences

*Legislative mandate and the process of law review—*need to be responsible to the general public interest; the intervention of special interest groups; and the requirements for efficient management and administration.

*Policy and procedures of related subsystems within criminal justice—*need to account for and coordinate with the operational goals as reflected in the policy and procedure of agencies responsible for police, courts and prosecutorial services.

earlier presentations it should be clear that the making of law is a political act which is located apart from any of the individual bureaucracies of government. Even when law is made with regard to one particular activity of government, its development involves the consideration of issues and concerns not specific to that activity. It follows that correctional law[6] is made not only with regard to the requirements of correctional management and administration, but with consideration for the general public interest and for the desires of special interest groups both inside and outside government.

In one sense, law is the ultimate policy upon which corrections establishes its mandate and directs its operations. For its part, legislative review also may be undertaken either on the basis of initiatives arising within the correctional system or proceeding as a result of initiatives external to the system. In any case, legislative review itself is an external activity — once initiated, it brings a whole series of outside forces to bear on the review process.[7]

Any law review which proposes to establish new legislation in the correctional field, or which is geared to amend or to repeal related legislation, affects correctional policy regardless of the results stemming from the review. This is a point which must be emphasized: correctional policy is not only influenced and directed by legislation which has been passed and proclaimed; it also is influenced whenever such laws become subject to review. The *process* of reviewing the correctional mandate, as established in law, forces corrections to reassess its purpose in either a general or a particular way. Accordingly, correctional policy is effected either through the discovery of new directions or the affirmation of old ones.

But legislative review is not restricted to the political exercise associated with the making of law. Legislation is also reviewed as an activity of the courts. In the United States, there has been a deluge of litigation resulting in court reviews of decisions taken by correctional administrators related to the care and custody of persons in their charge. As Shover (1979, 249) states:

> Possibly the single most important stimulus to change has been the flood tide of litigation brought by convicts primarily in the federal courts, during the past decade . . . some indication of its magnitude can be gained from examining changes in the numbers of suits filed by prison inmates in the federal district courts for each year from 1961 through 1975 . . . we can see that in 1961 the rate of suits (per 1,000 inmates in state and federal institutions) was 11.85 and by 1974 this had increased to 84.37 before declining to 80.25 in 1975.

While there has been similar litigation in Canada, the Canadian courts have generally limited their appraisal of criminal law to constitutional questions and have tended to concentrate on the issue of whether the body making the law had the power to do so.

With the advent of the *Charter of Rights and Freedoms* as part of the newly patriated Canadian Constitution, the latitude of the courts to review correctional law has increased. The Charter gives individuals numerous grounds on which to challenge both legislation and government action and likely will be interpreted to include the grounds for challenging the actions of public officers. Furthermore, the *Constitution Act* (1982) provides that any law which is inconsistent with the Constitution (which includes the Charter) is of no force and effect. At this time, it is not known what end result the Charter will have on correctional law, but it is evident that the Charter is already stimulating policy reviews within government. It is worth noting that initially these policy reviews were undertaken preparatory to the coming into effect of the Equality Rights section of the Charter (April 17, 1985).

The review of correctional law which has been stimulated by the adoption of the Charter is being promoted in at least two ways: by forcing government departments to reappraise legislation pertaining to their operations and by requiring the courts to assess the validity of current law in relation to the Constitution.

For example, the Solicitor General of Canada established a Correctional Law Review in 1983. In the second report of the Working Group appointed to this task, the following comment was made: "The most significant aspects of the Charter for our purposes is the fact that its protections apply to inmates and parolees. Thus, correctional legislation and practices are subject to the Charter. The impact of the Charter on offender rights and the correctional system will be examined in the discussion of entrenchment, enforcement, and limitation of charter rights. . ." (Solicitor General of Canada 1986, 4).

These developments will almost certainly have at least three effects: first, an increase in litigation relevant to correctional policy and practice; second, an expanded review of correctional law and the "rule of law" as it applies to corrections; and third, the establishment of a new body of case law concerning correctional matters (see Tarnopolsky 1982; Epstein 1982).

Short-Term Political Need

Although the making of law may be thought of as creating a long-term political effect, there is another category of political activity which might best be described as relating to short-term political need. This category of political activity is usually associated with the executive function of government while law making is seen to be a product of the legislative function. Consequently, issues emerging from short-term political need are normally associated with the government of the day and its desire to retain power. Out of this political interest, individual ministers, cabinet committees, or cabinet as a whole, may choose to establish policy on their own initiative or to direct the civil service to do so on their behalf.

While corrections is not often regarded as presenting issues of sufficient import to influence the ability of a political party to acquire power, correctional issues can emerge which disturb the governing party's sense of political stability.[8] Events such as the commission of a serious offence by a released offender, a rash of highly publicized escapes, a major incident in an institution, or criticism by the courts of a correctional program, become politically sensitive issues which can disrupt the equilibrium of government. Although from a political perspective these are not matters which exist at the same level of political awareness as inflation, unemployment, or energy self-sufficiency, they do tend to take the form of anomalies or problems that require attention. The "fixing" of these problems becomes translated into short-term political need. Considerable pressure, then, can be expected to descend upon the correctional enterprise to develop policies and procedures which will alleviate the political discomfort and which will reduce the possibility that a similar political effect will occur again.[9]

Given the politically sensitive backdrop against which the correctional enterprise carries out its mandate, correctional managers are continually aware that a policy or procedure might, at any time, promote an event which will become elevated to the political arena.[10] It is not surprising, therefore, that the bureaucratic interests within corrections constantly assess policies and procedures with a view to their potential political repercussions. And with or without political intervention, the attention given to the political interest may be seen as a characteristic of correctional policy.

Policy and Procedures of Related Subsystems within Criminal Justice

In Chapter 1, the concept of corrections as a subsystem within a larger criminal justice system was discussed. The effect on corrections of policy and procedure generated by other criminal justice organizations was noted, particularly with regard to the need for joint management initiatives. Regardless of whether or not a correctional organization exists in a context where joint management principles are applied, the influence of related subsystems upon its activities must be acknowledged. Corrections represents the final stage in a continuum of organizational activity, and spread across this continuum are "all the official ways in which society reacts to persons who have been accused of committing criminal acts . . ." (Reid 1981, 20).

The National Advisory Commission on Criminal Justice Standards and Goals (1973, 5-6) states:

> The contemporary view is to consider society's institutionalized response to crime as the criminal justice system and its activities as the criminal justice process. This model envisions interdependent and interrelated agencies and programs that will provide a coordinated and consistent response to crime. The model, however, remains a model — it does not exist in fact. Although cooperation between various components has improved noticeably in some localities, it cannot be said that a criminal justice "system" really exists.
>
> Even under the model, each element of the system would have a specialized function to perform. The modern system's concept recognizes, however, that none of the elements can perform its tasks without directly affecting the efforts of the others. Thus, while each component must continue to concentrate on improving the performance of its specialized function, it also must be aware of its inter-relationships with the other components. Likewise, when functions overlap, each component must be willing to appreciate and utilize the expertise of the others.

Each component of the criminal justice system is responsible for specific functions in the criminal justice process and each component tends to describe its purpose through statements of functional objectives. Policy and procedure developed by any one component consequently tends to direct itself to reinforcing the declared functional objectives chosen to guide its activities. Such objectives have been portrayed through a varied choice of language but generally they are as follows:

1. *Police Services*—to promote and maintain public security and

order under law by preventing, detecting, apprehending, and charging law breakers.

2. *Court Services*—to provide a forum for the resolution of civil and criminal disputes.
3. *Prosecutorial Services*—to prepare and present the Crown's position relative to the disputes at issue.
4. *Correctional Services*—to provide a range of activities related to the counselling, treatment, surveillance, or confinement of persons referred by the court process through dispositions available in sentencing.

As these statements of functional objectives suggest, each component of the criminal justice system has a fairly well-defined and explicit responsibility in the criminal justice process. Each component is able to make policy and procedure with regard to its own interests and without regard to the implications they may hold for any other component. Nonetheless, the illustrations given above also suggest that each component's activities are related to the others and that the policies and procedures of one component may *require* other components to adjust their operations to accommodate them. And because corrections represents the final stage in the continuum of organizational activity in the criminal justice system, it follows that correctional policy and procedures are subject to the influence of all the other components comprising the system.

By way of example, it is possible to select a category of offence and then examine the possible policies which may be established by each component in relation to that offence. In Canada, for instance, there recently has been renewed attention directed toward the policies and programs which address drinking/driving offences. Different jurisdictions have chosen their own ways to respond to the issue but all jurisdictions have tended to harden their approach to this particular offence. The increased concentration on drinking/driving, however, allows for the creation of a scenario which amply illustrates the effects of the policy of one component upon others in the criminal justice process.

In this instance, police services may produce policy to increase the potential for the detection and apprehension of drinking drivers that allows for the use of such methods as the development and deployment of special surveillance strategies and applied technologies (e.g., mobile breathalyzer units). Prosecution policy may be established to concentrate on the conviction of persons apprehended for drinking/driving as well as to seek the most severe sentence provided in law. Court Services may formulate policy to increase the efficiency of processing charged persons by creating special courts, extending court hours, or increasing the number of judges available to hear cases. Correctional Services may establish policy and procedure for the development of special programs which target persons convicted of drinking/driving offences, such as impaired drivers' courses or other specialized community programs.

In recent years, the policy and procedural illustrations given above have been adopted at one location or another across Canada. Moreover, it is clear that some of these policies have come into conflict with others: the tendency of correctional services to support non-penal sanctions for persons convicted of drinking/driving offences is potentially in conflict with the interest of police, prosecution, and courts to increase the number of persons apprehended, convicted, and sentenced to imprisonment. The severity of the conflict is underlined by the fact that the Continuing Committee of Heads of Corrections (Canada) has identified the issue as a major problem related to correctional policy and planning.[11]

This example illustrates the general point that whenever police, prosecution, or courts policy is established to concentrate on a specific category of offence, or to change the emphasis in the processing of accused persons, there will often be a direct and dramatic effect on correctional services. In this regard, the *B.C. Corrections Branch Research Report* (Province of British Columbia 1982, 4) notes:

> There has been a change in the B.C. justice system regarding drinking drivers, as well as for other motor vehicle related offences. A "get tough" stance has been adopted, and implemented with vigour. Based on data for January-February 1982, as compared with January-February 1981, admissions for drinking drivers have increased by 67.3% (502 sentenced admissions vs. 300) . . . . Thus it is possible to attribute the growth in the count to a large number of shorter term sentences, primarily drinking drivers, many of whom have failed to pay their fines. Policy (of the criminal justice system as a whole) and the economy are interacting to produce a dramatic shift in the nature of the "typical" adult offender being incarcerated in B.C.'s provincial institutions.

It is within the character of correctional policy and practice to try to account for developments which may occur elsewhere in the criminal justice system. Arguments with regard to the need for new or different correctional programs are often justified with reference to plans or proposed initiatives taken by other agencies in the system. While it is relatively easy to illustrate the effect of policy initiatives taken elsewhere, it is more difficult to identify the means by which these effects can be managed. This is a fundamental objective of planning in the correctional field, and is addressed in more detail later in Chapter 5.

Academic Research

The influence of academic research on correctional policy and practice is more difficult to document than other external influences outlined in this section. Nevertheless, academic research has had an influence on correctional policy and practice, both directly and indirectly, and this influence is growing. Shover (1979, 19), in a discussion on the role of sociologists in correctional research, makes the following assertion:

> Sociologists often lament their assumed lack of significant impact on the operations of correctional agencies. While they may be correct in this assumption, their impact on public discourse and the public's understanding of correctional matters seems more substantial. They have sometimes played a highly visible role in deliberations over correctional issues. Not only have they contributed theoretical and research work to books and journals, but they have served as consultants to departments of corrections, as reviewers of research proposals in the area of correctional research, and as members of governmental commissions that study correctional issues . . . . And we cannot overlook sociologists' impact as educators who have sent forth their students to assume positions in correctional bureaucracies.

This assertion could be made to refer with equal authority to all those disciplines which apply theoretical concepts or research methods to correctional issues. Sociologists, psychologists, lawyers, educational theorists, psychiatrists, urban planners, criminologists, statisticians, and other persons representing a broad spectrum of related disciplines have engaged in academic research on correctional matters. To one degree or another, they all have made a contribution to the science of criminology — a science which is itself beginning to emerge as an academic discipline with an increasing number of adherents.

Over the last several decades in Canada, for example, there has been considerable growth both in the schools of criminology and in the numbers of students attaching themselves to the discipline.[12] There is also a considerable potential in Canada for an increase in the quantity and quality of academic research related to correctional matters. Additionally, there is an increase in the numbers of persons entering the criminal justice field who have passed through schools of criminology or who have acquired research training from other disciplines.

Academic research influences correctional policy and practice in several ways: through the publication and promulgation of research results; through the participation of university-based researchers as consultants to government on correctional matters; and through use in the training and education of persons who assume positions in correctional bureaucracies. If academic research is defined as a "type" of inquiry rather than as an inquiry occurring within a special location such as a university, then it can be said to occur within correctional bureaucracies through the work of personnel employed by government, through the activity of private research agencies operating on an entrepreneurial basis, and through the activity of colleges and universities related to teaching. Each of these locations presents its own set of problems concerning the performance of such research. However, each can influence correctional policy and practice.

As the list of disciplines presented above indicates, academic research which is applied to the correctional enterprise generally emanates from the social and behavioural sciences and falls under the general heading of "social science research." Waller (1979, 202) has provided a useful definition of social science research, as it applies to the general field of criminal justice:

> Social science research is a process based on explicit, controlled, and replicable procedures whose objective is to increase knowledge. It must be possible to communicate to other people both the specific research process and the knowledge obtained. It should provide a descriptive and often quantitative understanding of the phenomenon. In the case of criminal justice research, the subjects include crime itself, victimization, the operation of the criminal justice system, and public reaction to crime and its control. Social science research should provide knowledge that can be generalized from one situation to another and that aids in our understanding of the future. (I. Waller, "Organizing Research to Improve Criminal Justice Policy: A Perspective from Canada," *Journal of Research in Crime and Delinquency,* vol. 16, (July 1979), p. 202. Copyright © 1979 by the National Council on Crime and Delinquency. Reprinted by permission of Sage Publications, Inc.)

Waller's definition helps to identify the criteria for scholarly research in the social sciences as well as some areas of its application in criminal justice. What, then, are some of the uses of scholarly research that are specific to corrections?

Shover (1979, 18) states that:

> The correctional contributions of American sociologists during the past

fifty years have largely clustered in eight substantive areas:
1. Parole prediction theory and research.
2. Theory and research on the structure and functioning of correctional agencies, primarily prisons and training schools.
3. Theoretical applications of sociological theories to the prevention or control of criminality, usually in urban neighborhoods.
4. Theoretical applications of sociological and social psychological theories to the correction of offenders.
5. Research on some of the social psychological changes attendant to being corrected.
6. Evaluative research on the systemic and social psychological effects of correctional treatment and programs.
7. Research on the exercise of discretion in decision making by correctional personnel.
8. Theory and research on "violent" and "dangerous" offenders and violent behavior, especially in the prison setting.

Shover's commentary adequately encompasses the general areas of academic research related to corrections, not only in America, but in Canada and other countries as well. It is interesting, however, to consider the way in which correctional administrators pose research questions to researchers. Duxbury (1980, 67-73) lists some examples as follows (in these, the term "youthful offenders" can be used interchangeably with the term "wards"):

What is the effect of reducing the number of wards in an open dormitory setting? Is it cost-effective?

If wards are allowed to earn time-cuts by voluntarily participating in institutional programs, will they do so? Can institutional population be reduced this way — without increasing the risk to the community?

How many wards in institutions are in need of psychiatric treatment or special counselling programs? The programs for alcohol abusers?

How effective are our psychiatric programs? Our special counselling programs? With which types of wards are they most effective?

What skills do parolees need to survive on the job? Can these skills be taught effectively to institutionalized wards prior to their parole?

What kinds of academic achievement gains do incarcerated wards make?

How many wards need and receive educationally handicapped services?

What are parole staffs' opinions regarding training received, supervision, job satisfaction, communication, safety, and carrying fire arms?

What is the effect of juvenile visitation programs, such as shown in *Scared Straight?*[13]

Can intervention with youth street gangs reduce homicides and other violence? If so, what techniques contribute to the reduction?

What are the factors which contribute to wards' success on parole?

The relationship between the questions administrators pose and the issues of interest to academic research can be seen from the two lists presented above. Although the interests may be similar, the perspective each group brings to them are often quite different and the influence of academic research on correctional policy and practice is most positive when there is good communication between them. Moreover, such communication can reduce the potential for suspicion and conflict that may result from misperceptions surrounding the motives and interests each side carries into the interaction; it can increase the understanding on both sides regarding the problems and potentials associated with the application of research findings; and it can help to ensure that the priorities for decision making in correctional practice are more compatible with the knowledge arising from research. Biles (1981, 64) addresses this issue as follows:

> Persons engaged in criminological research (researchers) may have different perceptions of the purposes and value of such research than do the decision makers, administrators and policy makers (users) for whom the research results are intended. Perhaps over-stating this dichotomy, researchers generally are more concerned with methodological elegance, originality, publishability and achieving prestige among their peers, whereas the users are more concerned with the political acceptability, practical implications and cost-effectiveness of proposals emanating from research. To the extent that this is true, it follows that the determination of priorities is likely to be different for researchers and users . . . as I have said elsewhere, "the public service ethic of uncritical loyalty does not rest easily with the academic spirit of free enquiry and criticism".
>
> Differences between users and researchers in the determination of priorities would be reduced, if not eliminated, if users were more forthcoming in stating their needs and if researchers were more frank about what they had to offer. There is a need for stronger bridging between users and academic researchers. . . .

It seems apparent that academic research will have a growing influence on correctional policy and practice in Canada. The growth in the number of schools developing an emphasis in criminology, the increase in public criticism and the corresponding political sensitivity to correctional matters, as well as the increasing resource demands made by a system which is becoming more and more complex, all contribute to the potential for increased research commitments related to corrections. On the one hand, this trend has the potential to enhance correctional decision making and to improve correctional practice. On the other, it may well add to the confusion and complexity of an already troubled system. Whatever the eventual outcome may be, academic research will continue to provide an external influence on correctional policy and practice — a theme that is developed in more detail in the chapter on Correctional Reform.

Further discussion on the application of research to specific correctional tasks is presented in Chapter 5 (the role of research in correctional planning), and Chapter 7 (the role of research in the development and implementation of correctional treatment programs).

Internal Influences on Correctional Policy

Professional Interests

For corrections, one result that has been produced by the influence of the social and behavioural sciences has been the growth in emphasis upon programs and treatment applications which involve staff with specialized education and training. These staff can be said to reflect a growing "professional interest" in corrections; this trend has tended to create a partition between such professional staff and the personnel primarily responsible for custodial or "control" activities. This polarization is often referred to as the security/treatment split in correctional practice; it became most pronounced under the rehabilitative model of corrections following World War II.

However, "professional interests" can be identified in other ways as well. For instance, it is possible to describe management and administrative personnel as representing a type of professional interest which may not be totally compatible with the professional interests displayed by either treatment or custodial personnel. Additionally, politicians responsible for ministries which include corrections often portray a professional interest that may be associated with a political career.

Here it is important to more carefully define what is meant by "professional interest." Any individual or group may portray a professional interest without necessarily being identified as belonging to one of the organized professions (e.g., psychology, social work, law, or medicine) or without having obtained the credentials required to gain admittance to a professional fraternity. Consequently, the term "professional interest" involves more than simply a discussion of the influence brought to bear on correctional policy and practice by a professional organization. Indeed, the real influence of a professional organization in this regard is normally indirect and results from the membership of correctional employees in such an organization rather than from the intervention of the organization itself in the correctional enterprise. In common usage, the word "profession" refers to a vocation or calling, entered into by choice, where the primary measure of competence results from the evaluation of peers (i.e., others who have chosen the same vocation or calling).

As discussed previously, the common image of a profession is one which involves some branch of advanced learning or science. In fact, any vocation which requires a special skill, unique tools or technologies, and special structures within which the work takes place may be called a profession. Persons who engage in such work may therefore be said to share a professional interest. Accordingly, it is appropriate to refer to the "professional soldier," the "professional carpenter," the "professional administrator," and the "professional correctional officer." But individuals can perform their work using specialized skills in a specialized environment and still not be regarded as professionals, if they do not view their employment as a vocation for which a dedicated commitment is made. Consistent with this interpretation, the soldier who is conscripted and does not chose to re-enlist likely should not be regarded as a professional, since he or she does not view the work as a calling. Consequently, the conscript is not as likely to give significant weight to the evaluation of his or her peers in the performance of duties as a soldier.

Similarly, the correctional officer who is "filling in," until such time as more satisfying work can be found, is not usually considered a professional and probably cannot be said to exhibit a professional interest in the work performed. For purposes of this discussion, therefore, a professional interest in corrections is defined as being present whenever the following exist:

1. A correctional employee has satisfied the requirements for admission to an organized professional group or is a member of such a group.
2. A correctional employee has chosen corrections as a vocation and is interested in developing that career in association with

and supported by his/her peers.
3. A correctional manager has chosen public sector management as a career and seeks advancement through the acknowledgement received from his/her peers.
4. A politician responsible for corrections has chosen politics as a career and wishes to advance his/her political credit through the good management of the corrections portfolio.

The "professional interests" found throughout the correctional enterprise interact to affect the development of correctional policy and to influence the nature of correctional practice. In Canada, professional interests in corrections are acknowledged to have an influence upon the work performed. No deliberate attempt, however, is being made to effectively measure the extent of the influence or to develop ways in which it can be used to improve correctional practice.

That such an attempt has not been made is more striking when the movement toward entrenching "professional interests" in the Canadian corrections establishment is considered. For example, jurisdictions at both the federal and provincial levels have established management associations to develop and reinforce the professional interests of managers in the public sector. Since the early 1970s, correctional employees have been increasingly organized into collective bargaining units which display relative sophistication in pursuing the enhancement of the correctional work force's professional interests.[14]

All of these developments signify something about the nature of the "professional interests" expressed in corrections. Additionally, the high turnover rate among incumbents[15] in the federal corrections portfolio suggests that the professional interests of politicians may not be well served by assuming the mantle of political responsibility which corrections offers. Conversely, public sector management careers in corrections and career choices related to correctional programs seem to be increasing and becoming more organized.

An earlier reference was made to some of the effects professional interests exert upon correctional policy and practice, particularly at the political level. Clearly, the relationship between professional interests in the correctional enterprise, the conflicts they generate, and the need to account for them in planning and program development strategies must not be overlooked.

Resource Capability

Another important internal influence on correctional policy is the capacity of a correctional organization to acquire and manage its resources. Not only is this capability central to the implementation of policy, it is also an essential factor in determining what policies are made. It is not uncommon, for instance, that a significant change in resource capability often triggers a requirement for policy review. The resulting review can take several forms. First, it can be aimed either at limiting or increasing the interventions which result from policy, consistent with the decrease or increase in available resources. Second, it can be aimed at reviewing the basic operational goals that are reflected in policy in order to determine whether or not their restatement would provide for a more efficient use of resources without altering the social purpose which the policy is intended to support. In recent Canadian history, shifts in the correctional enterprise's resource capability have produced an almost constant process of policy review which addresses both the demand for increased efficiency and the redefinition of operational strategies.[16]

Correctional resources can be divided into two general categories of expenditure: (1) operational costs (personnel and material); and (2) capital costs.[17] Earlier in this chapter, it was pointed out that corrections, as a service to government, is labour intensive and that personnel costs account for the bulk of operational expenditures. However, capital costs, which do not appear as operational expenditures in most budgets, are significant across many categories of correctional work. The most obvious example is the cost associated with the building of a prison.

Due to the nature of most correctional programs, the development of a new program area commonly requires an increase in both capital costs and operational costs. It is far from surprising, therefore, that many correctional programs are hard pressed to adjust to changing economic circumstances or to any other factors which affect their resource capability. And because corrections does not have the ability to effectively control intake or to change many of the strategies required to carry out its mandate, changes in resource capability often are profoundly difficult to accommodate.

Furthermore, the resource capability is directly related to factors associated with quality of service. For some, quality of service is seen to be directly influenced by the employment conditions under which correctional staff exercise their duties. In this regard, collective bargaining can be said to have brought about an improvement in the work conditions experienced by many correctional employees, particularly with respect to salary increases, reduced work hours and similar related benefits. However, an increase in the employee benefits received by corrections staff may result in a decrease in the number of staff positions that are affordable within the correctional enterprise. Where the financial supply required to operate a correctional program remains constant, but the salary costs escalate and the hours worked by each employee decline, then staffing levels at work stations must be adjusted accordingly.

While improvements in working conditions may or may not have a direct correlation with improvements in service quality, the level of education and training possessed by correctional personnel most certainly does. Although the correctional resource capability may be viewed quantitatively in terms of capital and operational costs, it cannot be over-emphasized that the fundamental resource which enhances the quality of service resides in the expertise of individual employees. When setting out to understand how the resource capability affects correctional policy perspectives, therefore, it is essential to appreciate that the real foundation of service quality is located in staff training. Accordingly, staff development is probably the most important factor associated with the resource capability where the development and maintenance of policy initiatives are concerned.[18]

The ability to acquire necessary resources during times of fluctuating economic prospects, the capacity to compete successfully with other government services for an adequate share in available resources, the skill needed to achieve a balance between quality and quantity, and the strength of vision necessary to effectively address the social purposes that are reflected in policy are all central to the management and operation of the correctional enterprise. In times of budgetary constraint and resource limitations, the management process becomes more complex and the effect on policy is rendered more evident. Donald Evans (1981, 7-8) addresses this problem as follows:

> Managing is becoming an art in this decade. It will require an awareness of the political and economic environment, a development of skills in restraint management and increased effectiveness in working with others. It is clear that managing in an era of growth is quite different from managing in a restraint era. Greater emphasis must be placed on flexibility, collaboration and innovation as the essential ingredients in getting the job done.

Operational Maintenance Needs

Earlier in the text the problems associated with "crisis centred" policy advice were identified. It was suggested that policy which seeks only to resolve crisis-needs in order to maintain operations is unsatisfactory since it is likely to reinforce bad practices while failing to acknowledge the broader social purpose correctional work is intended to serve. In this section, the nature of operational maintenance needs, and the way in which they affect policy, will be described in more detail.

Jayewardene and Jayasuriya (1981, 39) discuss the nature of operational maintenance in an institution as follows:

> Most institutions have been in operation for some period of time and during that period, have developed, both by design and by accident, a routine of work to which most workers at the institution have got accustomed. In this development, the resources that are available to the institution and the constraints that have been placed on it, have been taken into consideration, both by accident as well as by design. The development has associated with it the generation of a sort of philosophical orientation for the institution. This orientation ensures it of a continuity but at the same time endows it with a structural rigidity and functional inflexibility which may sooner or later make it incompetent to handle its production task.

It is in the nature of institutions and organizations to evolve toward the establishment of a comfortable routine which allows staff members to function at the lowest possible level of stress. Moreover, structural supports are built into institutions through forms and procedures which maintain and reinforce the daily operational routines. Their success is judged on their ability (*1*) to predict operational needs, (*2*) to organize resources which address those needs, and (*3*) to express themselves in such a way that their use by employees is both comfortable and familiar.

Policies are necessary to assure that the criteria needed to secure the structural supports are satisfactorily met. These may include policies related to the function of the information systems and planning programs which are geared to increase the ability of the organization to predict its needs. Policies also may be needed to define the criteria for establishing priorities, to make decisions related to the acquisition of resources, or to assure adequate training and education of staff. As previously discussed, all such policies must be developed with due attention to the purpose of the work performed.

Given the direct influence maintenance needs exert upon the

development of policy, whenever there is a failure to satisfy any of the criteria associated with successful operational maintenance, a "crisis" is likely to occur. In turn, any crisis that arises will disrupt the routine of the organization and will adversely affect the degree of comfort experienced by its employees. If there is a loss of ability to predict operational needs, if the resource base changes, or if staff are provided with inadequate training, then the stress level within the institution will increase. This situation will result in growing agitation with a concurrent demand for an organizational response which will return the institution to a more comfortable and less stressful position.[19] Where the inability to meet the criteria for operational maintenance is persistently present, the organization can be said to exist in a constant state of "crisis management." And where crisis management predominates, it is not difficult to see the effect it will have on the policy-making process.

One of the reasons why correctional organizations are accused of operating in a crisis management mode stems from their consistent and traditional inability to satisfy the three criteria for operational maintenance outlined above. Adding to the problem, corrections intake is subject to a number of factors beyond the direct control of the organization itself. Consequently, the ability to predict operational need is always in question. And because corrections operates at a relatively low level of political priority, it is not always possible to know the extent of the resource commitment that correctional programs will receive or that they will be allowed to maintain.

Many correctional programs also have traditionally suffered from high turnover rates among staff, which result in relatively larger numbers of personnel being placed on the job without adequate training.[20] Further, correctional organizations tend to receive low-level commitments for both pre-service and in-service training, regardless of the rate of staff turnover. When these many factors combine, workers in the correctional enterprise are placed in a situation that is often more stressful and less comfortable than the efficient maintenance of operations demands.

CONCLUSION

As with any area of government service, there are many factors which interact to shape and direct correctional policy. An understanding of Canadian corrections requires an awareness of these factors and the ability to identify the general context within which they interact. More specifically, an understanding of the policy-making process is essential for planning and the effective management of correctional programs. In the following chapters, the relationship of planning and the structures of management and administration to correctional policy is discussed.

Notes

1. Larsen (1982, 47-50) discusses the various ways organizational theorists have defined or construed the term "policy." This analysis illustrates the difficulty others have had in coming to agreement on the meaning of the word and the processes associated with it. Larsen concludes that policy "be construed as a decision which establishes the *overall direction* which a given organization will take regarding a given issue . . . a policy must delineate a *general strategy* for dealing with the issue in question . . . (and) a policy must introduce *structural elements* which will serve to focus the making of administrative and/or operational decisions about the issue." Larsen concludes that "as long as these three criteria are satisfied, policy can result from either political or bureaucratic decision making."

2. A good example of a "maintenance" problem in corrections is overcrowding in secure settings. This is a type of problem which threatens the ability of the institution to maintain itself. The more overcrowded a secure setting becomes the less capable it is of maintaining its own order and ensuring the safety of both staff and inmates. In this type of situation, policies tend to be implemented primarily for the purpose of relieving the pressure on the institution. Examples of such policies might be to expedite applications for early release; to transfer prisoners in selected categories to less secure settings; to change classification policy to provide for direct admission into less secure settings; and, to change prosecution or probation policies concerning recommendations made to the court in sentencing. Often policies such as these are not assessed with regard to any implications beyond the immediate maintenance problem to be solved.

3. Ekstedt (1983, 301), in discussing the policy-making process associated with the development of juvenile containment centres in British Columbia, states "researchers and program evaluators tend to know very little about the nature of the policy disputes out of which various programs and procedures are developed. Partially this is a result of difficulties in accessing data since much of the knowledge of policy disputes is based on participation in the dispute or access to the content of negotiations which may be primarily informal and which reflect belief systems which are difficult to document."

4. Larsen (1982, 30-34) defines "open" and "closed" systems and identifies some of the major characteristics of each. He argues that social organizations should be regarded as "open" systems and that "an open system . . . is one in which the constituent parts interact with the external environment as well as with each other." He further states "in an open system . . . external factors are constantly being introduced through the interfaces. These new factors either create new critical variables or alter existing ones. As a result, the existing equilibrium is upset and the system commences to search for a new equilibrium which can co-exist with the new critical variables. Thus the process of homeostasis in open systems can be described as a constant search for the means to account for an ever-changing set of critical variables. This characteristic is instrumental in precipitating changes to the goals and values of a given system."

5. The term "moral obligation" has been defined as "a duty which is valid and binding in conscience and according to natural justice, but is not recognized by the law as adequate to set in motion the machinery of justice; that is, one which rests upon ethical considerations alone, and is not imposed or enforced by positive law" (*Black's Law Dictionary*, 5th edition, 1979).

6. While correctional law includes legislation specific to correctional matters and case law resulting from litigation related to prisoners' rights and the validity of administrative decisions, in this case, our discussion of correctional law refers only to the legislative process which results in enabling legislation. Examples of this in Canada are the *Prisons and Reformatories Act* (1970), the *Penitentiary Act* (1970), the *Parole Act* (1970) and Acts of the provinces specific to corrections.

7. Phelps (n.d., 2), in an unpublished paper titled "Inmates' Rights: The Case Law and Its Implications for Prisons and Penitentiaries," states: "Where court decisions are contrary to administrative requirements, the law may be changed to re-establish the administrative requirements as legal." An example of this occurred in British Columbia, where the court had determined that the Correctional Service of Canada did not have authority to conduct strip searches. The Cabinet changed the law, clearly permitting strip searches because these searches are considered to be essential to the safety of citizens, staff and inmates.

The above statement illustrates one way in which legislative review can affect correctional policy. Another type of legislative review occurs when the jurisdiction responsible for the making of criminal law (in Canada, the federal government) chooses to initiate a review for the purpose of major reform in an area of criminal law. An example of recent interest in Canada has been the review associated with the *Juvenile Delinquents Act*, which was initiated with the intent to create new or amended legislation. This review took place over a time-span of approximately fourteen years and involved on-going federal/provincial negotiations as well as the submission of briefs and papers on the subject by a variety of public and private agencies. While the review ultimately resulted in new federal legislation (*Young Offenders Act, 1982*), it is interesting to note that in at least three provinces (Quebec, Ontario and British Columbia) *provincial* legislation related to young offenders was changed directly as a result of the on-going review initiated by the federal government. This is an example of how legislative review can affect correctional policy as a result of the review itself, without regard to the results anticipated by the original initiative. For a discussion on the history of this review see *Young Persons in Conflict with the Law* (a report of the Solicitor General's Committee on Proposals for new legislation to replace the *Juvenile Delinquents Act*), 1975, page 6.

8. Events surrounding the Clifford Olson murder case in British Columbia (1981-82) provide a good illustration of an event related to corrections which can be politically unsettling. The Vancouver *Sun* (January 22, 1982; p.6) quoted the

Leader of the Opposition party as follows: "The government's handling of the Clifford Olson murder case has destroyed the credibility of the Attorney General, shown the Premier to be a coward and shattered the peace of mind of British Columbians . . . the only way to restore peace of mind in B.C. is through a public enquiry . . . the Olson affair is 'an indictment of the whole justice delivery system.' " A number of issues associated with this case were politically unsettling, not all of which were correctional in nature. However, this case resulted in significant criticism directed at both the prison and parole systems. The British Columbia newspaper *The Columbian* (February 27, 1982; p.2) reported the opinion that "Clifford Robert Olson was a result of a network of indulgent penologists and judges . . . Olson was released time and time again on mandatory supervision and parole. Each time, it was revoked. And he kept on committing crimes." These statements (and many others like them) both reflected and created considerable disruptions in the political and bureaucratic processes associated with correctional matters. The effect on political sensitivities crossed jurisdictional lines and quickly became a national issue involving both the federal and provincial corrections systems, the National Parole Board and other related justice agencies.

9. Again, the Olson case provides an illustration of this point. Although the Solicitor General's Ministry had been reviewing matters related to conditional release for some time, the Olson case, at least partially, expedited the federal government's response on at least one matter related to conditional release. In the same *Columbian* article quoted above (page 2), the following statement was made: "Solicitor General Robert Kaplan's recent recommendations will be welcomed, although some critics will say he hasn't gone far enough. Under the new system, a prisoner will be given one chance at mandatory supervision. If he fails, it's back to jail for the rest of his sentence." Clearly, the correctional system, at least at the political level, found it necessary to declare public policy which would both "take the heat off" and reduce the possibility that such a political effect would occur again.

10. Holt (1977, 18), in a discussion on the management of correctional institutions, makes the following statement: "The warden's problem is that every prison is a potential scandal. On any given day there is enough going on to create a considerable public relations problem. The public itself makes contradictory demands on the system so that regardless of what approach is taken some powerful interest group will probably be alienated. The day to day level of inmate deviance (drugs, assaults, homosexuality) would be judged by most of the public as intolerable. The public's high level of expectations for staff's personal conduct cannot be met over any period of time. 'Mistakes at work' due to complacency or poor judgement are common place. Every weapon that is discharged is a potential source of embarrassment. The warden's lament is 'what if the newspapers got hold of this one?' while his subordinates remind each other to 'protect the old man.' "

11. The minutes from a workshop held by the Heads of Corrections concerning possible amendments or changes in the criminal law (July 15, 1982) indicates that a report was made by the Province of Saskatchewan in which it was pointed out that 25 percent of prison admissions in Saskatchewan were for impaired driving and that this situation presented serious logistical problems apart from the issue of whether or not imprisonment is an appropriate sanction for this type of offender. It was suggested in the workshop that these problems were shared by many jurisdictions across Canada. For example, in 1985/86 drinking/driving admissions accounted for 17 percent of all admissions to provincial facilities, ranging from a low of 5 percent in Northwest Territories to a high of 34 percent in Newfoundland and Labrador.

12. Larsen (1981, 5-7) identified six universities in Canada which offer programs at the graduate and/or undergraduate levels in criminology or criminal justice education.

13. *Scared Straight* is the title of a movie which was released in North America in 1979. It documented a program of shock incarceration which was in operation at the Rahway State Prison in New Jersey. The intent of the program, which is operated entirely by hard-core convicts, is to literally scare kids straight, through intimidation and confrontation. For a detailed critique of the *Scared Straight* program, see Finckenauer 1982.

14. The federal public service and every province's public service is now unionized. The organization of correctional workers, within these unions, differs according to jurisdiction, but generally it can be said that all correctional workers in Canada are now subject to some form of collective bargaining. Ross (1981, 273) states: "Complicating the prison manager's task in recent years has been an increasing activism not only among inmates but also among prison guards who are proclaiming, through a variety of means including strikes, their right not only for expanded career opportunities, improved salaries and other employee benefits but also their right to participate in policy making — their right to have some control over their working lives."

15. From 1963 to the present, the following persons have held the portfolio of Solicitor General: John Watson MacNaught (April 1963-July 1965), Lawrence Pennell (1965-1968), John Turner (April 1968-July 1968), George James McIlraith (July 1968-December 1970), Jean-Pierre Goyer (December 1970-November 1972), Warren Allmand (November 1972-1976), Francis Fox (1976-1977), Jean-Jacques Blais (1978-1979), Allan Lawrence (1979-1980), Robert Kaplan (1980-1984), Elmer MacKay (1984-1985), Perrin Beatty (1985-1986) and James Kelleher (1986-).

There has been a change in the Solicitor General's portfolio an average of once every two years since 1963. While it is difficult to assess the reasons for this, it is clear that consistent turnover in the Minister responsible for a portfolio like corrections is disruptive to the development and maintenance of correctional policy. This would be true even if such a rate of change were considered normal in the political context and not a result of any peculiarity within the portfolio itself.

It should be noted that the Ministry of the Solicitor General also includes responsibility for federal police, so any effect of the portfolio on the turnover rate of Ministers cannot be ascribed only to factors associated with the political management of correctional services.

16. In a document titled *Strategic Overview* published by the Solicitor General of Canada in 1981, the following statement (1981, 5-6) is made: "In terms of its ability to continue to deliver quality law enforcement, correctional and other criminal justice services, the Ministry faces an important dilemma and challenge in the 1980's. Growth in crime, increasing numbers of federal inmates, and the greater fear of crime and its consequences will result in public demands for more and more of the traditional criminal justice services. At the same time, overall economic conditions, greater restraint on public spending and the relatively low priority accorded criminal justice issues within the social area, will make it increasingly difficult for the Ministry to expand traditional criminal justice services at the same rate experienced in the past ... The analysis of the societal forces acting on the Ministry and the elaboration and priorization of future areas of policy development must take place within the context of the Ministry's long-range goals and themes."

17. Capital costs are normally regarded as those expenditures made on a one-time basis for a fixed item such as a building or a piece of equipment. They may also include costs associated with the maintenance and repair of such an item. Capital cost expenditures may be made in a single payment or over a period of time but always in relation to a fixed object. These costs are usually distinguishable from "operational costs" which provide for items like salary expenditures and those costs associated with the continuing operation of a fixed object such as lights in a building or gas for a car.

18. In *The Role of Federal Corrections in Canada* (Task Force on the Creation of an Integrated Canadian Corrections Service 1977, 20) the following state- is made: "Manpower planning, training and development within Federal Corrections will become more complex and challenging. Correctional agencies within the Federal Government are already facing a serious challenge with regard to the management of their human resources. It has always been difficult to obtain good, qualified people for corrections and there has been an even greater problem in keeping them. Many positions remain unfilled, staff turnover in some institutions is high and staff motivation and morale in some institutions and community supervision agencies is low. When compared to other forms of employment, prisons are not perceived as being the most attractive working environments. The demands on Federal Corrections will require a sincere commitment on the part of all management and staff."

19. Correctional organizations devise many means to assure equilibrium. For example, since 1973 a position called Correctional Investigator has existed within the Solicitor General's Ministry (federal). The role of ombudsman and the function of critical inquiry associated with this office assists the organization to move from crisis to crisis while maintaining reasonable "evenness." For an example of the type of inquiry which may be undertaken by this office, see Stewart 1984.

20. Griffiths et al. (1980, 224) state: "Despite the critical position of the prison guard in the operation of the prison, relatively little attention has been given to recruitment and training. Typically, correctional institutions experience a turnover rate of guards as high as 50% per year which effectively hinders continuity in correctional policy."

References

Bartollas, C. and S.J. Miller. 1978. *Correctional Administration: Theory and Practice.* New York: McGraw-Hill.

Biles, D. 1981. *Criminal Justice Research in California.* Canberra: Australian Institute of Criminology.

Black, H.C. 1979. *Black's Law Dictionary* (5th ed.). St. Paul, Minnesota: West Publishing Co.

Duxbury, E. (Summer-Fall) 1980. "Role of Research: What Do We Know About . . .?" *Youth Authority Quarterly*. 67-73.

Ekstedt, J.W. 1979. "New Directions in the Administration of Justice and Corrections, Province of British Columbia, Canada." In *Marking a Dynamic Decade — Proceedings of the Fourth International SEARCH Symposium*. Sacramento, Calif.: SEARCH Group Inc. 37-40.

_____. 1983. "History of Juvenile Containment Policy in British Columbia." In R.R. Corrado, M. LeBlanc and J. Trepanier, (eds.) *Issues in Juvenile Justice*. Toronto: Butterworths. 285-301.

Epstein, H. 1982. "The Anticipated Effect of the Canadian Charter of Rights and Freedoms on Discretion in Corrections." In *The National Parole Board Report on the Conference on Discretion in the Correctional System*. Ottawa: National Parole Board.

Evans, D. (Fall) 1981. "Management: A Lesson Learned." 1 *Correctional Options*. Ontario: Ontario Ministry of Correctional Services. 7-9.

Finckenauer, J.O. 1982. *Scared Straight! and the Panacea Phenomenon*. Englewood Cliffs, N.J.: Prentice-Hall.

Griffiths, C.T., J.F. Klein and S.N. Verdun-Jones. 1980. *Criminal Justice in Canada: An Introductory Text*. Vancouver: Butterworths.

Hartman, D.M. 1982. *The Development of Criminal Justice Performance and Activity Measures*. Victoria: Corrections Branch, Ministry of the Attorney General.

Holt, N. (Autumn-Winter) 1977. "Prison Management in the Next Decade." 57 *The Prison Journal*. 16-30.

Jayewardene, C.H.S. and D.J.N. Jayasuriya. 1981. *The Management of Correctional Institutions*. Toronto: Butterworths.

Larsen, E.N. 1981. *Report to the Department of Criminology*. Burnaby, British Columbia: Department of Criminology, Simon Fraser University.

_____. 1982. "The Implications of Cybernetics for Criminal Justice Policy: Juvenile Containment as a Case History." Unpublished M.A. Thesis. Burnaby, British Columbia: Department of Criminology, Simon Fraser University.

National Advisory Commission on Criminal Justice Standards and Goals. 1973. *Corrections*. Washington, D.C.: U.S. Government Printing Office.

Phelps, J.A. n.d. "Inmates' Rights: The Case Law and Its Implications for Prisons and Penitentiaries." Unpublished paper. Saskatoon: Regional Headquarters, Correctional Service of Canada.

Province of British Columbia. (May) 1982. "B.C. Correctional Institutions: A Turning Point." *B.C. Corrections Branch Research Report*. 1-4.

Reid, S.T. 1981. *The Correctional System: An Introduction*. New York: Holt, Rinehart and Winston.

Ross, R.R. 1981. *Prison Guard/Correctional Officer*. Toronto: Butterworths.

Rusk, J. (December) 1980. "Prison Closing Unfolds at Turtle Pace." *The Globe and Mail*, Toronto. 8.

Shover, N. 1979. *A Sociology of American Corrections*. Homewood, Illinois: The Dorsey Press.

Solicitor General of Canada. 1975. *Young Persons in Conflict with the Law.* Ottawa: Supply and Services Canada.

_____. 1981. *Strategic Overview.* Ottawa: Supply and Services Canada.

_____. 1986. *A Framework for the Correctional Law Review.* Correctional Law Review Working Paper No. 2. Ottawa: Solicitor General of Canada.

Stewart, R.L. 1984. Report on the Allegations of Mistreatment of Inmates at Archambault Institution Following the Events Which Occurred on July 25, 1982. Ottawa: Correctional Investigator.

Tarnopolsky, W. 1982. "The Anticipated Effect of the Canadian Charter of Rights and Freedoms on Discretion in Corrections." In *The National Parole Board Report on the Conference on Discretion in the Correctional System,* Part II. Ottawa: National Parole Board.

Task Force on the Creation of an Integrated Canadian Corrections Service. 1977. *The Role of Federal Corrections in Canada.* Ottawa: Supply and Services Canada.

Waller, I. (July) 1979. "Organizing Research to Improve Criminal Justice Policy: A Perspective from Canada." 15 *Journal of Research in Crime and Delinquency.* 196-217.

Legislation

Canada. *Parole Act.* R.S.C. 1970, c. P-2, s.1.

Canada. *Penitentiary Act.* R.S.C. 1970, c. P-6.

Canada. *Constitution Act.* 1982. Proclaimed in force April 17, 1982, Canada Gazette, Pt. III, Special Issue, September 21, 1982.

Chapter 5

Correctional Planning

Planning is a necessary activity in the life of any organization. This is true regardless of the degree of formality employed by the organization in identifying planning tasks or in assigning responsibility for carrying out those tasks. In some organizations, including corrections, there are special sections which have been given primary responsibility for organizational planning. These sections are often called "planning offices" and persons who work in them often are known as "planning officers." Where these structures exist, they usually are associated with the tasks of research and policy development and it is now common to find "policy planning divisions" or "planning and research sections" in many government agencies.

The movement by correctional organizations to reflect their planning interests in a more formal and structured way is relatively recent. In Canada, most of this activity has taken place since the late 1960s but there are still jurisdictions which have not formally structured their planning interests in a way which has resulted in any visible organizational change.[1]

The main reason for the increased attention to planning tasks is the heightened complexity of both correctional decision making and the problems of correctional programming. Part of the complexity results simply from the fact of systems growth — growth in the number and type of correctional programs; increases in personnel and associated costs; increases in the various categories of crime; and increases in the number of offenders placed in correctional programs. The complexity also is due in part to mounting demand for accountability, which places pressure upon politicians and senior civil servants to review policy and to explain both the purposes and procedures related to the operation of correctional programs.

While it is clear that these factors influence the structure and style used by correctional organizations to engage in planning, it is important to remember that the requirement for planning has always been present. Accordingly, it would be inappropriate to assume that the creation of a planning office indicates that the organization has finally "discovered" its need for planning, when in fact all that has transpired is that the form and emphasis given to the planning function has undergone change. In the discussion of planning which follows, concentration will therefore be placed on the *substance* of planning as a characteristic in the life of a viable organization. Some planning *structures* will be discussed, but only in terms of the value those structures might have in improving the quality and efficiency of planning under specific circumstances. By approaching the subject in this way, confusion between *form* and *substance* as it applies to planning can be avoided and planning can come to be understood as an ongoing activity of all correctional organizations, regardless of the *form* any given planning activity might take.

For the purpose at hand, planning may be defined as the application of present knowledge to anticipations of the future. Planning ought to be orderly, systematic, and continuous and ought to be applied whenever there is a need in decision making to respond to speculations about the future, to anticipate future needs, or to give direction to future events.[2]

Generally, there are two types of planning — *reactive* and *proactive*. While many planning activities involve elements of both types, it is important to distinguish between them. Reactive planning occurs when a management level decision has been taken which will require an organizational response in preparation for the future. In such cases, the planning activity relies upon existing organizational knowledge to assess the decision's anticipated effects and to establish arrangements which will allow the organization to accommodate them.

A good example of reactive planning can be taken from the manner in which a bureaucratic organization adjusts to changes in its resource base. During times of restraint, it is not unusual for line ministries of government to be notified that they will experience a percentage reduction in anticipated revenues over the next fiscal year. The affected organization must then plan a response which will allow it to adjust satisfactorily before the next fiscal year arrives.

Reactive planning also takes place in government whenever decisions are made at the political level as a result of pressure from special interest groups or for other reasons related to political need. Often the political decisions call for the addition of new programs or for changes to old ones. The government agency responsible for the service in question will then be required to plan operational adjustments in relation to the political need which has been expressed.

Proactive planning, on the other hand, occurs when the future circumstance at issue cannot be fully anticipated. This type of planning seeks to promote the most desirable future for the organization through an assessment of all the factors which contribute to its development. The planning activity sets out to describe a desired future and to contribute to the decisions that will help to give it shape and definition. Proactive planning pursues its task of projecting future needs by first assessing the present state of organizational knowledge in relation to the organization's declared purpose and then extrapolating forward the likely future need that can be expected to emerge. Proactive planning may be stimulated in any number of ways. As previously suggested, one example of proactive planning occurs when a decision to review the legislation governing a corrections agency requires a corresponding policy review within the agency.

But it should be understood that some situations may have the potential to result in either reactive or proactive planning. For instance, prison overcrowding may call for a total reassessment of a correctional agency's overall program application with a corresponding redefinition of organizational policy. Where such a planning activity is initiated in order to anticipate and to more effectively satisfy the agency's purpose at some future date, then it properly can be said to be proactive in nature. However, if the response is simply to adjust the prison environment so that it can more adequately house a larger number of persons, then the planning activity becomes reactive by seeking only to accommodate a known situation.

In reactive planning, the operational or program goal is usually known before planning begins. In proactive planning, the operational or program goal is not known and attention is given to establishing a policy direction that can be used to guide the development or adjustment of programs. For this reason, reactive planning is sometimes called program planning, and proactive planning is sometimes referred to as policy planning. This distinction between reactive and proactive planning has been discussed by Prince and Chenier (1980, 522) who refer to planning units or structures as assuming a reactive or proactive stance:

> A reactive unit does not serve as a source of innovative policy or program ideas; it merely appraises and maybe responds to suggestions emanating from other parts of the organization.

> A proactive unit, has, in its extreme form, a monopoly in the elaboration of innovative proposals in the organization. Such a unit may be considered necessary in cases where the organization does not have or has not

demonstrated a capacity to produce the strategies required to keep pace with changes in the environment.

Regardless of the subtleties involved, all planning activities require an adequate and usable information base. Speculations about the future are always grounded in present knowledge and speculations about the future that are based on misperceptions of the present can only result in perpetuating error. One of the primary tasks in planning, therefore, is to constantly assess and seek to improve the present knowledge base. In organizational terms, the knowledge base includes:

1. *The research base* — assessment of programs and services in relation to their purpose.
2. *The data base* — information related to the continuing maintenance and operation of the system.
3. *The policy base* — assessment of goals and strategies used by an organization to carry out its mandate.

The knowledge and understanding that emerges in each of these areas constitutes the knowledge base used by planners in carrying out their tasks. Each area of information requires a concentration of effort in order to ensure that the knowledge base is as accurate and up-to-date as possible. The more sophisticated an organization becomes, the more it will structure itself to accommodate information needs and to provide a competent knowledge base.

While the knowledge base is critical to the activity of planning, it does nothing more than provide the foundation upon which planning can take place. The particular skill required in order to plan competently concerns how the assembled information can be used in relation to decision making which anticipates or gives direction to the future. No matter how accurate or comprehensive the information base may be, it is useless for planning purposes if it cannot be translated into decision-making terms. It follows that the structure and style of planning must seek to promote the best possible decisions for the future and not simply the best possible understanding of the present. Accordingly, it is the transition from current reality to future possibility that is the real task of planning.

It also should be evident that much of the effectiveness of an organization in meeting future needs is related to the balance it maintains between reactive and proactive planning. A total emphasis on reactive planning tends to make an organization rigid and defensive in its response to change. In such an environment, planning is used to assure the internal maintenance of known systems in response to changes in circumstances which occur externally. Organizations which restrict their planning activities to a reactive mode also tend to view external demands, such as budget changes or political initiatives, as threats to their continuing existence.

Conversely, if there is too much emphasis placed on proactive planning, an organization is likely to be chaotic and unstable. Such an organization may view maintenance interests or demands for operational stability as threats and may then begin to promote change for its own sake.[3] It is therefore important for most organizations, including corrections, that the planning emphasis be balanced and directed in such a way that the decision-making needs of the organization can be served to their optimum benefit. With these principles in mind, the style and structure of planning in corrections can now be addressed.

ORGANIZING THE DATA BASE

It is evident that planning, whether reactive or proactive in nature, requires an organized and continuously updated data base. The fundamental information set required for planning purposes in corrections can be referred to as the *offender data base*. Its principal components are as follows:

1. Since correctional services are client-centred, the data base must be structured in a way which allows for an accurate accounting of clients (offenders) held under corrections' jurisdiction and placed within correctional programs.
2. Since corrections provides services and programs for persons who are admitted as a result of decisions taken by the courts, the data base must be organized to identify and account for factors related to intake from a variety of locations and under differing conditions.
3. The data base must identify and account for the factors associated with the release of offenders from the system, either as a condition of parole or upon completion of sentence.

Given the categories described above, it should be evident that the offender data base generally must be organized according to categories related to admission or intake, program distribution, and release. Within each category, the data can be developed to any degree of complexity depending on available resources and the degree of sophistication which the technology allows. In turn, the structure of data gathering may rely upon manual, automated, or computerized systems.

The most elementary form of data base is one which organizes information according to simple counts in relation to time and form of disposition. An information set, compiled in this way, records how many persons were received into a correctional system with a sentence of imprisonment or a probation order on any given day, month, or year; how many persons in total were under corrections' jurisdiction in each program category; and, how many persons were released from each program over the same period of time.

The offender data base can be developed to encompass any number of additional variables including the number of clients admitted, held, and released according to sex, age, length of sentence, offence, or number of previous admissions. Again, the degree of complexity is governed by the ability to provide detailed and consistent information from which the data base can be constructed, as well as the ability to manipulate the data base for purposes of isolating and correlating the variables it contains.[4]

While the offender data base provides the basic information required for corrections planning, additional information sets are needed in order to relate the offender data base to other factors which influence decision making. It is important that the information base include data on the material and manpower commitments necessary to manage the offender case-load. Like the offender data base, this information set can be gathered and organized to many levels of complexity. Basic data in this category generally are provided by program type such as secure institution, wilderness program, community correctional centre, probation or parole office. The *resource data base,* as this information set may be called, usually includes information relating the numbers of staff to the numbers of offenders, the per diem costs, the per annum material and manpower costs, and the capital costs for each program type.

The offender data base and the resource data base provide the information available *within the system* which can be used for planning and management decision-making purposes. When all the information generated by the system is comprehensively assembled, it may be referred to as the *operational data base.*[5] However, effective planning requires information which extends beyond the operational data base and there are a number of external elements which affect correctional planning that must be included as part of the *total information base* (see Table 5.1). For instance, factors such as legislation, geography, population characteristics, economic conditions, and public attitudes all contribute to the expanded information set. Variables within these

TABLE 5.1   The Data Base in Correctional Planning

┌────── **Total Information Base** ──────┐

Operational Data Base (information generated within the system)	Environmental Data Base (information generated outside the system) The environmental data base includes the following information sets:
Offender Data Base Number of offenders admitted, held and released. Organized according to such variables as sex, age, sentence length, offence, number of previous admissions and location.	caseflow data acquired from the police and courts information systems; population characteristics — usually organized according to geographical regions;
Resource Data Base Usually organized according to program category. Information includes: ratio of staff to offenders; per diem costs; per annum material and manpower costs; and capital costs.	information on relevant legislation including legislative amendments and case law; public attitude surveys; and economic data.
This data base provides the information necessary to determine resource requirements, measure program volumes and assess the cost for each unit of service delivery.	This data base provides information necessary to forecast resource requirements and predict variations in categories of service delivery.

The total information base allows for an assessment of program effectiveness in relation to goals, client response and community interests.

___

information categories can be analyzed and correlated with the information generated within the system itself.

The external information base may be called the *environmental data base*. In the case of corrections, the environmental data base will include accessed information generated out of the operational data bases of other subsystems within criminal justice, primarily out of police and court information systems.

It is becoming increasingly popular to describe the organization of operational and environmental data as a

Management Information System (M.I.S.). Aside from the other uses to which they may be put, Management Information Systems can serve as aids to planning. In *Towards Management Information,* a document produced by the National Work Group on Justice Information and Statistics (Porter 1980, 1), Management Information Systems are described as follows:

> Management is becoming increasingly aware of the need for quantitative information in order to manage. To obtain, organize and control such information requires some sort of Management Information System (M.I.S.). The Police Management Information System Study of the Federal Solicitor General defines an M.I.S. as "the process whereby data is collected, stored and retrieved to provide *specific information for decision making".*
>
> This applies to decision making at all levels of operations in management. An M.I.S. may require computers, if warranted by cost, timeliness and volume, but this is not necessarily so. Technologies, including computers, are merely the means by which an M.I.S. may operate.
>
> Information in an organization is a resource which may be costly to generate, store, copy, transmit, retrieve and disseminate but it has an impact far in excess of its cost. For an organization "information, like electricity, is a form of energy". It is both necessary and important but there is a need to manage and control it. The M.I.S. is merely the tool by which this management and control of information can be achieved.

Muirhead (1979, 21) describes the relationship between a Management Information System and planning as follows:

> An operational and management planning instrument, built upon the knowledge of what is actually occurring, whether those occurrences are efficient/effective or not, can at least indicate what might be done to achieve our goals and embody our beliefs. Upon the basis of this knowledge, we can move the planning process from the realm of goals into specific objectives, the objectives into targets; and finally, targets into successful programme output. Utilizing a computerized management information system, the measurement of objective-based programmes through quantification of programme output can be obtained. Accordingly, the main function of a Management Information System is to reduce the probability of error or chance in decision making. In the delivery of correctional services, administrators must consider budget, staff, and capacities in terms of variety of alternatives or activities.

For planning purposes, the data base must not only exist and be consistently updated, it must also be organized and systematized to provide for the type of analysis which can allow managers to choose between the variety of alternatives available in the delivery of correctional programs. The more sophisticated a Management Information System is, the greater the likelihood that it will be able to contribute to effective planning and decision making. A Management Information System which is most effective will probably include all of the following:

1. The production of reports dealing with measures of resource requirements, program volumes, and how much it costs for each specified unit of delivery. This is the organization and analysis of *operational data.*
2. The production of reports which assess program effectiveness in relation to policy goals, client response, community assessment and other externally generated data. This analysis includes information from both the operational and environmental data bases.
3. The production of reports which *forecast* resource requirements as well as program volumes. These reports rely heavily on the environmental data base (police information, population characteristics, legislation, etc.) in order to predict variations from current resource utilization and expenditure and illustrate the expected volumes and costs by activity or program. At the highest level of sophistication, managers can be provided with the means to analyze the methods which they can use to optimize resource allocation. More particularly, they can use computer simulations or other available techniques to project changes in program requirements.[6]

It should be apparent that the development of an organized data base is fundamental to a planning process which promotes effective management decision making. And it is not surprising that the demand for accountability and cost efficiency in an increasingly complex system has resulted in the development of a number of sub-specialities within correctional organizations which concentrate on the production and use of information systems for planning and management purposes.

THE RELATIONSHIP BETWEEN
PLANNING AND RESEARCH

In Chapter 4, the influence of academic research on correctional policy and practice was discussed. In this section, some principles related to the application of research in correctional planning are presented.

The knowledge base required for planning has been described as including the data base, the research base, and the policy base (see page 132). In turn, the research base has been defined as an information set which provides "assessments of programs and services in relation to their purpose." The research application uses the data base when making these assessments, but it also uses theoretical or methodological approaches which will allow the information included in the data base to be understood and analyzed in relation to a known purpose. Additionally, when research is performed as *part of* the planning process, it must be organized in such a way that it is directed toward a specific decision-making need — for instance, to assist the decision maker in choosing between alternatives — as opposed to research which is organized primarily for the purpose of contributing to the knowledge base itself.

Expressed another way, research which is associated with a planning task must be directed to "practical" ends. The planner or decision maker must be able to use the research to assist in choosing between alternatives. Consequently, the research must be evaluative in form and presentation. It follows that much of the research that is associated with planning tasks has come to be known as "evaluative research." Adams (1975, 3) makes the following comment on this subject:

> A "practical" approach to evaluative research does not deny the relevance or importance of two other well-known approaches to research: the methodological, and the theoretical. In actuality, the practical approach builds upon either or both of the others. But by bringing in additional information, particularly of kinds ordinarily considered unimportant to either method or theory, it sometimes makes discoveries or achieves impacts that would not have occurred under the other approaches.

Muirhead and Hartman (1978, 1) provide the following illustration:

> Consider an academic researcher observing, measuring and hypothesizing about the direction and velocity of a rolling ball. The guiding principle in his methodology is non-interference with the rolling ball. Evaluative social research, on the other hand, has as its guiding principle, active intervention with the object under study. Evaluative researchers use the same techniques and strategies as academic researchers, but we are required to recommend that the direction and velocity of the ball be changed by intervention and new conditions.
>
> As evaluators of correctional programs, our responsibility and obligation to intervene is much more necessary than in altering the path of a rolling ball. The goals and policies of corrections vitally affect the lives

of human beings; not objects, but a variety of individuals. The means by which we achieve these goals is through the expenditure of public monies. Consequently, we are accountable both financially and morally to inform with accuracy.

Evaluation has been defined by Adams (1975, 43) as "a procedure for ascertaining whether an event, process, or situation (real or conceptualized) is better than another. The procedure may include steps for measuring 'how much better' and for explaining the reasons for the difference."

MODELS OF EVALUATIVE RESEARCH

There are a number of ways to describe the types of studies used in evaluative research. For purposes of this discussion, a brief review of evaluative research approaches will be provided under the headings of non-experimental studies, quasi-experimental studies and controlled experiments. Each of these research models may be used in association with techniques of cost and systems analysis in order to conceive the best possible alternatives in program planning and to determine the effect of any given decision upon the organization as a whole. Consequently, a brief definition of the terms "cost analysis" and "systems analysis" will be included in this section.

Non-Experimental Studies

It has been suggested that non-experimental research comprises at least 80 to 90 percent of the evaluative studies performed in corrections (Adams 1975, 53). Among the variety of research methods used in non-experimental studies, the most common are the case study, the survey, the time series, the cohort analysis, and the before-after study. These methods are briefly defined as follows:

1. *Case Study.* In this type of study, "cases" are examined to ascertain the characteristics of a situation, what is happening within it, and the explanation which possibly may account for its nature. A "case" may be a person, group, place, event, program or experience.
2. *Survey.* A survey involves procedures, most often questionnaires or interviews, for the systematic collection of data from multiple sources. Usually the purpose is to draw conclusions based on an analysis of responses from combined sources rather than a

response originating from a single source.

3. *Time Series.* Time series involve measurements of events at periodic intervals over time. They are used to provide a picture of trends related to categories of programs or populations.

4. *Cohort Analysis.* A cohort analysis is a study which provides a record of a group's performance over time. The term "cohort" is taken to mean any group constructed according to some shared experience, such as being born in the same year, being admitted to prison in the same year, etc.

5. *Before-After Study.* These studies attempt to ascertain the condition or status of a group, both prior to being involved in a particular experience and after the experience has transpired.

It is not surprising that non-experimental studies comprise the majority of studies associated with evaluative research in corrections. They have the capacity to provide decision makers with organized research information that is well-suited to the tempo of executive decision making during times of rapid change. Non-experimental studies can be quickly executed and are generally inexpensive by comparison to other research options. Moreover, the methods used in non-experimental evaluations tend to be compatible with the perceptions of decision makers respecting corrections work. In this regard, corrections work is often described by managers in terms involving the organization of "cases," the process of "case management" or the administration of "case-loads." As a consequence, the idea of "case studies" fits well with the prevailing decision-making rhetoric.

Surveys seem to allow administrators the opportunity to have access to a broad base of opinion, particularly in relation to initiatives which may be considered potentially unpopular or which may be subject to criticism. Similarly, most managers understand the use of time series and the need to analyze trends. Prison, parole, or probation populations all provide data for time series studies which can prove useful in the analysis of space requirements or in budget planning. Correctional managers can also easily understand the usefulness of data related to the performance of cohorts, such as admissions cohorts, program cohorts, or release cohorts. And before-after studies appear central to the analysis and justification of new program initiatives.

However, there are weaknesses in non-experimental studies when they are employed to form part of the research base for decision making. As Adams (1975, 53) points out:

Their value is determined to a large extent by the experience, judgement and objectivity of the researcher; improperly used, they may create more confusion than enlightenment. Their procedures lack standardization, their reliability is uncertain, and their interpretation is sometimes difficult. Many of these characteristics are more troublesome to researchers than to administrators. The latter are constantly faced with unreliable and uncertain data in their decision-making processes and they are more accustomed to acting on such information, though often with questionable effect.

Quasi-Experimental Studies

Quasi-experimental studies employ research designs to evaluate information which describes a "treatment" group that is subject to a particular process or program. Moreover, the evaluation proceeds by comparing the "treatment" group to a "comparison" group which is chosen on the basis that it displays "similar" characteristics. In other words, an effort is made to assess equivalents between the two groups under study, but contrary to a controlled experiment, the comparison group is not formed by random selection. Accordingly, true equivalence is difficult, if not impossible, to effect.

Quasi-experimental studies are undertaken when the membership of a treatment group has been determined on criteria unrelated to the study itself — for instance, where an experimental program is introduced to an existing offender population. In order to conduct a comparative study under such circumstances, it is necessary to select a comparison group which resembles as much as possible the group that was involved in the program experiment.

In a quasi-experimental study of a correctional program, the comparison group might be formed by going to a records file of persons in the correctional population and selecting cases that resemble, at least roughly, cases within the treatment group. The study design would require that both groups exhibit essentially comparable experiences in the correctional system. The primary difference between them, therefore, would be that the treatment group was subject to the program being evaluated while the comparison group was not.

Quasi-experimental studies also are used when controlled experiments, which would randomly select subjects eligible for treatment into experimental and control groups, are resisted. Such resistance may result from the lack of willingness by administrators to withhold treatment from eligible persons, simply on the grounds that they have been randomly selected to form a control group for purposes of an experimental study. As well, there are circumstances where the random selection and assignment of cases into treatment and control groups is not possible due to operational complexities. As Adams (1975, 61) points out:

> In the assignment of individuals to several half-way houses from several different sources — prison, probation, courts, bail agency, and the parole board — the assignment disparities between experimentals and controls may become so great that the randomization process is no improvement over the equating process used in the quasi-experiment.

As already pointed out, the quasi experiment is necessary in those cases where the treatment program population has been selected prior to the study, or where a program which no longer exists is being evaluated.

Controlled Experiments

Shover (1979, 282) discusses the controlled experiment as follows:

> In the classic experimental design, an *experimental* and *control* group are randomly selected from the same population of offenders and a treatment (i.e. independent variable) is administered to the experimental group but withheld from the control group. In every other way, efforts are made to assure that the two groups are treated exactly alike. Since the groups are assumed, subject to laws of probability, to be equivalent because of randomization, and the occurrence of the independent variable is the only thing that differentiates the two groups, any subsequently observed difference on the criterion can be attributed to the occurrence of the treatment variable. Thus, in the classic experiment, the two groups to be compared are constructed through the process of random assignment.

While the controlled experiment presents a number of technical problems, particularly when applied in the social sciences (Adams 1975, 69ff; Shover 1979, 282ff), it is clear that the controlled experiment is the most satisfying model from a research perspective. However, in the discussion of quasi-experimental studies, some reasons were identified which suggest why a controlled experiment is often not acceptable as an evaluative research model from the perspective of managers or other decision makers. The controlled experiment works best within carefully structured situations, with ample time available to conduct the study. It is common, however, that the demands on decision makers are not compatible with the time and structural requirements of controlled experimentation. Consequently, the controlled experiment is less amenable to direct application for the purpose of planning and management decision making than other models.

This is not intended to suggest that the controlled experiment is unimportant in correctional research but its use in the planning and policy-making process is more difficult to visualize than some other research models. As Adams (1975, 71) states:

> The major issues tend to be resolved and major actions tend to be taken on the basis of configurations of information and interests, not on the findings of a crucial experiment. The information component in the process seems much more likely to come from non-experimental than from experimental models.
>
> Whether the experimental model will in the future find a more influential role in decision-making than it now occupies is unclear. If corrections moves from fluidity to a more structured, laboratory-like state, with experiment-minded administrators and experiment-promoting chiefs of research, the controlled experiment may rise in importance. If present trends toward change, toward increasing use of uncertain information, toward integration of process and structure in ever-widening systems continue, the controlled experiment may decline in importance.

Cost Analysis and Systems Analysis

For effective planning in management decision making, the contributions of evaluative research, using any of the models described above, require an assessment in relation to resource implications and systems effects. This area of interest is sometimes referred to as *operations research* and includes cost analysis (cost-benefit analysis) and systems analysis.

Cost analysis assists in evaluating the implications of alternative courses of action through the introduction of monetary values or economic values as a basis for comparison. Heyel (1980, 25) points out that "the term 'cost' is used . . . in its broad sense. Although dollars are the units most generally used in this type of analysis, any economic resource might, for a given problem, be the limiting factor — e.g., personnel."

Systems analysis is used to measure the effect on an organization of alternative programs. Alternative programs are assessed in relation to known organizational objectives through an analysis of performance criteria, cost, and the risk which may be associated with the continuation of an established program or the implementation of a new one. Systems analysis may involve the creation of "simulations" as a process of testing the effect alternative programs have upon the system as a whole. In this context, a "simulation" is any representation by a model of a system or process. Recent developments in computer technology allow for relatively sophisticated simulations which can demonstrate the effect of a program either on an organization as a whole or on any subcomponent within it.

STRUCTURING THE PLANNING PROCESS

The process of planning involves the activity of a system in proceeding from the establishment of an information base through to the confirmation of a policy or management-level decision. While this process may be somewhat complex depending on the sophistication of the systems employed, it can be seen to involve four basic levels of initiative — basic research, policy research, policy analysis, and policy making.

1. *Basic research* addresses the questions "what do we need to know to make a decision?" and "how do we acquire that knowledge?" Basic research establishes the knowledge base.
2. *Policy research* addresses the questions "what do we know?" and "how can this information be organized and described for decision-making purposes?" Policy research organizes the information base according to decision-making need.
3. *Policy analysis* addresses the questions "what interpretation can be made from what we know?" and "what are the constraints and limitations which must be considered?" Policy analysis presents the implications arising from the information base in relation to the ability of the system to implement alternatives. Cost analysis and systems analysis are employed here.
4. *Policy making* addresses the questions "what is the preferred option for decision making?" and "what is the strategy for implementation?" In policy making, the objectives or goals related to the decision are identified and the implementation strategy is developed.

The planning process in corrections involves an interaction between technicians, line personnel, managers, administrators, researchers, offenders, and the public-at-large. The nature of corrections work and the circumstances surrounding it make planning a difficult task that is subject to a variety of uncontrolled and uncontrollable variables. Correctional planning and policy development are intimately related to the structures of management and administration as well as to the quality and character of line-level correctional personnel. Chapter 6 addresses these influences on corrections policy and planning.

Notes

1. A review of organizational flow charts of federal and provincial correctional services provided in a publication of the Canadian Centre for Justice Statistics (Statistics Canada 1982) reveals the extent to which planning has been structured organizationally in the various jurisdictions. At the federal level, the Correctional Service of Canada has incorporated the position of Deputy Minister of Policy, Planning and Administration, and within the National Parole Board there is the office of Director of Policy, Planning and Evaluation. Provincially, it is difficult to draw the line between those jurisdictions which do have structured planning departments and those which do not, since a planning structure may be located within another division such as British Columbia's Program Analysis and Evaluation Division. Nonetheless, as of 1981, it appears that Nova Scotia, New Brunswick, Quebec, Ontario, Alberta, Saskatchewan, and British Columbia have formal planning structures, whereas Newfoundland, Prince Edward Island, Manitoba, the Yukon Territory, and the Northwest Territories do not.

2. A variety of definitions of planning may be found in the literature. All are similar in their emphasis. For example, Banki (1974, 199) defines planning as: "a systematic step-by-step method and process defining, developing and outlining possible courses of action to meet existing possible future needs, interests or problems." Similarly, Hartman (1982, 110) states: "Planning has various definitions but the following definition is suggested as being one of the more useful: an assessment of the future, the determination of desired objectives in the context of that future, a development of alternative courses of action to achieve such objectives, and the selection of course (or courses) of action from these alternatives."

3. An example of a possible emphasis on change for its own sake may be found in the organization of the federal public service over the past two decades. Policy and program planning in the federal public service prior to the 1960s was an informal function of administrators and management. The 1960s, however, brought with them a rapid proliferation of policy planning units in Canadian government services and by the mid-1970s there were no less than 3,500 planners holding positions in major departments of the federal government. Prince and Chenier (1980, 537) discussed this increase in planning structures and questioned the necessity of developing policy planning units within many of these departments:

> Policy units were apparently created to help public organizations cope with the rapidly changing or turbulent environment. Not many would argue against the position that the internal environment of the federal public service was undergoing significant change — new management systems, new language requirements, new organizations not to mention policy planning units. Indeed, for some it seemed a "topsy turvy" place. True, some major changes did take place over the period in question but how many of these were simply one-shot affairs?
>
> For many departments, the environment was reasonably placid given the lack of the competitive marketplace. Yet the departments were all treated the same. The policy unit model was a general one promoted and

154 CORRECTIONS IN CANADA: POLICY AND PRACTICE

adopted throughout the federal bureaucracy. Differences in departmental needs, environments and functions were not seen to be crucial factors in the decision to establish policy units.

4. The National Advisory Commission on Criminal Justice Standards and Goals (1973b, 87) outlines the minimum requirements for corrections data about the offender:

1. Official data, including the date of entry into the correctional system, offenses and sentences, concurrent or consecutive sentences, recommendations of the court, conditions of work release or assignment to halfway houses or other community supervision, and county (court) of commitment or entry into the correctional system,

2. Personal data, including age, race, and sex; marital/family status; intelligence classification, military experience; classification categories; other test and evaluative information, job placement, housing arrangements, and diagnostic data; and

3. Historical data, including family background, educational background, occupational record, alcohol and drug use background, and prior criminal history.

There is, however, no empirical research to indicate the relationship between the amounts and kinds of data collected on offenders and the validity of the decisions made about them. A notable characteristic of the corrections system is its tendency to generate large amounts of information on the offender that may be of limited utility in assessing the offender's requirements and in taking initiatives that will assist in reducing the incidence of criminal behaviour.

5. Jayewardene and Jayasuriya (1981, 63) broadly define operational information as "information that relates to the context in which the activities have to be carried out — information regarding what has happened during the immediate past and what is known to happen in the immediate future."

6. Archambeault and Archambeault (1982, 150) provide the following comment on computer simulation:

Unlike evaluative research, which requires that a policy be translated into a program or course of action before it can be evaluated, the computer simulation models allow planners and policy makers to test out the probable future impact of a policy alternative long before a program or course of action needs to be initiated. Thus, given the limitation that only a relatively small range of known contingency policies can be programmed into the computer, correctional policy of the future may possess a level of validity that had only been possible heretofore after a decade of trial and error. Both research and simulation models are likely to become increasingly more influential in future policy development.

References

Adams, S. 1975. *Evaluative Research in Corrections: A Practical Guide.* Washington, D.C.: U.S. Department of Justice.

Archambeault, W.G. and B.J. Archambeault. 1982. *Correctional Supervisory Management: Principles of Organization, Policy and Law.* Englewood Cliffs, N.J.: Prentice-Hall.

Banki, I.S. 1974. *Dictionary of Supervision and Management.* Los Angeles: Systems Research.

Hartman, D.M. 1982. *The Development of Criminal Justice Performance and Activity Measures.* Victoria: Corrections Branch, Ministry of the Attorney General.

Heyel, C. 1980. *The VNR Concise Guide to Management Decision Making.* New York: Van Nostrand Reinhold.

Jayewardene, C.H.S. and D.J.N. Jayasuriya. 1981. *The Management of Correctional Institutions.* Toronto: Butterworths.

Muirhead, G. 1979. "Design for the Development of Corrections Management Information Resources." 2 *B.C. Corrections Research Report.* 20-32.

Muirhead, G. and D.M. Hartman. (March) 1978. "The Philosophy of Evaluative Research." 1 B.C. Corrections Research Report. 1.

National Advisory Commission on Criminal Justice Standards and Goals. 1973a. *Corrections.* Washington, D.C.: U.S. Government Printing Office.

_____. 1973b. *Criminal Justice System.* Washington, D.C.: U.S. Government Printing Office.

Porter, T.A. (March) 1980. *Towards Management Information.* Ottawa: National Work Group on Justice Information and Statistics.

Prince, M.J. and J.A. Chenier. 1980. "The Rise and Fall of Policy Planning and Research Units: An Organizational Perspective." 23 *Canadian Public Administration.* 519-41.

Shover, N. 1979. *A Sociology of American Corrections.* Homewood, Illinois: The Dorsey Press.

Social Sciences and Humanities Research Council of Canada. 1982. *Annual Report, 1981/82.* Ottawa: Supply and Services Canada.

Statistics Canada. 1982. *Correctional Services in Canada, 1980/81.* Ottawa: Canadian Centre for Justice Statistics.

Chapter 6

Structures of Management
and
Administration in Corrections

While the point has previously been made in a number of ways, it is important to re-emphasize that corrections is a service of government and is therefore structured according to principles of public administration. As Archambeault and Archambeault (1982, 41) note:

> All correctional organizations may be considered to be public service organizations and as such must be operated consistent with principles of public administration rather than private business administration. . . .

The fundamental objectives of public service organizations are not the same as those assumed by private business organizations. This is evident when considering the problems associated with efforts to justify public service expenditures in relation to a designated service or anticipated "product." As Archambeault and Archambeault (1982, 41) go on to point out:

> The problem of measuring the effectiveness of correctional organizations or any public policy organization is complex. It is difficult, if not impossible, to accurately measure the dollar amount of benefit to society for each dollar of tax money spent on a correctional program. Frequently, another standard is used, namely, cost-effectiveness. Cost-effectiveness refers to the measurement of the dollar expenditure (cost) per unit of service (effectiveness). Hence, in Corrections the unit of service may be such criteria as the number of correctional officers per inmate population, number of probationers per agent, or numbers of persons served by a given program. In programs such as education or vocational training, where skill levels can be determined, cost-effectiveness may relate to cost per student per level of skill achieved. However, again the direct dollar benefit to society is difficult to prove. In any case, every correctional organization is forced to justify its continued existence in terms of quality and quantity of services provided.

In addition to the general problems of accountability associated with public service agencies, the nature of correctional work raises some further issues. In the report of the National Advisory Commission on Criminal Justice Standards and Goals (1973, 441-42), the particular nature of corrections as a public service organization is discussed as follows:

> Corrections is a "human resource" organization: that is, its material is people, its product, behavior. The unique features of this type of organization complicate its structural design and management and make both a central part of implementing programs. . . .
>
> Managing a human resource organization is probably even more difficult than managing other public agencies because many traditional management tools are not directly applicable. Data describing effects of the correctional process relate to behavior or attitudes and are subject to subjective, frequently conflicting interpretations. The feedback loops necessary for judging the consequences of policies are difficult to create and suffer from incomplete and inaccurate information. There has not been in corrections an organized and consistent relation between evaluative research and management action.
>
> The management of corrections as a human resource organization must be viewed broadly in terms of how offenders, employees, and various organization processes (communications, decision-making, and others) are combined into what is called "the corrections process".

The structure and techniques which are employed in the management and administration of corrections must reflect both the principles of public administration and the unique character of the corrections process. Moreover, the problem of justifying expenditures and accounting for results occurs within a structure which must recognize and support the inter-personal relations between employees and clients. Accordingly, the requirement for discretionary decision making on the part of employees is an important factor that must be taken into consideration.

THE DISTINCTION BETWEEN MANAGEMENT AND ADMINISTRATION

With regard to their literal meanings, the terms "management" and "administration" may be used interchangeably. But the meaning of these terms in practice is often determined by the context in which they are applied. In discussions of public service or corrections organizations, it is common to define "administration" as the overall *process* used both to organize and to manage the delivery system that brings the services of the organization to the client or consumer. When administration is defined in this way, it can be seen as a process which includes all of the specific tasks and responsibilities associated with the continuing maintenance of the agency.

"Management," on the other hand, can be defined as a task *within* the administrative process (see, for example, Coffey 1975, 20ff; Bartollas and Miller 1978, 71ff; Archambeault and Archambeault 1982, 47ff.). This method of distinguishing "management" from "administration" is helpful when the intention is to identify specific management responsibilities within a network of organizational components, all of which can be said to be part of the same process. The distinction is compatible with the use of the term "administration" in the phrases "administration of justice" and "administration of government."

The administration of justice involves the management of cases from an initial charge or the laying of an information, through to the point of adjudication and sentencing in the courts. Similarly, *Black's Law Dictionary* (5th edition, 1979, 41) states, under the definition of "administration": "In public law, the administration of government means the practical management and direction of the executive department, or of the public machinery or functions, or of the operations of the various organs or agencies." When defined in these ways, management can easily be seen to be *subsumed* within a broader process of administration.

This distinction between management and administration breaks down, however, when administration is perceived as a function or as tasks to be performed, rather than as a process. In common usage, an administrative function can be said to be quite different from a management function — in practice, managerial functions and responsibilities are normally considered superior to administrative functions or responsibilities.

In Canada, management classifications are reserved for those positions involving responsibility for the overall direction and control of an organization or of any major component within it, while administrative positions are normally regarded as "support" positions involved with the administration of forms and procedures to carry out the directives of management. The task of management is to set direction and to determine policy; the administrative task is to devise procedures and to develop the support systems that are used to implement and carry out policy initiatives.

Aside from the fact that the literal meanings of the terms are often used interchangeably, it also should be realized that it is possible for a single individual to perform both management and administrative tasks. However, the practical distinction between management as a policy task and administration as a task which establishes and maintains procedures is an important one and one that can be consistently applied throughout the structure of government services in Canada.[1]

In discussing the structure of management and administration in corrections, the terms management and administration will be used to define *tasks* involved in the delivery of correctional services. Management tasks are defined as policy-related and administrative tasks are defined as procedure-related. Consequently, a director of corrections is a manager and a director of finance within corrections is an administrator. The activity of the director of finance is to organize procedures for budgeting and financial control in order to carry out the policies authorized by the director of corrections. Using this definition, the structure of management and administration within corrections can be said to involve four basic levels: policy management, executive administration, management of operations, and supervision of operations (see Figure 6.1).

POLICY MANAGEMENT

Policy management in public service is defined as negotiations between senior civil servants and politicians to establish governing policy. In these negotiations, the overall mandate of the organization is either authenticated or reinforced and specific emphases within that mandate are determined. At this level, decisions may be taken with regard to elements of law and regulation as they apply to the operating agency; the targeting of specific client groups in the provision of services; the establishment of service priorities; and the determination of the amount of resources (both human and material) that will be committed to the organization for the purpose of exercising its mandate.

In the public service, the policy management task involves several decision-making levels, each of which is supported by an administrative system. At its highest level, the managers are politicians acting as ministers holding portfolios responsible for the delivery of government services. Together with the premier of the province or the prime minister, the ministers collectively make up the executive council or cabinet of the government in power. The full cabinet is normally organized into committees of ministries

FIGURE 6.1 Structure of Management and Administration in Corrections

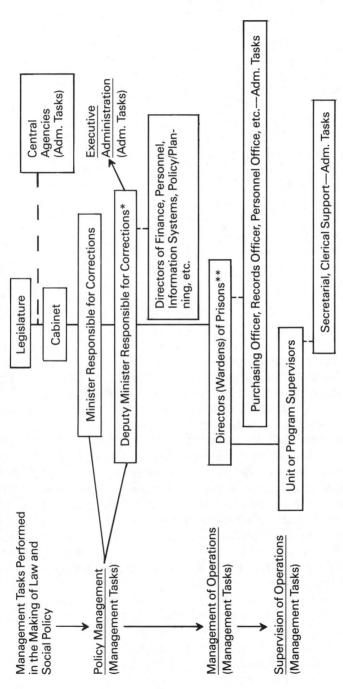

*In some jurisdictions, the senior civil servant responsible for corrections is called a Director or Commissioner. That person may report to the Minister through a Deputy Minister with broader ministerial responsibilities (such as a Deputy Attorney General or Deputy Solicitor General).

**Prisons are selected for illustrative purposes. The same general division of responsibilities applies to probation, parole or other non-institutional corrections services.

sharing similar categories of responsibility, such as a social services committee, or to address a specific category of decision making, such as a treasury board. The cabinet committees consider policy issues which extend beyond the authority of any individual minister to resolve (for an example of cabinet committee structure, see Figure 6.2). Individual ministers work within a mandate, usually established by legislation, which determines the latitude for independent policy making within their ministry.

In turn, the operation of each ministry is managed by a deputy minister. In most cases, the deputy minister is the senior civil servant responsible for the actual delivery of services within the ministry. It is often the case that deputy ministers may also be collectively organized according to committees similar to the committees of cabinet. It is the responsibility of deputy ministers to provide policy recommendations for consideration at the political level and to organize the ways and means of implementing policy decisions which are taken at that level. Since the civil service provides the stability required for the organization and management of government services, it is in the exercise of deputy ministerial responsibility that the key to the policy management process is found.

But it should be made clear that there are some decisions which cannot be made within the executive or cabinet structure of government. The requirement for new legislation or for legislative reform ultimately involves a decision of the legislature as a whole which includes the government in power, both cabinet and back benchers, and any opposition parties which may be sitting. As well, the estimates for all categories of government expenditure must be approved by the legislature for each fiscal year.

It is therefore possible to see that the policy management process may involve several different levels of decision making. Some issues may be resolved between a deputy minister and the minister responsible for the service in question. Some issues will be taken to cabinet committee for decision making and, occasionally, an issue will be considered by the entire cabinet. Furthermore, new legislative initiatives will proceed to the legislature as a whole. This then is the structure of the policy management process. The context within which this process occurs is illustrated in Figure 6.3.

As suggested previously, policy management is served by a variety of administrative support agencies. These agencies are normally referred to as the "central agencies" of government. The most common central agencies are the public service or civil service commissions responsible for procedures related to the recruitment, training and employment of personnel; the comptroller general, responsible for accounting policies and procedures, payroll and other cheque disbursements; public works, responsible for the development and maintenance of facilities used in the delivery of services; and purchasing commissions, responsible for procedures related to the purchase of the materials used in service delivery.

There may be any number of other agencies included in the administrative support network. A common one in Canada is the Queen's Printer, which is responsible for the printing and publication of all government documents. More recently, governments have been establishing central agencies responsible for computerized information systems which also service government as a whole. All of these agencies are subject to policy that has been established at the political level. In turn, they exist to provide information which may be used in the development of policy and to develop procedures which are used in the implementation of policy. The organization of the policy management process clearly illustrates the relationship between management and administration according to the task definition provided earlier.

EXECUTIVE ADMINISTRATION

Executive administration refers to the administrative tasks which are performed within a line ministry in order to organize the human and material resources required to reach the goals of policy management. At this level, the deputy minister or the director with responsibility over the services provided for by policy, establishes the procedures and organizes the resources which are to be used in order to implement that policy. Where such an activity takes place within public service, it provides a good example of a location in which responsibility for management and for administrative tasks overlaps.

For instance, deputy ministers or their counterparts are not usually responsible for managing the direct delivery of service such as the immediate management of operations within a jail. Instead, the deputy organizes the human and material supports required by the system as a whole in order to operate all of its programs. In doing so, the deputy performs a task which is essentially administrative in nature and which is subservient to the management task of making policy. At one and the same time, therefore, the deputy minister or director participates in the

FIGURE 6.2   Organization of the Government of British Columbia Cabinet Committee Structure (1979)

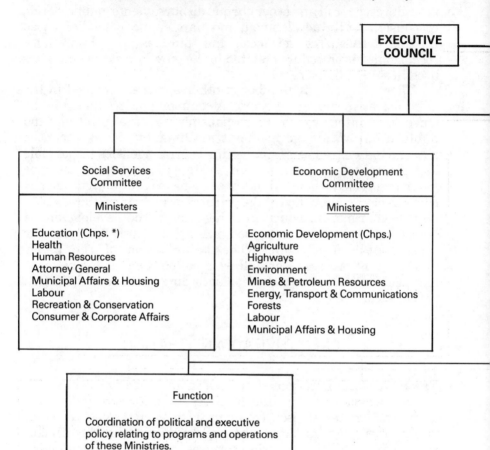

EXECUTIVE COUNCIL

Social Services Committee

Ministers

Education (Chps. *)
Health
Human Resources
Attorney General
Municipal Affairs & Housing
Labour
Recreation & Conservation
Consumer & Corporate Affairs

Economic Development Committee

Ministers

Economic Development (Chps.)
Agriculture
Highways
Environment
Mines & Petroleum Resources
Energy, Transport & Communications
Forests
Labour
Municipal Affairs & Housing

Function

Coordination of political and executive policy relating to programs and operations of these Ministries.

(Chps. *)—Chairperson

PREMIER'S OFFICE

Planning & Priorities Committee	Treasury Board
Ministers	Ministers
Premier (Chps.) Deputy Premier Finance Economic Development Education	Finance (Chps.) Premier Economic Development Education

Function	Function
1. Determination of political policies and strategy. 2. Determination of program priorities. 3. Approval of new program policies & initiatives. 4. Inter-governmental relations policy.	1. Central coordination & control of government operations. 2. Approval of Ministry organization structures; establishment levels; classification standards & levels; pay plans; & union contracts. 3. Establishment of administrative, personnel, & financial management policies, systems & procedures. 4. Establishment of budgetary procedures; coordination of government budgetary process; review, analysis, & approval of Ministry budget estimates. 5. Program analysis & review; analysis & approval of expenditure proposals.

FIGURE 6.3 The Context of Policy Management in Government

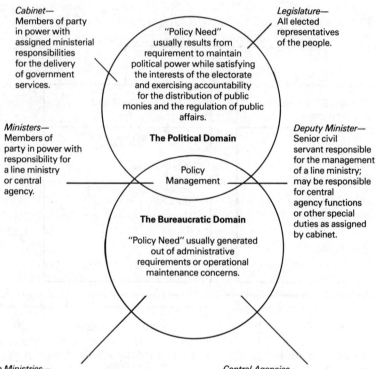

Cabinet—
Members of party in power with assigned ministerial responsibilities for the delivery of government services.

Legislature—
All elected representatives of the people.

"Policy Need" usually results from requirement to maintain political power while satisfying the interests of the electorate and exercising accountability for the distribution of public monies and the regulation of public affairs.

The Political Domain

Ministers—
Members of party in power with responsibility for a line ministry or central agency.

Policy Management

Deputy Minister—
Senior civil servant responsible for the management of a line ministry; may be responsible for central agency functions or other special duties as assigned by cabinet.

The Bureaucratic Domain

"Policy Need" usually generated out of administrative requirements or operational maintenance concerns.

Line Ministries—
Departments of Government responsible for delivery of specific government services.

Examples:
Attorney General: responsible for legal advice to government; prosecutorial services; administration of law enforcement policy; and, in some jurisdictions, courts and corrections administration.

Solicitor General: in some jurisdictions responsible for law enforcement, corrections and parole.

Education: responsible for administration of policy related to public and private schools.

Welfare or Social Development: responsible for administration of services to those citizens eligible for government subsidy.

Central Agencies—
Agencies of government responsible for specific aspects of the *overall* administration of government.

Examples:
Public Service Commission; responsible for administration of personnel policy.

Public Works: responsible for administration of government properties.

Comptroller General: responsible for administration of payroll and financial audit.

Purchasing Commission: responsible for administration of policy regarding purchasing of materials necessary for maintenance of government services.

management task of establishing policy and then is charged with the administrative task of organizing the resources needed in order for the policy to be carried out.

Consequently, the office of a deputy minister usually is structured to provide a variety of administrative services which are used to support more than one purpose: first, they provide information and advice for use in policy making; and second, they assist in the development of procedures which are used to allocate resources for service delivery. Accordingly, a deputy minister's or director's office will have other offices associated with it responsible for finance, personnel, facilities development, and purchasing — all of which are directed to the tasks associated with administration. These administrative support services, located at the line ministerial level, function for the ministry much in the same way that the central agencies of government support the broader political decision-making process. Moreover, like the central agencies of government, the ministerial administrative agencies function to serve managerial interests regardless of their location within the line ministry. Therefore, while these administrative services may be said to be located at a higher level in the organizational structure of a ministry (i.e., the deputy minister's office) than some other functions which are managerial in nature (i.e., the director of a jail), they still are intended to exist in a relationship which is subservient to management interests.

However, it seems to be within the nature of bureaucracies that this distinction is sometimes rendered unclear, and it must be understood that managers do not necessarily possess the arbitrary authority to violate or to bypass established administrative procedures. For instance, the authority over a financial procedure may rest with the director of finance who by definition is an administrator. Nevertheless, a finance director's authority over administrative procedures must be exercised in a way which is compatible with the management interests of the organization. More particularly, the finance director must not apply the administrative procedures under his control in such a way that they unduly restrict the policy authority. Instead, administrative procedures should be used for the purpose of both informing and servicing the policies established by the managers. In short, while managers cannot whimsically dismiss established administrative procedures, at the same time those procedures should not be used to circumvent the manager's policy authority.

THE MANAGEMENT OF OPERATIONS

The management of operations may be described as the organizational task of directing and controlling the achievement of those goals that have been defined by policy management. This category of management responsibility tends to be staffed by persons responsible for the major program components within an organization. In the context of corrections, persons responsible for the management of operations include the directors or wardens of specific institutions and the directors of probation or other community services. In the management of operations, the policy-oriented tasks involve the translation of organizational policy into operational policy. For example, policy managers in corrections may determine that the priority for program development will be centred in the establishment of alternatives to incarceration. The managers of operations will then be responsible for the development of policies within their programs which support and lead to the implementation of the policy management intention.

Within the management of operations, management responsibility tends to be more widely distributed than at the policy management level. Accordingly, there may be a number of persons holding managerial positions, depending on the size of any given program. A large institution, for instance, may have a director or warden supported by a number of assistant directors or wardens, with each responsible for a major program area within the institution. Within institutional corrections, various titles are used to describe these positions and they often reflect a paramilitary structuring. It is common, therefore, that managers of operations hold such titles as director, warden, officer-in-charge, chief or principal officer. It is also common that this category of management responsibility is sometimes referred to as "middle management."

Once again, there are a variety of administrative support services available at this level of management responsibility, which duplicate in kind the administrative support services at the policy management or executive administration level. Each major program component is likely to have a finance officer and a personnel officer. Additionally, institutional programs might include administrative positions such as "records officer" or "purchasing officer."

SUPERVISION OF OPERATIONS

According to Coffey (1975, 90):

> The role definition of supervisors in the correctional field is far less clear
> than the role definition of higher levels of correctional management . . .
> However, we can say that there is at least one expectation accompanying
> this role, regardless of function or variety of organization: that the
> supervisor "connects" the management process and the operational
> process.

Archambeault and Archambeault (1982, 56) point out that supervisors are charged "with responsibility for the day-to-day operations of specific areas within major organizational units":

> the first-level supervisor makes specific job assignments; makes routine
> first-level decisions; maintains close contact with operative employees;
> makes detailed and short-range operating plans; provides for motivation,
> control, direction, and training of subordinates; initiates employee
> grievances and other personnel actions responsible for the
> implementation of agency and institutional policies, rules, regulations at
> the employee level; and so on.

In corrections, the supervision of operations is the level of management responsibility most closely associated with direct service delivery to the client or offender. Moreover, it is at this level of management responsibility that policies either become implemented or are subject to failure. It also can be argued that there have been many policy intentions established at the policy management level which have failed either as a result of misunderstanding on the part of supervisors of operations or because of disagreements between policy makers and those responsible for delivery.

The administrative tasks which are associated with the supervision of operations tend to be clerical and secretarial in nature. Generally, they involve the use of forms and procedures established by executive administration since the supervisor's main responsibility is to manage the human resources associated with direct service delivery to clients. The procedures, applying to both employees and their clients, tend to be established at the level of executive administration or within the central agencies of government.

The way in which line ministries structure themselves to reflect the distinction between the categories of management and administrative responsibilities (described above) is illustrated in

Figure 6.4 (Organization of the Secretariat of the Federal Solicitor General's Ministry) and Figure 6.5 (Organization of the Ministry of Corrections, Province of Ontario).

MANAGEMENT STYLES

While the general relationship between management and administrative tasks is consistent across all public service organizations, the style that is established by any given organization to govern the relationship may reflect an individualized approach. In this regard, there are a number of theoretical approaches that may be employed within an organization to "set the tone" of management and administration. In turn, the chosen approach will do much to determine the character of the organization, including the way in which contributions are made to decision making.

Most theoretical approaches to management and administrative practice are represented in the conceptual framework developed by Douglas MacGregor (1960) in his work *The Human Side of Enterprise*. In a later work, MacGregor (1966, 5) propounded two basic theoretical views related to "management's task in harnessing human energy to organizational requirements." He termed these theoretical perspectives "Theory X" and "Theory Y."

Coffey (1975, 62) summarizes MacGregor's Theory X as follows:

> MacGregor points out that from the framework of Theory X, management has outlined various means of accomplishing its task by either reward or punishment. As he saw it, management was confronted with two alternatives inherent in the concept of accomplishing work "through other people"; the "hard management approach" — relying on coercion and threat with stringent control as the mode in directing employee behavior, or the "soft management approach," which included satisfaction of employee demands through permissiveness and focus on harmony, hoping that people managed in this manner would accept organizational direction.

According to MacGregor (1966, 5), Theory X is based on the underlying assumption that "without this active intervention by management, people would be passive — even resistant — to organizations' needs. They must be persuaded, rewarded, punished, controlled — their activities must be directed." Also according to MacGregor, this underlying assumption applies to both the "hard" and "soft" management approaches as defined

FIGURE 6.4 **Organization of the Secretariat of the Federal Ministry of the Solicitor General**

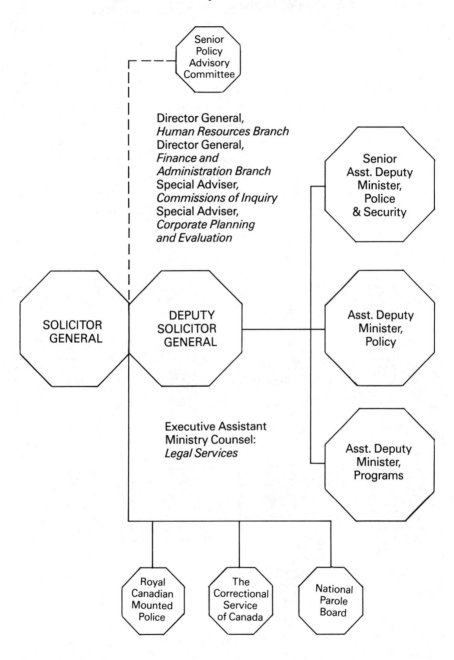

SOURCE: Solicitor General of Canada. 1983. *Annual Report. 1981/82,* p.2.

FIGURE 6.5   Organization of the Ministry of Corrections, Province of Ontario (1981)

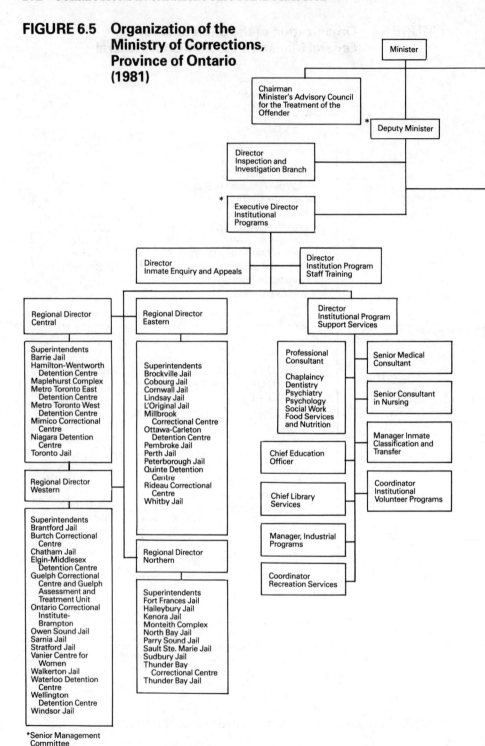

*Senior Management Committee

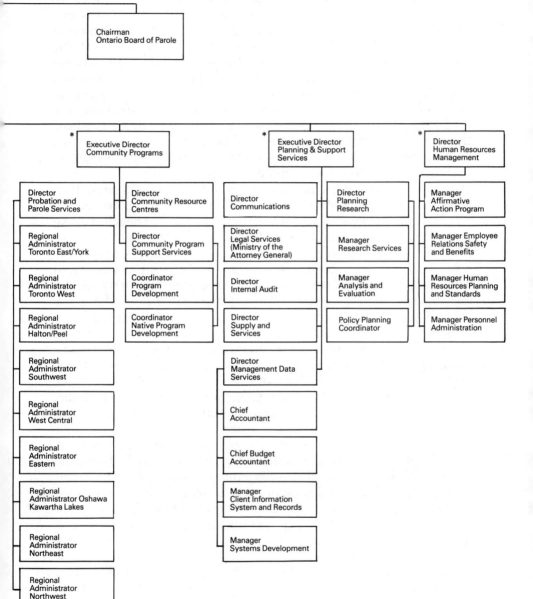

SOURCE: Statistics Canada. 1982. *Correctional Services in Canada, 1980/81.* p. 233.

within Theory X.

In proposing Theory Y, however, MacGregor suggested that another basic assumption is possible based on a re-evaluation of managerial assumptions, including the findings of the behavioural sciences: when given the opportunity, employees can be regarded as having the desire to "do meaningful work." On the basis of this point of view, management and administrative tasks will be organized "in terms of creating opportunities, removing obstacles, providing guidance rather than control, releasing potential and above all else, encouraging growth" (Coffey 1975, 3).

In summary, MacGregor's Theory X is based on the assumption that a manager must use systems of reward and punishment to control and direct the activities of employees. Theory Y proposes that an organization is best served through the positive motivation of employees and, consequently, that the management task is to structure the organization in a way which fosters this potential.

While it is arguable that some elements of both theories are at work in the life of all organizations, the distinctions made by MacGregor are important because they allow managers to assume a predominant position in the development of managerial style. They may adopt a traditional or "command" approach, as encompassed in MacGregor's Theory X, or they may develop a more humanistic or positive style, as suggested in MacGregor's Theory Y.

Since the mid-1960s, there has been a tendency to modify managerial approaches in Canadian corrections toward an increasingly humanistic or participatory style. A number of factors have contributed to this development. As illustrated earlier, there has been a definite movement away from reliance upon a "closed" system of prisons as the primary structure within which programs are delivered. Complementing this trend, there has been a corresponding movement toward creating a wide range of community services which require a much closer liaison with the community-at-large and a higher degree of individual discretion on the part of employees. There also has been a growing tendency to consider corrections as a subsystem within a larger criminal justice system. In turn, such a tendency requires a new emphasis upon promoting coordination and cooperation between criminal justice system components at all levels of operations. Additionally, the paramilitary style of prison administration has been extensively criticized and a variety of public and professional interest groups have pressed for a prison system which is more efficiently and humanely run. All of these factors, coupled with the growing interest in management and organizational theory that is being generated out of the behavioural sciences, have given impetus to the movement toward a less traditional and a more humanistic and participatory style of correctional management.

Resulting from these developments, a number of organizational strategies based on management theory are now being incorporated into corrections management practice. Among them, the two strategies that have received the most attention in recent years are Management by Objectives (MBO) and Organizational Development (OD). Although there are a number of other management strategies which have emerged to influence the correctional enterprise, these two will serve as appropriate illustrations of the general movement.[2]

Organizational Development is a strategy which is employed when a decision is being taken to change the structure of an organization in order to reflect a more humanistic and participatory style. According to Beckhard (1969, 139):

> Organizational Development is an effort (1) planned, (2) organization-wide and (3) managed from the top to (4) increase organization effectiveness and health through (5) planned interventions in the organization's processes using behavioral science knowledge.

The National Advisory Commission on Criminal Justice Standards and Goals (1973, 442-43) discussed Organizational Development as follows:

> Within the organization, individuals are encouraged to develop mutual trust, be candid, openly discuss conflict, and take risks. A premium is placed on the individual's self-actualization fulfillment of his needs within the organization's overall goals and objectives.
>
> A variety of specific interventions are used to implement these ideas and are limited only by the creativity of the change agent. Team building, intergroup problem solving, surveys, reorganization, training in decision-making and problem solving, modifying work flows and job enrichment are examples of the types of techniques frequently employed. An OD program usually involves an outside consultant to begin with, but it is essential to have (or develop) a capability for continuing the program within the organization. Generally, these techniques and processes are used in the work situation — the functions to be performed — to integrate the factors necessary for employee effectiveness (interpersonal skills, individual performance objectives, etc.) with the goals of the organization. OD practitioners feel that this complex process is necessary to relate organization design, planning, objectives, and employee performance.

Bartollas and Miller (1978, 311) support the use of Organizational Development in correctional organizations, stating that:

this approach to organizational renewal can be very helpful in ensuring that correctional institutions become more humane, in developing better teamwork among all levels of staff, in enlarging the commitment of all staff to participatory management, in developing system-wide planned change, and in effecting staff development.

While Organizational Development is a strategy employed to move from a traditional to a participatory style of management, Management by Objectives is a strategy that is adopted in an organization once the commitment to a participatory style has been made. In short, Management by Objectives is a strategy which is applied in the continuing operation of an organization. According to Archambeault and Archambeault (1982, 91): "Management by Objectives is an administrative management system which directs subordinates through mutually agreed-on goals, objectives, and procedures for attainment." Where it was previously assumed that the management task is primarily to maintain the efficiency of current roles and functions, the emphasis now is on the task of determining objectives against which the usefulness of present or future organizational activities can be assessed. Terwilliger and Adams (1969, 227) point out:

> Some of the larger correctional agencies are beginning to focus more sharply on the matter of objectives. Correctional administrators are combining managerial competence with correctional competence for the solution of pressing social problems. It is axiomatic that both the production and the use of tested knowledge tend to force increased attention to ends as well as means.
>
> Specifying objectives and using these objectives as guides for conducting organizational activities is becoming increasingly characteristic of "modern" management in all fields. These techniques are elements of a new managerial model — "management by objectives".
>
> Minimizing reliance on trial and error, rule of thumb, ideology and tradition, this model provides rational guidelines for ordering and allocating manpower, equipment, and fiscal resources. It facilitates the decision-making, simplifies the assessment of performance and, ideally, encourages employees to become self-directing and self-motivating when they identify with organizational goals. (C. Terwilliger and S. Adams, "Probation Department Management and Objectives," *Crime and Delinquency*, vol. 15 (April 1969), p. 227. Copyright © 1969 by the National Council on Crime and Delinquency. Reprinted by permission of Sage Publications, Inc.).

There are a variety of methods which may be used when applying Management by Objectives, but in order to determine whether or not a Management by Objectives strategy is being employed in an organization, it is usually sufficient to observe the manner in which basic functions of the organization are carried out. For instance, the budgeting process is fundamental to the life of any organization. In an organization which is structured to reflect the principles of Management by Objectives, the budgeting process will be geared to promote the highest degree of employee participation possible and will relate financial considerations to the organization's stated objectives.

Pursuing the example further, there are at least two budgeting strategies that may be used in Management by Objectives and that are becoming more common in the development of correctional budgets. These are the techniques of Zero-Base Budgeting (ZBB) and the Program, Planning and Budgeting System (PPBS). As Bartollas and Miller (1978, 93) point out:

> Like most of the participative approaches to management, PPBS and zero-base budgeting enable correctional personnel to understand correctional goals. Both managers and non-managers are urged to participate in the goal setting of their overall organization and of the units in which they work; hence, all are helped to a better understanding of correctional problems.

The National Advisory Commission on Criminal Justice Standards and Goals (1973, 448) defines PPBS as:

> a system-oriented effort to link planning, budgeting, and management by objective processes through programs. Under this system an agency or organization first would ask itself: "what is our purpose, and what goals are we attempting to realize?"
>
> Once our purposes or objectives have been determined, action programs to achieve these objectives would be identified or, if nonexistent, designed.
>
> Next, each such program would be analyzed. In existing programs, the analysis would be in terms of the extent to which they were oriented to achievement of the organization's objectives. Reference would be made to the level of effectiveness at which they were functioning toward such attainment. In the case of newly formulated, objective-oriented programs, the analysis would be in terms of their anticipated costs and expected contribution to accomplishment of organizational objectives.
>
> Finally, in terms of the decision-making process, existing and new alternative programs would be analytically compared as to their respective costs and anticipated benefits. Should an alternative, on the basis of such a cost-benefit analysis, be deemed preferable to an existing program, the latter would be discarded and the alternative adopted.
>
> Implicit in this management system is a longer-range programming perspective coupled with a continuous process of reevaluation of objectives, programs, and budgetary amounts as circumstances change.

Zero-Base Budgeting is a method of making budget decisions which is similar to PPBS but narrower in scale. In the Zero-Base Budgeting process, all of the more important functional goals pursued by subunits within the organization are identified. Next, each manager responsible for a subunit determines the program costs associated with each budget cycle by reassessing the total program in relation to the goals which have been determined for it and in relation to the functions that are expected of it. Zero-Base Budgeting also requires that the managers of each of the subunits strive for common agreement on goals in order to coordinate the activities of the collective subunits in relation to the overall objectives of the organization. The primary purpose of such an exercise is to avoid duplication of both cost and function.

In Zero-Base Budgeting it is not assumed that any approved expenditures for one year will be carried over into the next year. This forces all units of the organization to constantly reassess their programs and associated costs in relation to the goals expressed by the organization as a whole. As Bartollas and Miller (1978, 94) note:

> Much of the appeal of zero-base budgeting lies in its compatibility with MBO and other types of participative management. All personnel are helped to understand how their organization functions and the budgetary problems of its managers and administrators. Lower-level participants, in addition, help to define the scope of department efforts and the costs thereof. Upper-level managers also can have confidence that all alternative courses of action have been considered before proposals reach them. Since the alternatives are described, they can be reviewed if necessary to determine why some were rejected. Finally, planning must take place on the organizational level, and zero-base budgeting forces personnel to make the essential evaluations. (From *Correctional Administration: Theory and Practice*, 1978, New York: McGraw-Hill. Reproduced with permission.)

TRAINING AND EDUCATION
OF CORRECTIONAL PERSONNEL

In the final analysis, it is the people that count. This is particularly true in correctional organizations where all policies, structures, material and "systems" are geared to support a series of relationships between people, among whom the offender is the central figure.

FIGURE 6.6 Distribution of Average Per Diem Costs—Federal Corrections 1980-81

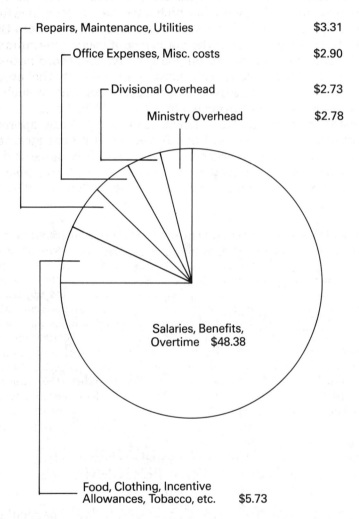

Repairs, Maintenance, Utilities	$3.31
Office Expenses, Misc. costs	$2.90
Divisional Overhead	$2.73
Ministry Overhead	$2.78

Salaries, Benefits,
Overtime $48.38

Food, Clothing, Incentive
Allowances, Tobacco, etc. $5.73

It is important to remember that corrections is a labour intensive activity of government and that personnel costs account for approximately 70 percent of the total operational budget of the Canadian correctional enterprise[3] (see Figure 6.6 for example of cost distribution).

Corrections does not produce a measurable product. At best, its process, as well as the activities within that process, can be evaluated in relation to some broad and intangible set of goals such as contribution to public safety, fairness and efficiency in the provision of dispositions for offenders, or presenting opportunities for rehabilitation and treatment. It is within the nature of correctional work that personnel are expected to exercise a high degree of latitude and discretion in the provision of services. It follows that management policy must address the training and education requirements of staff to be effective.[4]

All correctional policies attempt to address these and similar goals. And the structures of planning, management and administration contribute to the development and implementation of those policies. But since the goals are intangible and subject to continual flux and change resulting from social, political and economic circumstances, and since the substantial product is unmeasurable (how does one measure justice?), the best a correctional organization can do is to provide policies and support systems which offer the greatest opportunity for the system's employees to relate to the system's clients in ways that most closely approximate the organization's policy intentions.

The key to service delivery in corrections is found in the manner in which correctional employees exercise their discretion when working directly with correctional clients. This is true whether those clients are considered to be members of the public-at-large, representatives of other operating subsystems within criminal justice, or offenders. In corrections, the use of discretion at the line level is central to effective policy implementation. For discretionary decision making to remain faithful to the policy intentions of a system which is subject to continual change and growing complexity, a foundation of training and education is required. Therefore, the commitment of correctional organizations to training and education is central to their ability to make and implement policy.

The movements within corrections to develop structures for management and administration which promote and support participation of corrections personnel has already been noted. These movements recognize that corrections is essentially a human-relations activity and that the motivation, attitude, and sense of commitment of personnel is especially important. But to manage a system which recognizes and promotes the proper use of discretion on the part of its personnel requires special skills. Consequently, training and education programs are necessary at the management level.

The increasing sophistication and use of technology to provide information for decision making and the development of effective procedures for service delivery also involve a commitment to training and education at the administrative level. This is particularly important in order to ensure that systems and technologies do not override or diminish the ability of personnel to use their discretion in an effective way. The ability of line personnel to understand policy intentions and to work within the limits of law and regulation further requires a significant commitment to training and education. The degree to which any participant in the organization suffers from a lack of support for training and education is directly related to the ability of the organization to develop and to successfully implement its policies.

The use of the terms "training" and "education" is not accidental. These are distinct emphases within the learning process, particularly in a system where the implementation of policy depends so much on the exercise of individual discretion. In a report of the Justice Institute of British Columbia (1980, 62) the difference between training and education is discussed and the following comment is made:

> While both activities involve learning, their objectives vary. The transfer of knowledge that education deals with is produced out of academic exploration that is value-laden and open-ended. Training, on the other hand, involves instruction that is finite and task-specific.

Archambeault and Archambeault (1982, 320-21) also discuss the distinction between training and education:

> Criminal justice (criminology) draws a major distinction between training and education, a distinction that is currently held by many academicians . . . training is generally considered to be specific job-oriented knowledge or skills instruction which prepares a person to work in a given job in a given agency or type of agency. Education, on the other hand, reflects a liberal arts orientation and is defined as developing a person's general knowledge and power of critical reasoning, derived from the study of criminal justice (criminology) literature and theory, and making a person able to adapt to a broad range of criminal justice or criminological settings.

Correctional organizations have been severely criticized for their lack of commitment to the training and education of personnel at all levels. Traditionally, the learning opportunities provided for correctional personnel have concentrated on the provision of minimum levels of training associated with the tasks to be performed in particular job settings. In institutional programs, it has not been uncommon for persons to be employed with no training whatsoever and to work for some considerable period of time before minimal training opportunities are provided.[5]

Where training has been made available, it has often tended to be *ad hoc* and unrelated to any overall plan for the training and education of employees. Some commentators regard this as the reason for the rigidity of many correctional organizations and for the difficulties which have been encountered when adjusting to change or to the implementation of new policies.[6]

In Canada, as elsewhere in North America, progress is now being reported with regard to the training and education of correctional personnel. However, such positive indications have only recently begun to emerge and no major initiatives in correctional staff development are evident prior to the 1970s. In the United States, the National Advisory Commission on Criminal Justice Standards and Goals (1973) found it necessary to make a firm recommendation that "correctional agencies immediately should plan and implement a staff development program that prepares and sustains all staff members." In discussing this recommendation, the following comment was made (1973, 494):

> While low priority continues to be given to the development of correctional staff in some sections of the country, the picture is changing in others . . . substantial funds have been pumped into corrections for staff development. But use of these funds is uneven, with many agencies failing to participate through lack of interest and others operating training programs of poor quality.

The federal/provincial Deputy Ministers responsible for Corrections established a task force on manpower planning in 1974, in recognition of the need to improve, upgrade, and standardize correctional manpower training and education in Canada. As a result of this initiative some considerable improvement has been made regarding the nature of training and education programs provided for staff — particularly at management and supervisory levels. Similarly, individual provinces have taken a variety of initiatives in recent years to improve their correctional staff development programs.

In the Province of British Columbia, for instance, correctional staff development has been merged with an overall criminal justice training and education program provided through the Justice Institute of British Columbia. This program, as well as others across the country, has attempted to coordinate the development of specialized training programs with education opportunities provided through universities and community colleges. The Correctional Manpower Planning, Training and Development Project[7] reported that "British Columbia, Ontario and the Canadian Penitentiary Service have sizeable training staffs and make use of specialized staff training facilities. In other jurisdictions, staffs are relatively more modest or non-existent and specialized training facilities are not in use" (Segal and Hawes 1976, 19).

However, since this report was written, a number of new initiatives have taken place. For example, in Alberta, a new centralized staff training unit has been developed within the correctional services division. The *Annual Report, 1979/80* of the Office of the Solicitor General of Alberta (1981, 43) states:

> Training for recruits consists of a 180 hour program spaced during the first six months of employment as a correctional officer. This course is recognized by Provincial community colleges as 14 credits toward a certificate in criminal justice. The remainder of the credits (21) are offered on a voluntary basis via community college instruction. These voluntary courses are being transformed into a self-study format whereby recruits and in-service officers can commence and complete job-related courses at their own rate.

General developments of this nature, occurring across North America, lead Bartollas and Miller (1978, 327) to comment:

> Staff development is becoming an important concern in corrections today. The major factors in its growing popularity are as follows: the increasing demand for professionalism in corrections; the series of national commissions that challenged corrections to give the public more for its money; the growing number of civil lawsuits resulting from unprofessional handling of offenders; the fact that professional organizations which deal with the areas of management, social work, psychiatry, and psychology all emphasize the importance of highly skilled and trained practitioners; and the emerging expectations of both the private and public sectors that staff development is a required component of organizational life.
>
> As a result of these pressures, a growing number of correctional institutions either are providing staff development programs or are encouraging personnel to attend training programs elsewhere. Achieving the goal of developing more staff who are able to understand the needs of correctional clients, to work with them humanely, and to help them achieve full citizenship would allow administrators to add many more to a small cadre of staff in every organization who are genuinely concerned about helping offenders. Our experience in correctional institutions leads us to believe that the staff member who cares and responds to the resident as a human being does make a difference. (From Bartollas and Miller,

Correctional Administration: Theory and Practice, 1978, New York: McGraw-Hill. Reproduced with permission.)

SUMMARY

It has been illustrated that correctional policy and planning involves a series of relationships which include public interests, political interests, management and administrative interests, and the interests of line personnel. In keeping with the mandate which applies to all correctional agencies, these combined interests ought to be centred on the provision of services to persons who have been found guilty of an offence in law and for whom a penalty has been prescribed.

Additionally, in this and the two preceding chapters, there has been an attempt to provide an overview of the organizational structures, decision-making processes, tools and technologies which can be brought to bear on the exercise of the corrections mandate. The following chapters provide a description of the correctional programs which exist in Canada as a result of the policy, planning, and management processes.

Notes

1. If one looks at annual reports of different government services, the operational definitions of management and administrative tasks become apparent. For example, the Public Service Commission of Canada (1981, 44) defines a management category as follows:

> An occupational category . . . which encompasses senior personnel having responsibility for policy development; program formulation and delivery; the design and operation of management machinery; and management of personnel, finances and public affairs."

On the other hand, a clear illustration of the manner in which administrative tasks are perceived may be found in the 1981/82 *Annual Report* of the Social Sciences and Humanities Research Council of Canada (1982, 107):

> The responsibilities of the administrative services section are to provide and coordinate the council requirements of goods and services, accommodation, material and contract management, records management and other administrative support services.

2. Numerous other terms have been used to discuss emphases or strategies employed by management. In the corrections context, Jayewardene and Jayasuriya (1981, 2-8) used the terms "traditional autocracy" and "participatory management" in their discussion of types of management styles which have been or may be employed in correctional settings. Management by Objectives and Organizational Development would be placed under the general category of participatory management. Watson (1981) has coined the phrases "results-oriented managing" and "activities-centered management." Donald (1967, 122) discusses the concept of "management by exception" and Drucker (1977, 358ff) discusses the concept of "management by drives." All of these terms are intended to depict a style or emphasis which is employed organizationally by managers to accomplish the management task.

3. The *Justice Information Report — Correctional Services in Canada 1978/79, 1979/80* (National Work Group on Justice Information and Statistics 1981, 43) reports that "salaries, wages, and other personnel costs accounted for over 65% of the total National Parole Board and Correctional Service of Canada expenditures in both years." This report (1981, 343) also calculates the personnel expenditures for provincial and territorial correctional services as a percentage of total correctional expenditures. On average, personnel expenditures accounted for 76.8 percent of the total correctional expenditures by provincial and territorial governments for the fiscal year 1979/80.

4. In *The Role of Federal Corrections in Canada* (Task Force on the Creation of an Integrated Canadian Corrections Service 1977, 112) the following comment is made: "The climate in a penitentiary is attractive to few, there is a continuing problem with recruitment and a very high turnover. The correctional staff face the conflict between the "coercive" and "helping" roles in a direct and personal way. No amount of good planning or effective management can be sufficient without staff support and staff understanding of management's intentions, programs and methods."

5. In the report to Parliament of the Sub-Committee on the Penitentiary System in Canada (MacGuigan 1977, 52), the following comments were made with regard to staff training:

Along with the lack of discrimination in recruitment the Sub-Committee was greatly struck by the lack of training of those who work on the front line . . . Correctional officers have been assigned to work in institutions prior to receiving their induction training . . . Correctional officers have been employed for 15, 20 and even 27 years without receiving any training subsequent to their initial induction course.

Hawkins (1976, 106-107) comments on the training of correctional officers in the United States as follows:

The truth, as it emerges from the few studies which pay attention to prison guards and view them objectively, is simply that these guards were and are for the most part ordinary human beings with ordinary human failings and virtues. They have in the past been asked to perform impossible tasks without being properly trained to perform even possible ones. It is an extraordinary feature of the history of prisons that it was not until the 1930s that the first formally organized training programs for prison guards and custodial officers appeared in America. Many institutions still provide no full-time preparatory training for them before they start work. At the same time, they are the lowest paid of all correctional employees. We shall achieve nothing — worse, we are likely to do active harm — in prison until we carefully select, train as thoroughly as we know how, and properly recompense the prison officer of the basic grade. (G. Hawkins, *The Prison: Policy and Practice.* © 1976 The University of Chicago. Reprinted with permission.)

6. Segal and Hawes (1976, 52), in a study based on interviews with 569 institutional, probation and parole staff across Canada, reported that "post-employment training courses offered to probation and parole workers appeared to be effective in increasing the workers' awareness of organizational goals. Only 59% of those with two or fewer courses feel clear about organizational goals. This figure increases to 79% for those with three or more training courses." This report generally concluded that due to a lack of appropriate training programs "a large proportion of both probation, parole workers and institutional staff do not feel they have the necessary knowledge required to perform the tasks associated with their work." See also, Willet 1983.

In the report *Perspectives in Correctional Manpower and Training* (Joint Commission on Correctional Manpower and Training 1970, 108-109) the following comments are made:

It may well be said that the effectiveness of an organization is directly related to the quality of its training programs for new employees . . . when performance of familiar tasks is below expectations, training is an appropriate strategy. But training is even more essential when major changes in goals and procedures are contemplated. Employees, as individuals and groups, must learn new tasks and new contexts for familiar tasks. New divisions of labor and systems of inter-relation must be learned. Because change breeds insecurity, training provides understanding that is essential to staff morale.

7. This task force on manpower planning came to be known as the National Advisory Network on Correctional Manpower Planning, Training and Development. The National Advisory Network sponsored a correctional manpower planning, training and development project which was undertaken by Carleton University in Ottawa. This project resulted in the publication of three research reports on the subject authored by Brian Segal and Grant Hawes.

References

Archambeault, W.G. and B.J. Archambeault. 1982. *Correctional Supervisory Management: Principles of Organization, Policy and Law.* Englewood Cliffs, N.J.: Prentice-Hall.

Bartollas, C. and S.J. Miller. 1978. *Correctional Administration: Theory and Practice.* New York: McGraw-Hill.

Beckhard, R. 1969. *Organizational Development: Strategies and Models.* Reading, Mass: Addison-Wesley.

Black, H.C. 1979 *Black's Law Dictionary* (5th ed.). St. Paul, Minnesota: West Publishing Co.

Coffey, A.R. 1975. *Correctional Administration: The Manpower of Institutions, Probation and Parole.* Englewood Cliffs, N.J.: Prentice-Hall.

Donald, A.G. 1967. *Management Information and Systems.* Toronto: Pergamon Press.

Drucker, P. 1977. *An Introductory View of Management.* New York: Harper's College Press.

Hawkins, G. 1976. *The Prison: Policy and Practice.* Chicago: University of Chicago Press.

Jayewardene, C.H.S. and D.J.N. Jayasuriya. 1981. *The Management of Correctional Institutions.* Toronto: Butterworths.

Joint Commission on Correctional Manpower and Training. 1970. *Perspectives on Correctional Manpower and Training.* Washington, D.C.: U.S. Government Printing Office.

Justice Institute of British Columbia. (April) 1980. *1980-85: A Plan for the Future.* Vancouver.

MacGregor, D. 1960. *The Human Side of Enterprise.* New York: McGraw-Hill.

_____. 1966. *Leadership and Motivation.* Cambridge, Mass.: MIT Press.

MacGuigan, M. (Chairman). 1977. *Report to Parliament by the Sub-Committee on the Penitentiary System in Canada.* Ottawa: Supply and Services Canada.

National Advisory Commission on Criminal Justice Standards and Goals. 1973. *Corrections.* Washington, D.C.: U.S. Government Printing Office.

National Work Group on Justice Information and Statistics. 1981. *Justice Information Report — Correctional Services in Canada, 1978/79, 1979/80.* Ottawa.

Public Service Commission of Canada. 1981. *Annual Report.* Ottawa: Supply and Services Canada.

Segal, B. and G. Hawes. 1976. *Correctional Manpower, Planning, Training and Development Project.* Ottawa: National Advisory Network on Correctional Manpower, Planning, Training and Development. Carleton University.

Social Sciences and Humanities Research Council of Canada. 1982. *Annual Report, 1981/82.* Ottawa: Supply and Services Canada.

Solicitor General of Alberta. 1981. *Annual Report, 1979/80.* Edmonton: Queen's Printer.

Solicitor General of Canada. 1983. *Annual Report, 1981/82.* Ottawa: Supply and Services Canada.

Statistics Canada. 1982. *Correctional Services in Canada, 1980/81.* Ottawa: Canadian Centre for Justice Statistics.

Task Force on the Creation of an Integrated Canadian Corrections Service. 1977. *The Role of Federal Corrections in Canada.* Ottawa: Supply and Services Canada.

Terwilliger, C. and S. Adams. (April) 1969. "Probation Department Management and Objectives." 15 *Crime and Delinquency.* 227-30.

Watson, C.E. 1981. *Results-Oriented Managing: The Key to Effective Performance.* Toronto: Addison-Wesley.

Willet, T.C. (January) 1983. "Prison Guards in Private." 25 *Canadian Journal of Criminology.* 1-18.

Chapter 7

Correctional
Treatment Programs

The emergence of the rehabilitative model of corrections in the years following World War II, facilitated by the recommendations of the Archambault Report (1938) and the findings of the Fauteux Commission (1956), resulted in the development of a wide range of programs in federal and provincial institutions designed to treat and rehabilitate offenders.

Implicit in the term "rehabilitation" is the notion of change and an attempt to modify the attitudes and behaviours of offenders so as to reduce the incidence of criminal behaviour. Smith and Berlin (1981, 45) define treatment as including the techniques of "reeducating, conditioning, counseling and reinforcing aimed at changing the criminal into a conforming member of society." One of the major cornerstones of this change effort is the medical model, which views criminal behaviour as a manifestation of an underlying disorder within the offender. Diagnosis of this disorder by behavioural science professionals, followed by appropriate therapeutic intervention, would serve to correct the disorder and thereby reduce or eliminate the individual's criminality.

During the 1950s and 1960s, "treatment" and "rehabilitation" were used frequently (and quite loosely) to describe various policy and program initiatives in federal and provincial corrections. As Marshall (1981, 23) notes:

> After the introduction of the rehabilitation model in corrections, virtually everything done with, for, or to the offender after conviction was labeled "treatment". . . . A wide variety of programs and correctional measures have been included under the catch-all term "treatment", ranging from teaching an inmate how to make a license plate to solitary confinement to intensive forms of individual psychotherapy.

In this chapter, we will examine "treatment" initiatives that have been implemented in Canadian correctional facilities. These include education and vocational training programs, which are the oldest types of institutional programs, as well as specific treatment modalities. Of particular concern in our discussion will be the objectives of the various treatment initiatives and the continuing debate over their effectiveness.[1]

Much of our discussion will address programs in federal institutions. Given the relatively short period of time that offenders spend in provincial institutions under the two-year rule, and the diversity among the provinces in their correctional operations, a systematic examination of provincial correctional programs is beyond the scope of this text.

THE CLASSIFICATION PROCESS

A critical component of the correctional treatment process that must be addressed, prior to a consideration of specific program initiatives, is classification. This is the process by which offenders are assigned to specific institutions to serve their term of confinement. This, in turn, determines the types of treatment programs to which the offender may be exposed, as well as the institutional environment in which such programs are carried out.

In the Canadian criminal justice system, classification assumes a very important role in the correctional process, as the judge does not sentence an offender to a specific correctional institution, but rather for a period of incarceration that places him/her under the jurisdiction of either the federal or the provincial correctional system[2] (see Chapter 2 for a discussion of correctional jurisdiction). In addition, classification is a critical component of the rehabilitative model of corrections, the Ouimet Committee (1969, 311) defining it as "a continuous process through which diagnosis, treatment-planning and the execution of the treatment plan are coordinated to the end that the individual inmate may be rehabilitated."

Those offenders whose sentence length places them under federal jurisdiction are classified in the provincial institution to which they have been remanded. The sole exception is in Quebec, where a regional reception centre for federal offenders still operates. Classification boards and classification officers are responsible for classifying persons directly from the provincial remand centre to the appropriate federal institution. For those offenders whose sentence places them under provincial jurisdiction, each province has a classification unit which is responsible for both the assessment of the offender's security level and needs and the institutional placement decision.[3]

The classification assessment on which the initial placement decision is made for federal offenders is conducted by parole officers of the Correctional Service of Canada. In classifying offenders, a Benchmark System is used. The offender is interviewed by a placement officer who makes a needs analysis, including the training, treatment, and security requirements of the offender. The predominant factor at this stage of classification is the security requirements of the offender, although assignment to a specific institution may be affected by available bedspace.

Traditionally, the system of classification for federal offenders employed three broad levels of security that were based on the degree of likelihood that the offender would escape and on the potential harm to the community should he do so. These are as follows:

1. *Maximum security:* the inmate is likely to escape and, if successful, would be likely to cause serious harm in the community;
2. *Medium security:* the inmate is likely to escape if given the opportunity but should not cause serious harm in the community;
3. *Minimum security:* the inmate is not likely to escape and would not cause harm within the community if he did so.

During fiscal year 1981/1982, a new policy designating institutions at one of seven security levels was implemented. The levels range from Level 7, which are the Special Handling Units (super-max) for violent and extremely dangerous offenders, to Level 1, which are community corrections centres. At Level 6 are situated the maximum security facilities, while Levels 3, 4, and 5 represent different degrees of medium security. Level 2 facilities are minimum security, including forestry and work camps. In Table 7.1, the correctional facilities operated by the Correctional Service of Canada are categorized by security level.[4]

The classification of offenders in federal corrections has come under increasing scrutiny and criticism in recent years. The MacGuigan Subcommittee (1977, 130) described the federal classification system as "disorganized" and expressed concern about the "overclassification" of inmates and the regional variations in classification decision making. The Carson Committee (1984) also raised questions about the viability of the seven-level security system and the practice of "cascading" inmates (that is, moving them to progressively lower levels of security over the course of their confinement). Concern has also been expressed regarding the "overclassification" of offenders,

TABLE 7.1 Federal Correctional Institutions by Security Classification

| Minimum Security | | | Medium Security | | Maximum Security | | Multi-Level |
S1	S2	S3	S4	S5	S6	S7	ML
Carlton (N.S.)	Westmorland Farm (N.B.)	La Macaza (P.Q.)	Springhill (N.S.)	Leclerc (P.Q.)	Dorchester (N.B.)	Regional Reception Centre (P.Q.)	Regional Reception Centre (P.Q.)
Sand River (N.S.)	Montée-St-François (P.Q.)	Bowden (Alta.)	Cowansville (P.Q.)	Collins Bay (Ont.)	Archambault (P.Q.)	Sask. Pen. (Sask.)	Kingston Pen. (Ont.)
Parrtown (N.B.)	Ste-Anne-des-Plaines (P.Q.)	Mountain (B.C.)	Drummond (P.Q.)	Stony Mountain (Man.)	Laval (P.Q.)		Prison for Women (Ont.)
Bencit XV (P.Q.)	Bath (Ont.)	William Head (B.C.)	Federal Trng. Centre (P.Q.)	Matsqui (B.C.)	Millhaven (Ont.)		Regional Psychiatric Centre (Ont.)
Laferrière (P.Q.)	Beaver Creek (Ont.)		Joyceville (Ont.)		Edmonton (Alta.)		Regional Psychiatric Centre (Sask.)
Martineau (P.Q.)	Frontenac Farm (Ont.)		Warkworth (Ont.)		Kent (B.C.)		Sask. Pen. (Sask.)
Ogilvy (P.Q.)	Pittsburgh Farm (Ont.)		Drumheller (Alta.)				Regional Psychiatric Centre (B.C.)
Pie IX	Rockwood		Mission				

(P.Q.)

Annex
(Sask.)

Keele St.
(Ont.)

Grierson
(Alta.)

Montgomery
(Ont.)

Elbow Lake
(B.C.)

Portsmouth
(Ont.)

Ferndale
(B.C.)

Osborne
(Man.)

Oskana
(Sask.)

Altadore
(Alta.)

Portal House
(Alta.)

Pandora
(B.C.)

Robson
(B.C.)

Sumas
(B.C.)

SOURCE: Statistics Canada. 1986. *Adult Correctional Services in Canada, 1985-86*. Ottawa: Canadian Centre for Justice Statistics.

NOTE: S1/S2: open facilities with normal household locks; S3/S4: moderately controlled facilities with perimeter fences (may include armed posts); S6/S7: highly controlled facilities with perimeter fences, internal physical barriers, and armed posts; ML: multi-level facilities, all or part of which may be highly controlled and may house all levels of classification.

particularly in maximum security institutions, the Subcommittee (1977, 131-32) noting: "Since the overcrowding is particularly serious in medium security institutions, there are a large number of inmates presently in maximum security who would, under normal conditions, be in medium security" (see also Gosselin 1982).

The difficulties associated with the proper classification of offenders and the fact that such a process is often subjective rather than premised on established predictive guidelines must be a major consideration in any discussion of correctional treatment.

PRISON EDUCATION PROGRAMS

Throughout the 1800s the primary task of the penitentiary was punishment and the emphasis was on hard labour and solitary confinement enforced by a strict code of discipline. This in turn was supported by the extensive use of corporal punishment. Although the Brown Commission had recommended the creation of education programs in its 1848 report, attempts to introduce basic literacy courses in the Kingston, Ontario penitentiary encountered considerable opposition. Critics argued that such programs detracted from the regimen of hard labour and discipline necessary for the reformation of criminal offenders. The literacy training programs which did eventually develop during this time were closely allied with the religious efforts in the penitentiary. Cosman (1980) points out that prison education was thought of in association with spiritual development and was viewed as the responsibility of the prison chaplain. Similarly, Weir (1973, 40) has observed that

> the chapel was the classroom for the forty-minute daily period of instruction, the chaplain was the schoolmaster, and the Bible the text in the sense that the objective of the basic literary program was to enable the scholar to become familiar with the Bible.

During this time, education was seen in terms of its moral value and it was not until the late 1800s that educational programs began to assume a separate identity, although participation in them by inmates was viewed as a privilege. Weir (1973, 41) cites the *Report of Penitentiaries* in 1879: " 'the rules and regulations for school' encourage the enforcement of strict discipline and allow only those convicts noted for good conduct after a minimum of three months in prison to take part in classes. The opportunity to attend school was considered one of the highest rewards that could be bestowed on convicts." However, Weir (1973, 41) is quick to note that education continued to play only a secondary role in the reformation of convicts: "According to the 1888 Penitentiary Act, Rules and Regulations, the schoolmaster was under the immediate supervision of the chaplain; his speaking with inmates outside of his teaching task was prohibited."

While the 1914 *Report of the Royal Commission on Penitentiaries* was the first public recognition of education as a valuable component of the reformation process, numerous difficulties were encountered, as Weir (1973, 42) observes: "in 1927 educational lectures were not permitted; in 1933 while individual studies were permitted, no books were provided, and in the same year subscriptions to magazines and periodicals, while tolerated, were subject to rigorous censorship."

Perhaps the strongest influence on the development of prison education programs were the recommendations of the Archambault Report (1938), which called for a complete reorganization of the educational system. However, it was not until the post-World War II years that any real initiatives in prison education occurred.

Further impetus for the development of elementary and secondary school programs was provided by the Fauteux Report in 1956. The authors of the Report expressed dissatisfaction with the correctional system's lack of progress in developing education programs and identified prison education as a major component of the treatment process.

During the 1950s and 1960s, educational programs providing literacy training and elementary and secondary school courses were widely introduced in federal correctional facilities.[5] Since the early 1970s, post-secondary school programs have been operating in federal institutions in British Columbia, at Stony Mountain prison in Manitoba, at Laval, Quebec, and at the federal prison at Collins Bay, Ontario. Of particular note is the internationally acclaimed program operated by Simon Fraser University in British Columbia, which has been used as a model for prison education programs in the United States and overseas.[6]

The distinguishing characteristic of the Simon Fraser University post-secondary school program is its conceptual foundation. Duguid (1979, 83-84) summarizes the philosophy of the program, which focuses on the moral development of the offender:

> The program emphasizes the role of cognitive growth in producing changes in moral reasoning which in turn facilitates changed behavior. This . . . is based on two premises . . . First, the criminal has been more a

decision-maker than a victim . . . despite environmental, family, and class factors, there remains a strong element of choice in the act of becoming a criminal . . . The second premise . . . is that the decisions of the criminal are made in the context of a certain stage of cognitive/moral development and that this stage can be altered in order to facilitate different decisions within the same or similar environment (see also Kohlberg et al. 1974; Duguid 1980, 1981a, 1981b, 1983).

Despite the expansion of elementary, secondary, and post-secondary courses in federal institutions, numerous problems have plagued prison education programs. The MacGuigan Subcommittee (1977) reported from its investigation that education programs suffered from a lack of qualified teachers, as well as deficient curricula. Similarly, Griffin (1978, 72, 74) has argued that physical facilities for educational programs are inadequate in most institutions, that there has been a failure to establish standards for the selection and training of educational staff in institutions, and that there is no uniformity in measuring the educational achievements of inmates among the different institutions.

Griffin (1978, 62) notes that while many observers view prison education as a means of moral reformation, others see it as a means of increasing the employability of the inmate upon release.

A major obstacle encountered by prison education programs is the incompatibility between the learning process and the environment of the prison. Duguid (1979, 88) notes:

The university program takes place in almost complete isolation from the surrounding prison environment. The students arrive in the morning and return in the late afternoon. Thus part of their day is spent in an extremely authoritarian environment and the other in a much more democratic environment. This, of course, produces confusion and tension as one switches roles each day and frequently tries to apply the wrong practices to the wrong community.

The attributes of initiative, democracy, and independence of thought which characterize the learning process may conflict with the custody and control goals of the institution, which demand compliance, passivity, and dependence.

Campbell (1974, 128) has also noted that education programs may get caught in the tension between the rehabilitative goals of the prison and the concerns for security and control: "Custody personnel will feel that problems of education and other treatment efforts interfere with their custodial function. Treatment personnel, equally, will contend that the opposite is true. The rationale through which the one is harmonized with the other has yet to be developed." Each of these factors, the conflict between the goals of various treatment initiatives and those of the prison, as well as the tensions between the treatment staff and the custody staff, are discussed in greater detail in Chapter 8. At this point, suffice it to say that such conflicts and tensions have significant implications for the operation of prison education programs (and other treatment initiatives), and may significantly affect their ultimate success in facilitating the rehabilitation of the offender.

One of the major difficulties in assessing the efficacy of prison education programs in reducing or eliminating the criminal behaviour of participating inmates is the lack of evaluative research. Waldo (1973, 369) notes that several early evaluations conducted by Lanne (1938), Schur (1948), and Saden (1962) reported significant differences in post-release behaviour of men who had participated in educational programs while confined and those who had not. On the other hand, Lewis (cited in Greenberg 1977, 121) found no differences in the recidivism rates of inmates who had participated in a college education program in a U.S. prison and those who had not. Lewis reported that, at the end of a 33-month period following release, approximately 33 percent of those released from each group had been returned to prison.

Few evaluations have been conducted on the effectiveness of prison education programs in Canadian institutions. Duguid (1981a) reports the results of an evaluation of the University of Victoria program which revealed that in a followup study of 75 program alumni, virtually all were employed, and in the three-year term of the study, only 15 percent had been reincarcerated as compared to a rate of 55-65 percent for those not in the program. Further, Duguid (1981a, 155) notes that "among many of the students there are stated and acted upon ambitions to continue their academic endeavours upon release with the intention of using their education to begin a new career" (see also Linden et al. 1984; Gendreau et al. 1985). However, a major problem with this and most other investigations of the effectiveness of prison education programs is the lack of proper controls in the evaluation.[7]

Perhaps one of the most extensive and well-designed evaluations of the impact of the effectiveness of prison education programs was conducted by Glaser (1964) and reported in the volume *The Effectiveness of a Prison and Parole System.* The findings of the study with respect to prison education were as follows:

1. For most inmates, prison education is statistically associated

with above average post-release success only when the
education is extensive and occurs in the course of prolonged
confinement;
2. For most prisoners, especially those with extensive felony
records, the usual duration and types of involvement in prison
education are associated with *higher than average post-release
failure* (emphasis added);
3. A small amount of education in prison frequently impairs post-
release prospects of inmates indirectly, by inspiring them with
unrealistic aspirations, or by the education's being pursued
instead of alternative prison programs which could provide
more useful preparation for post-release life.

Glaser's findings indicated that inmates attending school
during a longer period of confinement and who advanced through
several grade levels had higher rates of success upon release than
those who attended for only shorter periods of time or not at all.
Further, Glaser raises the possibility that education may prove
dysfunctional for the inmate, both in terms of there being other
more viable options for treatment within the institution and in
terms of unrealistic expectations that it may raise in the inmate.
However, in a review of these findings (1973, 351), he cautions that
the results may be due to the selection of inmates for school or the
initial attributes of those inmates who advance in grade level as
opposed to those who do not, rather than being due to the effects of
the education program itself.

Our brief consideration of prison education programs indicates
that while such initiatives have a long history in Canadian
correctional institutions, numerous obstacles have been
encountered that have limited their effectiveness. Further, it can
be argued that, despite the recommendations of the Archambault
Commission (1938) and the Fauteux Report (1956), Canadian
corrections has not been successful in establishing a uniform
system of prison education including provision for adequate
facilities, staffing, and curriculum. McCarthy (1985, 451) has been
particularly critical of the "half-hearted" support for prison
education by the CSC, and argues that the development of a viable
and effective nation-wide program is not a high priority.

As will become evident in our discussion of the effectiveness of
correctional treatment, when such initiatives are perceived to fail
in reducing criminal behaviour, the inclination is to challenge the
viability of the programs. At this early juncture, it is suggested
that the historical materials presented provide conclusive evidence
that, as with many other treatment initiatives, prison education

has continued to be plagued by problems that hinder its operation. It remains unknown whether education for incarcerated offenders, if conducted within a supportive environment and involving certain types of offenders, might have a positive impact on post-release behaviour (see Morin 1981).

VOCATIONAL TRAINING PROGRAMS

From our discussion of the history of corrections in Chapter 2, it will be recalled that in the mid-1700s and the early 1800s, the Province of Nova Scotia encountered considerable opposition to its attempt to develop a system of workhouses similar to those which had first appeared in England in the 1500s. These were designed to instill the Protestant work ethic in the dependent and deviant populations. Further, in what was one of the first efforts of organized labour in Canada, the mechanics in Kingston successfully opposed the teaching of craft skills to inmates in the newly completed penitentiary. This resistance, in conjunction with the prevailing view of criminal offenders, resulted in convict labour being utilized primarily for the maintenance of the institution.

In considering the similar types of problems encountered in the U.S., Marshall (1981, 23) points out that "although hard work was a guiding reform principle of the nineteenth century penal practitioners, its presumed rehabilitative value probably was less important than its contribution to the institutional financial picture." Similarly, Lightman (1982, 37) argues that in the nineteenth century, "prisoners in both the United States and Canada were viewed primarily as a cheap and readily exploitable source of labour: by their work activity making products such as boots, shoes and clothing, inmates could help contribute to the costs of their upkeep" (see also Chunn 1981).

The importance of providing meaningful work experiences for inmates was noted in the 1927 *Report of the Superintendent of Penitentiaries* (cited in Gosselin 1982, 22), which concluded that government should furnish more work for inmates and that those inmates whose conduct within the institution had been good should receive a salary for their labour. In 1938, the Archambault Commission recommended the implementation of vocational training programs in federal institutions. Vocational training programs, designed to provide inmates with marketable skills to be utilized upon release from confinement, were expanded during the movement toward the rehabilitative model of corrections in the 1950s. The programs included auto mechanics, welding, furniture repair, carpentry, drafting, and plumbing and heating.

Jarvis (1978, 169) identifies the following tenets of vocational training programs in correctional institutions:

1. Successful social living requires a secure economic base;
2. Most sentenced offenders do not have a trade or skill by which to earn a living;
3. If former offenders are returned to society with a trade or skill, they can earn a living and will not return to crime;
4. By training offenders in a skill, we will increase their opportunities for employment; and
5. Rehabilitation can be provided through a correctional program that includes vocational training.[8]

As with the initiatives in prison education, vocational training programs and the related prison industries have encountered numerous obstacles that have hindered their effectiveness. Fifty years after the Archambault Report (1938), the MacGuigan Subcommittee (1977) reported that vocational training programs in federal institutions were inadequate due to *(1)* the limited number of programs offered, *(2)* the low rate of inmate participation (approximately 15 percent of the total inmate population) in programs, *(3)* the lack of qualified instructors, and *(4)* the use of machinery to train inmates which was incompatible with that in use in outside industry. From his examination of vocational training programs in federal institutions, Griffin (1978, 93) concluded that "the vocational training curriculum throughout the Canadian Penitentiary System is a strange hodge-podge of courses, reflecting the prevailing view of earlier times that inmate training must benefit the institution."

Another problem afflicting vocational training programs is the difficulty of securing recognition for apprenticeship work. Many of the provinces often do not recognize time spent in prison vocational training programs as counting toward apprenticeship credits in various skills which would assist the inmate in securing employment upon release. There is also concern as to the usefulness of the vocational training experience once the offender is released from confinement.

While Griffin (1978, 182) found that a high percentage of the federal prison inmates interviewed considered vocational training programs as valuable and as more beneficial than other activities for preparation for life outside the institution, the experiences of many inmates once they are released are often considerably different. The MacGuigan Subcommittee (1977, 111) expressed concern about the quality and the applicability of vocational training programs:

> A complaint commonly heard from ex-inmates is that the vocational
> training they received in our institutions was in fact useless to them once
> they were released. Many of them found that, after having taken courses in
> plumbing, carpentry and the like, their achievements were not recognized
> as valid by outside employers, since the courses given to them by the C.P.S.
> were either insufficient or outdated.

Such findings are similar to following studies conducted in the
United States which have found that only a small percentage of
released offenders utilize their prison work experience or
vocational training in post-release jobs (Waldo 1973).

Closely related to vocational training programs for inmates are
prison industry programs, which are often a major mechanism for
teaching inmates skills and work habits. Griffin (1978, 12), in
discussing prison industry, distinguishes between *maintenance
functions,* which involve physical and service maintenance in the
prison, and *production work,* which involves the manufacture of
goods that are consumed by other departments of the government
or by non-profit organizations.

In our discussion of the history of Canadian corrections, we
documented the extensive opposition to any attempts to develop
prison industry programs. Lightman (1982, 37) notes that in the
mid-1800s various schemes were introduced whereby private
entrepreneurs used cheap inmate labour to produce goods which
were then sold on the open market. These arrangements, however,
were short-lived due to the continuing opposition of the labour
unions. Today goods are produced primarily for government or
institutional use. In its report, the MacGuigan Subcommittee
(1977, 109) recommended that the *Penitentiary Act* be amended to
allow the products of inmate labour to compete on the open market
and that a national prison industries corporation be established.[9]

Macdonald (1982, 4) notes that prison industry programs have
traditionally suffered from poorly defined and often conflicting
program objectives, dull work assignments, outdated work
equipment, and inadequate incentives for both inmates and
program staff. Macdonald concludes that "Successful programs
have been the exception rather than the rule." CORCAN, the
federal prison industries corporation, is afflicted by operating
deficits and high production costs.

From his consideration of the current status of prison industry
in Canadian federal institutions, Macdonald (1982) proposes the
development of "self-sustaining" prison industries that would
provide meaningful work experiences for inmates while at the

same time producing sufficient financial returns to cover all direct and indirect program costs. One of Macdonald's major arguments is that correctional policy makers and administrators may have overestimated the extent of public and private opposition to prison industry programs. A survey of the attitudes of a variety of groups in the community, including labour unions and business representatives, revealed clear support for the proposition that offenders should be paid for the work they performed; the survey also uncovered support for the sale of inmate-produced goods on an open market so long as prison industries were not given unfair competitive advantage through subsidies. On the basis of these and other findings, Macdonald (1982, 80-81) concluded that the trade unions, business community, and the general public supported the development of prison industry programs, as long as the products of these programs were not given unfair advantage on the open market.

While the work of Macdonald (1982) would seem to suggest that there is fertile ground for the development of meaningful work in prison industries, it remains to be seen whether such initiatives will be forthcoming in Canadian corrections, particularly given the economic realities confronting Canadian society in the 1980s. Further, a change in the perceptions of correctional policy makers and administrators may also be required, and heed will have to be taken of Miller's (1972, 21) admonishment:

> Correctional personnel (as well as politicians) need to realize the dysfunctional effects of using inmates for meeting institutional maintenance goals under the guise of on-the-job training (simply because it is convenient and inexpensive on a short-term basis). They also need to realize that work for the sake of work has virtually no payoff except for the institution.[10]

Our brief consideration of vocational training and prison industry projects indicates that despite the recognition of both types of initiatives as potentially beneficial for the incarcerated offender, the Correctional Service of Canada has been largely unsuccessful in creating meaningful programs with continuity in either area. This failure is even more unfortunate when one considers the vast untapped source of creativity and manpower in prison populations and the potential positive impact of meaningful employment programs on the prison environment (see Cullen and Travis 1984).

CORRECTIONAL TREATMENT MODALITIES

While education and vocational training programs have a relatively long history in institutions, the development of specific treatment modalities occurred only following the Second World War with the advent of the rehabilitative model of corrections. This was accompanied by the introduction of professional treatment staff into correctional facilities, including psychiatrists, psychologists, and psychiatric social workers who were charged with implementing the medical model. Until this time, the role of professionals in corrections had been primarily limited to religious officials, school teachers, and vocational training instructors. As Marshall (1981, 24) states: "The recruitment of behavioral experts into the correctional setting guaranteed residential 'surgical' services to cut out (figuratively) the diseased material responsible for the offender's problem." The rehabilitative model resulted in the development of a wide range of programs and intervention strategies under the rubric of "treatment," Marshall (1981, 25) observing that "there are nearly as many different treatment programs as there are correctional experts to implement them."

In Chapter 2, we discussed the relationship between the perceptions of criminality and the response to offenders by society. Similarly, there is a close relationship between the perceived causes of the criminal behaviour of the offender and the type of treatment employed in the correctional setting. Smith and Berlin (1981, 68) note the different perspectives assumed by sociologists, who emphasize the role of social factors and societal institutions as causal factors in producing criminal behaviour, and psychologists, who focus on the inner drives, motivations, and conflicts within the individual, as causal factors in criminality:

> The sociologists stress the fact that criminal behavior is learned behavior. Factors influencing and shaping the offender are social, economic, ethnic, sub-cultural affiliation, and family influence ... The psychologically oriented regard criminal behavior as a symptom of internal, intrapsychic maladjustment... [T]he criminal act is an attempt to release the inner tension generated by an emotional conflict.

In his discussion of correctional treatment, Gibbons (1965) identified two major categories of strategies: *(1) psychological therapies,* which include individual and group psychotherapy, reality therapy, transactional analysis, and client-oriented therapy, and *(2) environmental therapies,* which include group therapy and milieu-management. Each of these two major orientations, as well as the individual treatment programs within them, make certain assumptions about criminal behaviour, have specific objectives, and define a technique for achieving these objectives. The major correctional treatment modalities are summarized in Table 7.2.[11]

A cursory examination of the various treatment techniques described in Table 7.2 reveals that a majority of them have a heavily psychological orientation. Marshall (1981, 24) has observed that the psychological perspective is ideally suited to the medical model of corrections:

> The "sick" premise underlying the behavioral theories of certain psychologists, psychiatrists, and social workers assumed that criminal behavior is a symptom of some underlying psychopathology. Individual psychotherapy, psychoanalysis, or other forms of individual counseling were thought to alleviate the underlying pathological condition and to help offenders gain insight into their problems and learn how to deal with them effectively.

While the majority of programs implemented under the rehabilitative model had strong psychological underpinnings, several treatment modalities did develop that considered the group context. These group treatment strategies included group counselling, group therapy, group psychotherapy, and the therapeutic milieu (or therapeutic community), all of which "attempt to directly manipulate and modify the nature of the offender's group relations, social roles, group identifications . . . in such a manner that law-abiding attitudes and values squeeze out criminal attitudes and values" (Marshall 1981, 24).

While there is a wide range of treatment strategies, the introduction and utilization of a particular treatment technique in a correctional institution is generally not the consequence of a policy decision by the Correctional Service of Canada, but rather the result of initiatives at either the regional, provincial, or institutional level. Both the Archambault (1938) and the Fauteux (1956) Reports, as well as numerous provincial commissions and task forces (see Chapter 2), concluded that prisons should be charged with the task of reformation and rehabilitation. However, other than identifying the need for more educational and vocational training programs, no direction was provided as to the specific treatment techniques to be employed in pursuing and achieving these objectives. Rather, the use of particular treatment modalities is generally a decision of the treatment staff at the institutional level.

Further, the decision to terminate a correctional treatment

TABLE 7.2   Correctional Treatment Modalities

Type	Origins	Treatment Goal	Technique
A. Individual and Group Psychotherapy	Freudian psychology; early life experience and past conflicts important determinants of behaviour; offender cannot change unless past addressed.	Facilitate the growth process so individual can manage own affairs; encourage individual to resolve past conflicts which cause personal problems, and become responsible for own behaviour.	Therapist working on individual basis with offender or within group setting.
B. Reality Therapy	Dr. William Glasser; emphasis on present behaviour; past not important; basic problem of the offender is irresponsibility; assumption that all people need to give and receive love; basic human needs are relatedness and respect that are satisfied by actions that are realistic, responsible, and right (the 3 R's of reality therapy); all persons have basic needs and act in an irresponsible manner when they are unable to fulfill them.	Assist the offender to become responsible for himself; to accept reality and meet his needs within it; offender must address the moral aspect of his behaviour and decide right from wrong.	Therapist becomes involved with offender to assist adaptation by being a model and a mirror of reality; inmate forms honest and real relationship with therapist; therapist indicates that offender is accepted but irresponsible behaviour is not.

TABLE 7.2   continued

Type	Origins	Treatment Goal	Technique
C. Transactional Analysis (TA)	Dr. Eric Berne, author of *Games People Play*; human relationships often involve "games"; each person has three ego states: parent, adult, and child, each of which perceives a different reality; and each of which operates in the "games people play."	Develop spontaneity and a capacity for intimacy; use of games, psychodrama, and script analysis; offender to understand how each ego state controls behaviour; help offender to use adult ego state, which represents the responsible and mature self, more often.	Use of a TA group; leader teaches offenders to identify game-playing behaviour and learn new approaches to inter-personal relationships.
D. Erhard Seminars Training (EST)	Created by Werner Erhard in 1971.	Force offender to examine the belief systems that govern his life, so as to become the source rather than merely the agent of his behaviour; offender to take control of own life and recreate it on own terms; develop a positive response to life.	Sixty-hour training conducted by an est-trained therapist.
E. Transcendental Meditation (TM)	Founded by Maharishi Mahesh Yogi.	Reduce anxiety, insomnia, neu-rosis, tension, depression, irritability.	Offender sits in quiet setting for 20 minutes twice daily, repeat-ing a phrase to relax mind and allow clear thinking and reduce stress.
F. Psychodrama	Introduced into U.S. in 1925 by Jacob Moreno; individuals can reveal their problems through psychodrama.	To develop individual behav-iour; to develop a greater understanding of their behav-iour through acting out their emotions.	Drama takes place on stage and performers spontaneously act out their emotions to group members.

Program	Basis	Purpose	Methods
G. Client-Centered Therapy	Based on work of Carl Rogers and his associates.	To assist the offender in understanding his problems in a secure, non-threatening setting.	Creation of a psychologically secure atmosphere in which the patient can interact with therapist; therapist assumes reflective role, attempting to see problems as the offender sees them; includes individual and group counselling.
H. Behaviour Modification	Theories of B.F. Skinner; behaviour is controlled in its consequences; deviant behaviour learned in the same manner as all other behaviour; undesirable behaviour can be eliminated, modified or replaced by taking away the reward value.	Elimination of undesirable behaviour; application of principles of conditioning and learning to solve behaviour problems among offenders.	Use of techniques to reinforce behaviour and extinguish negative behaviour; positive reinforcers include attention, praise, money, food and privileges; negative reinforcers are threats, confinement, punishment, and ridicule.
I. Therapeutic Community	Evolved from work of Maxwell Jones, *Social Psychiatry in Prisons* (1968); focus on the importance of creating a total environment within which change can occur.	Give greater authority to inmates in the operation of their living units; acceptance of responsibility for past behaviour; confidence in offender's ability to judge situations; inmate acts as therapist for other inmates; inmate learns to understand self emotionally.	Utilizes for therapeutic purposes all of the resources in the institution; non-hierarchical structure with no sharp division between inmates and staff; creation of open dialogue between offenders; use of the living unit plan and living unit officers.

program is often not the result of evaluative findings that the program has no appreciable impact on post-release behaviour of the offenders participating in it. And, even in those instances where evaluative results are cited as justification for decisions regarding correctional programs, numerous problems with the design of such evaluations make the use of such results highly questionable.

One notable exception to the general lack of direction from federal inquiries was the recommendation of the MacGuigan Subcommittee (1977) that the therapeutic community arrangement be implemented in medium and maximum security facilities.

Creation of the Therapeutic Community

The development of the therapeutic community was an attempt to include the entire environment of the group in the treatment process. The conceptual foundations of this approach are summarized by Fenton et al. (cited in Trojanowicz and Morash 1983, 260):

> This program bridges a communication gap between staff and inmates typically found in correctional institutions and also utilizes inmate peer influence — the self-help concept — to help inmates gain self-awareness and a more responsible outlook. Inmates who live and work together meet with the staff regularly with an expressed goal of improving post-release performance. By employing, under staff direction, open communication, confrontation, as well as other treatment methods, inmate participants can model and adjust their behavior through learning, testing, and fixating newer and more effective modes of perceiving and relating to others.

In Canada, the attempt to create a therapeutic community in correctional institutions is reflected in the Living Unit program of the Correctional Service of Canada. In 1971, the *Report of the Working Group on Federal Maximum Security Institutions Design,* under the chairmanship of Hans Mohr, recommended that a residential unit program be adopted in all maximum security institutions. Subsequent to this recommendation, the Living Unit concept was introduced initially at Springhill Institution in Nova Scotia and in Warkworth Institution in Ontario (see Gamberg and Thomson 1984).

Under the Living Unit program, the offender is assigned to a Living Unit upon entering the institution. In addition, each inmate has a Case Management Team composed of a case management supervisor, a Living Unit Officer, and, depending upon the needs and requirements of the offender, a psychologist, a security officer, or a member of the educational or medical staff. According to the *Annual Report* of the Solicitor General (1983, 65): "*Case Management* provides coordinated management and administration of the entire sentence of offenders, ensures that inmates receive maximum benefits from all available program opportunities, maintains assessment on all federal offenders and makes recommendations to the National Parole Board for conditional release on full parole, day parole or temporary absence." Throughout the period of confinement, the Case Management Team monitors the progress of the inmate and assists in the development of a plan that considers both the short- and the long-term needs of the offender. The team also meets with the offender on a regular basis to inform the inmate of its assessments and discuss the inmate's progress toward release.

The Living Unit arrangement is a primary mechanism through which the Case Management of the offender is carried out. Under the Living Unit concept, the traditional role of correctional officer (or guard) was abolished, and replaced by the position of Living Unit Officer. The Living Unit Officer wears ordinary street clothes rather than a uniform and has a case-load of five to ten inmates. The officer is assigned to a particular cell block on a regular basis and works with the residents in the role of counsellor, as well as assuming responsibility for security in the Living Unit. In short, the Living Unit concept was designed to break down the traditional split between inmate and staff relations, while creating an environment that would facilitate the development of positive attitudes and values among the residents. In 1986, the Living Unit program in federal institutions underwent a change with the introduction of Functional Unit Management. Citing the increased operating costs associated with the Living Unit program, CSC assigned lower-paid, uniformed security personnel to Living Units to assist in the control function.

In Chapter 8, when we discuss the conflicting mandates of the prison we shall see that, since its introduction in 1973, the Living Unit Program has been beset by difficulties that have seriously hindered its effectiveness. The introduction of Functional Unit Management also has significant implications for both the Living Unit program and the patterns of staff/inmate interaction.

THE EFFECTIVENESS OF CORRECTIONAL TREATMENT

The effectiveness of correctional treatment programs has been one of the most highly debated areas of contemporary corrections, and the controversy involves not only a consideration of the efficacy of specific treatment modalities, but also the operation of the correctional enterprise as a whole. In this section, we attempt to provide an overview of this controversy, identifying the major arguments as well as the conceptual issues that are involved.

Despite the initial optimism accompanying the adoption of the rehabilitative model of corrections in the late 1940s and early 1950s, and the subsequent introduction of various treatment programs in Canadian institutions throughout the following two decades, by the mid-1970s the rehabilitative model was under increasing criticism and questions were being raised about the effectiveness of correctional treatment programs. This concern was expressed in several federal reports, beginning with the Ouimet Committee in 1969, followed by a 1975 report of the Law Reform Commission entitled *Imprisonment and Release* and the 1977 Task Force Report, *The Role of Federal Corrections in Canada* (see Chapter 2 and Chapter 10). All of these reports concluded that the rehabilitation of the offender within the penitentiary was an unrealistic and unattainable goal that should be abandoned in favour of an increased emphasis on community-based corrections and the implementation of an opportunities model within federal correctional institutions.

This shift in correctional philosophy in Canadian corrections was precipitated by the controversy over the effectiveness of correctional treatment that reached its zenith in the mid-1970s in the United States. A widely accepted conclusion at this time was that treatment programs operating in correctional institutions were not successful in reducing criminal behaviour among inmate participants. However, in the discussion below we suggest that correctional policy makers may have been too hasty in discarding the rehabilitative model and may have failed to consider all of the issues involved in this complex topic.

Our discussion reveals that it has not been conclusively established that correctional treatment programs are ineffective in reducing or eliminating criminal behaviour. While we are unable to resolve all of the issues involved in the debate over the effectiveness of correctional treatment programs, nevertheless, it is incumbent upon us to address them, for this controversy permeates the whole of the correctional enterprise and is likely to do so for many years to come.

Robert Martinson and "Nothing Works"

With few and isolated exceptions, the rehabilitative efforts that have been reported so far have had no appreciable effect on recidivism (Martinson 1974, 25).

In 1974, Robert Martinson and his associates reached this conclusion from a survey of 231 evaluations of correctional treatment programs conducted between 1945 and 1967, and fired the shot heard round the correctional world. The "nothing works" finding, while certainly not the first instance (or the last) in which the efficacy of correctional treatment had been questioned, came at a time when the rehabilitative model of corrections was under increasing attack, and it had a significant impact on correctional policy in both Canada and the United States[12] (see Lerner 1977; Halleck and White 1977).

In fact, questions had been raised about the effectiveness of correctional treatment in the late 1950s and they continued throughout the 1960s, as evidenced by the following conclusions:

Evidence supporting the efficacy of correctional treatment is slight, inconsistent, and of questionable reliability (Bailey 1966, 159).

There is no evidence to support any program's claim of superior rehabilitative efficacy (Robison and Smith 1971, 80).

At present, this society is not able to reduce recidivism measurably by exposing the offender to treatment or rehabilitation programs either in prison or in the community (Citizens' Inquiry on Parole and Criminal Justice, Inc. (1975, 178).

Many correctional dispositions are failing to reduce recidivism . . . . Much of what is now done in the name of "corrections" may serve other functions, but the prevention of return to crime is not one of them . . . The blanket assertion that "nothing works" is an exaggeration, but not by very much (Greenberg 1977, 140-41).

Rehabilitation treatment has not been shown to be effective in reducing recidivism. The recidivism rates of those treated in different programs by different methods do not differ from those not treated at all (van den Haag 1975, 188).

In Canada, Jobson (1977, 256) has based his arguments for dismantling the criminal justice system on the conclusions of Martinson et al., noting: "The promoters of the rehabilitative ideal 'jumped the gun'. The research reports are clear: there is no empirical evidence to show that criminal justice sanctions or programs are effective in bringing about reform, generally, or in reducing recidivism." In fact, Cousineau and Plecas (1982) point out that the conclusive, uncritical acceptance of Martinson's findings has resulted in the argument by such scholars as Hackler (1978) that further research on correctional treatment is of limited usefulness.

In support of these conclusions, correctional observers document the apparent failure of correctional treatment programs to have a measurable effect on the post-release behaviour of offenders. One of the most widely cited treatment "failures" was the program of intensive group counselling implemented in several California institutions in the early 1960s. Kassebaum et al. (1971) note the following tenets of the group counselling modality (cited in Shover 1979, 68):

1. an open, permissive group setting is an excellent one for individuals to learn what effect they have on others and how others perceive them.
2. the permissive nature of small groups and the processes of group development and interaction are such that members may feel a degree of uncritical acceptance that they have not experienced before.
3. in the process of discussing and trying to resolve the problems of others within the group, each member necessarily assumes a therapeutic role and learns to view himself differently.
4. because the members of the group have had similar backgrounds and problems, they are best able to deal with similar problems in others.
5. in the process of group interaction and discussion, the individual may learn more constructive means of handling personal problems by learning from the experiences and suggestions of others.

From an extensive six-year study and followup of approximately 1,000 offenders who had been members of either a control group or who had participated in one of the intensive counselling experimental groups, Kassebaum et al. (1971) reported that inmates who had participated in the intensive counselling sessions *(1)* were *not* less hostile to prison staff during their period of confinement, *(2)* did *not* commit fewer or less serious violations of prison rules and regulations, *(3)* did *not* violate their parole less frequently, *(4)* did *not* stay out of prison longer before committing a violation of their parole, and *(5)* did *not* commit less serious crimes on parole than the offences for which they had originally been sent to prison.

From these findings, Kassebaum et al. (1971) concluded that not only had the group counselling failed to have an impact on post-release behaviour, but that a major reason for the failure of the program was the constraints of the institutional environment. We explore these and other obstacles to correctional treatment programs in Chapter 8. At this juncture, the relevance of the Kassebaum et al. study is that it was utilized by many correctional administrators and scholars as conclusive evidence that correctional treatment programs were not effective.

Despite the widespread support for the "nothing works" conclusion among both scholars and correctional policy makers, a close examination of the issues reveals that such conclusive statements may not only have been premature, but were not premised on sound empirical investigation. In fact, in a little known turn of events, Martinson (cited by the National Council on Crime and Delinquency in their *Criminal Justice Newsletter* 1978, 4) publicly negated his "nothing works" conclusion, conceding that the criteria that he and his associates had utilized to assess the success of the reviewed treatment evaluations had resulted in the exclusion of several studies that may have showed a significant impact on the post-release behaviour of offenders. Martinson (1979, 244, 252) subsequently undertook a re-evaluation of correctional treatment programs, employing new criteria, and concluded:

> Contrary to my previous position, some treatment programs do have an appreciable effect on recidivism. Some programs are indeed beneficial . . . New evidence from our current study leads me to reject my original conclusion . . . The evidence in our survey is simply too overwhelming to ignore.

As the discussion below reveals, data-based evaluations often suffer from numerous methodological difficulties which render questionable any conclusive statements about the efficacy of treatment. Further, in Chapter 8, it is suggested that the majority of observers supporting the "nothing works" conclusion have done so without considering the various factors that may have hindered the success of correctional treatment modalities which, if offered within an appropriate setting and with proper organizational support, may have provided a useful rehabilitative tool for the offender.

Challenging the "Nothing Works" Verdict

The first major criticism of the Martinson study came from Ted Palmer, a criminal justice administrator, who attacked the report on methodological grounds and specifically challenged the criteria that Martinson and his associates had used to assess the effectiveness of correctional treatment programs. Palmer's response is instructive, for he raised a number of issues that are critical to an understanding of the debate over the effectiveness of correctional treatment.

In a treatise entitled "Martinson Revisited," Palmer (1975) argued that a major limitation of the survey was the inclusion of studies only up until 1967. Further, Palmer pointed out that the investigators had failed to include all types of treatment programs and had tended to ignore the effects of some treatment programs on individual offenders. For example, Palmer notes that in asserting the success of a particular program, Martinson et al. concentrated on whether the treatment strategy was effective in all of the studies in which it was tested. The "differential value" and "degree of effectiveness" of the program were not considered. In addition, such an analysis obscured the impact of treatment on the individual offender.

In a re-examination of the evaluations reviewed by Martinson et al., Palmer (1975) found that 48 percent of the programs produced positive results. In concluding his critique, Palmer (1975, 150) argued that rather than asking "what works?" we should be asking "which methods worked best for *which* types of offenders and under *what* types of conditions or in *what* types of settings?"[13] At the conclusion of this chapter, and again in Chapter 8, we return to a consideration of the concept of differential treatment — the notion that certain offenders may benefit from a particular treatment modality in a specific institutional setting.

A more recent challenge to the "nothing works" conclusion has come from two Canadian criminologists, Paul Gendreau and Robert Ross (1979), who conducted an extensive survey of the results of the evaluations of 95 treatment programs conducted between 1973 and 1978. While many of the intervention strategies reported by Gendreau and Ross were utilized with juvenile offenders, nevertheless their findings constitute a significant contribution to the literature on correctional treatment.

In reviewing the debate over the effectiveness of correctional treatment, Gendreau and Ross (1979, 464-65) offered the following observations: "The arguments are persuasive, the language used often brilliant, the metaphors appealing, and the objectivity sadly lacking. The antagonists . . . seem to be more intent on winning arguments than on seeking truth." Cognizant of the criticisms of the criteria utilized by Martinson et al. in assessing treatment evaluations, Gendreau and Ross (1979, 469) established the following requirements for a treatment program evaluation to be included in their review:

1. the study had to employ at the minimum a quasi-experimental design;
2. the study had to contain a statistical analysis of the data; and,
3. the study had to provide a report on the followup of the offenders for at least a six-month period of time following release from confinement.

Using these criteria, these investigators surveyed the results of evaluations of 95 treatment programs conducted between 1973 and 1978, which included family and community intervention, contingency management, counselling, diversion, and biomedical assistance. The authors concluded that there were several types of correctional treatment programs that "worked" for offenders. Elaborating on their findings a year later, Ross and Gendreau (1980, 23) argued that while a "box score" analysis of the effective programs was not appropriate, "certainly 95 intervention studies reported since late 1973, of which 86% reported success, should and cannot be ignored."

Cousineau and Plecas (1982) have also made a significant contribution to the discussion of the effectiveness of correctional treatment. While deliberately not taking sides in the debate, these authors raise important points relating to the widespread acceptance of the Martinson findings and the impact of the report on correctional policy and practice.

According to Cousineau and Plecas (1982, 311), there were several factors operating which assured the widespread acceptance of the "nothing works" finding and the lack of critical scrutiny that would have revealed the numerous methodological weaknesses of the Martinson inquiry, including *(1)* an ideological climate regarding criminal behaviour that was conducive to a hardening of the response toward criminal offenders, *(2)* a low readership of the Martinson study, which was expensive to purchase and cumbersome to read, *(3)* highly laudatory reviews of the study by well-known criminologists and social scientists, and, *(4)* what Cousineau and Plecas (1982, 311) note as the "impression of thoroughness and rigour" created by the authors in the opening pages of the report.

Cousineau and Plecas (1982, 311) argue that while the findings of Martinson have been challenged, "criticism *has not* been directed towards a re-assessment of the methodological adequacy of the studies reviewed . . . For the most part the criticism is aimed at the conclusions offered, the manner in which the findings are presented, and to a lesser degree, the methods employed by Martinson." In their treatise, Cousineau and Plecas admonish scholars for accepting the findings of Martinson et al. at face value and failing to exhibit what Storer (cited in Cousineau and Plecas 1982, 308) has termed "organized skepticism," a norm which embodies the principle that "each scientist should be held individually responsible for making sure that previous research by others on which he bases his work is valid."[14] The authors (1982, 308) then proceed to examine four of the best studies evaluated by Martinson and conclude that, "contrary to the high regard for these studies, they are shoddy and produce no plausible 'finding' at all." (For an insightful look into the methodological issues involved in evaluating correctional treatment, see Gottfredson 1979.)

   Given the profound implications, for both the offender and the correctional enterprise, of discarding the rehabilitative model, in the following discussion we examine the difficulties of measuring the success of correctional treatment.

MEASURING TREATMENT SUCCESS

From our discussion, it is evident that the controversy over the effectiveness of correctional treatment has not been resolved. In addition to the highly emotional debate over the efficacy of correctional treatment and the failure of the litigants to exercise "organized skepticism," there are two additional factors for this unsettled state of affairs: *(1)* the severe methodological shortcomings of the evaluations of correctional treatment conducted to date, and *(2)* the criteria for success traditionally utilized by evaluations to assess the effectiveness of correctional treatment. As Conrad (1981, 1725) concluded from a review of the evaluative literature: "The research done to test rehabilitation is a considerable mass, chiefly remarkable for its sterility. We are no wiser about crime, criminals, or the changing of criminals than we were when we started."

Problems in Evaluation

Many correctional observers have argued that the methodological inadequacies of correctional evaluations are so great as to prevent conclusive statements about what works. Shover (1979, 304), for example, cites the work of Adams (1975) who discovered in a survey of correctional evaluations that no more than 10 percent of the studies of correctional treatment programs had employed a true experimental design. Similarly, Gendreau and Ross (1979, 466) reported the work of Bernstein (1975), who surveyed 236 evaluations of correctional treatment programs and found that "75 percent did not use an experimental or quasi-experimental design, 41 percent did not use random selection of the subjects, 50 percent used biased samples, and 65 percent did not include a statistical analysis of the data."

There are numerous reasons for the poor methodological design of correctional program evaluations, many of which are beyond the control of investigators. The organizational demands of correctional institutions often hinder the random assignment of offenders to experimental and control groups, and the maintenance of inmates in these groups may be difficult over time. Marshall (1981, 33) notes that the random assignment of offenders to experimental and control groups may conflict with management and security concerns within the institution. There are also many legal and ethical questions surrounding the use of controlled experimentation with inmates, including the extent to which informed consent to participate in a correctional treatment program can be given.

In addition to these factors, attempts to implement and sustain the integrity of an evaluative research design are hindered by inmate turnover, intentional or inadvertent changes in the treatment program by the prison administration or treatment staff, or events independent of the treatment program that may have a significant impact on the offender's behaviour and attitudes (see also Sommer 1976; Sechrest et al. 1983). Due to these contingencies, Marshall (1981, 33) concludes: "It becomes very tenuous [*sic*] to conclude whether observed changes in the offenders' behavior or attitudes are the result of their participation in the treatment program, or whether influences beyond the researcher's control are responsible for the change."

Recidivism Rates

The second major item that has seriously hindered efforts to assess the effectiveness of correctional treatment is the traditional reliance by evaluation researchers on recidivism rates as a measure of program success. Gendreau and Ross (1979) have argued, for example, that the strict adherence to recidivism rates has limited an understanding of the total impact of treatment. Briefly stated, recidivism rates refer to the number of offenders who, once released from confinement, are returned to prison either for a technical violation of a condition of their parole or mandatory supervision, or for the commission of a new offence.

Despite the widespread use of recidivism rates, however, there is disagreement among correctional observers as to their usefulness and appropriateness as a measure of the effectiveness of correctional treatment programs. Support for the use of recidivism rates among correctional observers is reflected in the comments of Waldo (1973, 368-69) that "unless the program has been effective in reducing recidivism, in the final analysis we cannot say we are achieving our primary goal in corrections."

On the other hand, there are an increasing number of researchers who argue that the simple counting of the number of offenders who return to prison is too gross a measure of the success or failure of correctional treatment. Conrad (1981, 1720), for example, contends that:

> Recidivism rates produce the wrong answers to whatever questions it is important to ask about the rehabilitation of offenders. In every treatment program, the essential information is the achievement or non-achievement of the intended primary benefits of the program itself.

Conrad and others suggest that the use of recidivism rates, which result in the exclusive reliance on the rates of official contact with the criminal justice system following release, obscures the extent to which the goals of specific treatment modalities may have been achieved for the individual offender. Such positive influences, which are not measured by recidivism rates, would include the development of a positive self-image, increased communication skills, the attainment of a certain level of education, or the acquisition of vocational skills. This position is most succinctly stated by the authors of *Struggle for Justice* (American Friends Service Committee 1971, 44):

> Although treatment ideology purports to look beyond the criminal's crime to the whole personality ... it measures its success against the single factor of an absence of reconviction for a criminal act. Whether or not the subject of the treatment process has acquired greater self-understanding, a sense of purpose and power in his own destiny, or a new awareness of his relatedness to man and the universe is not subject to statistical study ... and so is omitted from the evaluation.

These comments suggest that, while the rehabilitative model of corrections was designed to treat underlying disorders in the offender, the baseline measurement of the success of these efforts is a control measure — whether or not the offender was subsequently returned to prison. No provision is made to assess other areas of improvement in the offender.

There are several additional difficulties with using recidivism rates as the measure of effectiveness of correctional treatment programs. First, using legal criteria of subsequent contact with the criminal justice system makes no provision for the "relative" improvement of the offender. If, for example, offenders who previously committed serious crimes are subsequently returned to prison for a relatively minor offence, they may be viewed as "relative" successes. Similarly, while offenders who commit technical violations of their parole conditions and those who commit new offences while on parole are both returned to the institution and classified as failures, there may be considerable differences between them.

A second difficulty in using recidivism rates is the question as to how long after release from confinement the offender's behaviour is to be monitored. While some studies have followed the offender for only a short while, other investigations have followed the offender for periods of up to three years, even after completion of parole. This makes it difficult to compare the findings of various evaluative studies.

A third problem with the use of recidivism rates is that they depend upon the detection of offender behaviour by agents of the criminal justice system. In fact, the offender may have returned to criminal activity and not have been detected.

A fourth problem is that there is considerable evidence to suggest that the success or failure of an offender upon release (parole) may be due in large measure to the level and type of supervision that he or she receives, as well as other organizational factors not directly related to behaviour. Ohlin et al. (1956), for example, identified three types of parole officer, each distinguished by their conceptions of parole work, which were, in turn, reflected in the manner in which they supervised parolees: *(1)* the "punitive officer," who assumes a central orientation, emphasizes protection of the community and who attempts to coerce the offender into behaving in an appropriate fashion through the use of threats; *(2)* the "protective agent," who vacillates between protecting the community and assisting the offender, resulting in an ambivalent stance toward the offender; and *(3)* the "welfare worker" whose orientation is toward the welfare of the client. Further, Takagi (cited in Irwin 1970, 129-41) devised a typology of parole officers on the basis of their emphasis on assistance to the released offender, or on control. Thus the parole outcome must be viewed as a consequence not only of the parolee's behaviour but also of the activities of the system's agents and agencies.

A final difficulty in utilizing recidivism rates is that one cannot assume that the behaviour of an offender, once released from prison, is in any way related to the correctional treatment received during incarceration. In fact, there are many reasons why an individual may cease violating the law, including the efforts of a supportive family or spouse, the fact of securing permanent employment, or maturation. As Conrad (1981, 1724) argues: "The difficulties of accounting for success after release from custody are almost insurmountable, but the links between interventions and success are exactly what we need to know but can at best measure poorly." Thus, even in the most tightly controlled evaluation, it is difficult to determine with certainty that the post-release behaviour of the offender was a direct or even an indirect consequence of exposure to a specific treatment modality while in confinement.

By the same reasoning, given the large number of factors that may contaminate the treatment effort, both within the prison and in the community once the offender is released, it may be inappropriate to conclude that a treatment program, per se, is not effective, even though the offender is ultimately returned to prison.

In an attempt to address these and other difficulties associated with the use of recidivism rates as a measure of the effectiveness of correctional treatment programs, several observers have suggested more refined measures of post-institution behaviour. Glaser (1964, 31-58), for example, has proposed the following system of classification that is designed to avoid the present success/failure dichotomy:

1. *Clear reformation:* those offenders who have been on parole, have good jobs, are steady workers, and are not associating with criminals.
2. *Marginal reformation:* those offenders who have not returned to prison, but who have failed to keep their jobs, are associating with criminals, or have committed minor offences.
3. *Marginal failures:* those offenders who are returned to prison for violation of parole conditions or for minor crimes.
4. *Clear recidivists:* those offenders who commit a major crime and are returned to prison.

This classification scheme broadens categories of released offenders and provides a distinction between those offenders who are returned to prison for minor offences and those who commit major offences while under supervision. However, Glaser's classification system is still premised on contact with the criminal justice system as a measure of success and, other than examining the employment of the offender and his association patterns, includes no provision for measuring improvements in other areas of the offender's life. Further, it is important to note that, despite the alternative suggestions of Glaser (made nearly 20 years ago) and others, evaluation researchers and correctional policy makers continue to utilize recidivism rates as a measure of program success.

Differential Treatment Effectiveness

In addition to criticizing the use of recidivism rates as a measure of the effectiveness of correctional treatment programs, many observers challenging the "nothing works" finding argue that no attempt has been made to assess the impact of treatment modalities on the individual offender. Rather, evaluations have generally examined the influence of treatment on groups of offenders, ignoring the varying backgrounds among offenders, the extent of involvement in criminality, and the interface between their law-violating behaviour and the adherence to conventional values and attitudes.

Warren (1977, 360) argues that the conventional method of measuring program success — focusing on those programs that "work" for all offenders in all settings — is inappropriate, and the focus should shift to the extent to which the specific treatment modality meets the specific needs and requirements of the individual.

> Treatments, to be effective for some, need not be effective for all ... effective treatment may best be identified by asking which type of treatment method is most effective with which type of offender, and under what conditions or in what type of setting. . .

When the measurement of the effectiveness of correctional treatment is done on a group rather than an individual basis, Warren argues that "masking" may occur—that is, while the overall success rate of a particular treatment program may be low, this summary rate, which includes all of the offenders who participated in the program, masks the possibility that certain types of offenders may have benefitted from the treatment and performed better than the other offenders in the group (see also Austin 1977). The concern with the differential effectiveness of correctional treatment is directly related to the issue of the appropriateness of treatment initiatives for individual offenders, which we address in the following chapter.

Notes

1. At the outset of our discussion, it should be noted that there is considerable disagreement among correctional observers as to what programs in correctional institutions constitute "treatment" (see Gibbons 1965, 6-12). And, as our discussion in this chapter indicates, programs such as vocational training and prison industries are often utilized to fulfill functions other than attitudinal and behavioural change in the offender.

2. It should be noted that there is considerable variation among correctional institutions, even those at the same security level, in the structure and operation of treatment programs. Differences in administration, staff-inmate relations, physical facilities, and other organizational attributes, including the size of the inmate population, will have a significant effect on the development and implementation of correctional treatment programs, as well as the types of obstacles that such initiatives will encounter. The seven-level security classification system at the federal level is a useful mechanism for ascertaining differences among institutions and their populations.

3. While often not so recognized, the sentencing process is an important component of the correctional system. Nettler (1978, 48-52) outlined six justifications that are commonly used for imposing a criminal sanction: *(1)* deterrence, *(2)* education, *(3)* incapacitation, *(4)* retribution, *(5)* rehabilitation, and *(6)* restitution. These justifications may operate singularly or in combination for a particular offender and have a significant influence on the disposition given to the offender. (For a detailed discussion of the sentencing process in Canada, see Griffiths et al. 1980, 171-97.)

4. During the course of confinement, offenders are often moved to lower levels of security as they progress toward release. This is known as "cascading." In addition, under federal/provincial agreements, offenders may be exchanged between federal and provincial institutions.

5. During 1985/86, 1,185 inmates were employed in prison industry programs; 2,652 were students in education and training programs, and 415 were employed in agriculture-related activities. In federal prisons, inmates attend school on a voluntary basis and receive remuneration for their participation. The per-day wage received is dependent upon the pay level and security level of the institution.

6. The prison education program began under the auspices of the University of Victoria, and was first offered in the B.C. Penitentiary at New Westminster in 1972 and expanded to the Matsqui Institution at Abbotsford in 1973. With the closure of the B.C. Penitentiary in 1979, the program was transferred to the new Kent maximum security institution at Agassiz and in the following year was introduced in the adjacent Mountain Institution and at William Head Institution near Victoria on Vancouver Island. The program at Matsqui offers courses at all post-secondary levels, providing an opportunity for students to complete a general B.A. degree in one of five subject areas: Psychology, English, History, Anthropology, and Sociology. The Kent/Mountain programs and the program at William Head offer courses at the first and second year levels, although full-time faculty do, on occasion, offer senior level courses to small groups of qualified students. Approximately 200 inmates are enrolled in the program annually (see Duguid and Hoekema 1985). The Ministry of the Solicitor General announced in February, 1983, that effective March 31, 1983, funding would no longer be provided for post-secondary school programs. Under intense pressure, the federal government subsequently reinstated post-secondary education programs. In 1984, Simon Fraser University assumed operational control of the prison education program.

7. To measure the impact of participation in a particular treatment program on post-release behaviour, an experimental group and a control group of inmates are required. The experimental group is composed of those inmates who participate in the program, while the control group are those offenders who are similar in all measurable respects to the offenders in the experimental group, with the exception that they do not participate in the treatment program. Further, there must not be any bias in the assignment of inmates to either the experimental or the control group. Any differences between the two groups in post-release behaviour are then ascribed to participation in the program (see Chapter 5).

8. The 1985/86 *Annual Report* of the Solicitor General of Canada notes that the Industries Division manufactures goods at 22 institutions in 92 different shops, ranging from small operations producing one or two units at a time, to larger operations producing high volumes of a few products on a production line basis. Major products produced include upholstered and modular office furniture, mail transfer boxes, mail bags, shoes, and clothing. During 1985/86 a total of 1,185 inmates were employed in prison industry.

9. The Correctional Service of Canada does operate several industry programs with private sector participation. In a federal institution in Ontario, inmates earn minimum wages for assembling automotive components for a private company, and in another, inmates earn union wages working in a privately owned meat processing plant. Such arrangements with private industry, however, are the exception. For a discussion of the major issues surrounding private-sector involvement in prison industries, see Gandy and Hurl 1987.

10. In 1986, a five-level pay system for inmates was implemented. The daily wage earned is dependent upon the security level of the institution in which the inmate resides and work performance. In contrast to previous wage systems, the amount an inmate may earn is not restricted by the type of work done. Inmates enrolled in school programs, for example, are not limited in the daily wage they may earn.

11. For a detailed discussion of correctional treatment modalities, see Smith and Berlin 1981 and Trojanowicz and Morash 1983. Many of these modalities are also applied in community corrections settings as well as in correctional institutions. There are also a variety of other programs in federal and provincial institutions designed to prepare inmates for re-entry into the community. Notable examples are life skills programs and anger management programs.

12. The article by Martinson (1974) was extracted from a larger study entitled *The Effectiveness of Correctional Treatment* (1975), co-authored by D. Lipton, J. Wilkes and R. Martinson.

13. The debate over the effectiveness of correctional treatment has been characterized by a high degree of emotion and subjectivity that has often

obscured an objective analysis and assessment of the topic. This is poignantly illustrated by the heated exchanges that took place between Palmer and Martinson. One of Palmer's criticisms was that Martinson had not been a major contributor to the survey project; Palmer cited the comments of the former Director of Research and Planning for the City of New York, who stated that Martinson joined the project after it had been in progress for two years and that he had added little to the number of cases analyzed "except for several major distortions of fact . . . (and) the false claim that it was his study." Responding to Palmer's criticisms, Martinson (1976, 182) attacked Palmer's own research, stating: "To review one of Palmer's research reports is a formidable undertaking, something like translating the Moscow telephone book into Swahili."

14. In discussing evaluation research, Cousineau and Plecas (1982, 318) assume Bernstein's position that "social scientists involved in evaluation research are more likely to be guided by the norms of an 'entrepreneurial model' than the norms of the social science 'academic model' " with the result that there is a "lower conformity to the prescribed norms of methodology in social science." A similar criticism is voiced by Ross and Gendreau (1980, 4): "The debate about the 'impotence of treatment' is bogged down in rhetoric. Where one would expect to find reasonable and objective analysis and interpretation of data, one finds hyperbole. The task of testing one's view by seeking and critically evaluating new evidence . . . seems to have been studiously avoided by both sides in their struggle to upstage their opponents."

References

American Friends Service Committee. 1971. *Struggle for Justice.* New York: Hill and Wang.

Archambault, J. (Chairman). 1938. *Report of the Royal Commission to Investigate the Penal System of Canada.* Ottawa: King's Printer.

Austin, R.L. 1977. "Differential Treatment in an Institution: Reexamining the Preston Study." 14 *Journal of Research in Crime and Delinquency.* 177-94.

Bailey, W.C. (June) 1966. "Correctional Outcome: An Evaluation of 100 Reports." 57 *Journal of Criminology, Criminal Law and Police Science.* 153-60.

Bernstein, I.N. (March) 1975. "Evaluation Research in Corrections: Status and Prospects Revisited." 39 *Federal Probation.* 56-57.

_____. (March) 1978. "Social Control in Applied Social Science: A Study of Evaluation Researchers' Conformity to Technical Norms." 7 *Social Science Research.* 24-47.

Campbell, D.D. (April) 1974. "Developing Continuing Education in the Correctional Institution: Some Principles and Practices." 16 *Canadian Journal of Criminology and Corrections.* 117-32.

Carson, J. (Chairman). 1984. *Report of the Advisory Committee to the Solicitor General on the Management of Correctional Institutions.* Ottawa: Supply and Services Canada.

Chunn, D. (Fall) 1981. "Good Men Work Hard: Convict Labour in the Kingston Penitentiary, 1835-1850." 4 *Canadian Criminology Forum.* 13-22.

Citizens' Inquiry on Parole and Criminal Justice, Inc. 1975. *Prison Without Walls: Report on New York Parole.* New York: Praeger.

Conrad, J.P. (Winter) 1981. "A Lost Ideal, A New Hope: The Way Toward Effective Correctional Treatment." 72 *Journal of Criminal Law and Criminology.* 1699-1734.

Cosman, J.W. (Spring) 1980. "Penitentiary Education in Canada." 20 *Education Canada.* 42-47.

Cousineau, F.D. and D.B. Plecas. (July) 1982. "Justifying Criminal Justice Policy with Methodologically Inadequate Research." 24 *Canadian Journal of Criminology.* 307-21.

Cullen, F.T. and L.F. Travis. 1984. "Work As An Avenue of Prison Reform." 10 *New England Journal of Civil and Criminal Confinement.* 45-64.

Duguid, S. 1979. "History and Moral Education in Correctional Education." 4 *Canadian Journal of Education.* 81-92.

_____. 1980. "Post Secondary Education in a Prison: Theory and Praxis." 10 *Canadian Journal of Higher Education.* 29-35.

_____. (April) 1981a. "Moral Development, Justice and Democracy in the Prison." 23 *Canadian Journal of Criminology.* 147-62.

_____. (October) 1981b. "Prison Education and Criminal Choice: The Context of Decision-Making." 23 *Canadian Journal of Criminology.* 421-38.

_____. (July) 1983. "Origins and Development of University Education at Matsqui Institution." 25 *Canadian Journal of Criminology.* 295-308.

Duguid, S. and H. Hoekema. 1985. *University Education in Prison — A Documentary Record of the Experience in British Columbia, 1974-1985.* Burnaby, British Columbia: Continuing Studies, Simon Fraser University.

Fauteux, G. (Chairman). 1956. *Report of a Committee Appointed to Inquire Into the Principles and Procedures Followed in the Remission Service of the Department of Justice of Canada.* Ottawa: Queen's Printer.

Gamberg, H. and A. Thomson. 1984. *The Illusion of Prison Reform: Corrections in Canada.* New York: P. Lang.

Gandy, J. and L. Hurl. 1987. "Private Sector Involvement in Prison Industries: Options and Issues." 29 *Canadian Journal of Criminology.* 185-204.

Gendreau, P. and R.R. Ross (October) 1979. "Effective Correctional Treatment: Bibliotherapy for Cynics." 25 *Crime and Delinquency.* 463-89.

Gendreau, P., R.R. Ross and R. Izzo. 1985. "Institutional Misconduct: The Effects of the UVIC Program at Matsqui Penitentiary." 27 *Canadian Journal of Criminology.* 209-217.

Gibbons, D.C. 1965. *Changing the Lawbreaker: The Treatment of Delinquents and Criminals.* Englewood Cliffs, N.J.: Prentice-Hall.

Glaser, D. 1964. *The Effectiveness of a Prison and Parole System.* Indianapolis: Bobbs-Merrill.

_____. 1973. "The Effectiveness of Correctional Education." In A.R. Roberts (ed.) *Readings in Prison Education.* Springfield, Illinois: Charles C. Thomas. 351-63.

Gosselin, L. 1982. *Prisons in Canada.* Montreal: Black Rose Books.

Gottfredson, M.R. (January) 1979. "Treatment Destruction Techniques." 16 *Journal of Research in Crime and Delinquency.* 39-54.

Greenberg, D.F. 1977. "The Correctional Effects of Corrections: A Survey of Evaluations." In D.F. Greenberg (ed.) *Corrections and Punishment*. Beverly Hills, Calif.: Sage Publications. 111-48.

Griffin, D.K. 1978. *Ontario Institute for Studies in Education: Review of Penitentiary Education and Training, 1978-1979. Phase I: Report to Reviewers*. Ottawa: Education and Training Division, Canadian Penitentiary Service.

Griffiths, C.T., J.F. Klein and S.N. Verdun-Jones. 1980. *Criminal Justice in Canada: An Introductory Text*. Vancouver: Butterworths.

Hackler, J. 1978. *The Great Stumble Forward*. Toronto: Methuen.

Halleck, S.L. and A.D. White. (October) 1977. "Is Rehabilitation Dead?" 23 *Crime and Delinquency*. 372-82.

Irwin, J. 1970. *The Felon*. Englewood Cliffs, N.J.: Prentice-Hall.

Jarvis, D.C. 1978. *Institutional Treatment of the Offender*. New York: McGraw-Hill.

Jobson, K. (July) 1977. "Dismantling the System." 19 *Canadian Journal of Criminology*. 254-72.

Kassebaum, G., D.A. Ward and D.M. Wilner. 1971. *Prison Treatment and Parole Survival*. New York: John Wiley and Sons.

Kohlberg, L., K. Kaufman, P. Scharf and J. Hickey. 1974. *The Just Community Approach to Corrections: A Manual, Part I*. New Haven, Conn.: Moral Education Research Foundation, Harvard University.

Law Reform Commission of Canada. 1975. *Working Paper 11: Imprisonment and Release*. Ottawa: Information Canada.

Lerner, J.J. (August) 1977. "The Effectiveness of a Definite Sentence Parole Program." 15 *Criminology*. 211-24.

Lightman, E.S. (January) 1982. "The Private Employer and the Prison Industry." 22 *British Journal of Criminology*. 36-48.

Linden, R., L. Perry, D. Ayers and T.A.A. Parlett. 1984. "An Evaluation of a Prison Education Program." 26 *Canadian Journal of Criminology*. 65-73.

Lipton, D., J. Wilks and R.M. Martinson. 1975. *The Effectiveness of Correctional Treatment*. New York: Praeger.

Macdonald, G. 1982. *Self-Sustaining Prison Industries*. Vancouver: Institute for Studies in Criminal Justice Policy, Simon Fraser University.

MacGuigan, M. (Chairman). 1977. *Report to Parliament by the Sub-Committee on the Penitentiary System in Canada*. Ottawa: Supply and Services Canada.

Marshall, I.H. 1981. "Correctional Treatment Processes: Rehabilitation Reconsidered." In R.R. Roberg and V.J. Webb (eds.) *Critical Issues in Corrections: Problems, Trends, and Prospects*. St. Paul, Minnesota: West Publishing Co. 14-46.

Martinson, R.M. (Spring) 1974. "What Works? Questions and Answers About Prison Reform." 35 *The Public Interest*. 22-54.

_____. 1976. "California Research at the Crossroads." 22 *Crime and Delinquency*. 180-191.

_____. 1979. "New Findings, New Views: A Note of Caution Regarding Sentencing Reform." 7 *Hofstra Law Review*. 243-58.

McCarthy, B. 1985. "The Nature of Education Within Canadian Federal Prisons." 27 *Canadian Journal of Criminology*. 441-453.

Miller, M.J. (September) 1972. "Vocational Training in Prisons: Some Social Policy Implications." 36 *Federal Probation.* 19-21.

Mohr, J.W. (Chairman). 1971. Report of the Working Group on Federal Maximum Security Institutions Design: Design of Maximum Security Institutions. Ottawa: Solicitor General of Canada.

Morin, L. 1981. *On Prison Education.* Ottawa: Supply and Services Canada.

National Council on Crime and Delinquency. (24 October) 1978. *Criminal Justice Newsletter.* Hackensack, N.J.: National Council on Crime and Delinquency.

Nettler, G. 1978. *Explaining Crime.* 2d edition. New York: McGraw Hill.

Ohlin, L.E., H. Piven and D.M. Pappenfort. (July) 1956. "Major Dilemmas of the Social Worker in Probation and Parole." 2 *National Probation and Parole Association Journal.* 211-25.

Ouimet, R. (Chairman). 1969. *Report of the Canadian Committee on Corrections — Toward Unity: Criminal Justice and Corrections.* Ottawa: Information Canada.

Palmer, T. (July) 1975. "Martinson Revisited." 12 *Journal of Research in Crime and Delinquency.* 133-52.

Robison, J.O. and G. Smith. (January) 1971. "The Effectiveness of Correctional Programs." 17 *Crime and Delinquency.* 67-80.

Ross, R.R. and P. Gendreau. 1980. *Effective Correctional Treatment.* Toronto: Butterworths.

Sechrest, L., S.D. White and E.D. Brown. 1983. "The Prospects for Rehabilitation." In L.F. Travis, M.D. Schwartz and T.R. Clear (eds.) *Corrections: An Issues Approach,* 2d edition. Cincinnati, Ohio: Anderson Publishing Co. 200-15.

Shover, N. 1979. *A Sociology of American Corrections.* Homewood, Illinois: The Dorsey Press.

Smith, A.B. and L. Berlin. 1981. *Treating the Criminal Offender.* 2d edition. Englewood Cliffs, N.J.: Prentice-Hall.

Solicitor General of Canada. 1983. *Annual Report, 1981-1982.* Ottawa: Supply and Services Canada.

_____. 1986. *Annual Report, 1985-86.* Ottawa: Supply and Services Canada.

Sommer, R. 1976. *The End of Imprisonment.* New York: Oxford University Press.

Takagi, P. and J.O. Robison. (January) 1969. "The Parole Violator: An Organizational Reject." 5 *Journal of Research in Crime and Delinquency.* 78-86.

Task Force on the Creation of an Integrated Canadian Corrections Service. 1977. *The Role of Federal Corrections in Canada.* Ottawa: Supply and Services Canada.

Trojanowicz, R.C. and M. Morash. 1983. *Juvenile Delinquency: Concepts and Control.* 3d edition. Englewood Cliffs, N.J.: Prentice-Hall.

van den Haag, E. 1975. *Punishment: Concerning a Very Old and Painful Question.* New York: Basic Books.

Waldo, G.P. 1973. "Research in Correctional Education." In A.R. Roberts (ed.) *Readings in Prison Education.* Springfield, Illinois: Charles C. Thomas. 364-76.

Warren, M.Q. (December) 1977. "Correctional Treatment and Coercion: The Differential Effectiveness Perspective." 4 *Criminal Justice and Behavior.* 355-76.

Weir, J.D. 1973. "History of Education in Canadian Federal Corrections." In A.R. Roberts (ed.) *Readings in Prison Education.* Springfield, Illinois: Charles C. Thomas. 39-47.

Chapter 8

The Delivery of Correctional Treatment

In the preceding chapter, we considered the development and implementation of various correctional programs and techniques in Canadian institutions and concluded that the debate over the effectiveness of correctional treatment is unresolved and is likely to remain so for the foreseeable future. However, in addition to the difficulties of measuring the success of correctional treatment and the failure to consider differential treatment effectiveness, there are several issues in the delivery of correctional treatment that may significantly influence the effectiveness of treatment initiatives. Several of these can be grouped under one of two categories: (*1*) the organizational context within which correctional treatment programs operate, and (*2*) the "therapeutic integrity" of correctional programs. In addition, concerns about the ethics of correctional treatment have been raised by many observers.

While space limitations prevent a detailed examination of the myriad issues involved within each category, we will address some of the more critical components of each.

THE ORGANIZATIONAL CONTEXT OF CORRECTIONAL TREATMENT

There are at least three factors that may hinder the effectiveness of correctional treatment programs. All of these factors are related to the organizational structure of the prison and its operation: (*1*) the prison as a total institution, (*2*) the interaction among and between the inmates and the staff, and (*3*) the conflicting mandates of the prison.

The Prison as a Total Institution

One of the more significant contributions to the corrections literature was made over 20 years ago by Erving Goffman (1961) who introduced the concept of the prison as a total institution. According to Goffman (1961, xiii), a total institution is "a place of residence and work where a large number of like-situated individuals, cut off from the wider society for an appreciable period of time, together lead an enclosed, formally administered round of life."

In his treatise, Goffman (1961, 6) outlined the major attributes of life inside total institutions, among which he included mental hospital and prisons:

First, all aspects of life are conducted in the same place and under the same single authority. Second, each phase of the member's daily activity is carried on in the immediate company of a large batch of others, all of whom are treated alike and required to do the same thing together. Third, all phases of the day's activities are tightly scheduled, with one activity leading at a prearranged time into the next, the whole sequence of activities being imposed from above by a system of explicit formal rulings and a body of officials. Finally, the various enforced activities are brought together into a single rational plan purportedly designed to fulfill the official aims of the institution.

The predominance of these characteristics in correctional institutions led Thomas and Peterson (1977, 39) to conclude that "a major obstacle to corrections is the correctional institution itself" (see also Thomas 1973).

While all correctional institutions share a common identity as total institutions, there is considerable variability from one prison to another. To differentiate between correctional institutions and the patterns of interaction that occur between the staff and the inmates (and the consequences of such interaction for correctional treatment programs), a rough "continuum of correctional institutions" can be constructed, based on the extent to which the structure and regimen of a particular institution approximates Goffman's description. This variability among correctional institutions has been noted by Thomas and Peterson (1977, 42-43):

Prisons, like any other type of organization, vary in such important regards as size; resources . . . who is being processed . . . the characteristics of the inmate population . . . security classifications . . . and a variety of other demonstrably significant characteristics. All of these influences have a major effect on the structure of the prison organization, the types of problems and pressures that confront the inmate population, the manner in which inmates respond to the conditions of confinement, and the consequences that these responses have for both the inmates and the movement of the organization toward the acquisition of its goal or goals.

In the federal prison system, a major distinguishing characteristic of correctional institutions consists of the S-levels outlined in Chapter 7 (see Table 7.1). From this system of classification, it would be expected that the patterns of interaction among the staff and inmates in a forestry camp situated at Level 2 or in a community corrections centre at Level 1 would be different from those in a maximum security institution at Level 6. Needless to say, these differences may have significant implications for the implementation and operation of correctional treatment programs.

The Inmates and the Staff

A major consequence of the prison as a total institution is a split between the inmates and the prison staff. Goffman (1961, 7) observes: "Each grouping tends to conceive of the other in terms of narrow hostile stereotypes, staff often seeing inmates as bitter, secretive, and untrustworthy, while inmates often see staff as condescending, high-handed, and mean." The patterns of interaction among the inmates, who occupy a position of powerlessness and deprivation within the institutional hierarchy, and between the inmates and the staff, or correctional officers, who enforce the rules and regulations on the line level, may have a significant influence on the treatment process.

The Inmates

Upon entering the prison, offenders undergo what Goffman (1961, 18-20) has labelled a process of "mortification" during which they are transformed from "free" citizens into inmates. This psychological and material stripping of the individual, which involves a series of "status degradation ceremonies," includes the issuing of prison clothing, assignment of an identification number, the loss of certain personal possessions, and the end of unhindered communication with the outside community (see Cloward 1969). These procedures provide the mechanism by which the offender is moved from residency in the community, with its attendant freedoms, to the world of the prison, with its rules, regulations, and social systems.

Once confined, the offender will become a member of the inmate social system, which evidences a hierarchy of power and privilege, social roles, and behavioural norms (see Sykes 1958; Garabedian 1963; Thomas and Peterson 1977; Caron 1978). In his classic work *The Society of Captives,* Sykes (1958) argued that the inmate social system emerged as a collective response by incarcerated offenders to the deprivations or "pains of imprisonment" that exist inside prisons. These included the loss of liberty, personal autonomy, and security, as well as the lack of access to goods and services, including heterosexual relationships.

Early research on the inmate social system suggested the existence of an unwritten code among the inmates which included among its tenets a prohibition against exploiting other inmates and an oppositional stance toward initiatives by the staff and administration of the prison (see Sykes and Messinger 1960). Clemmer (1940), a pioneer in the study of the prison community, coined the term "prisonization" to identify the process by which the offender becomes socialized into the inmate social system, with its attendant behavioural and attitudinal prescriptions. Subsequent research has suggested, however, that the extent to which the offender becomes "prisonized" is dependent upon a variety of factors, including relationships and lifestyle prior to incarceration and the particular groups that the individual becomes involved with once confined (see Wheeler 1961; Thomas and Foster 1977).

The socialization of the offender into the inmate social system has potentially significant implications for treatment programs that are designed to produce attitudinal and behavioural changes. This is particularly critical given the oppositional stance of the inmate social system. Marshall (1981, 31) observes:

> The inmate subculture tosses overboard almost anything designed to facilitate the implementation of treatment programs and the initiation of pro-social changes . . . The greater the extent to which the inmates accept the goals and norms of the inmate culture, the lower the chance that correctional treatment programs will be successful.

Marshall's comments suggest that the inmate social system may be a major obstacle to correctional treatment initiatives.

While there is extensive documentation of the existence of the inmate social system in correctional institutions, little research has been done on the extent to which adherence to its tenets varies along the "continuum of correctional institutions." Further, the degree to which inmates subscribe to the behavioural code is open to some question. Studies of prison populations have revealed that inmate relationships and interaction are characterized by a considerable amount of violence and exploitation (see Porporino and Marton, 1984; Campbell et al. 1985). Similarly, in contrast to what might be expected from individuals who subscribe to a code of behaviour that ascribes little legitimacy to institutional initiatives, inmates do participate extensively in treatment programs and often voice complaints about the lack of program opportunities in confinement. While such participation on the part of many inmates may be an attempt to manipulate the treatment process to obtain an early release, nevertheless, inmates give at least implicit legitimacy to treatment initiatives by their involvement in them.

The Staff

The prison staff, or correctional officers, who are involved in the day-to-day surveillance and control of the inmate population, occupy a critical position in the institution. Due to their close proximity to the inmates, as well as their involvement in regulating the movement of offenders throughout the institution, the correctional officers may either facilitate or hinder the treatment process.[1]

Despite the strategic position of the correctional officer in prisons, until recently little attention was given to either the recruitment and training of officers or to the contingencies which they encountered in carrying out their tasks. Interviews with correctional officers have revealed that the primary motivations for entering correctional work are job security and economic benefits rather than an interest in helping offenders in confinement (see Willett 1977 and 1983; Jacobs 1978). In addition, the MacGuigan Subcommittee (1977, 52) found serious deficiencies in the formal training of correctional officers in Canada, reporting several cases in which officers had been employed for periods of up to 27 years without any formal training after their initial orientation to the job. (For a further discussion on correctional officers, see Ross 1981.)

A major consequence of the role and position of the correctional officers in the prison is the development of relationships with the inmates, prison administration, and treatment staff that may have significant implications for the effectiveness of correctional treatment programs. There is considerable evidence to suggest that newly hired correctional officers often have little understanding of their role, and experience considerable difficulty in adjusting to the daily regimen of the prison (Willett 1977).

The stress and uncertainty of the correctional officer is heightened by the traditional failure of the prison administration to provide a clear sense of direction for correctional officers or to evidence sensitivity to the problems encountered by officers in carrying out administrative directives on the line level. In his study of correctional officers in a Canadian prison, Willett (1977, 49) reported that officers expressed "a serious lack of confidence in high management which was seen as remote and ineffective." In fact, several observers have suggested that, due to their perceived powerlessness in the organizational hierarchy of the prison and the lack of empathy from the administration, correctional officers may come to identify more closely with the inmates than with the administration (see Webb and Morris 1978). As a correctional officer cynically stated to one of the co-authors: "We are just as much prisoners of this place as the inmates are — the only difference is that the inmates are eligible for a parole and we aren't."

The failure of correctional administrators at the institutional level to more clearly define the role of correctional officers in the treatment process is particularly unfortunate given their close proximity and contact with the inmates on a daily basis and the potential for officers to assume the role of change agents (see Johnson 1966).

As a further consequence of their position in the prison, accommodative relationships often develop between the staff and the inmates. The inmates may refrain from creating unnecessary disturbances in exchange for the correctional officers exercising their discretion to allow flexibility in the application and enforcement of the rules and regulations of the institution (see Duffee and Fitch 1976; Sykes 1978). Through such accommodative arrangements, life within the prison is made easier for both the inmates and the correctional officers. These relationships, however, in conjunction with the sense of alienation from the prison administration among many of the officers, may serve to undermine correctional treatment efforts.

In addition to the poor relationship that often exists between correctional officers and the prison administration, interaction between the correctional officers and the treatment staff may be characterized by strain and conflict. While the correctional officers are generally assigned the tasks of providing custody and control of the inmates, the treatment staff are involved in initiatives designed to develop self-initiative and responsibility in the offenders. Correctional officers often see the treatment staff as undermining their efforts at control, and may not cooperate in the treatment programs that are established.

The conflicts that exist between correctional officers and prison administration and treatment staff, and the resulting consequences for the operation of treatment programs, are, in large measure, due to the conflicting mandate under which the prison operates. While federal and provincial correctional agencies have given increased attention to the recruitment and training of correctional officers in recent years (see Chapter 6), Griffiths et al. (1980, 227) caution that

> merely developing better recruitment and training procedures for correctional officers will not be sufficient to overcome many of the problems currently existing in correctional institutions ... Once the procedure and techniques for recruiting and training correctional officers are developed and implemented, there still remains the fact that the environment of the prison may render the use of the correctional officer's skill somewhat difficult.

As our discussion below will suggest, even when a concept such as the therapeutic community is implemented on a system-wide basis, the conflicting objectives of the prison, in conjunction with the total institution environment, may severely limit the efficacy of correctional treatment programs.

The Conflicting Mandates of the Prison

Throughout our discussion of the history of corrections in Canada, we have seen that the prison was initially designed to confine and punish offenders and that little or no thought was given to the reformation and treatment of the inmates. It was not until the recommendations of the Fauteux Committee in 1956 that the prison was publicly charged with the task of rehabilitating offenders.

With the advent of the rehabilitative ideal in corrections and the development of a wide range of treatment programs premised on the medical model in the years following World War II, a conflict emerged between the custody and control objectives of the prison and the mandate to treat and rehabilitate. This resulted in what many observers have called the "split personality of corrections." As Vigod (1974, 411) notes: "There is the demand for the infliction of pain through restriction of freedom, while at the same time, there is the demand to initiate and maintain a non-punitive program of treatment." While we noted earlier that the stated philosophy of Canadian corrections has shifted from the rehabilitative ideal, nevertheless, considering the conflicting objectives under which the prison operates will further our understanding of the treatment enterprise and its apparent demise.

The conflicting mandate of Canadian prisons was highlighted in the report of the Ouimet Committee (1969, 311) which identified the two objectives of correctional institutions: (1) to hold the inmate in custody, and (2) to prepare the individual for permanent return to community living as a law-abiding and contributing citizen. These objectives charge the prison with carrying out a retributive function by confining the offender in order to protect the community, while at the same time effecting changes in the attitude and behaviour of the offender through treatment initiatives.[2]

In examining the structure and operation of correctional institutions, several observers have attempted to locate prisons on a continuum, according to the relative emphasis that they place on either custody or treatment goals. Cressey (1965), for example, discusses prison organizations in terms of two "ideal types" — the punitive/custody prison and the treatment prison — and outlines the patterns of interaction and communication that occur within each type and the consequences of these patterns for both staff and inmates (see also Berk 1966; Leger and Stratton 1977).[3] Despite these attempts to classify correctional institutions on the basis of the objectives they pursue, critics of this approach contend that the primary objectives of all prisons are custody and control.[4]

In fact, there are many observers who argue that, even with the advent of the rehabilitative model of corrections, there was not a corresponding change in the structure and regimen of the prison:

> Prisons as formal organizations have really not changed significantly. Initially established to provide custodial control . . . their basic structure has undergone relatively little change even though the goals they purport to seek have changed quite extensively . . . the general response to changing statements of purpose has been the addition of sub-units within an organizational structure that has remained constant (Thomas and Peterson 1977, 20-21).

These comments suggest that the treatment effort within correctional institutions assumed only an adjunct status, rather than being fully integrated into the organizational structure of the prison. As Murton (1976, 65) contends:

In terms of physical facilities, "custodial security", and penal philosophy in general, prisons are more similar than dissimilar to prisons 100 years ago. Historical antecedents are allowed, often unconsciously, to limit thinking, innovation, and departure from tradition.

The sources of the intransigency of the traditional prison structure are noted by Irwin (1980, 46-47):

> The new correctional institutions were not created in a vacuum but planned in ongoing prison systems which had long traditions, administrative hierarchies, divisions, informal social worlds, and special subcultures among the old staff . . . the old timers, many of whom were highly antagonistic to the new routines, resisted change, struggled to maintain as much control as possible, and were always successful in forcing accommodation between old and new patterns. . . .

A key role in the maintenance of the control/custody objectives within correctional institutions is played by prison wardens and superintendents. It is to the prison administrator that the task of reconciling the conflicting objectives of imprisonment falls. However, for a variety of reasons, occupational and organizational, prison administrators have not traditionally been a source of either innovation for rehabilitation programs or support for the creation of institutional environments that are conducive to the operation and success of treatment initiatives.

In his critique of correctional administrators, among which he included the managers of correctional institutions, Cohn (1976, 124-26) argued that an overwhelming concern with security and the avoidance of risk-taking were two of the major reasons mitigating against wardens and superintendents assuming a leading role in the treatment process (see also Adamson 1983). As Cullen and Gilbert (1982, 267) note, "Correctional officials *get paid to maintain order and not to rehabilitate*" (emphasis in original). The report of the Carson Committee (1984) found that Canadian prison wardens had little autonomy and, because of the excessive centralization of control by the CSC, were often reduced to "paper-shuffling" bureaucrats.

Another factor contributing to the perseverance of custody and control goals in the prison has been the susceptibility of the correctional system and institutions to public and political pressures. As a consequence of the influence of outside pressures from legislatures, the media, public interest groups, and the general community, treatment efforts may be severely hindered:

> The kinds of treatments which the correctional authorities are able to offer are often limited by society's demands for painful prison conditions . . .

Programs that attempt to create an environment where a useful treatment atmosphere can be developed are commonly attacked as "country club prisons" that do not provide enough pain (Travis et al. 1983, 178-79).

Public criticism of treatment programs may be particularly severe in those instances where offenders are provided with facilities and opportunities not freely available to members of the outside community. The controversy over university education programs for inmates in federal institutions in Canada provides a recent illustration of this phenomenon. As Travis et al. (1983, 179) point out:

> Quite understandably, a person who cannot afford to go to college . . . might be upset to find out that college courses are available inside a local jail or prison at no cost to the offender. The argument that such a program is a "treatment" which offers the hope of reducing criminal behavior is not sufficient to counter the claim that those who maintain a law-abiding life-style are sometimes unable to receive the benefits that society grants to those who are convicted of a crime.

This line of reasoning was used by the Solicitor General of Canada, Robert Kaplan, in defence of the decision by the federal government in 1983 to terminate (or substantially modify) the university programs operating in several federal institutions.[5]

Custody vs. Treatment: The Therapeutic Community

The overriding concern with custody and control in correctional institutions has had a major impact on the operation and success of treatment programs. Conrad (1981, 1721) observes that "there is considerable clinical opinion casting doubt on the feasibility of therapy under the conditions of coercive control in the artificial environment of the prison." In fact, many correctional observers contend that the experience of incarceration makes offenders *less* likely to become law-abiding members of the community (see Thomas and Peterson 1977; Irwin 1970; Thomas and Poole 1975). In discussing the failure of a program of intensive group counselling to have a significant impact on the post-release behaviour of inmate participants, Kassebaum et al. (1971, 321) concluded:

> Treatment programs . . . (such as) group counseling, set forth therapeutic goals such as the acquisition of greater insight and self-responsibility. By contrast, the regulations and procedures in the prison are, openly and

obviously, aimed at instilling habits of obedience and docility in inmates, both while confined and later in the outside world.

Perhaps most illustrative of the consequences of the conflicting mandates of the prison and the perseverance of the traditional structure and operation of the prison are the difficulties encountered in implementing the therapeutic community concept in Canadian federal institutions. Despite the adoption of the Living Unit program in nearly all medium and maximum security institutions, there has been considerable concern expressed over both its viability and its effectiveness.

Many of the problems with the Living Unit concept were discovered by the MacGuigan Subcommittee (1977), who were told by an inmate at Springhill Institution that the program was "a beautiful concept fouled up." In its report, the Subcommittee (1977, 122) noted the lack of an extensive training program to prepare staff for their new roles as Living Unit Officers and documented the inadequacy of the orientation courses.

The training component of the program was critically important, as many individuals who were formerly uniformed correctional officers applied and were hired as Living Unit Officers: "Guards are not changed into Living Unit Officers simply by wearing civilian clothes." The Subcommittee (1977, 122) also expressed concern with the potential conflicts encountered by Living Unit Officers who had to fulfill the combined roles of security and counselling. While identifying these and other difficulties with the Living Unit program, the Subcommittee (1977, 122) nevertheless recommended that the Living Unit concept should become an ordinary theory of staff management at every institution.

Despite this recommendation, the MacGuigan Subcommittee did not spell out the specific initiatives that would be required to overcome the documented deficiencies and make the Living Unit concept viable. The findings of other correctional investigators who have examined the therapeutic community operation suggest that major structural changes are required.

In a discussion of the operation of the therapeutic community in the prison, for example, Vigod (1974, 412) notes that the important features of the concept are egalitarianism and de-centralized decision making, whereby decision-making responsibility is shared equally by the staff and the inmates: "Decentralized decision making is seen as important in promoting the therapeutic milieu because it lessens the inmate's suspicions of authority and provides the opportunity for the inmate to play a responsible role." In examining the concept in operation however, Vigod (1974, 414) found that Living Unit Officers experienced considerable difficulty in attempting to carry out both custody and treatment functions:

> The therapeutic community officer is expected to relax in custodial and disciplinary matters but he is not expected to relax too much ... if he enforces rules strictly, he risks being regarded as rigid and "just another guard" because such enforcement is seen to threaten the therapeutic milieu. If his failure to enforce rules creates a threat to prison security and orderliness, he is failing in his custodially oriented tasks. These varying role expectations tend to decentralize decision-making without providing specific criteria on which decisions are to be based.

From his analysis of the patterns of activity and decision making and the extent to which the inmates actually participated in the program, Vigod (1974, 418-19) concluded that the overwhelming concern with custody and control of inmates and maintenance of order in the institution diluted the emphasis upon the treatment and change goals of the therapeutic community. The findings of Vigod (1974), the MacGuigan Subcommittee (1977), and others, suggest that not only is there considerable role conflict experienced by Living Unit Officers, but also that custody and control objectives tend to undermine the treatment component (see also Arboleda-Florez 1978).

The decision to implement Functional Unit Management in federal facilities, a decision made largely on cost considerations, does little to address the concerns raised about the Living Unit concept and the suggestions made to improve its effectiveness. In fact, it might be argued that the re-introduction of uniformed security personnel into the Living Units will only serve to dilute the Living Unit concept and create additional tensions between the Living Unit officers and security personnel, and between staff and inmates.

The clear incompatibility of the regimen of the correctional institution with treatment initiatives and the failure of the correctional system to modify the organizational structure of the prison to accommodate treatment initiatives has led many observers to argue that prisons were destined to fail at the task of reformation. These observers assert that no further efforts should be undertaken within the current structure of correctional institutions (see Tittle 1974). In his discussion of correctional treatment, Conrad (1983, 221-22) presents this view quite succinctly:

The hypothesis that rehabilitation can be systematically administered in prison is absurd on the face of it . . . *Rehabilitation is not an objective of corrections.* No further research should be commissioned, undertaken, or supported to determine whether "rehabilitative" programs have any effect at all on the reduction of recidivism . . . To suppose that retribution can be combined with a *systematic* program of rehabilitation that can be measured by needle readings on a gauge of recidivism is to fly in the face of common sense. . . . (Emphasis in original).[6]

THE INTEGRITY OF
CORRECTIONAL TREATMENT PROGRAMS

In addition to the impact of organizational attributes of correctional institutions on treatment programs, there are numerous issues relating to the therapeutic integrity of correctional treatment programs.

Cullen and Gilbert (1982, 171) contend that the integrity of a majority of treatment initiatives can be questioned on at least one of the following grounds: (1) the conceptualization of the program and the extent to which the program is grounded in empirical evidence; (2) the actual delivery of treatment to the inmates; and (3) the appropriateness of the correctional treatment for the inmates involved in the program.

The Conceptual Basis of Treatment:
Reconsidering the Medical Model

In Chapter 7, we noted that the medical model, which views criminal behaviour as a manifestation of an underlying disorder in the offender requiring clinical diagnosis and intervention, has provided the conceptual basis for a wide range of treatment modalities in federal and provincial institutions. With the advent of the medical model, behavioural treatment specialists assumed key roles in correctional institutions and there was increased optimism that, through scientifically based techniques, offenders could be "cured" and criminal behaviour reduced.

Both during the tenure of the rehabilitation model of correctional practice and after its abandonment as an objective of confinement, however, serious questions were raised about the medical model and its assumptions about criminal behaviour and the appropriate treatment. The major difficulties with the medical model as a conceptual basis for correctional treatment programs had to do with its failure to clearly define the objectives of treatment and to provide a body of empirical evidence which treatment specialists could utilize in designing and operating programs. Further, many correctional observers view the medical model and the programs that developed under it as "correctional panaceas" — as products of the elusive search for correctional cure-alls — and contend that the unfulfilled promises of the advocates of the medical model actually hastened its abandonment.

We noted in the opening paragraphs of Chapter 7 that the terms "treatment" and "rehabilitation" were used to describe a wide range of programs and techniques introduced in correctional institutions following World War II. However, Gibbons (1965) and others have pointed out that the terms were never clearly defined and remained only broad orientations with no systematic guidelines. Further, Tittle (1974, 385) argues that while the term "rehabilitation" has been extensively used, discussions of its specific meaning remain vague and general: "Presumably, rehabilitation implies the correction of certain 'unhabilitating' defects that characterize offenders. But there is little concrete evidence about what defects might be 'unhabilitating' or how to correct them, much less how to determine when they have or have not been corrected." This sentiment is echoed by Conrad (1981, 1721) who contends: "So uncertain is our knowledge about the treatment of correctional clients that we still have no model that specifies who needs what treatment, for how long, and what should be expected when treatment comes to an end."

Compounding the failure of the medical model to clearly define the objectives and operational mechanisms of the terms treatment and rehabilitation were the difficulties experienced by treatment professionals in establishing reliable criteria for the diagnosis of offenders and for the identification of the particular disorder from which offenders were suffering.

The lack of understanding of the causes of criminality and the inability of treatment professionals to diagnose specific maladies in offenders had profound consequences. From his observations of treatment professionals, Gibbons (1980, 154) found widespread use of "unshared and largely intuitive procedures . . . compounded out of gross behavioral theories and speculative hunches arrived at by trial and error in the work setting." In a similar study, Shover (1974, 357) reported that individual treatment agencies operated on a basis of *ad hoc* theories of criminal behaviour and treatment that were given professional legitimacy by the use of "scientific verbal gloss." These findings suggest that, from the outset, the rehabilitative ideal and the treatment programs that were developed on the basis of the medical model lacked a clearly defined conceptual framework.

A major attribute of the rehabilitative model of correctional practice was the indeterminate sentence. Under indeterminate sentencing schemes, the release of inmates from confinement became dependent upon a determination that the offender had been rehabilitated, and this resulted in pressures on both the inmates and the treatment staff.

For the inmates, the realization that release was closely tied to participation in treatment programs often resulted in manipulation of the treatment process. Inmates participated in correctional treatment programs not with the goal of self-improvement, but with the intent of securing early release from prison (see Manocchio and Dunn 1970; Murton 1976). Many inmates became extremely sophisticated at playing the treatment "game" without showing any significant alterations in their attitudes or behaviours. Treatment personnel, on the other hand, were confronted with the difficult task of determining when the offender had been rehabilitated and was ready for release from the institution, and of predicting the future behaviour of offenders.[7]

Contributing to the difficulties of the medical model in providing effective strategies for the treatment of offenders is what has become known as the "panacea phenomenon" or the seemingly endless search by corrections for a cure-all for criminal behaviour. This quest has traditionally made corrections fertile ground for the uncritical acceptance of models of correctional practice, acceptance given without a close examination of the viability and empirical validity of the assumption upon which such models are premised (see Finckenauer 1982). As Ross and McKay (1978, 281) note, "In corrections novelty frequently serves as a substitute for efficacy." This phenomenon has had profound implications for the treatment effort; Glaser (1975, 3) notes wryly that "The highway of corrections is paved with punctured panaceas."

Two of the more notable casualties of the panacea phenomenon were group counselling and behaviour modification, both of which were widely adopted in Canadian institutions and highly touted as effective treatment strategies. In his discussion of the "lost ideal" of rehabilitation, Conrad (1981, 1734) argues that group counselling personified the naive assumptions and unrealistic expectations of programs that were developed under the medical model:

> We have expected of counseling far more than the most expert counseling could deliver to willing clients in a free society. We have supposed that the insight gained from such counseling would move criminals from their acceptance of crime as a natural course toward personal satisfaction. This illusion, grounded on wishful thinking, haphazard planning, and

unthinking administration, is the rehabilitative ideal as we have known it in corrections for the last thirty or forty years. . . . It is to be dismissed now as an embarrassing absurdity.

Another example of a "punctured panacea" is behaviour modification, which Ross and McKay (1978, 280) discuss as an example of how treatment strategies in corrections are often "adopted wholeheartedly and foolheartedly [sic]; at times exclusively, and often with little question as to their applicability to the population in the field." In examining the implementation of programs based on behaviour modification, these authors (1978, 281) note that the decision to employ this particular modality in correctional institutions was premised "more on promise than accomplishment" and that there was little or no empirical evidence as to the rehabilitative efficacy of the technique. Given this background, it is not surprising that published evaluations of behaviour modification programs have shown results that are "singularly unimpressive."

In critiquing treatment modalities such as group counselling and behaviour modification, the intent of observers such as Ross and McKay (1978) and Conrad (1981; 1983) is not to argue for the abandonment of the treatment effort. Rather, they are attempting to identify the erroneous assumptions upon which a large number of treatment modalities were premised and, in so doing, move corrections away from the panacea phenomenon and toward the creation of more effective correctional strategies.

The Delivery of Correctional Treatment

A second major difficulty affecting the therapeutic integrity of correctional treatment programs is the manner in which they were operationalized in correctional institutions. Several observers have noted that there was often a major discrepancy between the original program and the manner in which it was implemented. This was due not only to the contingencies imposed by the institutional environment, but also to the manner in which such programs were administered. As Gendreau and Ross (1981, 39) note: "When successful treatments are taken from the developmental site and implemented elsewhere they are often altered and diluted." Similarly, Roesch and Corrado (1983, 405) concluded that, while many of the evaluative results have been discouraging,

many of the interventions have not had a fair test. The theories underlying interventions have often been subverted when the interventions have been implemented ... Factors such as individual and organizational self-interests, differing ideological perspectives, and political pressures and constraints can affect the way in which an intervention develops.

In our earlier discussion of the organizational attributes that may affect correctional treatment, it was noted that the traditional structure and regimen of the prison were not conducive to treatment initiatives. Similarly, while correctional administrators were assigned the task of reforming and treating offenders, often the rhetoric of rehabilitation was adopted without the necessary facilities being developed. Thomas and Peterson (1977, 36) state that

> it is not uncommon for an institution that houses a thousand or more inmates to define itself as being committed to rehabilitation when there is no full-time staff member who holds an advanced degree in any of the helping professions or, when there are full-time and more or less adequately qualified staff members, to find that the ratio of inmates to qualified treatment staff is a hundred or more to one.

There is considerable evidence that treatment initiatives in many institutions were undertaken on a token basis (see Murton 1976).

As a consequence of the failure to commit resources and personnel to the treatment effort, in many institutions there were low rates of inmate participation in treatment programs. Petersilia (cited in Cullen and Gilbert 1982, 172), for example, reported the results of one survey which revealed that no more than 40 percent of the offenders in state prisons in the United States participated in treatment programs while incarcerated, and that only "one in five inmates with identified needs participated in prison treatment programs related to these needs."

In his critique of the intensive counselling project evaluated by Kassebaum et al. (1971), Quay (1977) reported that circumstances surrounding the delivery of counselling therapy to the inmates seriously hindered its effectiveness:

> There was no consistency in the counseling modality. The sessions were weekly. The training of the counselors, even those whose training was "enhanced," was superficial. Many of the counselors had little confidence in the real value of what they were doing; they were involved in the interest of their own career advancement. The supposition that such a program could produce a lasting effect on those who were exposed to it should have strained credulity (cited in Conrad 1981, 1715).

In addition, Quay (1977) reported that most of the counsellors were not professionals, that training sessions for the counsellors had been poorly attended, and that inmate participation in the program was voluntary. Travis et al. (1983, 177) have also been particularly critical of the quality of counselling programs in correctional institutions and concluded that the poor therapeutic integrity of the intensive group counselling program evaluated by Kassebaum et al. (1971), rather than the technique itself, was the major reason for the program's apparent failure.

The Appropriateness of Correctional Treatment

One of the major assumptions that treatment professionals made in utilizing the medical model was that offenders who were incarcerated in correctional institutions suffered from disorders that required treatment. A related difficulty was the failure of correctional treatment personnel to recognize the variability among inmates in terms of their treatment needs and requirements.

Warren (1977) and Waldo (1973) have suggested that there may be considerable variability among offenders as to the most appropriate treatment setting and, further, that some offenders are more amenable to certain treatment modalities than are others. While some offenders may be best treated in a community-based setting, for example, others may be more responsive to treatment within an institutional setting. In addition, the "treater" and the type of treatment modality must be matched to the needs of the individual offender.

The importance of these considerations in the treatment process are illustrated by the findings of Adams (cited in Travis et al. 1983, 175). From an examination of the impact of a program of intensive counselling on post-release behaviour, Adams found that, while those offenders who had been identified as "amenable" to counselling improved following participation in the program, "those who were designated as 'non-amenable' and were given counselling fared worse than that group of non-amenables who were not given counselling." This finding led Adams to conclude that "counselling persons who were not amenable to therapy *decreased* their chances of success following treatment. As a group, they would have fared better if no treatment at all had been given." The "treatment-for-everyone" approach that developed under the medical model may have, in many cases, actually diminished the post-release prospects of inmates.

Closely related to the failure to individualize correctional treatment was the extensive reliance by the treatment programs upon single methods of intervention with offenders, an approach which ignored the complexities of criminal behaviour. From their review of the correctional literature, Gendreau and Ross (1981, 44) reported that programs relying on a single method of treatment had notably less positive results than those programs employing a multi-faceted treatment approach.[8]

In sum, there are numerous issues relating to the therapeutic integrity of correctional programs that may have contributed to their inability to have a significant impact on the behaviour of the inmates participating in them. Gendreau and Ross (1981, 43) provide a concise summary of the ingredients that are critical in the delivery of correctional treatment to clients, yet which were generally ignored by programs implemented under the rehabilitative ideal:

> There are no curealls in corrections. Programs that "work" with some offenders may fail or even have deleterious effects with other offenders. Treatment outcome seems to depend not only on the nature of the program but on the characteristics of the client and the therapists and the quality of their relationship. It also depends on the setting in which it is provided and the nature of the posttreatment environment. It all seems to depend upon who does what to whom, where, when, and how long.

THE ETHICS OF CORRECTIONAL TREATMENT

The introduction of the medical model of correctional practice and the involvement of inmates in the treatment process raised numerous issues regarding the ethics of correctional treatment. This debate, which many observers credit with contributing to the demise of the rehabilitation ideal, centred on the coercive nature of treatment in correctional institutions, a concern that such treatment constituted additional punishment of the offender, and the debate over whether the state had the right to force offenders to participate in treatment programs as a condition of their confinement and release.

As we have previously noted, the advent of the medical model resulted in a shift of attention from the crime to the offender. Behavioural experts, in an attempt to cure offenders of their underlying disorders and produce individuals who would conform to societal rules upon release, were given unfettered discretion in the classification, diagnosis, and treatment of offenders. While the interventions were designed to "help" the offender, the use of such techniques as electroconvulsive therapy, drug therapy, and various behavioural modification schemes, raised images of George Orwell's *1984* (1961) and of the fate of the leading characters in *One Flew Over the Cuckoo's Nest* (Kesey 1962) and *A Clockwork Orange* (Burgess 1965).

According to critics such as the authors of *Struggle for Justice* (American Friends Service Committee 1971, 146), the use of strategies designed to modify behaviour raises serious moral questions: "Treatment mixed with coercion is scientifically unfeasible and morally objectionable." Many observers argue that such treatment actually constitutes additional punishment of the offender, Gaylin and Blatte (cited in Arboleda-Florez 1983, 49) asserting that rehabilitation is nothing more than "punishment clothed in a therapeutic rationalization" (see also Irwin 1970; Mitford 1974).

The opponents of forcing inmates to participate in correctional treatment programs argue that the mandate of the criminal law is to respond to behaviour, and not to the psychological and sociological condition of the offender. As such, the state does not have the right to force inmates to participate in treatment programs: "People have a right to behave badly and to suffer the consequences of their actions if that is their desire; the state has no right to attempt to enforce behavior change" (Sechrest et al. 1983, 208).[9]

Similarly, Cullen and Gilbert (1982, 116) contend that the coercive nature of correctional treatment not only violates the civil liberties of offenders and exceeds the powers of the state, but also creates deep resentments among inmates toward institutional staff. These comments suggest that, rather than facilitating the development of prosocial attitudes and behaviours, "forced" correctional treatment has deleterious effects on inmates.

The origins of inmate perceptions that correctional treatment constitutes punishment are noted by Travis et al. (1983, 178):

> The offender knows full well that he is in a prison, and has been sent there by society for punishment. Once there, he is forced to take part in a program which he finds personally painful, and does not wish to be a part of. It is not hard to see how the offender may come to see this treatment program as one more pain or punishment he must bear in prison.

Such perceptions are no doubt intensified by the previously noted lack of inmate input into the treatment process. Had offenders been consulted and become active participants in the treatment programs developed under the medical model, rather than being merely recipients of the decisions of behavioural "experts," it is likely that such feelings would have been diminished. (For a critique of the ethics of correctional treatment from the radical-elitist perspective, see Gosselin 1982, 161-68.)

In Canada, the debate over the ethics of correctional treatment is best illustrated by the controversy surrounding the establishment of the Regional Psychiatric Centres by the federal government in 1972. While the opening of these institutions was accompanied by considerable optimism that the programs would successfully address the problems of the mentally ill offender, criticisms were voiced by observers such as Desroches (1973), who expressed concern about the potential for coercion of offenders and the violation of civil liberties under the guise of treatment. More recently, Arboleda-Florez (1983) has raised questions about the role conflict experienced by psychiatrists and other treatment staff working in the Regional Psychiatric Centres, which are classified as both maximum security penitentiaries and as hospitals.

It is likely that, in the next several years, the newly adopted Charter of Rights and Freedoms will provide the basis for an increased concern with the legal rights of incarcerated offenders and with issues related to the ethics of correctional treatment.

Notes

1. The term "correctional officer" is used to identify personnel who are charged with the control and surveillance of inmates within the prison. With the shift to the rehabilitative model of corrections in the 1950s and 1960s, the term correctional officer replaced the traditional designation of prison guard, although in most instances, the actual role and responsibilities of the individuals in the position did not change. Under Functional Unit Management, both Living Unit officers and uniformed security personnel are assigned to manage inmates. In provincial institutions, however, the Living Unit concept was not adopted and the uniformed correctional officer, whose responsibilities are custody and control, has been retained.

2. The split personality of corrections is evident in many long-standing controversies in Canadian corrections. The debate over conjugal visiting, for example, highlights the tension between punishment and treatment objectives. While, on the one hand, it is argued that permitting offenders to have overnight visits from spouse and family facilitates the stability and survival of the family unit, many critics contend that the offenders should be deprived of such contact as part of their punishment.

3. Ideal types are constructs that represent a pure form. No one institution would exist in this form; rather, according to those observers who subscribe to the punitive/custody–treatment continuum concept, an institution may have a preponderance of characteristics and approximate one ideal type or another.

4. Empirical support for the argument that few, if any, differences exist in the success rates of inmates released from institutions classified as "custody-oriented" and from those identified as "treatment-oriented" are provided by Wheeler (1961, cited in Garabedian 1971, 49) who found that "once the relevant offender characteristics have been taken into account, there are very few differences between offenders released from treatment-oriented institutions and those released from custody-oriented institutions."

5. While public opinion and concerns are often employed by correctional administrators and policy makers as a justification for particular decisions, actual empirical evidence of public opinion is rarely available. In actuality, it could be argued that the public is generally ill-informed on many issues in corrections, relying to a large extent upon the media for the information they receive on various correctional issues and controversies. Many correctional observers argue that the correctional system has made little effort to educate the public about corrections and the complexities of the issues involved in the confinement and treatment of offenders and further, that the public, if properly informed, could be an ally in the correctional enterprise. In contemporary corrections, the role of the public is generally a reactive one, with communities responding to particular initiatives of the correctional system, such as the decision to build a correctional facility in a community, or to specific events, such as the escape of a prisoner from an institution (see Tully et al. 1982).

6. It is significant that in reviewing the recommendations of the Task Force on the Creation of an Integrated Canadian Corrections Service (1977) and the MacGuigan Subcommittee (1977) that the prison relinquish the task of rehabilitation, little attention was given to examining the structural and operational attributes of correctional institutions that had hindered treatment initiatives such as the therapeutic community. Rather, the recommendations tended to focus on the perceived shortcomings of the medical model and on the need to assign greater responsibility to the offender, as well as, ironically, the importance of shifting treatment efforts to community-based programs. This is particularly evident in the MacGuigan (1977) report, which documented conditions in Canadian institutions similar to those discovered by the Brown Commission in 1848-49 (see also Ellis 1979).

7. Under the medical model, inmates who adapt well to the prison environment and conform to the expectations of treatment personnel, staff, and administration were often deemed "cured" and ready to re-enter society. However, as Cullen and Gilbert (1982, 114) appropriately note: "The regimen and realities of the society of captives have little or nothing in common with life in the wider society . . . many who might be model citizens within the confines of a structured environment may not possess the skills or personal strength to negotiate the rigors of an independent existence. Alternatively, those who fall prey to the intense pressures of imprisonment and respond with sporadic outbursts of resentment and rebelliousness may, notwithstanding, be equipped to adapt far better upon release." Thus, the behaviour of the inmate within the artificial world of the prison may be unrelated to how the offender will act upon release.

8. A predominant characteristic of the correctional treatment process that has hindered the selection of appropriate intervention strategies is the general lack of input by the clients (the inmates). It has traditionally been assumed that correctional administrators and treatment professionals have the necessary expertise to identify the treatment needs of offenders, who are relegated to a

passive rather than an active role in the reformation effort. Under current correctional policies, exemplified by the opportunities model, inmates are assigned a greater responsibility for taking the initiative for improving themselves, although actual inmate input into the programs and treatment modalities through which such self-improvement is to occur is negligible.

9. It might be argued that, under the opportunities model of correctional practice, which places the responsibility on the offender to participate in his or her own reformation, an inmate is given the choice of either participating or not participating in correctional treatment programs while confined. However, as our discussion of the decision making of the parole board in Chapter 9 reveals, the chances of an inmate being granted a parole are considerably enhanced by participation in treatment programs and by evidence that the inmate has made an effort to "better" himself while confined. Thus, while under the current model of correctional practice in Canada, the federal corrections system no longer assumes an ability to diagnose and treat criminality, the criteria for release remain very similar to those employed under the medical model. The parole board, as we see in Chapter 9, is very much interested in whether the inmate has exercised the opportunity during confinement to participate in a program of reformation.

References

Adamson, C.R. (October) 1983. "The Breakdown of Canadian Prison Administration: Evidence from Three Commissions of Inquiry." 25 *Canadian Journal of Criminology.* 433-37.

American Friends Service Committee. 1971. *Struggle for Justice.* New York: Hill and Wang.

Arboleda-Florez, J. (July) 1978. "Some Ethical Issues in the Treatment of Offenders at the Regional Psychiatric Center (Abbotsford)." 20 *Canadian Journal of Criminology.* 301-07.

. (January) 1983. "The Ethics of Psychiatry in Prison Society." 25 *Canadian Journal of Criminology.* 47-54.

Berk, B.B. (March) 1966. "Organizational Goals and Inmate Organization." 71 *American Journal of Sociology.* 522-34.

Burgess, A. 1963. *A Clockwork Orange.* New York: W.W. Norton.

Campbell, G., F.J. Porporino and L. Wevrick. 1985. *Characteristics of Inmates Involved in Prison Incidents.* Ottawa: Solicitor General of Canada.

Caron, R. 1978. *Go Boy: Memoirs of a Life Behind Bars.* Toronto: McGraw-Hill Ryerson.

Carson, J. (Chairman). 1984. *Report of the Advisory Committee to the Solicitor General of Canada on the Management of Correctional Institutions.* Ottawa: Supply and Services Canada.

Clemmer, D. 1940. *The Prison Community.* Boston: Christopher Publishing Co.

Cloward, R.A. 1969. "Social Control in the Prison." In L. Hazelrigg (ed). *Prison Within Society: A Reader in Penology.* Garden City, N.Y.: Doubleday. 78-112.

Cohn, A.W. 1976. "The Failure of Correctional Management." In G.G. Killinger, P.F. Cromwell, Jr. and B.J. Cromwell (eds.) *Corrections and Administration: Selected Readings.* St. Paul, Minnesota: West Publishing Co. 119-31.

Conrad, J.P. (Winter) 1981. "A Lost Ideal, A New Hope: The Way Toward Effective Correctional Treatment." 72 *Journal of Criminal Law and Criminology.* 1699-1734.

_____. 1983. "What Prospects for Rehabilitation? A Dissent from Academic Wisdom." In L.F. Travis, M.D. Schwartz and T.R. Clear (eds.) *Corrections: An Issues Approach.* 2d edition. Cincinnati, Ohio: Anderson Publishing Co. 216-26.

Cressey, D.R. 1965. "Prison Organizations." In J.G. March (ed.) *Handbook of Organizations.* Chicago: Rand McNally. 1036-48.

Cullen, F.T. and K.E. Gilbert. 1982. *Reaffirming Rehabilitation.* Cincinnati, Ohio: Anderson Publishing Co.

Desroches, F. (April) 1973. "Regional Psychiatric Centres — A Myopic View?" 15 *Canadian Journal of Criminology and Corrections.* 200-18.

Duffee, D. and R. Fitch. 1976. *An Introduction to Corrections: A Policy and Systems Approach.* Pacific Pallisades, California: Goodyear Publishing Co.

Ellis, D. (Winter) 1979. "The Prison Guard as Carceral Luddite: A Critical Review of the MacGuigan Report on the Penitentiary System in Canada." 4 *Canadian Journal of Sociology.* 43-64.

Finckenauer, J.O. 1982. *Scared Straight! and the Panacea Phenomenon.* Englewood Cliffs, N.J.: Prentice-Hall.

Garabedian, P.G. 1963. "Social Roles and Processes of Socialization in the Prison Community." 11 *Social Problems.* 139-52.

_____. (January) 1971. "Research and Practice in Planning Correctional Change." 17 *Crime and Delinquency.* 41-55.

Gendreau, P. and R.R. Ross. 1981. "Correctional Potency: Treatment and Deterrence on Trial." In R. Roesch and R.R. Corrado (eds.) *Evaluation and Criminal Justice Policy.* Beverly Hills, California: Sage Publications. 29-57.

Gibbons, D.C. 1965. *Changing the Lawbreaker: The Treatment of Criminals and Victims.* Englewood Cliffs, N.J.: Prentice-Hall.

_____. 1980. "Some Notes on Treatment Theory in Corrections." In D.M. Peterson and C.W. Thomas (eds.) *Corrections: Problems and Prospects.* Englewood Cliffs, N.J.: Prentice Hall. 153-66.

Glaser, D. (September) 1975. "Achieving Better Questions: A Half-Century's Progress in Correctional Research." 39 *Federal Probation.* 3-9.

Goffman, E. 1961. *Asylums: Essays on the Social Situation of Mental Patients and Other Inmates.* Garden City, N.Y.: Doubleday.

Gosselin, L. 1982. *Prisons in Canada.* Montreal: Black Rose Books.

Griffiths, C.T., J.F. Klein and S.N. Verdun-Jones. 1980. *Criminal Justice in Canada: An Introductory Text.* Vancouver: Butterworths.

Irwin, J. 1970. *The Felon.* Englewood Cliffs, N.J.: Prentice-Hall.

_____. 1980. *Prisons in Turmoil.* Toronto: Little, Brown and Co.

Jacobs, J.B. (April) 1978. "What Prison Guards Think: A Profile of the Illinois Force." 24 *Crime and Delinquency.* 185-96.

Johnson, R. (August) 1966. "Ameliorating Prison Stress: Some Helping Roles for Custodial Personnel." 5 *International Journal of Criminology and Penology.* 263-73.

Kassebaum, G., D.A. Ward and D.M. Wilner. 1971. *Prison Treatment and Parole Survival.* New York: John Wiley and Sons.

Kesey, K. 1962. *One Flew Over the Cuckoo's Nest.* New York: Signet.

Leger, R.G. and J.R. Stratton. 1977. *The Sociology of Corrections: A Book of Readings.* New York: John Wiley and Sons.

MacGuigan, M. (Chairman). 1977. *Report to Parliament by the Sub-Committee on the Penitentiary System in Canada.* Ottawa: Supply and Services Canada.

Manocchio. A. and J. Dunn. 1970. *The Time Game: Two Views of a Prison.* Beverly Hills, California: Sage Publications.

Marshall, I.H. 1981. "Correctional Treatment Processes: Rehabilitation Reconsidered." In R.R. Roberg and V.J. Webb (eds.) *Critical Issues in Corrections: Problems, Trends, and Prospects.* St. Paul, Minnesota: West Publishing Co. 14-46.

Mitford, J. 1974. *Kind and Usual Punishment. The Prison Business.* New York: Alfred A. Knopf.

Murton, T.O. 1976. *The Dilemma of Prison Reform.* New York: Holt, Reinhart and Winston.

Orwell, G. 1961. *1984: A Novel.* New York: New American Library.

Ouimet, R. (Chairman). 1969. *Report of the Canadian Committee on Corrections — Toward Unity: Criminal Justice and Corrections.* Ottawa: Information Canada.

Porporino, F.J. and J.P. Marton. 1984. *Strategies to Reduce Prison Violence.* Ottawa: Solicitor General of Canada.

Quay, H.C. (December) 1977. "The Three Faces of Evaluation: What Can be Expected to Work?" 4 *Criminal Justice and Behavior.* 341-54.

Reid, S.T. 1981. *The Correctional System: An Introduction.* New York: Holt, Reinhart and Winston.

Roesch, R. and R.R. Corrado. 1983. "Criminal Justice System Interventions." In E. Seidman (ed.) *Handbook of Social Intervention.* Beverly Hills, California: Sage Publications. 385-407.

Ross, R.R. 1981. *Prison Guard/Correctional Officer.* Toronto: Butterworths.

Ross, R.R. and H.B. McKay. (July) 1978. "Behavioural Approaches to Treatment in Corrections: Requiem for a Panacea." 20 *Canadian Journal of Criminology.* 279-95.

Sechrest, L., S.D. White and E.D. Brown. 1983. "The Prospects for Rehabilitation." In L.F. Travis, M.D. Schwartz and T.R. Clear (eds.) *Corrections: An Issues Approach.* 2d edition. Cincinnati, Ohio: Anderson Publishing Co. 200-15.

Shover, N. 1974. " 'Experts' and Diagnosis in Correctional Agencies." 20 *Crime and Delinquency.* 347-59.

Sykes, G.M. 1958. *The Society of Captives: A Study of a Maximum Security Institution.* Princeton, N.J.: Princeton University Press.

_____. 1978. *Criminology.* New York: Harcourt, Brace and Jovanovich.

Sykes, G.M. and S.L. Messinger. 1960. "The Inmate Social System." In R.A. Cloward, D.R. Cressey, G.H. Grosser, R. McCleery, L.E. Ohlin, G.M. Sykes and S.L. Messinger (eds.) *Theoretical Studies in the Social Organization of the Prison.* New York: Social Science Research Council. 5-19.

Task Force on the Creation of an Integrated Canadian Corrections Service. 1977. *The Role of Federal Corrections in Canada.* Supply and Services Canada.

Thomas, C.W. (March) 1973. "The Correctional Institution as an Enemy of Corrections." 37 *Federal Probation.* 8-13.

Thomas, C.W. and S.C. Foster. 1972. "Prisonization in the Inmate Contraculture." 20 *Social Problems*. 229-39.

Thomas, C.W. and D.M. Peterson. 1977. *Prison Organization and Inmate Subcultures*. Indianapolis: Bobbs-Merrill.

Thomas, C.W. and E.D. Poole. (February) 1975. "The Consequences of Incompatible Goal Structures in Correctional Settings." 3 *International Journal of Criminology and Penology*. 27-42.

Tittle, C.R. 1974. "Prisons and Rehabilitation: The Inevitability of Disfavor." 21 *Social Problems*. 385-95.

Travis, L.F., M.D. Schwartz and T.R. Clear. 1983. *Corrections: An Issues Approach*. 2d edition. Cincinnati, Ohio: Anderson Publishing Co.

Tully, H.A., J.P. Winter, J.E. Wilson and T.J. Scanlon. (July) 1982. "Correctional Institution Impact and Host Community Resistance." 24 *Canadian Journal of Criminology*. 133-39.

Vigod, Zena L. (October) 1974. "A Prison Therapeutic Community and its Decision-Making Structure." 16 *Canadian Journal of Criminology and Corrections*. 411-20.

Waldo, G.P. 1973. "Research in Correctional Education." In A.R. Roberts (ed.) *Readings in Prison Education*. Springfield, Illinois: Charles C. Thomas. 364-76.

Warren, M.Q. (December) 1977. "Correctional Treatment and Coercion: The Differential Effectiveness Perspective." 4 *Criminal Justice and Behavior*. 355-76.

Webb, G.L. and D.G. Morris. 1978. *Prison Guards: The Culture and Perspective of an Occupational Group*. Coker Publishing Co.

Wheeler, S. (October) 1961. "Socialization in Correctional Institutions." 26 *American Sociological Review*. 697-712.

Willett, T.C. (Summer) 1977. "The 'Fish Screw' in the Canadian Penitentiary Service." 3 *Queen's Law Journal*. 424-49.

———. (January) 1983. "Prison Guards in Private." 25 *Canadian Journal of Criminology*. 1-17.

Chapter 9

Community-Based Corrections

In our discussion of Canadian correctional history in Chapter 2, we documented the adoption of the reintegration model of corrections in the early 1970s, which resulted in the expansion of community-based correctional programs. This shift in correctional philosophy was prompted, in part, by the debate over the effectiveness of treatment in correctional institutions and the recommendations of several task force reports, centring on the argument that the rehabilitation of the offender would best be accomplished in the community. In Chapter 3, we outlined the operation of the reintegration model and provided an overview of several community-based programs including temporary absence, attendance centres, community-based correctional centres, community service order programs, and probation and parole.

In this chapter, we examine community-based corrections more closely, with particular emphasis on the goals of the various programs and the extent to which they are successful in achieving their objectives. Our discussion includes *(1)* probation, *(2)* the pre-release programs of temporary absence and day parole, *(3)* community-based facilities, and *(4)* parole. In addition, we consider work release as an example of a pre-release program that has been widely utilized as a community corrections program.[1] Diversion. which is often considered to be a community-based program, is examined in Chapter 10, as illustrative of an initiative within the broader context of justice reform in Canada.

COMMUNITY CORRECTIONS: CONCEPT AND CONTROVERSY

Our consideration of correctional treatment programs in Chapter 7 revealed that the failure of correctional policy makers and practitioners to define such key terms as "treatment" and "rehabilitation" hindered not only the operation of programs, but also assessments of their effectiveness. There have been similar difficulties surrounding the term "community-based" corrections. Doeren and Hageman (1982, 16) note that many definitions have failed to consider the key ingredient of *community relationships* and, further, that programs are often erroneously labelled as community-based or assumed to be community-based corrections, when they in fact are not.

Perhaps the most concise definition of community-based corrections has been provided by Doeren and Hageman (1982, 16):

> Community-based corrections may be defined as: any correctional-related activity purposively aimed at directly assisting and supporting the efforts of offenders to establish meaningful ties or relationships with the community for the specific purpose of becoming reestablished and functional in legitimate roles in the community.

A further delineation of the purposes of community-based corrections is provided by the *Report of the Task Force on Community-Based Residential Centres* (Outerbridge 1972, ix) which outlined the following objectives: *(1)* to divert persons entirely from the criminal justice system and incarceration; *(2)* to shorten the length of incarceration; and *(3)* to provide temporary relief from incarceration. In Canada, diversion programs and probation are designed to fulfill the first objective. Parole fulfills the second, and pre-release programs, such as Temporary Absences and day parole, under which the offender may reside in a community correctional centre or halfway house, achieve the third.

Table 9.1 is a summary of the community-based services for adults provided by provincial/territorial correctional agencies. All of the provinces/territories provide probation services, operate temporary absence and community service order programs, and utilize volunteer and outside agency services. With the exception of P.E.I. and the Yukon, all provincial/territorial jurisdictions have community-based centres, operated either by the province/ territory or by private agencies under contract, such as John Howard, Elizabeth Fry, St. Leonard's, or the Salvation Army. Table 9.1 also reveals that the provinces of British Columbia, Quebec, and Ontario have provincial parole boards, a situation that is discussed in greater detail later in the chapter.

A review of the extensive literature on community corrections indicates that three justifications have traditionally been employed in support of community-based programs (see Shover 1979; Roberg and Webb 1981; Doeren and Hageman 1982; Hylton 1982):

1. Community-based programs are more humane than incarcerating offenders in correctional institutions.
2. Community-based programs are less costly than institutional services.
3. Community-based programs increase the chances of the successful reintegration of the offender into the community.

In addition to these justifications, proponents of community-based programs contend that such initiatives have positive psychological benefits for the offender, assist in maintaining the viability of the offender's family, and lead to a greater understanding by the public of offenders and their problems. Community corrections has also been supported on the basis that, as the major intent is reintegration, the conflict between treatment and control that has long afflicted the correctional enterprise is avoided.

While community-based programs have proliferated in the last decade, many correctional observers have taken serious issue with the concept of community corrections and the extent to which specific community-based initiatives are successful in achieving the above-noted objectives (see, generally, Greenberg 1975; Lerman 1975; Chan and Ericson 1981; Scull 1982; Hylton 1982).

In Chapter 2, we noted the controversy over whether community corrections emerged as a consequence of humanitarian concerns or as an attempt to reduce the costs of incarceration. In their analysis of decarceration in Canada, Chan and Ericson (1981, 39) take issue with Scull's interpretation, arguing that rather than de-escalating the costs of social control, the decarceration movement has been accompanied by a "substantial growth of the criminal control apparatus." As support for this assertion, the authors (1981, 42, 44) note the record levels of persons incarcerated in federal and provincial institutions and the increasingly larger number of persons being placed under probation supervision in the community: "In Ontario the rate of adult persons under probation supervision has risen from 275.4 to 503.7 per 100,000 population from 1972 to 1978, and during the same period the rate of incarceration has risen from 52.2 to 71.1 per 100,000 population." Similarly, there was an 11 percent increase in the number of offenders on probation during the five-year period 1980/81 to 1985/86 (Statistics Canada, 1986, 93).

On the basis of such figures, Rothman (1980, 9) has argued that "innovations that appeared to be substitutes for incarceration have become supplements to incarceration," and Chan and Ericson (1981, 55) conclude that "people are not diverted *from*, but *into* and *within* the system."[2]

TABLE 9.1   Community Programs for Adults Provided by Provincial/Territorial Correctional Agencies

Community Services	NFLD	PEI	NS	NB	PQ	ONT	MAN	SASK	ALTA	BC	YK	NWT
Probation	×	×	×	×	×	×	×	×	×	×	×	×
Provincial Parole				×¹	×	×				×		
Community Service Orders	×	×	×	×	×	×	×	×	×	×	×	×
Temporary Absence Program	×	×	×	×	×	×	×	×	×	×	×	×
Drinking/Driving Program	×			×	×	×	×	×		×	×	
Fine Option Program				×	×	×	×	×	×		×	×
Victim-Offender Reconciliation					×	×						
Victim-Witness Program		×		×	×							
Bail Verification/ Supervision						×		×	×	×	×	
Restitution Program		×		×		×		×	×	×		
Community-Based/Halfway House Program	×		×	×	×	×	×	×	×	×		×
Volunteer/Outside Agency Services	×	×	×	×	×	×	×	×	×	×	×	×

SOURCE: Statistics Canada. 1986. *Adult Correctional Services in Canada, 1985–86*. Ottawa: Canadian Centre for Justice Statistics.

¹ The New Brunswick Board of Parole has authority only over adults convicted of Provincial Statute violations and young offenders charged under the *Young Offenders Act* (1984).

On a general systems level, then, a major concern of many observers is that the introduction of community corrections has resulted in an appreciable expansion of the criminal justice system, with an increasingly larger number of individuals being placed under some form of supervision and control.

Another major concern that has surrounded discussions of community-based corrections is the role of the community. It has been argued that the interface between the community and community corrections was never clearly defined and that, as a consequence, community correction programs were in, but not "of," the community. Irwin (1980, 175), for example, contends that the concept of community used by proponents of community corrections was naive and unrealistic:

> The idea that community corrections promotes the reintegration of the offender into the community distorts or stretches conceptions of community. The notion of a community is a holdover from rural or folk societies, and it is not exactly clear what it refers to in a modern city.

The failure of corrections to develop strategies to increase the role of the community in community corrections, despite the reports and recommendations of commissions such as the Task Force on the Role of the Private Sector in Criminal Justice (1977), resulted in public resistance to community corrections initiatives. As Greenberg (1975, 24) notes:

> The architects of community corrections appear to have hoped that neighborhood residents would rush to embrace their prodigal sons and daughters returning to the fold. To say that this hope has not been fulfilled would be an understatement ... the abstractly desirable goal of rehabilitation can be forgotten very quickly when personal safety and property values are believed to be in jeopardy.

In addition to the arguments surrounding the conceptual aspects of community corrections, criticism has been directed at assertions that community-based programs are more humane, less costly and more effective in facilitating the reintegration of the offender than traditional institutional programs. Greenberg (1975), Cohen (1979), Hylton (1982) and others contend that the behavioural restrictions imposed on offenders under probation and parole supervision, as well as the rules and regulations of community residences, make such alternatives to confinement less humane than they were designed to be. Cohen (1979, 343) argues that community-based programs tend to "reproduce in the community the very same coercive features of the system they were designed to replace." Further, Hylton (1982, 349) contends that "the presumed inhumanity of correctional institutions and the ability of community programs to humanize the correctional system are seldom examined carefully. There is a tendency simply to assume the superiority of community programs without a thorough examination of their impact."[3]

There has also been considerable disagreement over the cost effectiveness of community-based programs as compared to maintaining the offender in a correctional institution. Greenberg (1975) and Hylton (1982), for example, have pointed out that, while community-based initiatives are often less expensive to operate, this may be a consequence of the fact that offenders in community-based programs often do not receive adequate services. Hylton (1982, 367), citing research by Scull (1977) and Dunford (1977), argues that there is often a severe gap in the delivery of services to offenders in community programs and further that, had the level of intended services been provided, the costs of community-based programs would more closely approximate those of institutional services: "Where savings are achieved, it is often because program objectives have been sacrificed." Similarly, in discussing the costs associated with the delivery of correctional services, Greenberg (1975, 6) argues that "if the goal of making educational and vocational opportunities or individual psychiatric counseling available to those who wanted these services were taken seriously, the cost might be considerable." Additional arguments relating to the cost effectiveness of specific community-based initiatives are considered throughout the chapter.

In addition to these considerations, there is debate over the rehabilitative efficacy of community-based correctional programs. From his review of the evaluative literature, Greenberg (1975, 4) concluded that not only is there a lack of conclusive empirical support for the notion that community-based programs are successful in reintegrating offenders into the community, but also that they are apparently no more effective than traditional institutionally based techniques. This position is shared by Hylton (1982, 348-49) who found in a review of several evaluations of community-based programs that "there is no evidence that the widespread adoption of community programs has reduced crime rates or the use of correctional institutions."

Similar to our discussion of the effectiveness of correctional treatment programs, a definitive resolution of the controversy over the efficacy of community-based corrections is hindered by a paucity of research findings and poorly designed evaluations. The assertions of both the proponents and critics of community corrections should be kept in mind as we consider the structure and operation of probation, pre-release programs, community-based facilities, and parole in Canada. Our discussion will draw heavily from the *Solicitor General's Study of Conditional Release* (Solicitor General of Canada 1981a), hereafter referred to as the Working Group. This report is perhaps the most thorough examination of the various forms of conditional release conducted by the federal government to date. At this juncture, the reader may want to review the discussion of the reintegrative model of corrections in Chapter 3, as background for the remainder of this chapter.

PROBATION

In our previous discussion of the origins of community-based corrections, we noted that probation was formally established in 1889 through legislation enabling judges to suspend the imposition of a sentence and to release the offender on "probation of good conduct." Subsequent legislation in 1921 provided for the supervison of probationers in the community, and during the 46-year period from 1921 to 1967, the provinces and territories enacted legislation creating probation services. In Chapter 3, we discussed probation as a cornerstone of the reintegrative model of corrections and noted that it is the only community-based program that is implemented by direct court order.

One consequence of the jurisdictional arrangements under which the provinces assume responsibility for the delivery of probation services is considerable variability in the organization of probation across the country, the duties of probation officers, and in the facilities and programs available to probationers. In addition to supervising adult offenders, probation officers may be involved in the supervision of juvenile probationers, preparing pre-sentence reports, coordinating community service orders and monitoring restitution agreements. Further, in the more rural areas of the country, probation officers are often charged with duties generally performed by social workers and federal parole officers, and in the provinces of Quebec, Ontario, Manitoba, Saskatchewan, Alberta, and British Columbia, probation officers supervise both parolees and probationers.[4]

While the practice of probation has a long history in Canada and has expanded appreciably in the last decade, there has been considerable debate over the concept and its application. In its report, the Ouimet Committee (1969, 293) defined probation as

a disposition of the court whereby an offender is released to the community on a tentative basis, subject to specified conditions, under the supervision

of a probation officer (or someone serving as a probation officer) and liable
to recall by the court for alternative disposition if he does not abide by the
conditions of his probation.

In an early work on the topic, Diana (1960) identified several
conceptions of probation, including probation as *(1)* a measure of
leniency, *(2)* a legal disposition, *(3)* a punitive measure, *(4)* an
administrative process, and *(5)* a form of social casework
treatment. While Diana's (1960) work is over two decades old, it
does suggest the various connotations of the practice of probation.
Griffiths et al. (1980, 254) concluded that while probation served
all of the functions identified by Diana, it should be viewed
primarily as a legal disposition "which allows offenders to retain
most of their freedom while simultaneously placing them under
the threat of punishment should they not adhere to the terms of the
probation order" (see also Barkdull 1976).

The justifications offered for the use of probation are similar to
those employed for community corrections programs in general.
That is, that probation assists the offender in avoiding the negative
consequences of confinement, promotes the reintegration of the
offender into the community, and is more cost effective than other
dispositional alternatives. Further, probation is seen to achieve the
dual purpose of maximizing the liberty of the offender, while at the
same time affording a measure of protection to the community.

Despite the widespread support for probation, several
observers have raised serious questions about its use, focusing on
the more punitive and control-oriented attributes of the concept. In
a critical analysis of the origins and evolution of probation, Boyd
(1978) argues that the development of probation for adults and
juveniles in the late 1800s and early 1900s was closely tied to
changes that were occurring in Canadian society. More
specifically, Boyd (1978, 361) contends that the urbanization and
industrialization of Canadian society produced a number of social
problems and that probation emerged as a mechanism of
behavioural control:

> The control of the probation system was to be used as a means of
> inculcating the middle-class values of the day. While the development of a
> probation system ostensibly had as its purpose the prevention of future
> criminality, the greatest energies were actually being directed towards
> eradication of the sinful habits of the lowest classes.

Contrary to probation as an alternative to incarceration, Boyd
(1978, 369) argues that it was an *adjunct* to incarceration and was
"a means of placing a greater number of individuals under the

control of the State" (see also Hagan and Leon 1980).

While Boyd's analysis is heavily premised on the activities of the "child-savers" who were concerned about the activities of lower-class juveniles in urban areas, the use of probation as a control mechanism extended to adults. The punitive/control nature of probation, Boyd (1978, 372) contends, is reflected in several sections of the *Criminal Code* of Canada which outline the conditions of probation and the requirements that "the probationer comply with any 'reasonable conditions' that have been considered 'desirable for securing . . . good conduct.' "

In the following discussion, we address the delivery of probation services in Canada and the effectiveness of probation as a community-based program.

The Pre-Sentence Report

The primary mechanism by which the suitability of an offender for probation is determined is through the Pre-Sentence Report (PSR) which provides information about the offender to the court to assist it in arriving at an appropriate disposition.

Pre-Sentence Reports, which are usually prepared by probation officers, contain socio-biographical information on the offender, such as age, marital status, residence, employment history, educational level, reports on alcohol and drug dependencies, as well as material relating to the offender's current offence, prior record, and previous probations and paroles. The PSR may also contain a recommendation by the probation officer as to the most appropriate sentence for the offender, as well as the conditions that should be attached to the probation order.

Despite the importance of the PSR as an information source in the criminal court and its role as a major mechanism by which offenders are recommended for probation, there has been little research on the construction and utilization of PSR's, particularly in Canada. In one of the few investigations of the construction of PSR's, MacDonald (1981, 93) found that the informational content of the document was dominated by socio-biographical data on the offender and, further, that the content of the PSR was influenced by a number of court-related and probation-related variables, including the perceived needs of the court, the administrative procedures of the probation office, and the personal idiosyncrasies of the probation officer.

While a considerable amount of information is compiled in the PSR on the offender, there is little conclusive evidence of the usefulness of this material in making a recommendation to the court, or the extent to which it influences the decisions of the sentencing judge. Wilkins and Chandler (1965) uncovered no consistent pattern among the probation officers they studied in the manner in which the officers priorized information about the offender and concluded that both the selection and utilization of information were heavily influenced by the orientation of the individual probation officer (see also Carter 1967). Further, studies by Carter and Wilkins (1967) and the work of Wilkins and Chandler (1965) revealed that only a small portion of the total amount of information gathered on the offender in the PSR was ultimately utilized in arriving at a recommendation for the court. Carter and Wilkins (1967) also found a high correlation between the recommendation of the probation officer and the disposition of the sentencing judge. In those cases in which the probation officer recommended that the offender be placed on probation, there was a high likelihood that the judge would concur.

Probation Supervision

Probation orders imposed by a judge in the criminal court can be for a period of time not exceeding three years and contain conditions that the probationer will be subject to during the period of supervision. *General conditions* are those restrictions to which all probationers are subject, including the requirement to obey the law and to report at established intervals to the supervising probation officer. *Specific conditions* are those directives aimed at the individual offender and his or her particular needs and requirements. These may include the payment of restitution, the completion of a period of community service, or participation in an attendance centre program.[5]

Once an offender has been placed on probation, there are several issues that emerge surrounding the role of the probation officer, the interaction between the probation officer and the probationer, and the decision by the probation officer to revoke probation and return the offender to the sentencing court. In carrying out their duties, probation officers must act in the role of both "enforcer" and "helper" — acting to protect the community while at the same time assisting the probationer to reintegrate into the community (see Tomaino 1975). While the control function of the probation officer is easily defined, it is less clear how probation officers act to facilitate reintegration. There are two major approaches to the supervision of probationers that have been identified in the literature: *(1)* casework treatment, and *(2)* brokerage, or community resources management. Each orientation provides a framework within which the probation officer carries out his or her duties, and results in specific types of relationships between the probation officer and the probationer.

Boyd (1978), Travis et al. (1983), and others have argued that in the early years of the development of probation and parole, officers attempted not only to control the behaviour of the offender, but also to enforce a set of moral values and a middle-class lifestyle. With the development of treatment modalities, the role of probation and parole officers shifted to that of therapeutic agents. Latessa (1983, 162) notes that the casework approach is premised on the medical model of corrections and the probation officer "through a one-to-one relationship, diagnoses the offender, formulates a treatment strategy, implements that strategy, and finally, evaluates the offender in light of the treatment." Within the casework approach, many of the treatment techniques identified in Table 7.2, including reality therapy, transactional analysis, and behaviour modification, were implemented in community-based settings. Within this framework, the PSR is a primary mechanism for assessing the treatment needs of the offender and specifying a plan of action for the offender on probation.

While the casework approach has been the predominant orientation of probation officers and agencies for many years, the role of probation officers as therapeutic agents has been hindered by the questionable validity of the treatment techniques employed. This factor, in conjunction with the difficulty of carrying out casework treatment in the community, precipitated the shift to a brokerage approach to probation supervision. Within this orientation, the main task of the probation officer is to assess the needs of offenders and arrange for the provision of services:

> The officer is not seen as the primary agent of treatment or change . . . It is the task of the probation or parole officer to assess the service needs of the offender, locate the social service agency which addresses those needs as its primary function, to refer the offender to the appropriate agency, and to follow up referrals to make sure that the offender actually received the services (Latessa 1983, 163).

In contrast to the casework approach, which is premised on the medical model, Latessa (1983, 164) points out that the brokerage orientation is based on the reintegration model "which emphasizes the needs of correctional clients for specialized services which can best be provided by established community agencies."[6]

During the tenure of the probation period, there are two conditions under which the probationary status of an individual may be revoked: *(1)* a technical violation in which the probationer fails to abide by either the general or specific conditions of the probation order, or *(2)* the commission of a new criminal offence. In both instances, the probation officer has broad discretionary powers in deciding whether to revoke probation, and there has been considerable concern over the manner in which such discretion is exercised.

There is some evidence to suggest that the revocation decision is influenced by the personal orientation of the probation officer, by the organizational attributes of the probation agency, and by characteristics of the probationer (Andrews et al. 1977; Hagan 1977). Jackson et al. (1982, 275) found, for example, that the socio-biographical attributes of the probationer played a significant role in the revocation decision: "If . . . the probationer maintained a stable domestic and economic life, then further supervision was seen as unnecessary and probation was allowed to continue despite nonadherence." These investigators found that in 44 percent of the cases examined, probation was completed despite non-compliance with court-ordered conditions[7] (see also Aasen 1985; Smith 1983-84).

It is clear that more research is required on the dynamics of probation officer decision making and the factors which influence the revocation and termination of probation.

The Effectiveness of Probation

We have previously noted that community-based initiatives, such as probation, are generally justified on the grounds that they are less costly and more effective in reintegrating offenders into the community than are traditional institutional programs. This perspective is represented by the comments of Hunter (1969,45), who concluded: "The weight of Canadian evidence suggests that probation, in addition to being a more humane approach to criminal behaviour than imprisonment, is also a far more effective method of rehabilitation." To support this assertion, proponents cite the largely descriptive studies of the Ontario Probation Officers Association (1967), Cockerill (1975), and Renner (1978), all of whom found "success" rates of over 60 percent for offenders on probation.

While the efficacy of probation is widely assumed, many correctional observers have argued that a paucity of research, poorly designed evaluations, and variation in the measurement of "success" among studies completed to date, preclude definitive statements. Madeley (1965) notes, for example, that there are several different criteria that could be used in measuring the success of probation, including *(1)* successful completion of the period of probation, *(2)* avoidance of criminal activity for a period of time following termination of probation, and *(3)* a measurable change in the offender, such as increased emotional maturity, by a standardized index.

Methodological considerations aside, observers have raised several concerns regarding the operation of probation and its efficacy. Hatt (1985) notes there is a continuing conflict between the use of probation as a rehabilitative device and as a control mechanism. It has also been pointed out that usually only the best risks — those offenders least likely to commit additional criminal offences — are placed on probation. Successful completion of a period of probation may be due to a supportive family or stable employment, rather than to the efforts of the probation officer. Among the findings of Gottfredson and Gottfredson (1980, 235-38) in their survey of probation evaluations was that there was differential effectiveness of probation in reducing the incidence of criminal behaviour, with some offenders being more "amenable" to probation than others. More specifically, probationers with no prior record of arrests and who were convicted of property crimes had the greatest probability of completing a period of probation successfully.

One defense to critics who challenge the efficacy of probation is that the large case-loads of most probation officers preclude effective supervision. However, research has revealed that case-load size is not a factor which hinders the success of probation, except perhaps in a manner not anticipated by probation proponents. In a major inquiry that has become known as the "San Francisco Project" (Lohman et al. 1964), probation and parole officers were randomly assigned to supervise varying case-load sizes: 20 (intensive), 50 (ideal), and 100 (normal). In addition, a group of probationers and parolees were required to submit only monthly reports (minimum) to supervising officers. An assessment was then made of the success rates for the various groups. The results of the project are summarized by Frank (1973, 212), who points out that

> when cases were randomly assigned to different degrees of supervision, offenders in minimum caseloads performed as well as would be expected had they been receiving normal supervision; the minimum and the ideal caseloads had violation rates which were almost identical; *and in intensive caseloads, despite 14 times the attention provided the minimum cases, the violation rate not only failed to decline but increased with respect to technical violations* (Emphasis added).

On the basis of this and other investigations of the role of case-load size on probation success, Griffiths et al. (1980, 255) concluded that "giving probation and parole officers more time to do things with offenders does not appear to have a significant impact upon the offender's performance. . ." (see also Vetter and Adams 1970). In fact, a fairly consistent finding is that the rate of technical violations is higher among probationers who are part of smaller case-loads, indicating that the additional time that the officer has tends to result in a higher failure rate rather than increased success.

While there are additional areas of concern in the operation of probation, our discussion illustrates that there are numerous unanswered questions about the use of this technique. Considerable research remains to be done on the impact of case-load size, establishing predictive mechanisms to identify those offenders most "amenable" to probation, in determining what types of information should be gathered on offenders in the pre-sentence report and in monitoring the behaviour of offenders under supervision and following the termination of probation. Given the extensive use of probation as a community-based program for offenders, it would seem that a major priority of the correctional enterprise would be to attempt to answer many of the questions that remain about probation.

PRE-RELEASE PROGRAMS:
TEMPORARY ABSENCE AND DAY PAROLE

Two types of release programs that provide an opportunity for inmates to participate in community-based programs are temporary absences and day paroles. Temporary absence (TA) programs are operated by the Correctional Service of Canada, for federal inmates, and also by correctional agencies in all of the provinces and territories, for provincial inmates. Day parole is available only to inmates in federal institutions. However, at the provincial/territorial level, TA's serve the same general function; the distinction is primarily in nomenclature.

TA programs and day paroles (and even full parole) are strategies of "risk reduction" and components of *gradual release* — the movement of inmates from higher to lower levels of security and supervision. The basic rationale of gradual release comprises two elements: *(1)* the step-by-step "decompression" of inmates is preferable to sudden release, and *(2)* partial or temporary release forms serve as a useful "test" of whether the offender is "ready" for a more liberal form of release[8] (Solicitor General of Canada 1981a, 26).

Temporary Absences

Temporary absence (TA) refers to a program of short-term absences granted to inmates serving time in federal and provincial institutions. TA's allow inmates to be absent from the institution for a specified period of time. At the federal level, TA's are usually for a period of less than 15 days, while provincial programs provide a range of time periods ranging from one day to an indefinite period of time. Temporary absences may be either escorted (ETA) or unescorted (UTA). Escorted TA's, which require the inmate to be accompanied by a representative of the penitentiary, may be granted to federal inmates any time after the commencement of sentence and are generally granted by the warden of the institution, under the authority of the Correctional Service of Canada. Authority for granting UTA's resides with the National Parole Board, under provisions of the *Penitentiary Act*, although in practice these decisions are also often made by the Correctional Service of Canada. Federal inmates are eligible for UTA's after serving six months of their sentence or one-sixth of their sentence, whichever is longer.

There are four general types of UTA's and ETA's in the federal temporary absence program:

1. *Medical:* allow the inmate to receive emergency medical care or treatment;
2. *Humanitarian:* allow inmate to attend to family matters, including funerals, illness, or hardship;
3. *Rehabilitative:* assist the offender in reintegrating into the community and provide an opportunity for job interviews, home visits, participation in community service projects, recreational or cultural events; and
4. *Administrative:* granted to inmates whose parole date or mandatory supervision date falls on a weekend to facilitate administrative processing on the preceding workday; also used for pre-parole or mandatory supervision interviews and evaluations.

During 1985/86 there were nearly 43,000 ETA's given to inmates, a 27 percent increase from 1981/82. Approximately 14,000 UTA's were awarded in 1985/86, a 92 percent increase since 1981/82 (Canadian Centre for Justice Statistics 1986, 42). Over 99 percent of ETA's and UTA's are successfully completed.

While TA programs have high completion rates, there has been little research on the decision making surrounding the granting of

TA's or on the program's success in assisting the reintegration of offenders into the community.[9] In its assessment of the TA program at the federal level, the Working Group identified several areas of concern, including an ongoing dispute between the National Parole Board and the Correctional Service of Canada over authority to grant TA's and the considerable disparity in the number of TA's granted in different regions of the country and between federal institutions at the same security level. In concluding, the authors of the report (1981a, 148) recommended several modifications, including the use of civilian volunteers as escorts for inmates on TA's and the addition of provisions to increase the use of UTA's in federal institutions.

At the provincial/territorial level, TA programs are available to inmates serving time in provincial/territorial institutions. Provision for provincial TA programs was made in the *Prisons and Reformatories Act, 1950.*[10] Over the past two decades, provincial legislation has been enacted to establish temporary absence programs. Temporary absences from provincial/territorial institutions are generally provided for medical, humanitarian, and rehabilitative purposes, may be escorted, and are for varying lengths of time. While there are variations in the actual operation of TA programs across the country, the TA program in Ontario can be used for illustrative purposes (see McFarlane 1979).

According to Fox (1971, 51), the overall objective of the Ontario temporary absence program is to

> provide a variety of alternative means whereby sentenced prisoners may be temporarily released from the institution in which they are confined. While the plan is concerned, in part, with short-term leave on medical, job-seeking, family, or compassionate grounds, it is primarily concerned with providing prisoners with work or educational opportunities which it would be impractical to duplicate within the walls of the institution.

In Ontario, TA's are granted for a variety of reasons and for varying lengths of time:

1-to-5 and 6-to-15 Day Absences. An absence of up to 15 days may be granted by the Superintendent for humanitarian or rehabilitative reasons.

Terminal 1-to-5 and 6-to-15 Day Absences. An absence of up to 15 days may be granted by the Superintendent immediately prior to an inmate's discharge.

Recurring Programs. These are a series of short-term absences (escorted or unescorted) of up to 5 days duration and may be granted for humanitarian or rehabilitative purposes, i.e., employment interviews, community service work projects.

Employment TA. Absences are granted on a day-to-day basis to enable selected inmates to work in the community during the day and return to the institution in evenings and on weekends.

Education TA. Granted for purposes of education or training in the community; inmates return to institution in the evenings and on weekends.

Medical TA. Granted for an inmate to obtain medical treatment.

Staff Escorted Group TA. Granted for escorted inmates attending activities in the community such as recreational activities, field trips, and community service projects.

Each provincial institution has a Temporary Absence committee which, along with Superintendents and staff, assesses and approves applications for TA's.

Day Parole

Day paroles are available to inmates incarcerated in federal correctional institutions and may involve a variety of arrangements, from residence in a minimum, medium, or maximum security facility with occasional release for specific purposes, to situations in which the offender resides in private accommodations in the community with the requirement to report to the institution at designated times.[11]

Day paroles are generally granted for a four-month period of time and are renewable for a period of up to one year. Inmates are eligible for day parole six months after the date of their sentence or after having served one-sixth of the time required for parole eligibility. Inmates on day parole often reside in community correctional centres (CCC's) or community-based residential centres (CBRC's).[12] Approximately 2,500 day paroles, including "limited day paroles," are granted annually, and about one-half of these preceded the granting of a full parole.

The general functions of day parole are *(1)* to gradually release and "test" inmates, *(2)* to mitigate punishment, *(3)* to facilitate employment of inmates on special projects, *(4)* to provide access to community resources and programs, and *(5)* to increase the cost effectiveness of correctional initiatives. The lack of both systematic descriptive data and empirical research on the use of day parole in Canada precludes an assessment of its efficacy. In concluding its assessment, the Working Group (1981a) called for a clear delineation of the objectives of day parole, as well as an articulation of the criteria utilized in assessing and granting applications for day parole. It was also recommended that there be an inquiry into the regional disparities which exist in the use of day parole.

WORK RELEASE PROGRAMS

One of the most common community-based programs is work release (or work furlough), under which the inmate leaves his or her place of confinement during working hours and returns at night. A close examination of work release programs, their objectives, and the results of research inquiries provides additional insight into community-based corrections.

In Canada, federal and provincial inmates generally participate in work release programs through TA programs or day paroles and often reside in community-based correctional facilities. The justifications offered for the operation of work release are similar to those presented for community-based corrections generally: (1) it has economic advantages as a cost-effective alternative to incarceration, (2) it facilitates the reintegration of the offender into the community, (3) it has a positive psychological impact on inmates, and (4) it results in numerous benefits to the offender's family.

These justifications are evident in the definition of work release provided by Doeren and Hageman (1982, 133), who described it as "a program of graduated release which is designed to help selected inmates prepare for release and to assist them in making a successful transition from the structured institutional environment back into the free community." Similarly, Jeffrey and Woolpert (1974, 406) note that the basic operating principle of work release programs is that offenders "may be better integrated into the community without increased risk to the community and at a measurable savings in cost to the community." However, from their extensive review of the literature on work release programs, Boyanowsky and Verdun-Jones (1977a, 49) concluded that many of the supposed advantages of work release are "based on common-sense reasoning rather than on hard, objective data." As our discussion below reveals, there is some considerable question as to whether work release achieves its objectives.

Cost Effectiveness

A major justification for the development and expansion of work release is that it is less costly to support an inmate in a work release program than in prison. Further, it is argued that the monies generated by inmates on work release can be used to contribute to the costs of their confinement, support their families and pay restitution to victims. Citing figures of wages earned by inmates on work release programs in several U.S. states, and the amounts contributed to family, restitution, room and board and other sources, Doeren and Hageman (1982, 150-52) concluded that work release was less costly than confinement and resulted in measurable savings to the community. This conclusion, however, is contrary to the findings of Jeffrey and Woolpert (1974) that the difference in per diem costs in maintaining an offender on work release or in an institution were minimal, and those of Rudoff (1975) who found that, while many of the families of work releasees were on welfare, the contributions made from the inmate's employment only supplemented welfare payments, rather than replacing them.

Boyanowsky and Verdun-Jones (1977a, 49) have been particularly critical of cost effectiveness studies that premise their arguments on the total amount of dollars earned by inmates and the amounts contributed to various sources: "A simple listing of figures is very misleading and only begins to take on meaning when other surrounding circumstances and factors are considered." From their review of the available materials on the cost effectiveness of work release, these authors (1977a, 52) concluded: "Whether work release programs are cost-effective or not is a question that has not yet been answered and it will not be answered until some rigorous, cost-benefit analyses have been performed" (see also Katz and Decker 1982).

Impact on Recidivism

Difficulties similar to those encountered in assessing the cost-effectiveness of work release programs hinder attempts to ascertain the efficacy of work release in assisting the reintegration of offenders into the community and reducing the incidence of criminal behaviour. Not only is there a paucity of research, but many of the studies that have been conducted suffer from serious methodological shortcomings, including the failure to match experimental and control groups and the tendency of administrators to grant work release to "low risk" inmates. Given these and other limitations, the findings of the research to date must be viewed with caution.

The results of investigations that have measured the success of inmates who have participated in work release programs during their confinement are mixed. Boyanowsky and Verdun-Jones (1977a, 53) cite the research of Adams and Dellinger (1969), who reported that the success rate of felons participating in a work release program was 75 percent, while the success rate of those offenders who had not participated in the program was 83 percent. They also cite Johnson (1969), who reported no significant differences in success on parole between those offenders who had been involved in a work release program and those who had not. Similarly, Waldo and Chiricos (1977) found that participation in work release had no significant impact on recidivism rates, nor did the length of time the inmate was involved in the program (see also Brookhart et al. 1976).

Perhaps the most tightly controlled study has been conducted by Jeffrey and Woolpert (1974). In a four-year followup of carefully matched groups of inmates in California, these investigators found that inmates who had participated in work release programs were convicted of significantly fewer crimes and had better arrest records than those inmates who had not participated in work release. Of considerable significance was the finding that the differences between the two groups were most pronounced during the first two years following release, the time period when offenders are at the highest risk to recidivate. However, the analysis also revealed that the differences between the two groups diminished in the third and fourth years following release.[13]

While the results of the study by Jeffrey and Woolpert (1974) suggest that work release may have a positive impact on the self-image of the offender and improve his identification with the community, Rudoff (1975) reported that the self-image of offenders participating in a work release program he examined were more *negative* at the time of release into the community than those of inmates who had not participated in the program. These findings are supported by Waldo et al. (1976) who found no improvements in the levels of perceived opportunities, achievement motivation, or self-esteem among offenders following participation in a work release program.

There are numerous reasons why work release may not be as successful as a community correctional program as originally thought. One possible explanation is that inmates on work release are often unable to secure jobs other than those which are unskilled or semi-skilled, and, further, that there are often difficulties in securing employment that makes use of vocational training received in the institution. Securing meaningful work positions for inmates may also be hindered by the general economic climate in the community. During periods of high unemployment in the community, not only may jobs be difficult to obtain, but also there may be considerable public hostility and resistance to work release programs that are perceived to take jobs away from the general public. Administrators of work release programs may also have to overcome resistance among potential employers to hiring inmates (see Sacks 1975).

A particularly significant contribution to the work release literature (and to the corrections literature in general) has been made by Katz and Decker (1982). In reporting the results of an extensive review of the evaluative literature on work release programs which revealed that little evidence existed to support the claims of proponents, the authors noted an inverse relationship between the methodological strength of evaluations and their findings: those studies that were the weakest methodologically tended to provide support for work release claims, while evaluations that were well designed consistently produced negative results.

In concluding their assessment, Katz and Decker (1982, 242) argued that while work release programs have expanded rapidly in recent years, a critical re-examination of their premises and objectives was in order:

> The mandate to the criminal justice system with respect to work-release programs is clear: Support for such efforts is misguided. It is based upon some basis other than rational criteria. For if rationality (that is, research findings) had an impact on funding and program effort, there would be little reason to expect work release to receive much support.

COMMUNITY-BASED FACILITIES

The construction of facilities for sheltering and providing assistance to offenders who were in transition from prison to the community emerged in England and Ireland in the early 1800s and spread to North America. In 1854, the Quakers founded the Issac T. Hooper House in New York City and in 1864, a facility named the "Temporary Asylum for Discharged Female Prisoners" was opened in Boston. During these early days and up until the 1930s, several more now-famous halfway houses were opened and operated by private and religious organizations including the Quakers, the Salvation Army, and a group known as the

Volunteers of America. Despite these early developments, the halfway-house movement suffered a serious setback during the years 1930 to 1950. Boyanowsky and Verdun-Jones (1977a, 21) observe that by 1950 "halfway houses were close to extinction." The reasons for the slow dissolution of halfway houses were numerous and included the expansion of parole services, the difficulty experienced by offenders in locating employment during the Depression and its aftermath, and the passage of legislation in many U.S. jurisdictions requiring offenders to have jobs prior to release into community-based facilities. During the 1950s, the halfway-house movement was revived and, with the shift to the reintegration model of corrections, there has been increased attention to the development of community-based facilities, variously known as halfway houses, transition homes, hostels, and community correctional centres.

In Canada, halfway houses are operated for both federal and provincial offenders, the majority of whom are on temporary absence or, if federal inmates, on day parole. In addition, there are a smaller number of offenders who are either on full parole or mandatory supervision. The federal government sponsors two types of community-based facilities: *community correctional centres* (CCC's), which are operated by the Correctional Service of Canada and in 1986 were 18 in number, and *community-based residential centres* (CRC's or CBRC's), which are operated on a "fee-for-services-rendered" basis by private, non-profit organizations including the John Howard Society, Elizabeth Fry Society, St. Leonard's, and the Salvation Army.

The increased involvement of private, non-profit organizations in the operation of community-based facilities is the consequence of major initiatives by the federal government in the early 1970s. The *Report of the Task Force on Community-Based Residential Centres* (Outerbridge 1972) and the recommendations of the Task Force on the Role of the Private Sector in Criminal Justice (1977) firmly established the policy of involving non-government agencies in community corrections. In documenting the emergence of community-based residential centres for federal offenders, Zeitoun (1978, 140) notes that non-governmental agencies were perceived to have a distinct advantage in providing community-based services to offenders, including better access to community resources, a greater ability to involve the local community in program initiatives, and the capacity to provide services beyond those mandated to government. While these and other supposed advantages of private involvement in community corrections resulted in the expansion of the practice of contracting, there is no evidence to indicate that non-governmental agencies are more successful than governments in operating such facilities. Further, it is not known whether offenders residing in halfway houses operated by the federal or provincial governments have higher or lower success rates once released into the community than those persons residing in facilities operated by private organizations.

At the provincial/territorial level, only Prince Edward Island and the Yukon Territory do not operate community-based centres. Provincial facilities are known by a variety of names, including community correctional centres, community resource centres and community-based correctional centres. Such facilities may be operated either directly by the provincial/territorial government or by private organizations under contractual arrangements similar to those at the federal level.[14]

Among federal and provincial community-based facilities, there is considerable diversity in the specific services provided to residents, ranging from the provision of room and board to highly structured treatment programs. In addition to providing housing for residents, facilities may offer assistance in securing employment, personal and vocational counselling, referral services, and opportunities for participation in community activities. Many facilities are specifically designed to address the requirements of specialized offender groups such as individuals with drug or alcohol dependencies or mental health problems.

A conclusive determination of the extent to which community-based correctional facilities are successful in achieving their stated objectives is hindered by the lack of well-designed research and the variety of methods that have been utilized to measure "outcome." While the success of facilities has most often been measured by recidivism rates of offenders following full release into the community, several studies have used in-program success as a measure of effectiveness, and still others have focused on improvements in employment stability, education level, family relationships and reduced dependence on drugs or alcohol (see Latessa and Allen 1982).

With these limitations in mind, we briefly review the general conclusions of the research conducted to date and conclude that, as with our discussion of other community-based initiatives, no consistent evidence exists to support many of the claims made by proponents of community-based facilities. It is evident that additional research is required before definitive statements can be made.

Cost Effectiveness

A major justification generally offered in support of community-based facilities is that it is cheaper to maintain offenders in a community setting than in a correctional institution. However, numerous obstacles have been encountered in attempting to assess the cost effectiveness of community correctional centres and, in conjunction with the seemingly ubiquitous weaknesses in the methodology of most research, make conclusive or even well-informed statements difficult.

Latessa and Allen (1982, 160) cite research findings indicating that while halfway houses generally operate at less cost than institutions on a per diem basis, they are more expensive than the traditional alternatives of probation and parole. Further, Boyanowsky and Verdun-Jones (1977a, 38) have pointed out that in determining the cost effectiveness of community-based facilities, the basis of comparison should not necessarily be the prison, but rather the type of program the majority of halfway house residents would be eligible to participate in:

> When residents at halfway houses are probationers or parolees, the proposition that halfway houses cost less than prisons really does not apply. In these cases, it would be more appropriate to compare halfway houses with the costs of probation or parole since they are the alternative dispositions, and not incarceration.

In concluding their consideration of the cost factor of community-based facilities, Boyanowsky and Verdun-Jones (1977a, 38) leave us with a now familiar conclusion that "one can only conclude that halfway houses can cost less than prisons; they can cost as much or more than prisons, and they can cost much more than parole and probation." Obviously, additional research and inquiry is required before more conclusive statements can be made.

Impact on Recidivism

While it is widely held that offenders residing in community correctional centres have a higher likelihood of post-release success, this assertion is not supported by the research conducted to date. Rather, there appears to be some disagreement among observers who have reviewed the evaluative literature. Boyanowsky and Verdun-Jones (1977a, 35) concluded that little evidence exists to support the assertion that "halfway houses can more effectively reintegrate the offender and thus reduce recidivism," a position shared by Sullivan et al. (1974) and Beha (1975). Carlson and Seiter (1977), on the other hand, reached a different conclusion regarding the efficacy of community correctional centres in assisting the reintegration of offenders. From a review of 55 evaluations of halfway houses, they (1977, 388-89) concluded that "community residential programs are *as* effective as their institutional alternatives, and there is fairly conclusive evidence that halfway houses are more effective than the traditional prison-parole cycle." However, in discussing the evaluations reviewed, Carlson and Seiter (1977) comment extensively on the methodological shortcomings which afflicted the studies, noting that very few of the inquiries employed true experimental designs in which offenders were randomly assigned to experimental and control groups. Further, the studies that did employ true experimental designs reported no significant differences in success on release between those offenders who had resided in a halfway house and those who had not.

In attempting to assess the effectiveness of community correctional centres in assisting the offender, whether measured by lower recidivism rates or by some other outcome, we are left with conflicting results produced by poorly designed research. The general consensus among many correctional investigators is that community-based facilities, for a variety of reasons, have not lived up to expectations as a mechanism to facilitate the reintegration of the offender.

Humaneness

In our introductory comments on community corrections we noted that one of the major justifications for community-based facilities and programs was that such initiatives are a humane alternative to the degradation and deprivation of prison life. The humaneness of correctional facilities in the community, however, is more widely assumed than demonstrated. Boyanowsky and Verdun-Jones (1977a, 40) point out: "It seems that the belief in the humanity of halfway houses (as opposed to prisons) is so universal and so dogmatic that research on the subject is seen as unnecessary." Critics argue that many offenders find life in community correctional centres coercive and restrictive and more similar than dissimilar to life inside prison. The rules and regulations of halfway houses, for example, often impose severe restrictions on the behaviour and activities of the residents and are enforced by the threat of return to prison. In interviews with residents of halfway houses, Greenberg (1975) found many who expressed resentment and frustration at being required to live in a community-based facility as a condition of their release. While many of the residents had initially welcomed the placement as an improvement over incarceration, they soon developed resentment and hostility in attempting to adjust to being "halfway free."

Greenberg's (1975) findings are supported by the limited amount of research that has been conducted in Canada on this topic. The Working Group (Solicitor General of Canada 1981a, 62) reported that "the régime of the CCC or CRC is not always well understood by inmates prior to their arrival, and the restrictiveness of the facility's rules and the closeness of the interaction with staff often come as something of a shock to inmates . . . The CCC/CRC environment continues to be a source of frustration and pressure for many inmates throughout their stay." Similarly, in a survey of residents of a halfway house, Hylton (1982, 351) discovered that "many residents indicated that they found the combination of some freedom and considerable structure to be extremely stressful, psychologically" (see also Hylton 1981).

There is some evidence to suggest that the extent to which residents develop resentment and experience difficulties in halfway houses is due to the environment of the facility they reside in. In their examination of two community correctional centres in British Columbia, Boyanowsky and Verdun-Jones (1977b, 37) found different atmospheres in the two facilities which resulted in differing perceptions by the residents: "One centre was perceived by many offenders as just being an extension of a closed institution whereas the other centre was perceived as encouraging a relaxed, home-like atmosphere." On the basis of this finding, the investigators (1977b, 38) concluded that, due to the diversity in administrative approach in managing halfway houses, "it seems impossible to measure whether [a] centre is more or less humane than a closed institution."

Problems of Community-Based Facilities

It is evident from our discussion that the lack of well-designed evaluations is a major impediment to assessing the extent to which community-based facilities are successful in achieving cost savings, providing a humane alternative to incarceration, and serving as a mechanism to assist the offender to adjust to life outside the prison. The limited data that are available suggest that such facilities may not be less costly than other non-institutional alternatives, may be viewed by residents as additional punishment, and may not serve to increase the offender's likelihood of success upon full release.

The apparent failure of community-based facilities is undoubtedly due to a variety of factors, a full consideration of which is beyond the scope of this text. Correctional observers have, however, suggested several major problems that have afflicted facilities and significantly hindered their success. These include:

1. The lack of adequate classification and screening procedures for determining which offenders would receive the most benefit from a placement in a community correctional facility.
2. The tendency of correctional administrators to utilize community-based facilities to relieve overcrowding in institutions, resulting in the placement of "marginal" and "high-risk" cases in residences.
3. The lack of segregation of offenders with specialized needs from one another in community-based settings.
4. The apparent inability of either governmental correctional agencies or private organizations under contract with federal and provincial governments to secure public support and cooperation in operating community-based facilities and programs.
5. Recurring problems with obtaining and retaining qualified staff and implementing training programs.

Further research is required into these and other dimensions of community-based facilities before an improvement in the delivery of services to residents will occur.

PAROLE

We have previously discussed the history of parole and its role as a major component of the reintegrative model of corrections. Despite its widespread use in North America as a community corrections program, it has come under increasing criticism, particularly in the United States where abolitionists have succeeded in eliminating it in several state jurisdictions (see American Friends Service Committee 1981; Citizens' Inquiry on Parole and Criminal Justice, Inc. 1975; O'Leary 1975; von Hirsch and Hanrahan 1978). While there has been only limited discussion in Canada on the abolition of parole, several critical issues surrounding its operation have emerged in recent years which must be addressed.

In this section, we outline the structure and operation of parole at the federal and provincial levels. In addition, we consider the selection of offenders for parole, the supervision of parolees, and the decision to revoke parole. An attempt is also made to ascertain the cost effectiveness of parole, its humaneness as an alternative to incarceration, and the success rate of offenders released on parole into the community.

At this juncture, it is important to distinguish parole from probation and mandatory supervision, with which it is often confused. While probation is a sentence of the court, parole is granted by an administrative tribunal (the parole board) following a period of confinement in a correctional institution. Probation and parole are similar in that each places the offender under supervision in the community for a specified period of time during which certain conditions must be adhered to. There are also similarities and differences between parole and mandatory supervision. Parole is granted, by the discretionary decision making of the parole board, as an early form of release from confinement after an inmate has served a minimum of one-third of the total sentence or seven years, whichever is the lesser period. Inmates in provincial institutions who are serving sentences of two years less a day are eligible for parole after serving one-third of their sentence. There are additional eligibility requirements for offenders serving life sentences or sentences of preventive detention.

In contrast to parole, mandatory supervision is a legislated form of release for those offenders, *not paroled,* who remain incarcerated until a minimum of two-thirds of their sentence has been served. By law, inmates may have up to one-third of their time in confinement shortened by the earning of remission or "good time." If the inmate is not granted a parole (or does not apply for parole) after serving two-thirds of the sentence, he/she is generally released on mandatory supervision. Under mandatory supervision, the offender is required to report to a parole officer and is required to conform to general and often specific conditions, the violation of which may result in return to the institution to serve the remainder of their sentence.

Under the *Parole Act,* the National Parole Board (NPB) is given the authority to grant full parole and day parole to federal and certain provincial inmates; to grant temporary absences to federal inmates; and to terminate/revoke parole or mandatory supervision releases. In addition, the NPB reviews applications for pardons under the *Criminal Records Act* (1970). The NPB is an independent administrative body, composed of 26 full-time members, 18 of whom are located in five regional offices across the country (Atlantic, Quebec, Ontario, Prairies and N.W.T., and British Columbia and Yukon). The remaining members of the board are posted to NPB Headquarters in Ottawa.

In addition to these full-time members, the NPB appoints temporary board members for terms of up to one year. Temporary board members have the same powers as regular members and assist the board during periods of heavy case-loads. There is also provision for designating Regional Community Board Members, individuals selected from the community, who participate in reviewing the cases of inmates serving life sentences as a minimum sentence and the applications of those inmates who are serving indeterminate sentences as dangerous or habitual offenders.

The NPB is required by law to review the cases of all inmates when they are eligible for parole, and at two year intervals (annually for some categories of offenders) thereafter, until parole is granted, or the offender is released on mandatory supervision, or the full sentence is served. Each member of the parole board has one vote and, in cases of a tie vote, either the Chairman of the board will break the tie or request an additional vote from another board member. The number of votes required for release varies by the length of the inmate's sentence:

- •2 votes — Inmates serving single or aggregate terms of imprisonment of less than 5 years
- •3 votes — Inmates serving a single or aggregate term of imprisonment of 5 years but less than 10 years
- •5 votes — Inmates serving a single or aggregate term of imprisonment of 10 years or more, including life as a maximum
- •7 votes — Inmates serving:
  - –a minimum sentence of life imprisonment (murder)
  - –preventive detention
  - –detention for an indeterminate period of time

Since September 1, 1978, through amendments to the *Parole Act*, the provinces have been given the option of establishing provincial parole boards. Subsequent to the enactment of this legislation, the provinces of Ontario (1978), Quebec (1979), and British Columbia (1980) created parole boards with jurisdiction over all inmates confined in provincial institutions (including federal offenders serving time in provincial facilities under federal-provincial agreements).[15]

Parole Board Decision Making

Other than the disposition of the sentencing judge, perhaps no other decision in the entire correctional process is as critical to the offender as the deliberations of the parole board relating to the granting of parole. With the implementation of the rehabilitative ideal and the medical model of corrections in the post-World War II years, offenders were sentenced to indeterminate periods of confinement, and the parole board became the final arbiter of when the offender was ready to be released back into the community. In fact, as we have previously noted, while the rehabilitative model has been officially discarded, there is some evidence to suggest that the parole board continues to utilize criteria relevant to the medical model.

Much of the controversy that has surrounded the parole board relates to the decision to grant parole. Many correctional observers have noted that parole boards exercise considerable discretion in deciding on release applications and that this results not only in disparity among decisions but also in an inability to predict what the outcome of the deliberations will be in any particular case. Criticisms of parole board decision making have centred on the lack of clearly articulated release criteria and the failure of the parole board to gather data on the relationship between its decisions and the ultimate success of offenders in the community.

The *Parole Act* outlines the following three criteria that are to be utilized in considering an inmate for release on full parole: *(1)* that the inmate has derived maximum benefit from imprisonment, *(2)* that the reform and rehabilitation of the inmate will be aided by the granting of parole, and *(3)* that the release of the inmate on parole will not constitute an undue risk to society. These criteria reveal the dilemma faced by parole board members in attempting to reconcile the demands for protection of the community with the interests of the offender (see Shewan 1985). Further, these criteria indicate the vague and ambiguous nature of the parole board's release guidelines. The Working Group (1981a, 63) concluded that the officially stated criteria for release are

> either too vague (how much of a risk is an "undue risk"? and risk of what: violence, criminal recidivism, technical rules violation?) or inappropriate and largely beyond assessment in individual cases (few releasing or even corrections authorities today would venture to describe what obtaining the "maximum benefit from incarceration" might entail, nor would many officials feel confident in saying that any given program will aid the "reform and rehabilitation of the inmate").

Concerns about the criteria for parole release had been raised a decade earlier by the Task Force on the Release of Inmates (Hugessen 1973, 32): "Neither inmates nor members of the Board are able to articulate with any certainty or precision what positive or negative factors enter into the parole decision." In short, decision makers on the parole board encounter many of the same difficulties that treatment professionals in correctional institutions faced in attempting to implement programs under the medical model (see Chapter 8).

A major criticism of the parole board is that the lack of specified criteria, applied in a consistent manner, results in considerable uncertainty among inmates as to what is required for release (see James 1971). In our discussion of correctional treatment in Chapter 8, we noted that inmates often play the "treatment game" in an attempt to improve their chances for a favourable decision.

The lack of clearly defined criteria for release has also resulted in variation in the rates of parole granting. Hann and Palmer (1980) examined the number of paroles granted annually by the NPB during the years 1967 to 1978 and found variations in the annual granting rate as well as differences in the number of paroles awarded by the five regional parole boards. Chitra (1980, 64) discovered similar variability in the annual rates of paroles granted from 1957 to 1976 and concluded: "Parole should be a planned system of supervised release based on a logical scheme of selection with consistent criteria. Large fluctuations in granting levels from year to year indicate that this is probably not the case."

Decision-Making Criteria

In an attempt to understand the factors that influence the decision making of the parole board, researchers have examined the role of socio-biographical attributes of the offender, the offence and criminal history, the inmate's institutional performance, as well as the influence of the orientations and personal belief systems of individual parole board members and the organizational context within which they work.

Generally, research studies have revealed that the criminal history of the inmate, including the severity of the most recent offence, exerts a dominant influence on the decision to grant or deny parole (Scott 1974; Demers 1978; Simkus et al. 1978; Nuffield 1982). In an examination of decision making by the NPB in Ontario, Carriere and Silverstone (1976, 138) observed that there were several types of information frequently utilized by parole board members in making decisions, including the release plans of the inmate, personality problems, level of maturity, personal resources, pattern of delinquency, dangerousness, and performance in the institution.[16] However, these investigators also reported that parole board members did not priorize these items of information, nor were all of them considered in each case decision. What these criteria do illustrate is the strong orientation of the board toward the types of information considered under the medical model of corrections (see also Dawson 1969; Genego et al. 1975; Schmidt 1977).

The research evidence with respect to the role of the socio-biographical attributes of the inmate in parole board decision making is less clear. While conflict theorists have long argued that certain inmates will be punished by the criminal justice system more for who they are rather than for what they have done, no *consistent* evidence has emerged indicating that parole boards discriminate against offenders because of their age, gender, race, or socio-economic status. Several studies, however, have uncovered patterns of parole board decision making that reflect a bias against certain individuals. Nuffield (1982) found that younger inmates were more likely to be paroled than older offenders, and Bynum (1981) reported from a study of native Indians and parole release in the U.S. that, due to the decision making of the board, natives spent longer periods of time incarcerated than their white counterparts. Given the limited nature of the research conducted to date, these findings cannot be extrapolated beyond the particular setting from which they emerged, and further research on the role of age, minority status, socio-economic position and other variables in the decision-making process of the parole board must be undertaken.

It is important to point out that, while research has tended to focus on the role of attributes of the offender in the parole decision, these factors have generally been unable to accurately "predict" parole board decision making, even though several studies have found that they are considered in the parole decision. The Working Group (1981a, 66) reported that case file information contributed only slightly to the variation in parole board decisions. In order to better understand the decision making of the parole board, future research must also consider the potential influence of legislation (such as the Charter of Rights and Freedoms), the personal beliefs of parole board members, shifts in correctional policy (and the possibility of the existence of competing perspectives), the concerns of the general public, and the "swinging pendulum" of perceptions of crime and criminals. Collins (185) has documented the impact of court decisions and the recommendations of investigative committees on the operating procedures of the NPB. And O'Connor (1985), while cautioning that the NPB will continue to exercise immense discretionary powers, reported that the Charter of Rights has significantly affected parole board decision making.

The lack of explicit parole policy, along with the concurrent paucity of information as to the factors that are reliable predictors of the success of inmates once released on parole, have significant consequences, many of which are manifested in the difficulties surrounding the use of parole case files. Parole case files are the major source of information for parole board members and are prepared by Parole Service Officers in consultation with the offender's Case-Management Team in the institution. The case file contains a wide range of information relating to the socio-biographical characteristics of the offender, criminal history and circumstances of the most recent offence, as well as reports on institutional behaviour and progress and the inmate's parole plans. The case file also contains a recommendation by the Parole Service Officer as to whether a parole should be granted.

Despite the importance of the parole service file in the deliberations of the parole board and the high correlation between the recommendation of the Parole Service Officer and the decision of the board, there are numerous difficulties with the material contained in them which may hinder their usefulness. In an examination of the content of a sample of case files on federal inmates, Carriere and Silverstone (1976, 40-64) found that case-file reports included statements that were vague and ambiguous, contained numerous inconsistencies in information about the offender and presented conclusions that appeared to be unsubstantiated by documentation. The researchers also found considerable variability among case files in the types of information presented about the offender and the completeness of the material. On the basis of their investigation, Carriere and Silverstone (1976, 64-67) recommended that guidelines be established for identifying the specific types of information to be gathered on offenders, that quality control be exercised in the construction of the case-file documents to ensure accuracy and consistency, and that inmates assume a more active role in the preparation of their case files for the parole board (see also Nuffield 1982; Casey 1982).

If the lack of explicit parole criteria are, in part, a cause of the difficulties associated with the case-file materials, it is even more evident in the use of such information by parole board members. It is widely argued that, when presented with large amounts of information with no mechanism by which to priorize or assess its relative importance, members tend to rely on a few selected items of information to the near exclusion of a large amount of material in the file. Carriere and Silverstone (1976, 138) discovered in their observations of parole board decision making that "members seemed to have individual parole philosophies to guide their deliberations with the result for us that their decisions appeared to be made almost intuitively." The absence of procedures for assessing the relative importance of material in the parole case file increases the likelihood that parole board members will utilize "gut feelings" and "guesstimates" in reaching a decision (see Gottfredson and Ballard 1966). Such a situation seems even more likely when it is considered that much of the material in the parole case file, even if presented in an accurate and consistent fashion, may have limited usefulness or validity in predicting the future behaviour of the inmate.

Parole Supervision

In addition to the release decision, serious concerns have been raised regarding the supervision of offenders placed on parole. While ostensibly designed to assist individuals in coping with the "pains of re-entry," it has been suggested that the conditions of parole as well as the discretionary decision making of parole officers often compound the parolee's problems in readjusting to life in the community.[17]

Once granted a parole, the offender must abide by a number of general conditions, including obeying the law and meeting social responsibilities, reporting to a supervising authority on a regular basis, securing permission for travel outside his or her area of residence, and obtaining approval prior to incurring debts or assuming additional responsibilities. In addition to these general or standard conditions, specific behavioural prescriptions may be attached to the parole by the board. These are designed to address particular needs and circumstances of the individual, such as abstinence from drugs or alcohol, prohibitions against associating with certain individuals, or fulfilling certain obligations in the community.

Criticisms similar to those voiced against the conditions of probation orders have been leveled against the restrictiveness of parole conditions. The Task Force on the Release of Inmates (Hugessen 1973, 37), for example, stated that the conditions of parole were "too vague and general in application," noting the requirement that the parolee 'fulfill all social responsibilities' "is so vague that it could form the basis for revocation of virtually any parole." From his review of parole conditions in the U.S., which are generally similar to those in Canada, Arluke (1969, 269) concluded: "Some parole conditions are moralistic, most are impractical, others impinge on human rights, and all reflect obsolete criminological conceptions." The Working Group (1981a, 79) reported that many of the parole officers and parolees interviewed complained of the intrusive nature of parole conditions.

In arguing for a reduction in the number of standard parole conditions, the Working Group (1981a, 80) stated:

> Many of the standard conditions (and some of the special ones) are considered to be unenforceable and used only to "justify" a suspension which is really motivated by other concerns. Conditions like obtaining permission to marry or to leave a small geographical area are not consonant with formal correctional policies of minimal intervention and retention by offenders of the rights of ordinary citizens.

Should the offender violate one or more of the parole conditions, or commit a criminal offence while on parole, parole may be suspended. Within 14 days of the suspension, the Parole Service will either cancel the suspension and rerelease the parolee or refer the case to the NPB for a revocation hearing and decision. If parole is ultimately revoked by the Board, the offender is returned to prison to continue serving the sentence of the court. (See Dittenhoffer et al. 1986).

One attribute of the parole officer's role in supervising parolees that has a significant impact on the activities of the officer, including his decision making, is the dual role of "helper" and "enforcer" that officers must assume. Shover (1979, 208) observes that parole officers "are combination police officers and social workers, simultaneously providing assistance to parolees and controlling and monitoring them to prevent the commission of new crimes."[18] In studying the manner in which parole officers carry out this dual role, researchers have identified several "types" of parole officers, distinguished by the extent to which they adopt either of the two roles (see Ohlin et al. 1956; Dembo 1972). Ohlin et al. (1956), for example, found that there were "punitive officers" who emphasized the protection of the community and the control of the parolee's behaviour; "welfare workers" whose activities were directed toward assisting the parolee and facilitating adjustment in the community; and "protective agents" who vacillated between assisting the parolee and protecting the community[19] (see also Prus and Stratton 1976).

This brief review has suggested that factors other than the behaviour of the parolee may play an influential role in the decision making of parole officers and contribute to the success or failure of the offender. Over the next several years, it will be interesting to observe the impact that the newly enacted Charter of Rights and Freedoms has on both the decision making of the parole board and the supervision of parolees in the community. (See Collins 1985; Johnson 1984; Mandel 1984-85).

Effectiveness of Parole

In this final section, we return to a consideration of the effectiveness of parole as a community-based corrections program. It will be recalled that proponents of such initiatives argue that these programs are less costly, more humane, and are more effective in facilitating the re-entry of the offender than traditional institutional activities. Our preceding discussion of the parole granting process and the supervision of parolees in the community has suggested, however, that there are several fundamental difficulties with parole that may hinder its effectiveness. Unfortunately, a paucity of research evidence and poorly designed evaluations have prevented a conclusive analysis of parole and its efficacy. Needless to say, there is considerable debate about parole, the extent to which it is a more cost effective, humane alternative to incarceration, and its effectiveness in assisting reintegration.

It has been consistently shown that parole is less costly than imprisonment. However, there is some disagreement as to the interpretation of the descriptive cost figures that have been utilized to establish this. Doeren and Hageman (1982, 116) assert that "there is a substantial savings to be recognized when utilizing a parole strategy over imprisonment." Mandel (1975) has argued that, while parole is cheaper than incarcerating offenders, it is still expensive to operate and consumes financial resources that might be better applied to alternative strategies, particularly in light of evidence that casts doubt on its effectiveness. He (1975, 504) further points out that parole has not resulted in cost savings through either the reduction in the portion of time spent by offenders in institutions or in the numbers of persons confined in correctional institutions, both of which could potentially reduce the operating costs of the corrections system. Given the considerable concerns surrounding the conditions under which offenders are released on parole, which impose severe behavioural restrictions within an often arbitrary system of supervision, there is also some reason to question whether parole is the humane alternative it was designed to be.

Perhaps the most attention in the debate over the efficacy of parole has centred on its ability to assist offenders in adjusting to life in the free community. A scathing attack on the practice of parole in the United States was delivered by the Citizens' Inquiry on Parole and Criminal Justice, Inc. (1975). From its investigation of the operation of parole in the State of New York, the Inquiry (1975, 166-85) called for the abolition of parole, citing the following reasons:

1. The discretionary release and community supervision functions of parole have failed dramatically and are beyond reform.
2. Parole rests on faulty theory and has unrealistic goals.
3. The parole system is often unnecessarily abusive and unfair, giving rise to many serious and legitimate grievances by offenders.

Many studies of parole effectiveness are descriptive. Glaser (1964) reported that two-thirds of a large sample of federal parolees in the U.S. successfully completed their paroles while Kassebaum et al. (1971) recorded a 50 percent success rate of the state parolees in their sample. The use of such figures, however, is problematic. First, the primary method by which success or failure is measured is by recidivism rates (see Chapter 7). Secondly, many studies have compared the success of offenders released on parole with those who were not granted parole but were released under some form of mandatory supervision. In his study of several hundred men released from federal institutions in Ontario, Waller (1974) found that inmates who had served to discharge (i.e. were not granted parole) had a 66 percent re-arrest rate, while the parolees had a 44 percent re-arrest rate. when the risk factors for the two groups were controlled, however, there were no differences in post-release success between the two groups. This and other findings led Waller (1974, 206) to conclude: "While parole may have other functions, such as the mitigation of sentences or the relief of overcrowding in prisons, it is not ... effective in terms of the primary aim of reducing the likelihood of future criminal behaviour" (see also Stanley 1976).

The lack of definitive evaluative research, coupled with the failure of the parole system to clearly define the criteria for release and the parameters of supervision decision making, led the Working Group (1981a, 75) to conclude:

> There are . . . no definitive answers at present to the question of what will
> be effective with parolees, under what conditions and to what degree. . .
> Very little, too, is known about "differential intervention": what effect
> different parole officers will have in doing different things with different
> offenders. It is known that correctional intervention apparently makes
> some people "worse" and others "better", but is is not known how to tell
> which effect will take place with whom.

Until these and other questions surrounding parole are answered,
there is little likelihood that it will successfully meet its intended
objectives.

A NOTE ON MANDATORY SUPERVISION

Earlier in the chapter, we distinguished parole and probation from
mandatory supervision. It was noted that mandatory supervision
(MS) is a legislated form of release under which offenders, who have
not been granted a parole by the National Parole Board, are
released from a correctional institution on the basis of earned
remission (time off for good behaviour). Given the controversy
which has surrounded this form of release, several additional
comments are in order.[20]

In its report in 1956, the Fauteux Committee (1956, 61)
suggested that the use of a "mandatory parole period" for inmates
would have "the beneficial result of providing a degree of
supervision and control for all persons released from penal
institutions at expiration of sentence." Following a similar
recommendation by the Ouimet Committee (1969), mandatory
supervision was implemented in 1970 under Section 15 (1) of the
Parole Act. According to the MacGuigan Subcommittee (1977, 151),
MS is "intended to provide an interphase between imprisonment
and release, during which the offender may adjust to his new life
while still being subject to some control." A recent report (Solicitor
General of Canada 1981b, 9) outlined the following tenets of MS:

1. no one should be released directly to the community without
some form of control and assistance,
2. MS releasees should be subject to at least the same degree of
control and assistance, and to the same kind of conditions, as
parole releasees,
3. supervision provides control, and
4. supervision provides assistance.

The decision to release offenders on MS is made by Correctional

Service of Canada personnel who exercise control over the granting of remission. Once released, the offender is subject to supervision by parole service officers and to the same general conditions as parolees, as well as to any specific conditions that may have been attached to the release. The procedures for the suspension and revocation of MS are similar to those for parole.

In 1986, the *Parole Act* and the *Penitentiary Act* were amended to give the National Parole Board authority to review all cases of offenders to be released on mandatory supervision and, utilizing criteria established in the Criminal Code relating to dangerous offenders and dangerous sexual offenders, to immediately suspend the MS of those federal offenders whom the NPB considered a threat to the community and likely to commit additional offences if released.

It remains to be seen whether this legislation will sufficiently address the difficulties surrounding the operation of MS in Canadian corrections. It is evident, as the authors of the *Solicitor General's Study of Conditional Release* (1981a) and *Mandatory Supervision: A Discussion Paper* (1981b) have noted, that additional research is required on MS and on the particular needs and requirements of offenders released on this form of supervision.

Notes

1. Earned remission, under which offenders may be given a reduction in the length of their confinement through the earning of "good time," is another method by which the offender may be released early from confinement. Inmates may earn a maximum of 15 days "good time" per month which may reduce their length of confinement by up to one-third. However, earned remission is not a community-based corrections program and is not considered in this chapter. For a discussion of the various issues surrounding earned remission in Canada. see Solicitor General of Canada 1981 and Ross and Barker 1986.

2. The increasing number of persons being placed under supervision in the criminal justice system has resulted in a substantial increase in personnel costs. For the five-year period 1981/82 to 1985/86, total expenditures on adult corrections at the federal level increased 36 percent. Seventy-one percent of all expenditures during 1985/86 were for staff salaries.

3. Somewhat ironically, constraints on the movements and activities of residents of community-based facilities are often the result of public concern about the danger posed by offenders in the community or resistance to the location of a correctional facility in a particular neighborhood. For a discussion of public resistance to community-based residential centres in Canada, see Zeitoun 1978. See also Fattah 1982.

4. For a detailed description of the organization and delivery of probation services in Canada, see Statistics Canada 1986.

5. For a detailed examination of a community service order program in a

Canadian province, see B.C. Ministry of the Attorney General 1977 and Plecas and Winterdyk 1981.

6. The casework treatment and brokerage models of probation practice are ideal types, with agencies and officers approximating one approach or another in their activities and decision making.

7. The research by Jackson et al. (1982) provides support for the assertion of Hagan et al. (1979) that probation is not closely integrated into the subsystem of the criminal court. Among the other findings of these authors (1982, 274) were that "even in cases where general reporting conditions were not satisfactorily complied with . . . probation was allowed to terminate. . . ." Further, interviews with probation officers revealed that probationers were often not charged with nonadherence to general or specific conditions if the supervising officer felt that there was "little to gain from such action."

8. For a detailed discussion of temporary absence programs and day parole, as well as the issues surrounding their use at the federal level, see Solicitor General of Canada 1981a.

9. One of the few studies to examine TA programs is a recent investigation of the decision to grant UTA's. Porporino and Cormier (1982) surveyed members of case management teams in two federal institutions and found a high consensus among the officers in the factors they felt should be considered in evaluating applications for UTA and in the priority of importance of various items of information relating to the offender's criminal history, institutional behaviour, community situation, and personality. Disagreement among the officers existed on some items, such as the assessment of the appropriate length of time an inmate should serve before being granted a UTA.

10. *Revised Statutes of Canada* 1952, Ch. 217, s. 37A.

11. It is important to distinguish day parole from temporary absences. When limits were placed on the amount of time offenders could be absent from institutions on TA's, day parole emerged as a mechanism by which the offender could be absent for a longer period of time. As the *Solicitor General's Study of Conditional Release* (Solicitor General of Canada 1981a, 48) observes: "TA's are . . . to be distinguished from day paroles in that any unescorted leave or leaves (other than for medical or humanitarian purposes) of greater than 72 hours in each quarter of the year must be through a day parole program of the NPB; if a Warden wishes to give a TA or a series of TA's which would exceed 72 hours per quarter, he must provide an escort." For a further discussion of the origins of day parole, see Hugessen 1973.

12. There is also a form of release called "limited day parole" which is utilized for community service projects or other irregular activities. Limited day paroles may last longer than one year.

13. Another significant finding of the Jeffrey and Woolpert (1974) study was that the work furlough program was most successful with inmates classified as "high risk" and who were least amenable to more traditional forms of correctional treatment. In our discussion of correctional treatment in Chapter 7, we noted research which suggests that certain offenders may be more amenable to specific treatment techniques than to others. Jeffrey and Woolpert (1974, 413) attributed the success rate of the high risk inmates to the fact that the work furlough program provided employment, even at the unskilled level, to individuals who would otherwise have difficulty obtaining work, and to the fact that the status of being a participant in the work release program may have had positive psychological benefits for the inmate.

14. For a description of community-based facilities operating at the federal and provincial levels, see Statistics Canada 1986.

15. For a discussion of the creation and operation of provincial parole boards, see Ekstedt 1979. There are no published studies of provincial parole board decision making.

16. Many observers have been particularly critical of the use of institutional performance by the parole board as a variable in decision making. Mandel (1975, 530), for example, has argued: "Study after study has failed to show any relationship between what one does in prison and what one does afterwards (criminally speaking) when the initial risk differences are controlled for." As we noted in Chapter 8, those offenders who evidence difficulty in adjusting to life inside the prison might be considered to be *better* risks on parole than individuals who easily adapt to the world of the total institution.

17. Perhaps the most insightful discussion of the contingencies encountered by offenders upon release from confinement is presented by Irwin 1970.

18. In recent years, like their counterparts in probation, parole officers have adopted more of a "brokerage" approach to supervision, in which they attempt to identify and secure services to meet the needs of parolees.

19. For an extensive discussion of the patterns of relationships that develop between parole officers and parolees, see Irwin 1970.

20. For a discussion of the development of mandatory supervision and the issues surrounding its use in Canadian Corrections, see Solicitor General of Canada 1981b, Pandak 1982, and Stewart 1983.

References

Aasen, J.N. 1985. "Enforcement of Probation in British Columbia." Unpublished M.A. Thesis. Burnaby, B.C.: School of Criminology, Simon Fraser University.

American Friends Service Committee. 1971. *Struggle for Justice*. New York: Hill and Wang.

Andrews, D.A., J.J. Kiessling, R.J. Russell and B.A. Grant. 1977. *Volunteers & 1 to 1 Supervision of Adult Probationers: An Experimental Comparison with Professionals and a Field-Discipline of Process & Outcome*. Ottawa: Canadian Volunteers in Corrections.

Arluke, N.R. (April) 1969. "A Summary of Parole Rules — Thirteen Years Later." 15 *Crime and Delinquency*. 267-74.

Barkdull, W.L. (December) 1976. "Probation: Call It Control — And Mean It." 40 *Federal Probation*. 3-8.

Beha, J.A., III. (July-August) 1975. "Halfway Houses in Adult Corrections: The Law, Practice, and Results." 11 *Criminal Law Bulletin*. 434-77.

Boyanowsky, E.O. and S.N. Verdun-Jones. 1977a. *A Pilot Study of Community Correctional Centres in British Columbia. Part I: Literature Review*. Burnaby, B.C.: Department of Criminology, Simon Fraser University.

_____. 1977b. *A Pilot Study of Community Correctional Centres in British*

Columbia. Part II: Report on Community Correctional Centres in British Columbia. Burnaby, B.C.: Department of Criminology, Simon Fraser University.

Boyd, N. (June) 1978. "An Examination of Probation." 20 *Criminal Law Quarterly.* 355-82.

British Columbia Ministry of the Attorney General. 1977. *The Community Service Order Program: The British Columbia Experience. Volume 1: Background Description of Initial Cases.* Victoria: Corrections Branch.

Brookhart, D.E., J.B. Ruark and D.E. Scoven. (December) 1976. "A Strategy for the Prediction of Work Release Success." 3 *Criminal Justice and Behavior.* 321-34.

Bynum, T. 1981. "Parole Decision Making and Native Americans." In R.L. McNeely and C.E. Pope (eds.) *Race, Crime, and Criminal Justice.* Beverly Hills, California: Sage Publications. 75-87.

Carlson, E.W. and R.P. Seiter. (Summer) 1977. "Residential Inmate Aftercare: The State of the Art." 1 *Offender Rehabilitation.* 381-94.

Carriere, P. and S. Silverstone. 1976. *The Parole Process: A Study of the National Parole Board.* Ottawa: Supply and Services Canada.

Carter, R.M. (July) 1967. "The Pre-Sentence Report and the Decision-Making Process." 4 *Journal of Research in Crime and Delinquency.* 203-11.

Carter, R.M. and L.T. Wilkins. (December) 1967. "Some Factors in Sentencing Policy." 58 *Journal of Criminal Law, Criminology and Police Science.* 503-14.

Casey, M. 1982. "Parole Guidelines: Are They a Worthwhile Control on Discretion?" In *National Parole Board Report of the Conference on Discretion in the Correctional System.* Ottawa: National Parole Board.

Chan, J.B.L. and R.V. Ericson. 1981. *Decarceration and the Economy of Penal Reform.* Toronto: Centre of Criminology, University of Toronto.

Chitra, M. (Summer) 1980. "Modern Trends in Parole Granting, 1957-1976." 5 *Queens Law Journal.* 46-72.

Citizens' Inquiry on Parole and Criminal Justice, Inc. 1975. *Prison Without Walls: Report on New York Parole.* New York: Praeger.

Cockerill, R.W. (October) 1975. "Probation Effectiveness in Alberta." 17 *Canadian Journal of Criminology and Corrections.* 284-91.

Cohen, S. (October) 1979. "The Punitive City: Notes on the Dispersal of Social Control." 3 *Contemporary Crises.* 339-63.

Collins, O.O. 1985. "The Impact of the Rule of Law on the Operational Procedures and Policy-Making of the National Parole Board." Unpublished M.A. Thesis. Burnaby, B.C.: School of Criminology, Simon Fraser University.

Dawson, R.O. 1969. *Sentencing: The Decision as to Type, Length, and Conditions of Sentence.* Boston: Little, Brown and Co.

Dembo, R. (August) 1972. "Orientation and Activities of the Parole Officer." 10 *Criminology.* 193-215.

Demers, D. 1978. *Discretion, Disparity and the Parole Process.* Unpublished Ph.D. Dissertation. Edmonton: Department of Sociology, University of Alberta.

Diana, L. (July-August) 1960. "What is Probation?" 51 *Journal of Criminal Law, Criminology, and Police Science.* 189-208.

Dittenhoffer, T., J.-P. Leroux, and R.B. Cormier. 1986. *The Suspension and Revocation Process in Canada: A Study of How and Why Federal Inmates Under Conditional Release Are Returned to Imprisonment.* Ottawa: Supply and Services Canada.

Doeren, S.E. and M.J. Hageman. 1982. *Community Corrections.* Cincinnati, Ohio: Anderson Publishing Co.

Dunford, F.W. (November) 1977. "Police Diversion: An Illusion?" 15 *Criminology.* 335-52.

Ekstedt, J.W. 1979. "Information Background — Statement on Purpose and Aims of Parole in the Province of British Columbia." Unpublished paper. Vancouver: British Columbia Board of Parole.

Fattah, E.A. (October) 1982. "Public Opposition to Prison Alternatives and Community Corrections. A Strategy for Action." 24 *Canadian Journal of Criminology.* 371-85.

Fauteux, G. (Chairman). 1956. *Report of the Committee Appointed to Inquire Into the Principles and Procedures Followed in the Remission Service of the Department of Justice of Canada.* Ottawa: Queen's Printer.

Fox, R.G. (March) 1971. "Temporary Absence, Work-Release, and Community Based Corrections in Ontario." 4 *Australian and New Zealand Journal of Criminology.* 46-61.

Frank, B. 1973. "Community-Based Correctional Programs: Models and Practices." In B. Frank (ed.) *Contemporary Corrections: A Concept in Search of Content.* Reston, Virginia: Reston Publishing Co. 207-23.

Genego, W.J., P.D. Goldberger and V.C. Jackson. (March) 1975. "Parole Release Decision Making and the Sentencing Process." 84 *Yale Law Journal.* 810-903.

Glaser, D. 1964. *The Effectiveness of a Prison and Parole System.* Indianapolis, Indiana: Bobbs-Merrill.

Gottfredson, D.M. and K.B. Ballard. (July) 1966. "Differences in Parole Decisions Associated With Decision Makers." 3 *Journal of Research in Crime and Delinquency.* 114-19.

Gottfredson, M.R. and D.M. Gottfredson. 1980. *Decision Making in Criminal Justice: Toward the Rational Exercise of Discretion.* Cambridge, Mass: Ballinger Publishing Co.

Greenberg, D.F. (Spring) 1975. "Problems in Community Corrections." 10 *Issues in Criminology.* 1-33.

Griffiths, C.T., J.F. Klein and S.N. Verdun-Jones. 1980. *Criminal Justice in Canada: An Introductory Text.* Vancouver: Butterworths.

Hagan, J. (March) 1977. "Criminal Justice in Rural and Urban Communities: A Study of the Bureaucratization of Justice." 55 *Social Forces.* 597-612.

Hagan, J., J.D. Hewitt and D.F. Alwin. (December) 1979. "Ceremonial Justice: Crime and Punishment in a Loosely Coupled System." 58 *Social Forces.* 506-27.

Hagan, J. and J. Leon. 1980. "The Rehabilitation of Law: A Social-Historical Comparison of Probation in Canada and the United States." 5 *Canadian Journal of Sociology.* 235-51.

Hann, R. and J. Palmer. 1980. *Determinants of Canadian Penitentiary and Prison Populations: Phase 1 Report.* Ottawa: Solicitor General of Canada.

Hatt, K. (July) 1985. "Probation and Community Corrections in a Neo-Correctional Era." 27 *Canadian Journal of Criminology*. 299-316.

Hugessen, J.K. (Chairman) 1973. *Task Force Report on Release of Inmates*. Ottawa: Information Canada.

Hunter, I. 1969. "Probation in Ontario." 27 *University of Toronto Faculty Law Review*. 29-51.

Hylton, J.H. 1981. *Reintegrating the Offender: Assessing the Impact of Community Corrections*. Washington, D.C.: University Press of America.

_____. (July) 1982. "Rhetoric and Reality: A Critical Appraisal of Community Correctional Programs." 28 *Crime and Delinquency*. 341-73. '

Irwin, J. 1970. *The Felon*. Englewood Cliffs, N.J.: Prentice-Hall.

_____. 1980. *Prisons in Turmoil*. Boston: Little, Brown, and Co.

Jackson, M.A., C.D. Webster and J. Hagan. (July) 1982. "Probation Outcome: Is It Necessary to Fulfill the Conditions?" 24 *Canadian Journal of Criminology*. 267-77.

James, L. 1971. *Prisoners' Perceptions of Parole*. Toronto: University of Toronto Press.

Jeffrey, R. and S. Woolpert. (September) 1974. "Work Furlough as an Alternative to Incarceration: An Assessment of Its Effect on Recidivism and Social Cost." 65 *Journal of Criminal Law and Criminology*. 405-15.

Johnson, H.R. (July) 1984. "Procedural Safeguards and the National Parole Board." 26 *Canadian Journal of Criminology*. 325-341.

Kassebaum, G., D.A. Ward and D.M. Wilner. 1971. *Prison Treatment and Parole Survival*. New York: John Wiley and Sons.

Katz, J.F. and S.H. Decker. (June) 1982. "An Analysis of Work Release: The Institutionalization of Unsubstantiated Reforms." 9 *Criminal Justice and Behavior*. 229-50.

Latessa, E.J. 1983. "Community Supervision: Research, Trends, and Innovations." In L.F. Travis, M.D. Schwartz and T.R. Clear (eds.) *Corrections: An Issues Approach*. 2d edition. Cincinnati, Ohio: Anderson Publishing Co. 159-70.

Latessa, E.J. and H.E. Allen. 1982. "Halfway Houses and Parole: A National Assessment." 10 *Journal of Criminal Justice*. 153-63.

Lerman, P. 1975. *Community Treatment and Social Control: A Critical Analysis of Juvenile Correctional Policy*. Chicago: University of Chicago Press.

Lohman, J., D.A. Wahl and R.M. Carter. 1964. *The San Francisco Project: A Study of Federal Probation and Parole*. Berkeley, California: School of Criminology, University of California.

Macdonald, K.D. 1981. "Information for the Court: An Analysis of the Adult Pre-Sentence Report." Unpublished M.A. Thesis. Burnaby, B.C.: Department of Criminology, Simon Fraser University.

McFarlane, G.G. (July) 1979. "Ontario's Temporary Absence Program: 'Phantom' or 'Phoenix' — Like Phenomena?" 20 *Canadian Journal of Criminology*. 310-37.

Madeley, St. J. 1965. "Probation" In W.T. McGrath (ed.) *Crime and Its Treatment in Canada*. Toronto: Macmillan. 220-43.

Mandel, M. (October) 1975. "Rethinking Parole." 13 *Osgoode Hall Law Journal*. 501-46.

Mandel, M. 1984-85. "Democracy, Class and the National Parole Board." 27 *Criminal Law Quarterly.* 159-181.

National Parole Board. n.d. *A Guide to Conditional Release for Penitentiary Inmates.* Ottawa.

Nuffield, J. 1982. *Parole Decision-Making in Canada: Research Toward Decision Guidelines.* Ottawa: Solicitor General of Canada.

O'Connor, F.C. (Spring) 1985. "The Impact of the Canadian Charter of Rights and Freedoms on Parole in Canada." 10 *Queen's Law Journal.* 336-391.

O'Leary, V. (May-June) 1975. "Parole Theory and Outcomes Re-examined." 11 *Criminal Law Bulletin.* 304-17.

Ohlin, L.E., H. Piven and D.M. Pappenfort. (July) 1956. "Major Dilemmas of the Social Worker in Probation and Parole." 2 *National Probation and Parole Association Journal.* 211-25.

Ontario Probation Officers Association. (January) 1967. "An Examination of the Results of Adult Probation." 9 *Canadian Journal of Corrections.* 80-86.

Ouimet, R. (Chairman). 1969. *Report of the Canadian Committee on Corrections — Toward Unity: Criminal Justice and Corrections.* Ottawa: Information Canada.

Outerbridge, W.R. (Chairman). 1972. *Report of the Task Force on Community-Based Residential Centres.* Ottawa: Information Canada.

Pandak, E.S. 1982. "A Review of Mandatory Supervision." Unpublished paper. Burnaby, B.C.: Department of Criminology, Simon Fraser University.

Plecas, D.B. and J.A. Winterdyk. 1981. *Community Service in the North Fraser Region: A Description and Analysis of Program Efficacy.* Maple Ridge, B.C.: Corrections Branch, Ministry of the Attorney General.

Porporino, F.J. and R.B. Cormier. (July) 1982. "Consensus in Decision-Making Among Prison Case Management Officers." 24 *Canadian Journal of Criminology.* 279-93.

Prus, R.C. and J.R. Stratton. (March) 1976. "Parole Revocation Decision Making: Private Typings and Official Designations." 40 *Federal Probation.* 48-53.

Renner, J.C. 1978. *The Adult Probationer in Ontario.* Toronto: Ontario Ministry of Correctional Services.

Roberg, R.R. and V.J. Webb. 1981. *Critical Issues in Corrections: Problems, Trends, and Prospects.* St. Paul, Minnesota: West Publishing Co.

Ross, R.R. and T.G. Barker. 1986. *Incentives and Disincentives: A Review of Prison Remission Systems.* Ottawa: Solicitor General of Canada.

Rothman, D. 1980. *Conscience and Convenience: The Asylum and Its Alternatives in Progressive America.* Toronto: Little, Brown, and Co.

Rudoff, A. 1975. *Work Furlough and The County Jail.* Springfield, Illinois: Charles C. Thomas.

Sacks, M.J. (July) 1975. "Making Work Release Work: Convincing the Employer." 21 *Crime and Delinquency.* 255-68.

Schmidt, J. 1977. *Demystifying Parole.* Lexington, Mass: D.C. Heath.

Scott, J.E. (March) 1974. "The Use of Discretion in Determining the Severity of Punishment for Incarcerated Offenders." 65 *Journal of Criminal Law and Criminology.* 214-24.

Scull, A.T. 1977. *Decarceration: Community Treatment and the Deviant — A Radical View.* Englewood Cliffs, N.J.: Prentice-Hall.

_____. 1982. "Community Corrections: Panacea, Progress, or Pretense?" In R.L. Abel (ed.) *The Politics of Informal Justice. Volume 1: The American Experience.* New York: Academic Press. 99-118.

Shewan, I. (July) 1985. "The Decision to Parole: Balancing the Rehabilitation of the Offender with the Protection of the Public." 27 *Canadian Journal of Criminology.* 327-339.

Shover, N. 1979. *A Sociology of American Corrections.* Homewood, Illinois: The Dorsey Press.

Simkus, A.A., E.L. Hall and C.T. Griffiths. 1978. "Parole Board Decisions and the Severity of Punishment: A Critical Reexamination of the Evidence." In E.E. Flynn and J.P. Conrad (eds.) *The New and the Old Criminology.* New York: Praeger. 285-98.

Smith, M.E. 1983-84. "Will the Real Alternatives Please Stand Up?" 12 *New York University Review of Law and Social Change.* 171-197.

Smykla, J.O. 1981. *Community-Based Corrections: Principles and Practices.* New York: Macmillan.

Solicitor General of Canada. 1981a. *Solicitor General's Study of Conditional Release: Report of the Working Group.* Ottawa: Supply and Services Canada.

_____. 1981b. *Mandatory Supervison: A Discussion Paper.* Ottawa: Communication Division.

Stanley, D.T. 1976. *Prisoners Among Us: The Problem of Parole.* Washington, D.C.: The Brookings Institute.

Statistics Canada. 1986. *Adult Correctional Services in Canada, 1985-86.* Ottawa: Canadian Centre for Justice Statistics.

Stewart, G. (April) 1983. "Mandatory Supervision: Politics and People." 25 *Canadian Journal of Criminology.* 95-104.

Sullivan, D.C., L.J. Seigel and T.R. Clear. (April) 1974. "The Halfway House, Ten Years Later: Reappraisal of Correctional Innovation." 16 *Canadian Journal of Criminology and Corrections.* 188-97.

Task Force Report on the Role of the Private Sector in Criminal Justice. 1977. *Report: Community Involvement in Criminal Justice, Vol. 1.* Ottawa: Supply and Services Canada.

Tomaino, L. (December) 1975. "The Five Faces of Probation." 39 *Federal Probation.* 42-45.

Travis, L.F., M.D. Schwartz and T.R. Clear. 1983. *Corrections: An Issues Approach.* 2d edition. Cincinnati, Ohio: Anderson Publishing Co.

Vetter, H.J. and R. Adams. (February) 1970. "Effectiveness of Probation Caseload Sizes: A Review of the Empirical Literature." 8 *Criminology.* 333-43.

von Hirsch, A. and K.J. Hanrahan. 1978. *Abolish Parole?* Washington, D.C.: U.S. Department of Justice.

Waldo, G.P. and T.G. Chiricos. (February) 1977. "Work Release & Recidivism: An Empirical Evaluation of a Social Policy." 1 *Evaluation Quarterly.* 87-108.

Waldo, G.P., T.G. Chiricos and L.E. Dobrin. 1976. "Community Contact and Inmate Attitudes: An Experimental Assessment of Work Release." In P.G. Boesen and S.E. Grupp (eds.) *Community-Based Corrections: Theory, Practice and Research.* Santa Cruz, California: Davis Publishing Co.

Waller, I. 1974. *Men Released From Prison.* Toronto: University of Toronto Press.

Wilkins, L.T. and A. Chandler. (January) 1965. "Confidence and Competence in Decision Making." 5 *British Journal of Criminology*. 22-35.

Zeitoun, L. (Winter) 1978. "The Development of Community-Based Residential Centres in Canada." 3 *Offender Rehabilitation*. 133-50.

Chapter 10

Correctional Reform

Correctional reform has been one of the dominant themes in modern correctional history, a theme which has been developed and promoted by politicians, professional interest groups, academic theoreticians and the public-at-large. It has been the subject of scholarly research, program experiments, and major negotiations between levels of government.

No study of corrections, involving any country or political system, is complete without a study of the issues associated with correctional reform. Reform implies change. But change must have a purpose. According to the *Oxford English Dictionary* (6th edition, 1976), "reform" is "the process of making a person, institution or procedure better by removing or abandoning imperfections, faults or errors." The factors which are influential in promoting correctional reform are the same as those factors involved in the creation and implementation of correctional policy — it is in the act of policy making that reform efforts are initiated or affirmed.

In this chapter, correctional reform is discussed as an issue which has generated unique and deliberate initiatives within the Canadian corrections system to identify "imperfections, faults, or errors" and to create changes in policy and procedure which will promote a "better" system. The areas of reform interest in modern correctional history are identified and the influence on the correctional enterprise as a whole is discussed.

ISSUES IN CORRECTIONAL REFORM

The primary issue in correctional reform is prison reform. As pointed out earlier in the text, prisons have been the centre of correctional programming in Canada since prior to Confederation, and in relation to prisons, correctional reform has tended to concentrate on one of two perspectives: either the reform initiative has been directed at changing the prison itself, or it has been directed at changing the correctional system to promote less dependence on the use of prisons as a form of correctional disposition.

As opinion on the purpose and efficacy of prison reform has evolved, a sense of negativism, if not hopelessness, is evident. Rothman (cited in Bartollas and Miller 1978, 306) has suggested:

> Every generation of Americans, from the first days of the Republic to our own times, has produced a dedicated coterie of prison and asylum reformers. Yet each generation, it seems, discovers anew the scandals of incarceration, each sets out to correct them, and each passes on a legacy of failure. The rallying cries of one period echo dismally into the next . . . We inherit, in essence, a two-hundred year history of reform without change.

Similar sentiments have been expressed with specific reference to Canadian corrections. Gosselin (1982, 22), in discussing the Report of the Parliamentary Sub-Committee on the Penitentiary System in Canada (MacGuigan 1977), comments as follows:

> The ultimate recommendations of the Sub-Committee were easy enough to predict — so easy that one could have taken instead the conclusions and recommendations of the 1927 Annual Report of the Superintendent of Penitentiaries. The differences are negligible . . . Fifty years have not wrought many changes in the pious statements mouthed by those responsible for the repression.

In contrast to the perception of prison reform evidenced in these statements, there is a body of opinion which views correctional reform, including prison reform, in a more positive light. From this perspective, the prison itself is seen as a testimony to correctional reform. Heijder (1980, 1) states: "For centuries, enforced confinement has been at the core of the assortment of punishments offered by penal law. Compared with the noose and the pillory, the prison is an improvement." While suggesting that prison may be an improvement over other forms of punishment, Heijder and other commentators acknowledge that the use of prisons raises a series of reform questions concerning both the purpose of prisons and the practices which occur within them. Heijder (1980, 1) goes on to point out that

> there is pervasive uneasiness about its [prison] use. The correctional institution is supposed to be a people-changing agency, yet we doubt whether prison really persuades offenders to abandon criminal behavior. We hope that prisons deter people from criminal inclinations, but we are not at all sure whether there is in fact a close link between general prevention, a professed goal of criminal justice, and the prison system (A. Heijder, "Can We Cope with Alternatives?" *Crime and Delinquency,* vol.

Much of the literature suggesting that progress in prison reform can be demonstrated, concentrates on issues related to prison practice and includes an assessment of the changes in both prison programs and the management principles associated with them. Faguy (1973, 9), for example, in commenting on the Canadian penal system, states that "the cafeteria system has been established in almost every institution. A far cry from the old cell style feeding." In discussing the history of jails and prisons, Kirkpatrick (1964, 407) declares that:

[The] Gaol Act of 1823 became the foundation of the English prison system. The justices were now required to govern the prisons according to prescribed principles. The jailer became their paid servant, the jails had to be inspected and reports were mandatory to the Home Secretary. . . .

Again, Kirkpatrick (1962, 163), discussing changes in prison discipline and penitentiary regulations over the previous century, states:

I am often asked if we are far behind in Corrections in Canada. My feeling about it, and I have seen prisons and services in many other countries, is that while we have much to do we are making considerable and speedy progress. Many of our problems are jurisdictional and organizational; but it seems clear that progressive ideas and plans are in the minds of the administrators of our correctional system. But the results to date indicate that we have had a serious failure rate in the past and that this should and can be improved. . . .

These perceptions of progress in prison reform, while acknowledging the continuing need for change, are often regarded with suspicion even by those who maintain that prison reform can occur and has occurred. For instance, Bowker (1979, 25) offers the following comment:

There is something to be said for an analytic history of a correctional institution. Official histories deal with a sequence of events without explaining what caused these events to occur. There is also a tendency to ignore problems and to reinterpret everything in terms of the historical progress of prison reform. Such a history is a little more than apology for Corrections industry. . . .

Any judgement about the desired ends of correctional reform, and whether or not reform has actually taken place, is directly related to the political, philosophical, or ideological perspective of the observer. As well, shifts in public attitudes and in the perspectives of the criminal justice system itself have a direct effect on the way in which reform is perceived. As observed previously, the development of policy and practice throughout Canadian correctional history clearly suggests that while each new emphasis in correctional practice is considered reformative in relation to the emphasis which preceded it, the dominant philosophy of the day also influences how reform is perceived *within* the models of practice which are intended to reflect that philosophy. Culbertson (1981, 317), in discussing the barriers to correctional reform, comments:

> The correctional component has the least political impact on the criminal justice system and is undoubtedly the most affected by ideological shifts in the system. For example, in the shift from utilitarian philosophy and the due process model to retributive philosophy and the crime control model, the entire correctional apparatus is forced to respond accordingly. Yesterday, treatment was heralded as reform. Today, it is an evil to be eliminated and replaced by punishment and the determinate sentence. The issue of goals is again important, as it becomes clear that the correctional process cannot establish a set of goals to guide its operations in the long-term. Rather, the corrections systems must be prepared to swing with the pendulum and suffer the inequities and inefficiencies that follow philosophical and political change.

JURISDICTIONAL REFORM IN CANADA

The frustration, confusion and uncertainty associated with the use of prisons and with the effectiveness of prison reform have shifted the interest of Canadian correctional authorities (both political and bureaucratic) toward a redefinition of the jurisdictional responsibility for the delivery of correctional services. This change in focus would indicate that Canadian correctional authorities believe that correctional reform, including prison reform, requires a reassessment of the management and administrative structures which determine correctional policy and which are responsible for correctional practice. In Canada this belief continues to exert significant influence on perceptions of correctional reform.

The change in emphasis away from program-specific reform issues and toward a redefinition of responsibility for making program decisions seems to have been occasioned by the following factors:

1. Correctional reform initiatives in Canada have consistently been subject to procedural difficulties arising from the present split in jurisdiction.
2. The increasing cost of criminal justice services has required attention to issues of cost effectiveness, particularly the desire to reduce the wasteful duplication of services.
3. There is an emerging view that substantial correctional reform and jurisdictional responsibility for corrections must be organized in a way which allows for the greatest possible compatibility with the authority structures providing other justice services.

Each of these factors has received considerable attention in recent years and every major inquiry into the correctional system since the 1930s comments on one or more of them. The following excerpts illustrate the point:

> It is obvious, for example, that if different than that [sic] recommended by your Commissioners is given to the prisoners in provincial institutions, if classification and segregation are not uniformly instituted, if a different discipline is in effect, and the administration is not supervised by the same authorities, the success of the system recommended by your Commissioners would be jeopardized, and the evils discerned in the antiquated treatment at present in existence would be permanently extended (Archambault 1983, 340).

> Our general conclusion concerning the legislative authority for the operation of Canadian penal institutions is that there is much confusion, if not actual contradiction, in the law. We consider that much could be done to achieve greater unity of purpose and treatment in the various provinces (Fauteux 1956, 50).

> The correctional services must be seen as an integral part of the total system of criminal justice and their aims should be consistent with and supportive of the aims of the law enforcement agencies and courts (Ouimet 1969, 277).

> The corrections field is further fragmented by the division of responsibility between federal and provincial governments and by different administrative patterns in various jurisdictions (Ouimet 1969, 275).

> Costly duplication of services and lack of continuity and inconsistencies in treatment must somehow be avoided and I would suggest to you that this will never really be accomplished until the responsibility for the total correctional process in any area is placed under one authority (Ontario Ministry of Correctional Services 1975a, 7).

The division of responsibility creates a basic weakness inherent in Canadian corrections. The concept of continuity in treatment and proper programming which is so necessary for the offender be he young or old is ignored. The balkanization of the correctional process is the necessary result of the two year rule (Ontario Ministry of Correctional Services 1975b, 3).

But we are most concerned, and it is here that I wish to focus my remarks, with the duplication, overlapping, lack of communication, inefficiency, ineffectiveness, and lack of rational basis characterizing the existence of two separate systems of corrections at the federal and provincial levels of jurisdiction, each system developing (and still expanding) a broad range of alternative correctional responses to those persons convicted and sentenced by the court to serve periods of confinement (Macdonald 1975, 3).

As a result of escalating concern over these issues, the Continuing Committee of Deputy Ministers responsible for corrections formed a Federal-Provincial Task Force in 1975 to "examine the long-term objectives for Corrections in Canada, with a view to assessing alternative splits in jurisdiction between the federal and provincial governments" (Federal-Provincial Task Force on Long Term Objectives in Corrections 1976, i). The Task Force presented its report to the Federal-Provincial Conference of Attorneys General and Ministers Responsible for Corrections in Ottawa on June 27th to 30th, 1977. No less than 13 options to the present division of jurisdiction were outlined (see Table 10.1). Of these options, the following four were selected for detailed description:

1. split in jurisdiction based on sentence length;
2. present split in jurisdiction with improvements;
3. total provincial administration of corrections; and,
4. total federal administration of corrections.

(For a detailed assessment of these options as presented to the Federal-Provincial Conference, see Table 10.2.)

On receipt of this report, the Ministers decided to proceed with a detailed study of the following four options:

1. the Government of Canada to assume full responsibility;
2. the provincial governments to assume full responsibility;
3. split jurisdiction to be maintained but on a different basis; and,
4. a federal/provincial crown corporation to be established to direct a unified system.

TABLE 10.1   Summary of Options Considered Related to the Federal/Provincial Split in Corrections Jurisdiction (1976)

1. Current situation with improvements
   (better coordinating and contracting mechanisms)
2. All *Federal* Corrections System
3. Federal Correctional Service Delivery
   (services presently delivered by provinces would be delivered under contract with the federal government)
4. All *Provincial* Corrections System
5. *Provincial* Correctional Service Delivery
   (services presently delivered by the federal government would be delivered under contract with the provinces)
6. Community-Institution Split
   (community services/provincial; institution services/federal)
7. Program Split
   (other than community/institutional)
8. Minor/Serious Offender Offences Split
   (minor/provincial; serious/federal)
9. Sentence Length
   (other than current two-year rule, e.g., six months)
10. Federal/Provincial Corrections Agency
    (crown corporation model)
11. Law Reform Commission Proposals
    (based on various recommendations of the Law Reform Commission of Canada re: Sentences and Dispositions)
12. Personal/Property Offences Split
    (personal/federal; property/provincial)
13. Split Based on Statute-Making Authority
    (persons convicted under federal laws and statutes/federal; persons convicted under provincial laws and statutes/provincial)

SOURCE: Summarized from Federal-Provincial Task Force on Long Term Objectives in Corrections 1976. *The Long Term Objectives and Administration of Corrections in Canada.* Ottawa: Solicitor General of Canada.

These options have been studied and discussed in numerous federal/provincial forums and have received comment by interest groups such as the Canadian Criminal Justice Association and the various provincial corrections associations.[1]

It is interesting that the Ministers chose to include the crown corporation option in their identification of alternatives for further study. There is no doubt that during these discussions the Ministers experienced considerable frustration in their attempts to resolve the issues of split jurisdiction through direct negotiation between the two levels of government. The idea of "cooperative

TABLE 10.2   Assessment of Options for the Split in Jurisdiction in Corrections

		Options			
		I	II	III A	III B
		Six month split — non-unified, and both centralized and decentralized	Present split with better coordination — non-unified and both centralized and decentralized	Totally provincially adminis-tered system unified within the provinces and decentra-lized	Totally federally administered system unified nationally and centralized
C R I T E R I A	**Philosophy**	•fed/prov split of secure facili-ties/community programs •less community in-volvement for offenders over 6 months	•fed/prov split of secure facili-ties/community programs •less community involvement for offenders over 2 years	•less focus for secure facilities versus com-munity programs •greater com-munity involve-ment	•greater focus for secure facilities versus commun-ity programs •less community involvement
	Service Delivery	•dual service delivery system •fewer program opportunities •some consist-ency in service delivery in provinces •increase in federal workload	•dual service delivery system •fewer program opportunities •some consist-ency in service delivery in provinces	•single service delivery system •more program opportunities •more consis-tency in service delivery in provinces •increase in provincial workload •may not be economical for certain provinces	•single service delivery system for sentences of imprisonment •more program opportunities •more consistency in service delivery nationally •increase in federal workload
	Administrative Structure	•same with some increase federally	•same with some economies	•increase in provincial structure •difficulties in joining 2 organizations	•increase in federal structure •difficulties in joining 2 organizations
	Standards	•good nationally for offenders sentenced over 6 months, but not necessarily in provinces	•good nationally for offenders sentenced over 2 years, but not necessarily in provinces	•good in provinces, but not necessarily nationally	•good everywhere
	Finance	•increase in federal responsibility	•same as present	•funding?	•funding?
	Coordination with C.J.S.	•same as present	•improved slightly	•probably improved	•probably decreased
	Coordination with other Social Service	•same as present	•improved slightly	•probably improved	•probably decreased
	Impact on Private Agencies	•same as present	•improved slightly	•better coordination	•better coordination

SOURCE: Federal-Provincial Task Force on Long Term Objectives in Corrections. 1976. *The Long Term Objectives and Administration of Corrections in Canada.* p. xxvii.

federalism," which has been viewed as central in the Canadian form of federalism, creates a situation where issues that must be resolved through agreement between the federal and provincial governments are often subject to inordinate delay and confusion. The issue of correctional jurisdiction is certainly no exception. As Prevost (1968, 52) states, "The Canadian Federated System is therefore at least in part responsible for the slowness in establishing a single philosophy throughout the entire corrections system."

As an issue related to correctional reform, it is important to recognize that the attention to jurisdictional matters is centred on the desire to create an organizational dynamic which will reduce the tendency of correctional systems in Canada to be in competition with each other — a competition which often results in the duplication of services and in conflicts over operating principles. It is not so much a question of "fixing" a single operating philosophy as it is a desire to assure that the operating philosophies and the strategies which result from them will be subject to consistent review. Furthermore, it is a desire to assure that reform, where required, will be efficiently, effectively and consistently administered. And as indicated earlier, in the current view, these desires can only be realized when correctional services are organized to ensure management integrity through clear lines of authority and when the responsibility for managing correctional reform is regarded as an activity associated with the goals and strategies of the criminal justice system as a whole.

Thus far it has been illustrated that correctional reform may be viewed as including everything from improvements in inmate food services to improvement in the way in which the entire correctional system is structured to determine priorities and to administer whole programs. There is evidence, however, that correctional reform which is approached through piecemeal improvements in specific areas of service delivery is less than satisfying. In fact, it can be argued that reform attempts of this kind promote disparity rather than reduce it. There is also the fundamental question of whether piecemeal reform works at all, either in the short or the long run. Therefore, the recent interest of Canadian correctional authorities in pursuing the fundamental issues of jurisdiction and in establishing a unifying philosophy may be a positive sign.

At this writing, the discussion of jurisdictional alternatives continues and no real resolution is in sight. The difficulties are recognized by the ministers themselves, and while their officials continue to study jurisdictional alternatives, they have also been given instructions to seek improvements in service delivery within the areas of discrete responsibility governed by the current jurisdictional split. Consequently, there have been two agenda items considered by correctional officials and their ministers since the presentation of the Task Force report in 1977. One is to continue to search for ways within the present jurisdictional arrangement to reduce duplication and to improve coordination in the delivery of correctional services. The other is to continue to press for reform in the jurisdictional arrangement itself.[2]

Within the present jurisdictional schema, there have been a number of political and administrative initiatives taken to address correctional issues requiring reform. In the following sections some of these initiatives are discussed and the major issues are identified.

CORRECTIONAL INVESTIGATIONS AND INQUIRIES

As indicated earlier, questions of jurisdiction, while a relatively recent emphasis in formal discussions at the political and bureaucratic levels, have emerged as a dominant issue in the studies of many investigative bodies over at least the last half century. Normally, commissions of inquiry and task forces have been formed to address specific issues or critical events within either the federal or provincial correctional systems. These groups invariably make numerous recommendations for reform, and their recommendations often concern the process through which reform decisions must be made, or the administrative requirements necessary to assure that reform initiatives will be maintained. Excerpts from some of these studies have been quoted above in the discussion on jurisdictional reform.

The issue of how reform can best be initiated must also be raised. The nature of the correctional system and its decision-making process must be taken into account by reform initiatives. But it must be realized that it is difficult for an operating bureaucratic system to reform itself — particularly when the primary service delivery functions of the system are performed in closed institutions. It, therefore, is generally the case that correctional systems are under greatest pressure to engage in reform when social and political conditions, or critical events, demand some form of external review.

It is something of an anomaly that even where an external review is demanded, it is often initiated by the authorities holding responsibility for the system being reviewed, and that the recommendations resulting from any review must be received and implemented by that same authority. This situation results in the rather persistent charge that political and bureaucratic authorities often use external reviews as a way to reduce political pressure or delay the implementation of required reforms. Many argue that the situation is compounded in Canadian corrections by the current split in jurisdiction: even when recommendations for reform are clear and are supported by one level of authority, it is often the case that agreement between jurisdictions must be established before the reform can be implemented.

However, in discussing the difficulties associated with the implementation of correctional reform, it is evident that there are factors involved which probably cannot be satisfactorily resolved by jurisdictional reform alone. Culbertson (1981) identifies a number of such "barriers to reform". In this context, one of the most important barriers has to do with the posture of correctional organizations when confronted with recommendations for change. Culbertson (1981, 322-23) comments as follows:

> Correctional processes are not unlike other components of the criminal justice system, and tend to resist the negative feedback which could enable the system to make corrections for errors in planning and management. Criticism of correctional agencies stimulates a host of defensive mechanisms and postures as agency personnel excuse, rationalize, and justify obviously bad practices that are not in the best interests of their clients. . . . Because the correctional apparatus has tended to be reactive rather than proactive, it has been plagued with (a) narrowness of perspective. . . . Under these conditions, reform is difficult if not impossible. If the system will not acknowledge the existence of data it has set out to collect, what chance do persons and groups outside that system have to make the kinds of input that would enhance potential for reform?

The response of the Solicitor General (Canada) to the Parliamentary Sub-Committee Report on the Penitentiary System of Canada (1977b) is instructive in this regard. The Solicitor General noted that the Parliamentary Sub-Committee had made 65 recommendations and states, "I have accepted 53 of the recommendations in whole or in part and have reserved my position in others that, because of their far-reaching implications, require further examination on an urgent basis by the departments and agencies involved."

However, the Solicitor General also noted (1977b, 2) that the Parliamentary Sub-Committee made the following statement:

> A crisis exists in the Canadian Penitentiary system. It can be met only by the immediate implementation of large-scale reforms. It is imperative

that the Solicitor General act immediately on this Report as a matter of the utmost urgency.

The Solicitor General's (1977b, 2) response to this statement indicates both a rejection of the critical nature of the situation and a defensive posture.

> The Solicitor General strongly supports the call for reform of the system, and evidence of his commitment is contained in this document itself, and in his pledge to implement those recommendations which further the goal of reform which he shares with the Committee. Approximately four out of five recommendations are accepted in principle, as this detailed response demonstrates. While there are serious problems which must be resolved, doubt is expressed about use of the term "crisis" to describe a situation which has been of ongoing concern for some time. It should also be noted that the Sub-Committee was established as a result of disturbances in 3 institutions in a system containing 54.

The resistance to change within the Canadian Correctional system is easily demonstrated and has been a source of frustration to many persons and agencies who have sought correctional reform.

SUMMARY OF MAJOR CANADIAN CORRECTIONAL INVESTIGATIONS AND INQUIRIES

In this section, the major Canadian correctional investigations and inquiries occurring in recent years are identified and summarized. For the most part, these inquiries are the work of politically appointed commissions which have been brought together out of the need to address an operational crisis that has been translated into a consequent need for a broader review of some aspect of the correctional enterprise.

Politically appointed commissions of inquiry have been used as a vehicle for conducting public investigations into correctional matters since the mid-nineteenth century. Over the years, the reports resulting from these inquiries have provided the locus for debate on correctional matters and have generated a variety of responses and further initiatives from the academic community, private sector agencies, public interest groups, the legal community (including the judiciary) and the political and bureaucratic systems responsible for correctional policy and practice. The documents produced by the inquiries offer insight into the development of correctional thought in Canada, including the frustrations expressed by the investigators as they attempted to assess correctional practice in relation to some understanding of correctional purpose. Comments and recommendations from some of these reports have been presented in earlier chapters.

Before proceeding with the discussion of the inquiries themselves, it must be noted that initiatives directed at correctional reform have historically come from a variety of sources ranging from private agencies and citizens' groups to the legal community and professional associations. From time to time, all of these groups have exerted considerable influence on the development of correctional thought and on the implementation of correctional reform. Some agencies, such as the John Howard Society and Elizabeth Fry Society, have been taking an active role in Canadian correctional reform for most of the twentieth century.[3] More recently, national and provincial corrections associations and civil liberties and prisoners' rights groups have been established for the primary purpose of stimulating correctional reform.

The reliance upon commissions to identify and resolve correctional problems is relatively recent and reflects a shift in the locus of correctional reform from the arena of private concern — religious, philanthropic, or voluntary interventions — to the arena of public concern, which views correctional reform as the responsibility of the state. The relationship between the public sector agencies responsible for correctional policy and practice and the private sector agencies interested in correctional reform has significantly changed.

Private sector agencies have found their ability to act as arbiters of correctional change blunted, as their relationship with government becomes more formal (contractual) and as their activities become more directly centred on the provision of correctional services. In recent years, this phenomenon has produced increased tension between those public and private sector agencies engaging in corrections work and has stimulated a number of initiatives which have sought to re-define and to clarify their relationship.[4] As a result, many private sector agencies and interest groups which were dedicated to taking a proactive stance in relation to correctional reform have been co-opted. Many have adopted a reactive stance, which is partially reflected in the growing tendency of these agencies to contract with governments for the provision of correctional services, and is partially reflected in the use of these agencies as "responders" to government-initiated investigations and inquiries.

The beginning of the "commission response" to correctional issues is usually associated with the Archambault Report (1938).

However, while the Archambault Report was certainly the first major commission report in modern Canadian correctional history, the "commission response" to correctional matters began much earlier. In a summary of inquiries into Canadian corrections published by the Solicitor General of Canada (1977c, 1) the following comment is made:

Since the Legislature of Upper Canada commissioned a report recommending the construction of Kingston Penitentiary in 1832, studies, investigations and inquiries on prisons and corrections in Canada have come thick and fast. Just 17 years later, in 1849, another committee was asked to look into conditions at the Kingston prison, and, in 1876, a federal commission investigated prison labour and the remuneration of officers.

The "1913 Commission" and the "1920 Committee" were two more major attempts to come to grips with the continuing questions of philosophy and management which plagued the prison system, and they were the forerunners of the Archambault Commission, which was appointed in 1936 "to inquire into and report, on the penal system of Canada. . . ." This report published in 1938, was a landmark in Canadian corrections, making 88 recommendations in the course of its 364 pages of text. Much of its philosophy remains influential today.

Two other commissions of great significance were established in later years — Fauteux (1956) and Ouimet (1969). Taken together with the Archambault Report (1938) and the report of the MacGuigan Sub-Committee (1977), they are considered by many to be the most influential correctional inquiries initiated in Canada to date.

For its part, the Fauteux Committee (1956) was established to "inquire into the principles and procedures followed in the Remission Service of the Department of Justice." Similarly, the Ouimet Committee (1969) was established "to study the broad field of Corrections, in its widest sense, from the initial investigation of an offence through to the final discharge of a prisoner from imprisonment or parole. . . ." The Fauteux Committee submitted its report in April, 1956, with "44 recommendations on everything from the philosophy of corrections, to the goals of the court at one end of the system right through to parole at the other" (Solicitor General of Canada 1977c, 5). In March, 1969, the Ouimet Committee submitted its report containing 118 recommendations.

According to the Solicitor General's Summary (1977c, i):

Archambault (1938), Fauteux (1956) and Ouimet (1969) — the three major inquiries into the corrections system — all focused on the rehabilitative and treatment role of the penal system. All saw it as central, all defended it for the same reasons, all perceived a failure in application, and all assumed the situation to be correctable.

While their review of correctional practice, their assessment of correctional philosophy, and their recommendations certainly had an influence on correctional practice and on the implementation of specific correctional reforms, perhaps the reports' most interesting effect was the stimulus they provided to the correctional enterprise in Canada to continue using this mode of inquiry. Not only have commissions been used to investigate both general and specific correctional issues, they have been relied upon to assist the correctional enterprise to restructure itself, particularly with regard to the dialogue between jurisdictions — a dialogue in part made necessary by the need to find a more satisfactory method of responding to the issues and recommendations made in the reports themselves.

With regard to the continuing use of this form of investigation, it is interesting to note that at least nine nationally significant external inquiries into corrections have occurred since the publication of the Ouimet Report in 1969: the Mohr Report (1971), the Swackhamer Report (1972), the Vantour Report (1975), the Farris Report (1976), the various working papers of the Law Reform Commission of Canada (1975, 1976), the MacGuigan Report (1977), the Carson Report (1984), the Correctional Law Review (1986), and the Canadian Sentencing Commission (1987). The area of concern investigated by each of these bodies can be represented as follows:

1. *The Mohr Committee,* in February, 1971, was asked to "determine the needs of inmates that the working group define as maximum security, determine the programs and staffing requirements necessary to satisfy these needs, and finally to determine the ideal institutional design and locations to facilitate implementation of these programs." This Committee's report was submitted in November, 1971, and contained 22 recommendations.
2. *The Swackhamer Commission* was asked to report on the specific causes and effects of the disturbances at Kingston Penitentiary and Millhaven Penitentiary between April 14 and April 18, 1971. In April, 1972, the Commission brought down its findings, including 55 recommendations. Having addressed the specific issues related to their mandate, the Swackhamer Commission expanded its mandate in order to "assist the Canadian Penitentiary Service in lessening the frequency and severity of penitentiary disturbances and devising techniques for management, control and settlement of such disturbances when they do arise."
3. *The Vantour Committee,* in April, 1975, was mandated to look at the question of dissociation in federal penitentiaries. The

Committee presented its report in December, 1975, with 57 recommendations.

4. *The Farris Commission* was asked to investigate "the particular events occurring between June 9 and June 11, 1975, at the British Columbia Penitentiary." This Commission did not choose to broaden its mandate and limited itself instead to very specific terms of reference in its investigation. Nevertheless, this report "pointed out clearly in its limited look at a particular incident the fact that the old promise and optimistic assumptions made by earlier reports had, in practice, proved to be much more difficult to achieve than anyone had thought" (Solicitor General of Canada, 1977c, 29).

5. *The Law Reform Commission of Canada* was established in 1970 to address a wide range of issues associated with the review of criminal law and criminal law procedure. As might be expected, its working papers and reports have addressed a variety of correctional issues and several of these papers make reference to the correctional inquiries which preceded them. In particular, the *Working Paper on Dispositions and Sentences* (1976) has had considerable influence on federal/provincial negotiations on correctional matters.

6. *The Parliamentary Sub-Committee on the Penitentiary System in Canada* was formed in 1977 to "inquire into the system of maximum security institutions maintained by the Canadian Penitentiary Service" (MacGuigan 1977, 6). During its inquiry, the Sub-committee examined various aspects of institutions, including security procedures, classification, correctional programs and the problems encountered by staff and management. In its final report, the Subcommittee proposed 65 recommendations, the majority of which were subsequently accepted by the Solicitor General.

7. The Advisory Committee to the Solicitor General of Canada on the Management of Correctional Institutions (Carson Committee) was commissioned on July 27, 1984. Its mandate was to review the management of the Correctional Service of Canada in response to earlier studies on suicide and violence in the service. Its report was submitted on November 30, 1984.

8. The Correctional Law Review (established in 1983 and still in existence at the time of writing) is one of fifty different projects that together will make up the Criminal Law Review. The Correctional Law Review is principally concerned with reviewing federal legislation and parts of the *Criminal Code* which relate to correctional matters. The Review aims to develop a framework for corrections that reflects the philosophy

of Canadian corrections, facilitates the attainment of correctional goals and objectives, and provides clear and specific authority in law for correctional agencies and their functions and activities.

9. The Canadian Sentencing Commission was established in 1984, in recognition of the serious problems which exist in the structure of sentencing in Canada. The mandate of the Commission was to examine sentencing and to forward proposals on how the process could be improved. The Commission found that the system is in need of fundamental changes in its orientation and practice. In its final report, the Commission made ninety-one recommendations which attempt to present a uniquely Canadian solution to the problems currently in existence.

The effect of these studies and reports on both the structure and content of negotiations at the federal and provincial levels of correctional jurisdiction can be illustrated. To do so requires a review of federal/provincial initiatives and their relationship to the various reports described above.

FEDERAL/PROVINCIAL INITIATIVES RELATED TO CORRECTIONAL REFORM

In this section, the more significant federal/provincial initiatives that have been taken in recent years to address issues of correctional reform are discussed. In turn, the discussion is broken into three parts. The first deals with the structure of dialogue which has emerged between the federal and provincial governments; the second concentrates on identifying the most important internal investigations and studies initiated by the levels of government either jointly or individually; the third discusses the leading initiative taken to reform correctional programs or elements of correctional practice.

The Structure of Correctional Dialogue

As indicated earlier, in recent years the attention of correctional administrators and politicians has been directed to refining the structure of joint participation when addressing correctional issues. There is no doubt that this interest has been stimulated by recommendations arising from all of the major inquiries, particularly their call for a review of correctional jurisdiction and their insistence that one of the major barriers to correctional reform is the difficulty, because of split jurisdiction, in developing and implementing consistent policies and practices.

The first political initiative of this kind was taken in 1958, when a joint meeting of Ministers Responsible for Corrections was held in Ottawa. Given the Fauteux Committee's concern about jurisdictional issues and its mandate to inquire into the Remission Service, it is quite clear that the Fauteux Report (1956) provided at least a partial stimulus for the meeting. High on the agenda was a discussion of matters related to the new *Parole Act*, an Act which replaced the *Ticket of Leave Act* and which established the first National Parole Board.

As a result of the meeting, mechanisms were established for the purpose of improving negotiations between governments at the bureaucratic level, and federal/provincial discussions between officials responsible for correctional services began to increase. However, 15 years elapsed before another meeting of Ministers Responsible for Corrections was convened.

There were undoubtedly a number of factors leading to the next meeting of the Ministers Responsible for Corrections, which finally did take place in December, 1973. The interaction of corrections officials which began in 1958, while slow in developing, undoubtedly had a stimulating effect. Equally important were improvements in the economy, concerns over increases in categories of "new" offences (such as drug-related offences), and movements, particularly in the provinces, to develop a wider range of community-based alternatives. As well, the increasing attention to constitutional matters also played a significant role.

However, two other events were instrumental in eventually bringing the Ministers back together. The first was the proclamation of the *Government Organization Act* (1966) which created the Department of the Solicitor General of Canada and which assigned responsibility for federal police, penitentiaries and parole to the new ministry. This initiative resulted in a renewed commitment at the federal level to address correctional matters. Accordingly, ministerial and bureaucratic responsibility was refocused and a better forum was created to initiate federal/ provincial dialogue.

The second event was the publication of the Ouimet Report (1969), a report still considered by many to have been the most important correctional inquiry in Canada. To a degree not previously experienced, it clearly provided impetus for a renewed dialogue on correctional matters involving both government and non-government agencies. Furthermore, the Ouimet Report was unique in at least one respect. While the other reports addressed problems, both in practice and jurisdiction, which seemed to be inhibiting the realization of accepted correctional goals, the Ouimet Report began to cast doubt on the goals themselves. As a consequence, the response to the Ouimet Report tended to be more substantial than that elicited by other inquiries; correctional authorities were forced into a discussion of first principles. And finally, the discussion of first principles resulted in a new demand for negotiation at the political level.

In preparation for the Federal/Provincial Ministerial Conference on Corrections held in Ottawa in December of 1973, the Solicitor General's Ministry issued a discussion document entitled *The Criminal in Canadian Society: A Perspective*. The document was heavily influenced by the Ouimet Report, particularly in the way in which it emphasized the role of Corrections within the overall framework of the criminal justice system. Furthermore, it signalled the beginning of two fundamental changes in emphasis with regard to the study of correctional matters.

The first change was to give vitality to the view that correctional reform could take place only as an activity associated with broader criminal justice reform. The second concerned the motivation given to the development of formal federal/provincial discussions and studies on correctional matters — activities which involved officials under the direct purview of the Ministers responsible for Corrections. Additionally, the Ministers and Deputy Ministers responsible for Corrections began to meet jointly with the Ministers and Deputy Ministers responsible for other justice services in order to assure that the broader interests of the criminal justice system were considered in any correctional review.[5]

Internal Investigations and Studies

Following the federal/provincial conference in December, 1973, a Continuing Committee of Deputy Ministers Responsible for Corrections was established and was given a mandate to identify correctional issues requiring review and to make recommendations with regard to legislative, administrative or program reform. This Committee generated its own studies through the formation of task forces (e.g., the National Advisory Network on Manpower Planning, 1974, and the Federal-Provincial Task Force on Long Term Objectives in Corrections, 1976). It also provided a forum for the discussion of reports and studies which either preceded the formation of the Continuing Committee or were initiated after it was established (e.g., Working Group on Federal Maximum Security Institution Design, Mohr 1971; Task Force on Community-Based Residential Centres, Outerbridge 1972; Task Force on the Release of Inmates, Hugessen 1973; and Commission of Inquiry into the Non-Medical Use of Drugs, LeDain 1973).

The formation of these federal/provincial mechanisms for dialogue provided the means to undertake to review studies. In theory at least, they also improved the capacity of the various jurisdictions to be responsive to reform initiatives. This movement increased the opportunity for reform ventures to be undertaken in both government and non-government locations and enhanced the possibility for joint discussion and joint action. For instance, in 1975, the Province of British Columbia entered into bilateral discussions on correctional jurisdiction with the federal government. Once this initiative was brought forward to the Continuing Committee of Deputy Ministers, it resulted in the Federal-Provincial Task Force on Long Term Objectives (1976). Similarly, the provincial Attorneys General established the National Task Force on the Administration of Justice (1976) for purposes of acquiring an improved data base on criminal justice programs across Canada. In turn, this initiative led to the establishment of the National Work Group on Criminal Justice Statistics (1979) and eventually to the formation of the Canadian Centre for Justice Statistics (1980).

The flurry of activity generated during this period of time improved both the capacity of government agencies to engage in dialogue with non-government agencies, and the communication between government jurisdictions, particularly when one jurisdiction sought to undertake a major structural or program venture. An example of the former is found in the Task Force on the Role of the Private Sector in Criminal Justice (1977), established in 1975 by the Continuing Committee of Deputy Ministers Responsible for Corrections, and resulting in a national dialogue between governments and representatives from private sector agencies. An example of the latter is the attempt made by the Solicitor General's Ministry to restate both the structure and the principles associated with federal corrections through the creation of a task force in 1973 "to develop and implement an integrated Canadian corrections service, which would include the Canadian Penitentiary Service and the National Parole service." The report of the task force was published in 1977 and resulted in a significant restructuring of the administration of federal correctional programs.

It is interesting to note that issues related to correctional jurisdiction — and to the broader questions surrounding the administration of justice — became part of the constitutional debate and received comment in the federal document *A Time for Action: Toward the Renewal of the Canadian Federation* (Government of Canada 1978), as well as in the first two reports of the Western Premiers' Task Force on Constitutional Trends (1977 and 1978). These matters also appeared on the agenda of the inter-ministerial meetings of Ministers on the Constitution. As a result, further impetus was given to the review of correctional reform issues.

Initiatives Taken to Reform Correctional Programs

Given the definition of reform provided earlier, it is worth stating again that judgements about whether or not reform has actually taken place depend very much on the political, theoretical, or ideological perspective of the observer. Additionally, any assessment of reform initiatives within public institutions proceeds best when reform is viewed in terms of both process and result.

The problem of inconsistency in the development of correctional goals and the implementation of strategies to realize those goals also has been previously noted. Some authorities argue that it is simply not possible for corrections to establish firm and consistent goals, since corrections is a reflection of movements and changes in social attitudes, "professional" perspectives and political beliefs. Therefore, it is within the general nature of correctional reform that it tends to seek either to "retain something" in the face of these movements and changes or to "move toward something" which affirms basic organizational, cultural, social, or political values, regardless of other shifts in attitude and beliefs which may occur.

These basic values include such things as the reasonable exercise of stewardship over public resources (cost effectiveness and cost efficiency), the avoidance of cruel and unusual punishment (humane treatment), the maintenance and promotion of respect for the law (equality in application) and the right of citizens in a free and democratic society to determine the parameters within which the state can make interventions on their behalf — including the requirement that the state be accountable to its citizens for any interventions made within those parameters. In Canada, correctional reforms are usually demanded or initiated as a result of these and similar values. Moreover, in the face of inconsistencies in goals and strategies — including jurisdictional problems — assessments of correctional reform might usefully consider whether or not these values are affirmed and whether or not they are reflected in the specific programs and practices which result.

In one sense, this approach provides a much more satisfying way to assess correctional reform than the activity of evaluating specific correctional programs to see if they "work." Work to do what? In a system where operational goals (other than those provided in law) are nearly impossible to establish or are inconsistently applied, it is difficult to see how reform initiatives could be adequately assessed by determining whether or not they successfully realize known operational objectives. This feature of the correctional enterprise may account for the propensity either to employ superficial measures in the assessment of correctional programs (e.g., recidivism) or to concentrate on the validity in application of programs geared to result in behavioural change. In both of these examples, it is difficult to relate findings to any clear and consistent statement of operational objectives.

Regarding the lack of clarity of some correctional program objectives, it is acknowledged that many experimental initiatives are embarked upon which are not based on any articulated social values. Instead, they are undertaken to determine whether something can be learned which will assist in establishing correctional program objectives which have practical utility. More often than not, they are initiated simply to determine how the man-management problems associated with the requirement to maintain order and discipline in correctional settings might be reduced.

It can be argued that reduced recidivism or behavioural change are examples of objectives which cannot be regarded as legitimate for any program associated with the sanctioning power of the state in a free society. Reduced recidivism or behavioural change may be acceptable or even desirable consequences of the activity of the state in the use of its sanctioning power. But they are not regarded as the *purpose* for sanctioning individual behaviour. And such effects are nowhere declared as a fundamental social purpose of the correctional enterprise in Canada. Thus, the assessment of program initiatives might be more fruitful if it were undertaken with regard to the social values which are fundamental to the correctional enterprise, such as the regard for individual rights, protection of the public, and the application of punishment in relation to the degree of harm done.

With these issues in mind, it is easier to understand why the general movement in Canadian correctional reform over recent years has concentrated on questions of cost efficiency and cost effectiveness, on establishing consistent and generally accepted principles, on issues of jurisdiction, and on clarifying the legal and constitutional mandate. Without clarification of these matters, any assessment that sets out to determine the value of programs with respect to achieving reform will be subject to confusion, frustration and uncertainty.

It has already been pointed out that the constitutional debate which resulted in the *Constitution Act* and the *Charter of Rights and Freedoms* continues to have an effect on correctional reform. The work of the Law Reform Commission, in its review of criminal law and criminal law procedure, also has provided a basis for improving the legal mandate of corrections, in ways which more appropriately reflect current social values. Moreover, the Commission's activities have led the federal government to engage with the provinces, municipalities and non-government interest groups in a project to review Canadian criminal law, for the purpose of rewriting the *Criminal Code* of Canada and other federal criminal laws. As a first step, the federal government produced a document entitled *The Criminal Law in Canadian Society* (1982). The mechanisms described above, which were established to improve the dialogue on correctional matters between federal and provincial governments, have also provided a context within which correctional authorites can both contribute and respond to the review's findings. Particularly important in this regard is the ability to enter into dialogue concerning the requirements affecting correctional practice which result from law reform.

There is little doubt that these initiatives, together with the studies and recommendations emanating from academic research, private sector agencies, task forces and commissions, have had an appreciable effect on the process of correctional reform. The *results* of this process, insofar as they are reflected in specific programs or practices, are debatable and remain the subject of continuing critical review.

However, the cumulative effect of these activities has been to stimulate changes in both philosophy and practice in Canadian corrections. Some of these changes are worth noting. The first of these is the general agreement among correctional authorities that the rehabilitation or "medical model" of treatment in correctional programs should be abandoned. This emphasis was partially stimulated by Ouimet (1969), who began to express doubts about the suitability of prison as a place for rehabilitation while nonetheless acknowledging that the goal of rehabilitation is legitimate for corrections. The Law Reform Commission (1975a, 11) took this concept further by stating:

> Experience and research in the social sciences now make it difficult to accept with easy assurance the usual justifications for imprisonment. Generally, it is difficult to show that prisons rehabilitate offenders or are more effective as a general deterrent than other sanctions.

The Law Reform Commission's report on dispositions and sentences (1976, 2-3) affirmed the necessity of prisons with the following rationale:

> Not because we expect that the offender will be reformed by this measure, not because such a measure will necessarily deter others from committing offences, but because there are cases in which the community has reached the limits of its tolerance.

These sentiments were further developed by the Task Force on the Creation of an Integrated Canadian Corrections Service (1977, 25-26), where the point was made that the rehabilitation model is based on

> the assumption that correctional practitioners are able to change or modify the personality of the offender, which further assumes that criminal behaviour is somehow an expression of some underlying personality disturbance which requires extensive therapy and treatment before the criminal behaviour ceases. As a correctional goal, these claims have been challenged as being unrealistic, unsubstantiated and unattainable. Continued emphasis on rehabilitation as *the* recognized goal in corrections will tend to mislead the public as well as the offender regarding the intent, capacity and capability of corrections.

The abandonment of the rehabilitation model has been evident in attempts by both federal and provincial correctional agencies to restate their philosophy and purpose[6], and in the statement of philosophy associated with the Criminal Law Review.[7]

However, it is important to clarify what relinquishing the rehabilitation model really means. It does not mean that rehabilitation, either as a concept or as a practice that may benefit individual offenders, has been removed from the correctional enterprise. It means that rehabilitation, particularly as expressed within the medical model, has been abandoned as an accepted *purpose* of imprisonment. In the words of the Law Reform Commission (1976, 37-38):

It is important to remember that rehabilitation cannot be used as a primary reason for imposing imprisonment in the first place . . . the timing of release and the transition from complete custody to lesser degrees of restricted freedom should ordinarily not be dependent on the offender's reaction to treatment but on his behaviour and acceptance of responsibilities.

In *The Role of Federal Corrections in Canada* (Task Force on the Creation of an Integrated Canadian Corrections Service 1977, 29-30) the following statement is made:

The new position of Federal Corrections with respect to rehabilitation is best summed up in a quote from Norval Morris's "The Future of Imprisonment" (1974, 14-15): " 'Rehabilitation,' whatever it means and whatever the programs that allegedly give it meaning, must cease to be a purpose of the prison sanction. This does not mean that the various developed 'treatment' programs within prisons need to be abandoned; quite the contrary, they need expansion. But it does mean that they must not be seen as purposive in the sense that criminals are sent to prison for 'treatment'. There is a sharp distinction between the purposes of incarceration and the opportunities for the training and assistance of prisoners that may be pursued within those purposes."

The issue to which Morris draws attention illustrates the difficulty encountered when assessing correctional reform, if some distinction is not made between the process of reform and the results it obtains in program practice. There is absolutely no question that the correctional enterprise in Canada has moved to forsake the rehabilitation model. It is equally apparent that the rehabilitation model continues to be expressed in correctional practice. It seems clear, therefore, that it is not usually possible to assess reform intent through a measurement of practice. However, if the reform intent is known, it is possible to assess correctional practice in order to determine the degree to which the reform intent is being realized. And it is at least an indication of some movement forward that reform intentions are now being formally expressed in statements of philosophy, goals and objectives which can be used as the basis for program evaluations.

A related emphasis in correctional reform which has recently emerged is the view that prisons should be regarded as an option of last resort within correctional practice. If the rehabilitation model is to be abandoned while the concept of rehabilitation is retained, it is clear that alternatives to incarceration must emerge as a primary element of correctional practice. Moreover, these alternatives must themselves be organized to take advantage of as many "normal" community resources as possible. As a consequence, the abandonment of the rehabilitation model has resulted in the acceptance of the reintegration model and, where imprisonment remains a requirement, the development of what Canadian Federal Corrections has termed the "opportunities model."[8]

Taken together, the disavowal of the rehabilitation model and the accompanying acceptance of using prison only as an option of last resort, have provided the impetus for almost every specific reform of Canadian correctional practice in recent years. However, the concept of prison as an option of last resort gives rise to a number of problems associated with assuring that program practice is compatible with reform intent. These problems are illustrated by two issues currently evident in Canada.

The first concerns the fact that the economic downturn, along with the resulting increased competition for resources, have made it easier for correctional authorities to justify prison expenditures and to effect cost-savings through the elimination of "softer," community-based programs. Accordingly, economic considerations have supported the use of prison as a form of correctional programming at a time when the intention is to limit the reliance on prisons and to promote community-based alternatives.

The second issue concerns the hardening of social attitudes that may be attributed in part to the difficult economic climate: there is an increasing public demand for the use of harsher sanctions in relation to a variety of offences. For instance, offences such as drinking/driving, which have historically been treated with a fair degree of leniency, are now resulting in sentences of imprisonment in an increasing number of cases. Here the problem of maintaining a consistent set of correctional objectives, when those objectives are so subject to fluctuating social, political and economic pressures, is illustrated once again. This is true even when the reform intent is relatively clear.

SPECIAL ISSUES IN CANADIAN CORRECTIONAL REFORM

In any pluralistic society, there are groups who, because of their minority status, demand special attention or create unique and pressing issues in the administration of justice. There are also groups, whether minority or otherwise, who create similar demands for special attention because of their position in the social hierarchy. Additionally, there are emphases in practice which emerge in the administration of justice as a response to changes in the prevailing ideological perspectives or shifting socio-economic conditions. While special interest groups and special issues affect policy and practice within corrections, they generally consume a small portion of the resources and committed energy of the operating system. However, they develop a high profile, either because they reflect a demand for reform or because they are viewed as reform initiatives in their own right.

In the following section, two special groups and two categories of alternate programming are discussed as Canadian examples of this phenomenon. The two special groups are natives and women. The two categories of alternate programming are diversion and services to victims. In recent years, each of these topics has stimulated increasing investigation, experimentation and debate related to correctional policy and practice. Furthermore, each of these topics has been regarded as a special issue in other arenas of social or political concern; they all have become fodder for academic investigation, editorial comment, political promises, bureaucratic initiatives and lobby groups representing a variety of special interests. And finally, they provide examples of groups and issues which influence correctional policy and practice and create pressure for reform *because* they are topics of relevance and concern in a context beyond the correctional enterprise.

Indeed, it is arguable that until an issue evolves as a matter of broad social concern — such as self determination for indigenous or minority groups, equal status for women or compensation for victims of crime — attempts to reform the practices of any social institution are likely to have little result. And although many commentators regard correctional reform as a myth (see, for example, Culbertson 1981, 316), on review it would appear that this opinion is usually offered when the issues in question either are not fundamental matters of public concern or when the issues of public concern somehow have a neutralizing effect on the desired reform.

This is not to say that the subjects discussed here will result in any clearer indications of correctional reform than might be indicated by other issues. But it is arguable that the issues associated with natives, women, diversion, and victims represent a different level of interest than many other areas of correctional reform. Moreover, it is theoretically possible that a different result will occur when the demand for correctional reform results from a broad social concern — for example, a concern for the rights of victims — rather than from a narrow professional concern such as the efficient management of prisons.

Natives

The position of native Canadians within the corrections system offers a clear example of the points made above. Indians are over-represented in many provincial, territorial, and federal correctional institutions, particularly in the Territories and in the Prairie provinces (see Birkenmayer and Jolly 1981; Jolly and Seymour 1983; Jolly 1983; Moyer et al. 1985).[9] The response (both emotional and intellectual) to this situation is much different from the response to statements such as "drinking drivers are clearly over-represented in provincial correctional systems."

It is arguable that on the basis of the same criteria used to claim that natives are over-represented in Canadian correctional systems, it can be easily demonstrated that drinking drivers are *much more* over-represented. But while both these issues have generated demands for correctional reform, the reform initiatives are distinctly different in kind. Correctional administrators are beginning to press for reforms in practice related to drinking/driving, in order to offset the pressure on institutions created by the escalation in prison sentences for drinking drivers. With regard to drinking/driving offences, the social attitude is clearly in favour of harsher penalties, including the increased use of prison sentences.[10] However, it is difficult to find an equivalent, organized bureaucratic initiative to deal with the alleged over-representation of native offenders.

Instead, political and bureaucratic reactions to issues surrounding native justice have been stimulated by the social activism of native groups and by the concomitant interventions of academic investigators and social commentators. More precisely, native over-representation in Canadian correctional systems is important as a reform issue *because* it is associated with the social concern about the treatment of native peoples in Canadian society generally, including the alleged paternalism and oppression fostered by the government (see Reasons 1975). And, as Mikel (1979/80, 35) notes, the concern related to native peoples in Canada is even reflected in international dialogue:

> The deplorable state in which our native people exist is a direct result of the treatment they have received by the white man. Whenever Canada attacks Russia for the treatment of Jewish people, or Israel for the treatment of her Palestinian captives, in the United Nations, Canada is also universally condemned for the treatment of her native peoples. Canada has kept its Indians in concentration camps, known as reserves, for about one hundred and twenty-five years and has regulated their behaviour in all aspects of their lives.

It is this type of sentiment, and the resulting collective guilt, which has recently placed natives in a position of prominence with regard to correctional reform. And when it is discussed as a correctional matter, this issue is consistently associated with broader social issues. In discussing natives and the correctional system in Saskatchewan, for example, Hylton (1982, 124-25) states:

In the next fifteen years, however, as the population ages, a large proportion of the Native population will grow into the 15 to 30 year age range — the high risk period in terms of admissions to provincial correctional centres. If the criminal justice system continued functioning in the manner it did in 1976, demographic changes alone would cause Native admissions to rise to about 80% of all admissions, while the absolute number of non-Native admissions could actually decline. The opening up of northern Saskatchewan, economic development, and increasing urbanization, could cause this figure to go still higher. On the other hand, a settlement of Indian land claims, the introduction of broad social, economic, educational and other programs, the settlement of jurisdictional disputes between the federal and provincial levels of government, reforms within the criminal justice system, and the greater involvement of the Native peoples themselves in determining their own destiny, would result in some overall improvements.

To summarize:
1. The experience of involvement with the justice system is a very prominent one for Canada's native peoples;
2. Most of the involvement is for minor infractions of the law and seems more indicative of "social" than of "criminal" problems;
3. There is no reason to believe that the situation will get any better for native people unless serious attempts are made to reform current practices.

The following statement appeared in the *Highlights of Federal Initiatives in Criminal Justice: 1966-1980* (Woods and Sim 1981, 64): "During the 1970s, the federal government engaged in a number of initiatives directed to the particular problems of the native offender." Much of this activity was intended to increase the level of cooperation between federal and provincial governments as well as between these governments and representatives of native organizations and interest groups. Following from these consultations, during the 1970s a number of program experiments were initiated at both the federal and provincial levels including native policing projects, native courtworker programs and the creation of coordinating roles for native offender programs. Specific initiatives included:

1. *The National Conference and Federal-Provincial Conference on Native Peoples and the Criminal Justice System (Edmonton, 1975)* which was attended by delegates from every major native organization in Canada and by federal and provincial cabinet ministers and other government officials;
2. *The Federal Advisory Council on Native People and the Criminal Justice System (1975)* which was established at the Edmonton Conference and was composed of representatives from six national native organizations and officials from five federal government departments;
3. *The National Consultant on Natives and the Criminal Justice System (1976),* which also was established in response to recommendations arising from the Edmonton Conference; and,
4. *The Metis and Non-Status Indian Crime and Justice Commission* which was established in 1975 to study the native inmate population and which reported to the Federal Department of Justice and the Solicitor General in 1977.

But what has been accomplished by all this activity? Earlier, it was suggested that reform can be assessed both in terms of process and results. In relation to the issue of natives and the criminal justice system, including corrections, it remains important to ask whether or not any results have been obtained during the last decade, or whether the process has been all "sound and fury, signifying nothing." As with all other topics that form the subject of correctional reform, this question can be endlessly debated. For every example where the reform intent has been affirmed, there is an example where it has been denied. And although the reform of social institutions is difficult and subject to much resistance, nevertheless, there is evidence that the reform intent with regard to native people continues to be expressed in a variety of ways, while specific results in practice remain disappointing.

It is clear from the list of initiatives identified above, that the National Conference on Native Peoples and the Criminal Justice System held in Edmonton in February, 1975, was a key event in addressing native justice issues. It was here that the reform intent was first deliberately and clearly stated. Warren Allmand, the Solicitor General of Canada at the time, addressed the Conference with the following statement:

> Our expectations of this conference are high, and so they should be. The right people are here. We share a determination to gain a better understanding of the problems we face and to move towards their solution (Solicitor General of Canada 1975, 3).

This Conference produced

guidelines for action (which) were regarded and adopted by the Minister as a statement of general philosophy underlying any approach to problems of natives within the criminal justice system.

1. Native persons should be closely involved in the planning and delivery of services associated with criminal justice and native peoples.
2. Native communities should have greater responsibility for the delivery of criminal justice services to their people.
3. All non-native staff in the criminal justice system engaged in providing services to native people should be required to participate in some form of orientation training designed to familiarize them with the special needs and aspirations of native persons.
4. More native persons must be recruited and trained for service functions throughout the criminal justice system.
5. The use of native para-professionals must be encouraged throughout the criminal justice system.
6. In policy planning and program development, emphasis should be placed upon prevention, diversion from the criminal justice system to community resources, the search for further alternatives to imprisonment and the protection of young persons (Solicitor General of Canada 1975, 38).

A number of initiatives resulting from the Edmonton Conference have already been mentioned.[11] Despite the increased concern with the over-representation of native Indians in federal and provincial correctional institutions, considerable difficulties have been encountered in translating the recommendations of the 1975 Edmonton Conference into policy. Griffiths and Yerbury (1982; 1984) argue that while the Conference served to identify many of the issues and concerns of natives, the recommendations were too general and did not address the many legal and cultural complexities surrounding native involvement in the criminal justice system. Further, no provision was made for ensuring that action would be forthcoming on the publicly stated commitments of natives and non-native leaders. In a report which surveyed government action on the recommendations of the 1975 Conference, Jolly et al. (1979) found that little or no progress had been made on many of the recommendations and that many of the senior level civil servants interviewed had not read the report on the Conference and were unfamiliar with the recommendations that were made. Many of those who were aware of the recommendations of the Conference expressed strong reservations regarding the creation of alternative justice structures for native Indians.

The response (or lack thereof), of the government to the recommendations of the 1975 Edmonton Conference must be examined in the larger socio-political context of native-government relations in Canada. Keon-Cohen (1982, 191-92) notes, for example, that while native Indian tribes in the United States exercise jurisdiction over criminal justice on the reservations, the Canadian government has traditionally resisted initiatives by Indians to assume jurisdiction in this area:

> In direct contrast to the U.S.A., but like Australia, Canadian natives have not in practice been accorded any inherent rights, be they sovereign or proprietorial . . . Therefore, tribal governments and justice systems based on inherent powers have not, to date, developed in Canada, nor it seems, have community government structures been developed pursuant to legislation . . . Canadian natives, like their Aboriginal counterparts, and unlike their American Indian brethren, are thus totally subject to, and processed by, the Anglo-Canadian legal system, as compared to separate tribal justice systems.

In discussing the consequence of federal initiatives in the area of natives and of the criminal justice system, Verdun-Jones and Muirhead (1979/80, 18-19) caution:

> Research has yet to determine the "success" of such developments. There is, of course, a certain irony in the attempt of the Federal and Provincial governments to deal with problems created by their predecessors in a manner which effectively requires natives to provide their own "solutions" through cooptation into the formal agencies of the criminal justice system. Furthermore, it is not clear whether these recent political developments reflect a genuine commitment to radical change or merely an overall governmental strategy of reducing costs by turning over part of its responsibility to volunteers and self-help groups of various kinds. Perhaps Canadian criminology may furnish its most significant contribution to the policy-making process in Canada by developing a broad theoretical framework capable of integrating socio-economic, socio-political, historical and anthropological perspectives; only then shall we know if programs are mere "band aids" tacked onto symptoms of social disintegration or whether they at least promise to set us upon the correct pathway towards coping with the problems generated by the status of native peoples in Canada.

The "broad theoretical framework" referred to by Verdun-Jones and Muirhead has not been developed, and native and non-native observers have raised numerous concerns about the extent to which provincial/territorial and federal correctional authorities have addressed the requirements of native offenders. One of the recommendations of the Edmonton Conference (Solicitor General of Canada 1975, 56) was that "programs, particularly of a social, cultural or educational nature, special counselling services and community-based programs, such as forestry camps, must be made more available to native inmates and must be tailored to their special needs."

McCaskill (1985, 68) argues, however, that there has been "little tangible change in the Correctional Service of Canada's policies or programmes" since 1975. Several reports and investigations have identified key areas in which reform is required, including the hiring of native Canadians in the correctional system and the development of custodial and non-custodial programs for native inmates (See Newby 1981; McCaskill 1985). The Correctional Service of Canada has introduced policies allowing native inmates to observe traditional religious practices, and there has been increased involvement of elders, the Native Brotherhoods and Sisterhoods, and native prison liaison workers in correctional facilities (Couture 1983).

A major issue which had hindered reform is the extent to which native Canadian offenders should receive special consideration in the development of correctional policies and programs. While McCaskill (1985, 75) found that "nativeness" was an important factor in self-identification for the majority of native inmates in Manitoba, there continues to be considerable resistance on the part of correctional authorities to the idea that separate policies and programs may be required for native Canadian inmates (Newby 1981; Haveman et al. 1984).

The Female Offender

Paralleling the discussion about native Canadians, the issue of women in the criminal justice system and, more particularly, women in prison, has generated considerable comment and review in recent years. Interest in the female offender is associated with a much broader interest in the reform of social institutions to better reflect the rights of women and the role of women in society. From a correctional perspective, however, issues surrounding female offenders are distinctly different from those affecting native offenders, especially because women cannot be said to be over-represented in correctional institutions. It is ironic that the reform of programs for incarcerated women is considered a problem precisely because women are under-represented in the system (see Berzins and Cooper 1982). As Berzins (1977, 6) states:

We are always saying that if we only had fewer men, we could really do something. What irony! Here we have a small number of women and instead of taking advantage of the situation, we use it as an excuse for not doing anything because the numbers don't justify the resources. . . .

Indeed, the number of incarcerated females in Canada is relatively small. During 1980/81, approximately 6 percent of the 108,575 sentenced admissions in Canada were female (Statistics Canada 1982, 29). Perhaps more telling is the Centre's information that in 1980/81 women accounted for 6.4 percent of the 103,788 sentenced admissions in provincial institutions across Canada, while they accounted for only 1.8 percent of 4,787 sentenced admissions in Federal institutions (1982, 26). These statistics indicate approximately 6,642 women were sentenced to provincial institutions, while approximately only 86 were sentenced to Federal institutions in the same year. Further, the average annual count for the Federal Prison for Women in 1980/81 was approximately 94 (Statistics Canada 1982, 72).

Canadian correctional initiatives with regard to the female offender have concentrated on the problems of incarceration. The primary interest on a national level has been with the Federal Prison for Women at Kingston, Ontario, and a variety of actions have been taken in an effort to effect reforms. It also should be recognized that every major correctional inquiry in Canada has commented on the Prison for Women. Archambault (1938) recommended closure of the Prison. Fauteux (1956), while supporting the idea of one central institution for women, noted that in such a large country as Canada, the problems of separating federal female offenders from family and friends would have to be addressed. Ouimet (1969) recommended closure of the Prison for Women, suggesting that inmates might be transferred to institutions in their own province.

In the 1970s, several national committees addressed the question of the female offender in Canada. These included:

1. *The National Advisory Committee on the Female Offender (1977).* This committee recommended that the Prison for Women be closed and emphasized the need for more community-based residences, temporary release, and better institutional programs linked (wherever possible) to the community.
2. *The National Planning Committee on the Female Offender (1978).* This Committee was established by the Continuing Committee of Deputy Ministers in 1977 to assess the National Advisory Committee report. Like the National Advisory Committee, it emphasized the need for the development of community-based residential centres for women and advocated

establishing regional Federal facilities for women, with at least one facility in the East and one in the West.

3. *The Joint Committee to Study Alternatives for the Housing of the Federal Female Offender (1978).* This Committee was appointed by the Commissioner of Corrections (Canada) and included representatives from the private sector. The Committee recommended that the Federal Government purchase Vanier Institution (near Toronto) from the Ontario Government for use as a central facility, and that one of the living units of Mission Institution (for males) in British Columbia be used as a "co-correctional" western facility. The Committee also favoured community-based facilities and the continued use of provincial institutions acquired through exchange of service agreements.

Major provincial initiatives also have tended to concentrate on the incarcerated female offender. For instance, in British Columbia, a Royal Commission on the Incarceration of Female Offenders was established in 1978 as a result of allegations of misconduct at the Oakalla Women's Correctional Centre in Burnaby. And, coincidentally, the B.C. Ministry of the Attorney General (1978b) published a study entitled *Incarcerated Women in British Columbia Provincial Institutions.*

Perhaps the main issue identified in the studies described above, apart from the problem of the numerically small representation of females in prison, is contained in a comment of the report of the Royal Commission on the Status of Women (1970). In a chapter entitled "Criminal Law and Women Offenders," the report (1970, 365) contends that "women who encounter ... correctional institutions are treated in accordance with the traditional concept of a woman's role that is no longer necessarily appropriate in the 1970's."

This statement can be interpreted as meaning that prison, as a microcosm of society, reflects all those "inequalities which discriminate against women, be their source historical, social or administrative convenience" (British Columbia Ministry of the Attorney General 1978b, 11). While most observers acknowledge these inequalities, there is disagreement about their nature and about the form of their expression. For instance, Chesney-Lind (1980, 29) states:

It is time to recognize clearly the notion of the liberated female crook as nothing more than another in a century-long series of symbolic attempts to keep women subordinate to men by threatening those who aspire for equality with the images of the witch, the bitch and the whore. Male dominance and other forms of social inequality produce female crime, and it is social and economic justice that will reduce its incidence.

Johnson (1980, 213), on the other hand, states:

Traditionally, women who have committed felonies are treated very differently from their male counterparts. In part, this stems from a reluctance to address the "weaker sex" as part of the bona fide criminal element, along with a view of women in the role of "motherhood and apple pie". This concept of womanhood and the element of the women's movement that maintains women are "the oppressed and downtrodden", creates a distorted image that women are second class and not capable of being responsible for criminal behavior.

Regardless of the ideological perspective taken, however, there is a general agreement that

the problem of female offenders has reached critical proportions. The neglect that has characterized female corrections becomes more alarming and more visible in light of the rapidly changing role of women in our society.

The criminal justice system no longer should ignore the inequities providing differential sentencing of women on certain charges, inadequate institutional programming, and lack of available research (National Advisory Commission on Criminal Justice Standards and Goals 1973, 379).

In recognition of these concerns, recommendations for reform within correctional institutions have tended to concentrate on two issues: administration and programming. These emphases are reflected in the commentary of the National Advisory Commission on Criminal Justice Standards and Goals (1973, 379):

Women's institutions, owing to their relatively small population and lack of influence, have been considered an undifferentiated part of the general institutional system and therefore have been subjected to male-oriented facilities and programming. Special requirements of the female offender have been totally ignored. Male domination often extends to administration of the institution.

Women in American society are taught to define themselves in terms of men and therefore depend on assistance. In institutions, intensive group counseling should focus on self-definition and self-realization. Included in such an approach should be the acquisition of social and coping skills — including family life education and consumer training — that will prepare the woman to deal with society without reliance on a welfare system or a temporary male guardian.

Of primary concern in women's prisons in the almost total lack of meaningful programming . . . Women do the laundry, sewing, and other "female" tasks for the correctional system. . . .

While these sentiments are generally affirmed, and while statements of reform intent with regard to them have become increasingly common, it is interesting to note the difficulty that presents itself when specific attempts are made to stimulate practical results in the reform of programs for incarcerated women. The *Report of the British Columbia Royal Commission on the Incarceration of Female Offenders* (Proudfoot 1978) is a case in point. In its report, the Commission (1978, 87) concluded:

> The so-called programmes which now exist are admitted by all those responsible to be woefully inadequate. Of the five programmes available — laundry, kitchen, sewing, beauty parlour, and education — three are for the maintenance of the institution. Women in Corrections express the opinion that "... there's a difference between working at a job which is to maintain an institution and working at something which is going to benefit you as an individual."

Despite these comments, the Commission curiously recommended (1978, 87) that these same programs should be expanded and improved on the basis that "the Commission also understands that in practice there is insufficient work to keep all the inmates engaged productively during a full day." The Commission (1978, 91) then applauded the sewing program as "the only one in the O.W.C.C. (Oakalla Women's Correctional Centre) which is functioning on a productive basis." Accordingly, the Commission recommended (1978, 85) that "the budget for the sewing program be increased and that this program be expanded" and that "staff members be assigned to supervise and train inmates in the beauty parlour and that modern equipment be installed." These are precisely the types of programs which the National Advisory Commission on Criminal Justice Standards and Goals (1973, 379) regarded as programs which do "nothing to prepare a woman for employment and in fact greatly increases her dependency." Many observers regard programs of this kind as contributing to the institutional oppression of women for "administrative convenience."

Madam Justice Patricia Proudfoot, the Commissioner responsible for the *Report of the British Columbia Royal Commission on the Incarceration of Female Offenders,* did acknowledge the possibility of other program alternatives for female offenders, but stated (1978, 94):

> The budget and facilities at OWCC make the provision of non-traditional training programmes impracticable at present. It is hoped that if new facilities for women are constructed they will include facilities for training inmates in work which is not traditionally female.

Thus, a major judicial inquiry not only failed to clearly define reform intent on an issue generally regarded as fundamental in the reform of prisons for women, but went so far as to state that it could not be done under present circumstances. The Commission, nonetheless, found it appropriate to make 57 major recommendations, many requiring significant expenditures of funds and which, taken collectively, would not result in a single program change of substance. On the contrary, the Commission recommended that several alternative residential programs already in place should be disbanded in favour of strengthening the current programs within the security setting of the Oakalla Women's Correctional Centre. This was justified (1978, 121) partially on the grounds that "This Commission has shown a good deal of concern with some of the costly projects undertaken by the Corrections Branch."

The Commission Report clearly points out that some of these alternative programs had experienced problems during their implementation, some of which were serious. The Report makes clear that a select number of these problems resulted from the resistance of staff employed in the traditional programs, in addition to community resistance and to problems in administration and planning. In this regard, the Commission made many useful recommendations. Yet it is ironic that the Commission was not established as a consequence of problems evident in any of the alternative programs, but rather as a result of serious problems and allegations of misconduct at the Oakalla Women's Correctional Centre itself. This inquiry, perhaps more than any other in recent Canadian history, illustrates the nature of the resistance to substantial correctional reform and the serious problems faced by persons and agencies identified with such reform efforts in the transition from traditional to alternative approaches in practice.

The reform of correctional programs for the female offender in Canada has taken another turn with a judgement of the Canadian Human Rights Commission rendered in December, 1981. This judgement resulted from a complaint lodged by the Women for Justice, a political action group, on behalf of federal female offenders, and read as follows:

Ruling on December 14th, 1981 that women are victims of discrimination in the federal penitentiary system, the assembled Commissioners directed conciliator Julien Delisle to ensure that effective remedies be developed to end discriminatory practices (Solicitor General of Canada 1982, 16).

It must be remembered that this Commission was asked to rule on whether or not women are victims of discrimination in the Federal Penitentiary System. It has already been noted that there is only one institution for female offenders in the Federal Penitentiary System — the Prison for Women at Kingston, Ontario. Therefore, the findings of the Commission concentrated on the implications for a national correctional system which provides only a single program for a specific class of offenders. As the Solicitor General of Canada (1982, 17-18) points out:

> The key finding of the Human Rights Commission was that, because the Prison for Women is the only Federal Penitentiary for Women, female prisoners have less access to training and rehabilitation programs than do male inmates. By the same token, they are also more likely to be far away from family and friends. Women prisoners have no choice of being transferred to a better prison than Kingston, the Commission states. And while men are segregated in minimum, medium or maximum security prisons, depending on the nature of their crime, women of varying security risks are all imprisoned together at Kingston.

In terms of cost effectiveness and utility, if the problem of developing decentralized alternatives to a single institution are considered problematic at the provincial level, how much more difficult are they likely to be at the national level? Indeed, the Commission (Solicitor General of Canada 1982, 18) itself acknowledged this problem:

> There were, however, no clear-cut tangible remedies immediately identifiable to the Commissioners. Hence the appointment of conciliator Julien Delisle. "This particular case," he explains, "is by definition a systemic complaint; the Commissoners found that Corrections Service Canada, as a whole system, discriminates against women."
>
> Delisle's role as conciliator will be to effect the settlement representing public interest in the outcome. "The Commission is concerned not only with needs of individuals presently in the prison, but also with the systematized policies at the root of the discriminatory practices."

One of the options which has been recommended to resolve this problem is to make use of institutions already in place for male offenders and to develop some form of "co-correctional" program within them which would allow for the housing of female offenders. It has been argued that such an approach would allow female offenders to be placed in a range of security settings; it would provide many female offenders with continuing access to family and community supports; it would reduce the requirement for developing new or additional facilities for female offenders; and it would "normalize" the environment of institutions used in this way with the result that both female and male offenders would benefit. As pointed out previously, the Joint Committee to Study Alternatives for the Housing of the Federal Female Offender (Solicitor General of Canada 1978d) also made this recommendation as part of a possible plan to close the Prison for Women.

Similarly, in the United States, the National Advisory Commission on Criminal Justice Standards and Goals (1973, 379) addressed this option in the following way:

> The correctional objectives, methodology, problems, and needs essentially are no different for females than for males. The correctional system should abandon the current system of separate institutions based on sex and develop a fully integrated system based on all offenders' needs. The coeducational program can be an invaluable tool for exploring and dealing with social and emotional problems related to identity conflicts that many offenders experience.
>
> Coeducation programs such as those in the Ventura and Los Guilucos Schools of the California Youth Authority have demonstrated clearly that a mixed population has a positive program impact. The Federal system also has converted at least two institutions, one for the juveniles at Morgantown, West Virginia, and one for adults at Forth Worth, Texas, to coeducational facilities. It is recognized, however, that in jurisdictions with a relatively large number of male institutions and a small number of women prisoners, coeducational arrangements cannot be universally feasible.

In the *Report of the Joint Committee to Study Alternatives for the Housing of the Federal Female Offender* (Solicitor General of Canada 1978d, 15-16) the following statement is made with regard to Canada:

> The Federal experience with co-correctional institutions is limited. The Committee, after examining the U.S. experience, felt that a co-correctional institution is a feasible idea.

While the majority of female offenders are housed in provincial institutions, the provinces are confronted by many of the problems facing the federal program. The provinces have generally been able to exercise greater flexibility in providing a range of security options for the less serious offender, but where there is a need to house female offenders in secure settings, the flexibility of the provinces is limited. The limitation is largely due to the small numbers of female inmates and to the fact that centralized institutions tend to emerge to produce an environment similar to the Federal Prison for Women. Canada is a very large country and the provinces within it are also large. Therefore, many women tend to be dislocated from family and community even when sentenced to a secure institution within a province. The costs associated with developing alternative security settings for women within the provinces have been prohibitive. Accordingly, the "co-correctional" option has been considered by the provinces as one possibility for resolving problems attendant upon the female offender.

In 1974 the Province of British Columbia made an attempt to introduce such a program in the male institution at Prince George. Prior to that time the only secure setting for female offenders in the province was the Oakalla Women's Correctional Centre near Vancouver. It must be understood that Vancouver is in the southern region of the province and Prince George is in the northern region, with approximately 500 miles separating the two cities. The program was established on the grounds that a security program for female offenders was required in the northern region; that alternatives were required to reduce the pressure of overcrowding at Oakalla; and that an experiment in co-corrections would be valuable, based on indications from the U.S. experience.

The *Report of the British Columbia Royal Commission on the Incarceration of Female Offenders* (Proudfoot 1978) discussed the "co-correctional" program and made recommendations regarding it. While it is clear that the program was subject to the traditional resistance encountered during the implementation of substantive reform, it appears that the most significant problem experienced was the disparity between the number of male and female offenders housed in the institution. While one living unit (26 cells) was set aside for female offenders, the male population fluctuated between 120 and 140 inmates. However, the average female population was approximately 11 inmates. Dr. Ekstedt (Proudfoot 1978, 83), in addressing the Commission on the Prince George program, stated that, while changes in attitude and program emphasis could certainly improve the program and assist it to realize its original intention, "too much of a disparity (in numbers) is self-defeating or counter-productive."

The Proudfoot Commission (1978, 83) summarized its position on the Prince George program in the following way:

> In a survey to determine the success of the Prince George "co-ed" program, the Chaplain, H.R. Morgan, was told by staff and inmates that there was a noted improvement in personal hygiene, improvement in dress and less use of abusive language. As well the male-female companionship boosted morale.
>
> Measured against this were disadvantages of conflicts and jealousies

(8 women for 140 men); sexual frustrations; intensified emotional depression; the detrimental effects of jail romances on outside life; and inmate-guard romances. The advantages seem superficial and are, in the view of the Commission, heavily outweighed by the disadvantages.

The Report of the British Columbia Ministry of the Attorney General, *Incarcerated Women in British Columbia Provincial Institutions* (1978b, 44), states:

> The overall impression of the physical facilities at the Women's Unit at P.G.R.C.C. (Prince George) is that they were designed as a part of the Men's Unit; they are not adequate for a separate female facility. The women have been accommodated by makeshift procedures devised by hardworking staff members trying to fit a program for women into a facility not designed for that purpose.

It appears evident that attempts to develop co-correctional programs are frustrated both by the disparity in numbers and the tendency to try to "fit" women into a men's program or men into a women's program. To date, there has not been a successful Canadian experiment in developing a co-corrections program in a security setting. It is interesting that the correctional enterprise, rather than attempting to learn from past experience in planning co-correctional programs, exhibits the tendency instead to withdraw from program experiments of this kind. For instance, the Proudfoot Commission (1978, 81) recommended that "the co-correctional programme at Prince George be discontinued immediately" and that "no further co-correctional facilities be established elsewhere in British Columbia."

Additionally, according to the Commission's own research, a similar trend is evident in the United States. The Commission's Report (Proudfoot 1978, 83) states:

> At its peak in the United States there were a dozen co-correctional facilities with populations up to 2,000. The trend today is away from mixing male and female inmates and only a few institutions remain "co-ed."

The problems involved in accommodating the female offender in correctional systems governed by male attitudes and geared to the male offender are significant and not subject to simple resolution. Given this atmosphere, there is a growing concern that the co-correctional option, even if carefully constructed, may not be a useful alternative. As Johnson (1980, 216) states:

> The atmosphere is of major importance: It is my belief that it is necessary for the agency to address the needs of the women and not be a co-ed facility

geared for men. Women in a co-ed facility have a tendency to regress to a stereotypical role expected of them. This type of atmosphere does not allow a woman to grow and develop the tools to make choices in and for her life.

Even where facilities have been set aside to provide programs exclusively for women, similar problems of "atmosphere" are evident. As Chinnery (1980, 225) observes:

> The Prison for Women operates under the same directives as provided for male inmates, and it is necessary to interpret these in different ways every day . . . I hope that some day the women will be governed by directives truly designed to meet their special needs.

The decision of the Canadian Human Rights Commission that women are victims of discrimination in the federal penitentiary system has set in motion another series of reviews and inquiries on the subject. The significance of the Commission's decision remains to be seen but, as *Liaison* (Solicitor General of Canada 1982, 21) reports:

> The legitimacy their decision has given to this concern may well provide the final impetus needed to bring this issue out of the wilderness and into the arena of public concern. Unless CSC (Corrections Service Canada) can prove to the satisfaction of the Human Rights Commission that it no longer discriminates against women, the legality of sentences to the Prison for Women may be challenged before the courts on the basis that they infringe on their fundamental rights. . . .
>
> What we are witnessing might just be the first few rumblings of the mouse that roared. . . .

Diversion

Diversion is a concept which achieved popularity in Canada in the 1970s. It is probably fair to say that the concept of diversion gained popularity partially as a result of the inability of the criminal justice system to satisfactorily address reform issues of the kind previously described. Levine et al. (1980, 584) define diversion as:

> . . . a policy in which adults accused of certain criminal offenses have their prosecution halted for a period of time . . . (it) attempts to side-step prosecution by inducing interested parties to negotiate an agreement to participate in community-based conflict resolution, counseling, or treatment programs. (From *Criminal Justice* by James P. Levine et al., copyright © 1980 by Harcourt Brace Jovanovich, Inc. Reprinted by permission of the publisher.)

These authors (1980, 426) offer the following explanation for the growth of diversion programs:

> Today, diversion from the entire criminal justice system is being turned to more and more because of dissatisfaction with the criminal justice system itself. Diversion involves taking individuals out of the criminal justice stream because it is believed that they cannot be rehabilitated within it.

Support for the concept of diversion, however, involves more than frustration with the apparent inability of the criminal justice system to effectively rehabilitate offenders. There are some who argue that rehabilitation, regardless of its potential as an activity of the criminal justice system, should not be regarded as a primary goal of diversion.[12] Instead, diversion can be viewed as a concept compatible with the philosophy and goals of reintegration — particularly given its emphasis on the community resolution of social conflict, including community-based correctional programs and restitution to victims. Diversion also has been seen as a means of reducing court backlog while at the same time reducing the possible stigma and negative influences which formal contact with the criminal justice system brings to those persons committing minor or first offences.

In this respect, the expectations related to diversion in practice have been high. As the report, *Diversion: A Canadian Concept and Practice* (Solicitor General of Canada 1978a, 10) states:

> Diversion is a promise!
>
> It is a promise that the poor, the uneducated, the disadvantaged and the abandoned who come in conflict with the law will receive the support and compassion of their communities. It's a promise that society is still capable of resolving relatively minor conflicts without recourse to the courts.
>
> Diversion is an alternative less formal than the court system which has the potential to reduce court backlog, provide compensation to the victims or the community, and present a mechanism to establish community support for many people in conflict with the law, while protecting the rights of the offender.
>
> It provides ordinary citizens with the opportunity to participate in the process of resolving problematic behaviour in the community, and gives the victim of such behaviour the benefit of restitution.

Yet the same report (Solicitor General of Canada 1978a, 11-12) goes on to acknowledge the dangers of diversion.

> The greatest danger is that the diversion process will become another layer of bureaucracy ... Another danger is that diversion might not always provide for due process, the protection of the individual's rights

under law ... Another danger is that where a diversion project exists, a police officer who previously might have dismissed an offender with a warning may feel compelled to refer the offender to the project ... Above all, diversion schemes must not preclude decriminalization of certain types of non-violent offences. Diversion efforts will not resolve existing problems within the criminal justice system and are not designed to do so. Exploration of improvements within the present system must be encouraged and continued, such as the development of sentencing alternatives.

The concept of diversion has had an appreciable effect on the process of reform within criminal justice and corrections in recent years. Diversion is a practice which has been widely applied in the area of juvenile justice (see for example, Coffey 1975; Levine et al. 1980; and Reid 1981) — especially since the philosophy and objectives of juvenile justice systems are generally sympathetic to practices which allow juveniles to avoid the stigma arising both out of formal contact with the criminal justice system and from the criminal record which may result.

As Doob (cited in Solicitor General of Canada 1978a, 11) has remarked: "The history of the Juvenile Court itself was a diversionary scheme from adult criminal courts." However, it has often been the case in recent years that popular concepts of practice in juvenile justice have made inroads into the adult criminal justice system. This certainly has been true with regard to diversion, and there have been an increasing number of attempts to introduce diversion programs for adults. As Levine et al. (1980, 470) point out in discussing this phenomenon in the United States, "Funds from the federal government in the last decade have been used to establish experimental adult diversion programs in over 50 metropolitan areas."

However, in discussing the growth of adult diversion programs, the authors (1980, 470-71) state:

> Paradoxically, the explosion of adult diversion programs has occurred at a time of disenchantment with and retrenchment in the area of juvenile diversion ... several scholars and practitioners argue that juveniles are coerced into such programs rather than volunteering for them through deliberative bargaining ... Originally intended to avoid stigmatizing youths with the label of "delinquent", diversion programs have expanded the institutionalization of youthful "clients", a fate as socially damaging as any delinquent label ... critics call for a fresh injection of due process into the juvenile justice system. They want closer supervision of discussions surrounding whether or not a youngster requires any of the treatment offered by diversionary programs ... this same criticism has been lodged against adult diversion programs. (From *Criminal Justice* by James P. Levine et al., copyright © 1980 by Harcourt Brace Jovanovich, Inc. Reprinted by permission of the publisher.)

In Canada, the debate continues concerning the potential and dangers associated with the development of diversion programs in the adult criminal justice system.[13] Yet there is no doubt that the diversion concept has influenced both the policy and practice associated with criminal justice reform in Canada, including correctional reform. Coffey (1975, 179) defines diversion as "the *systematic development of alternatives for selected offenders;* the alternatives consist of dispositions of cases outside the justice system, and handled by non-justice-system programming" (emphasis in original). Coffey (1975, 179) further suggests:

> The practice of diverting offenders from the justice system . . . is thought by some to be outside the scope of correctional responsibilities. But . . . diversion [is] an appropriate correctional operation, although it is a somewhat more coordinative function to administer than the relatively direct administrative links in the residence programs . . . the key is preventing deeper penetration into the system when alternatives are appropriate — when the danger to the offender and to the community is such that the potential value of some alternative exceeds that of the justice system.

The view that the criminal justice system, in all its parts, can act on the principle that it is legitimate to prevent "deeper penetration into the system when alternatives are appropriate" has resulted in a variety of Canadian initiatives by police and prosecutorial and correctional agencies in concert with private agencies, and local community interests. Beginning with the East York Community Law Reform Project in 1972 (Law Reform Commission of Canada 1975b), no fewer than 17 major adult diversion programs were in operation by 1977 (see also Solicitor General of Canada 1977a). Furthermore, almost all of the programs reported active involvement and support from police and prosecutorial and correctional agencies. And in many cases, the initiative which gave stimulus to the programs came from one or more of these agencies within the formal criminal justice system.

The diversion "movement" has had a positive effect on correctional reform by adding impetus to the "search for alternatives" and by helping to reinforce the attitude within Corrections that not all the solutions to correctional problems need to be determined or implemented within the correctional system itself. In at least a small way, the diversion movement has forced the correctional system to "think outside of itself." As a consequence, it has been more open and innovative in its approach to correctional reform than might otherwise have been the case.

While post-incarceration alternative programs cannot be

properly described as "diversionary", particularly when they are administered and operated by the correctional system itself, there is no doubt that many such programs have been viewed in this way. This perception is strengthened when diversion programs are regarded as providing alternatives to the traditional dispositions offered by the correctional system, in order to avoid the negative effects of "deeper penetration." Moreover, diversionary principles have influenced the administration of traditional correctional programs. The development of case-management practices in both institutional and probation programs, with their emphasis on the use of community resources and the early reintegration of the offender into society, has clearly been given impetus by the increased acceptance of diversion as a legitimate principle in criminal justice. However, Roesch and Corrado (1983, 388) caution that the proliferation of diversion programs has occurred despite the fact that "there is scant information about their effectiveness. Most studies have simply been descriptive, lacking control or comparison groups and other aspects of methodologically defensible research" (see also Roesch 1978).

Further, with the growth in diversion activity, many of the dangers alluded to earlier have been realized. In some cases, the emphasis on diversion has tended to increase bureaucratic layering with the result that diversion programs, rather than creating alternatives to the criminal justice system, become alternative programs *within* the criminal justice system. And, in too many cases, diversion programs have appeared to "widen the net" of the criminal justice system by drawing in persons who never should have been involved in official processing. While the degree to which this has happened remains a subject for further study, there is no doubt that the danger exists and that increasing numbers of persons are concerned with the negative possibilities which are present (see Hogarth 1978; Solicitor General of Canada 1978a; Levine et al. 1980; and Reid 1981).

Denial of due process and the creation of "double-jeopardy" situations in the administration of diversion programs also have been documented in Canada.[14] Furthermore, the lack of formality and defined goals which have been associated with the evolution of diversion projects in Canada have created disparity in practice and procedure, resulting in increased criticism of the diversion emphasis. Citing the works of Renner (1979), Blomberg (1980), and Baker and Sadd (1981), Roesch and Corrado (1983) have argued . that diversion programs have tended to involve relatively minor offenders who would not otherwise have been subject to prosecution and would have been released. In discussing the need to reduce the net-widening effect and to assist diversion initiatives to fulfill their original objectives, the authors (1983, 392) argue that the following criteria should be followed:

1. Projects should follow procedures that ensure that diversion occurs only after the filing of charges, so that diversion is a genuine alternative to the criminal justice system.
2. The scope of diversion should be expanded to include, and perhaps emphasize, defendants charged with more serious crimes.
3. Diversion programs should try true diversion, in which defendants are simply diverted out of the system, with no services from a diversion program.
4. The type of program offered by a diversion program should have a firm grounding in theory. A program should justify why a selected intervention, such as counselling, should be presumed to have an effect on recidivism, the participant's quality of life, or any other outcome variable.
5. More research on the effects of diversion programs is needed.

As a result of these problems, the diversion concept has become the subject of intensive review in both Canada and the United States. As Levine et al. (1980, 470) state:

> The "new diversion process", a phrase coined by Raymond Nimmer, has four characteristics: (1) it represents a planned reaction to both the problem of formal prosecution and the insufficiencies of traditional diversion; (2) it reduces the discretion available to individual prosecutors and judges in the final disposition of offenders; (3) it relies heavily on formal relationships with agencies outside the criminal justice system, and (4) it regularly involves the staff of non-criminal agencies in the disposition of cases. Rather than depending on the ad hoc decision-making of individual actors, "new diversion" relies on programs with established eligibility criteria, a variety of ways to help clients (e.g., treatment, counselling), and full-time staff positions filled by trained community residents and professionals. In short, it attempts to use organizations and rules as a means to assure that when the criminal label is withheld, it is done within a legal framework. (From *Criminal Justice* by James P. Levine et al., copyright © 1980 by Harcourt Brace Jovanovich, Inc. Reprinted by permission of the publisher.)

Studies on the legal framework for diversion and the criteria to be applied to diversion programs have been initiated in Canada (see, for example, Ekstedt and Harrison 1974; Whitson 1979; Ministry of Justice and Ministry of the Solicitor General 1979). Again as in other areas of criminal justice and correctional reform, the process is instructive, while the results, in terms of any measurable effect on crime and the criminal justice system, have yet to be determined.

Services to Victims

Probably the most recent trend which has had an influence on correctional reform can be found in the growing emphasis on services to victims. As reported in the Bureau of Justice Statistics *Bulletin* (U.S. Department of Justice 1981, 1);

> Traditionally, both public attention and the criminal justice system have focused on criminal offenders. Criminal justice resources have been used to pursue, apprehend, judge, and imprison offenders and have paid little attention to their victims. Recently, however, public attention has turned to the victims of crime as well. This concern is reflected in legislation proposed or enacted at both State and National levels, in various service programs to aid victims and/or compensate them for financial losses, and in a greater sensitivity within the criminal justice system to the treatment of victims (either as victims or as witnesses). Within the academic community, too, the study of the victims of crime is emerging as a new field.

This issue was also addressed in *The Criminal Law in Canadian Society: Highlights* (Government of Canada 1982, 13):

> The concern of the criminal justice system has historically been the conflict of the State versus the individual, whereas the civil system has provided the forum for conflicts between individuals. The criminal and civil systems could be made more responsive to the needs of victims in order to focus the criminal justice system more clearly on the positive goal of reparation rather than the negative goal of punishment.

The emphasis on services to victims represents a logical progression in the cycle of correctional reform. When first initiated, the reform movement concentrated on the purpose served by prisons and the conditions found in them. Reform interest then shifted away from improving prison conditions to expanding the range of options in prison practice, such as instituting varying security levels and specialized programs. Next, attention was directed to a new emphasis on non-institutional correctional programs for select categories of offenders. More recently, the reform emphasis has been placed on developing programs which involve offenders in community activities that are considered both rehabilitative and reparative. And yet another shift in reform interest focuses attention on establishing diversion programs which allow offenders to avoid a "deeper penetration into the system" and which provide opportunities to repair the damage done.

Throughout this cycle, the emphasis has been on the offender, although increasing attention has been given to the relationship between the offender and the community, and to repairing the damage caused to both the community and individual victims. The shift which has most recently occurred takes this movement one step further. Now an attempt is being made to look at both the offence and the state's response to the offender from the point of view of the victim.[15] Moreover, the reform interest in providing services to victims involves more than merely the State's providing offenders with programs that can result in victim restitution. The new emphasis also includes the broader objective of restoring the relationship between the victim, his or her community and, where possible, the offender. Included, as well, is the objective of restoring the confidence of the victim in the efficacy of the criminal justice system. As Stookey (1975, 5) states:

> It has become almost a platitude to suggest that the crime victim is the neglected party within the administration of criminal justice . . . We shall attempt to show theoretically the potential consequences for the criminal justice system of continued failure to consider the plight of the victim and will argue that restitution in its present form is not totally an adequate solution.
>
> Briefly, our argument is that the act of victimization will cause the victim to question seriously the legitimacy and usefulness of the criminal justice system. The rationale behind this is that the individual will consider his/her victimization a consequence of the system's failure to serve its function of protection. Therefore, the unresponsive system is not worthy of support . . . The only way to regain the support of the victim subpopulation is for some means to be devised to make the victim "whole" again after the victimization.

Similarly, Letkemann (1981, 60) offers these comments:

> The recognition that a just system of justice must consider the needs of those who were victimized, and that crime involves human relationships, either more or less directly, brings us quite logically to the question of what might be done to repair broken relationships between offenders and victims. A fair system of State compensation to victims of crime would meet the victim's financial loss. Restitution suggests that in some cases the offender himself should be responsible for all or part of these losses. Reconciliation goes even further — dealing directly with emotional and social injuries which cannot be touched by restitution alone.

As Norquay and Weiler (1981, 34-46) point out, there are basically five areas of victim services which have emerged in Canada. They are as follows:

1. *Services that deal with the crisis of victimization.* These include services for specific types of victims (e.g. the disabled, the elderly, natives, recent immigrants, abused children, sexually assaulted women and abused spouses) and general crisis services offered by voluntary community agencies, social welfare, or police agencies. Crisis centres and emergency telephone "crisis-lines" are in this category.
2. *Services that assist victims and witnesses to participate effectively in the criminal justice system while protecting their rights.* This includes the activity of police departments to inform victims and witnesses about the criminal justice process, procedures to inform crime victims about the status of their case, and programs to assist both victims and witnesses with regard to their appearance in court.
3. *Services aimed at compensating the victim for personal damages incurred as the result of a crime.* This includes compensation paid for a victim's out-of-pocket expenses, loss of income due to injury or permanent disability, pain and suffering, and loss to dependents resulting from the victim's death.
4. *Services aimed at achieving restitution, reconciliation, or both between the offender and the victim.* This includes the payment of money or services by offenders to victims and a variety of reconciliation and mediation programs.
5. *Services to assist the victim to locate and use appropriate existing services.* Information and referral services have been established with increasing frequency in Canada to assist citizens to locate and use appropriate social service agencies in relation to a variety of problems. Many such agencies are including an emphasis on the capacity to provide information and referral for victims of crime.

Additionally, short-term programs to encourage potential victims to protect themselves more effectively from specific types of crime are becoming more popular in Canada. Programs such as "Lock It and Pocket the Key" to reduce auto theft, and "Neighbourhood Watch" to reduce the incidence of break and enter, are examples of crime prevention activities which are victim-oriented. Other programs focus on the prevention of shoplifting, bank fraud, vandalism, sexual assault, purse snatching, and child abuse.

The emphasis on services to victims has both influenced

correctional reform and been stimulated by specific correctional reform initiatives. As the *Report* of the National Workshop on Services to Crime Victims (Solicitor General of Canada 1981a, 16) points out:

> Correctional services staff are often knowledgeable about the criminal justice system in general and local community social development services in particular. Many recent programs — diversion initiatives, for example — affect the victim and involve corrections staff resources. These and other factors have resulted in an increasing number of persons working in the corrections field committing themselves to the development of specifically victim-related services. . . .

The types of victim-related services which are initiated by federal or provincial correctional systems tend to fall in category four (4) above.

In the Province of British Columbia, "Project Restore" provides an example of a justice system project to assist victims of crime. This project was established in the Fraser Region of the B.C. Corrections Branch and was overseen by a regional justice management group, which includes representation from the R.C.M.P. and municipal police, correctional managers, court administrators, provincial court judges, and provincial prosecutors. As reported in the leading provincial newspaper (Vancouver *Sun*, April 12, 1983; p. A12):

> . . . an official with the B.C. Corrections Branch . . . coordinates a new project in which a group of policemen, prosecutors, court administrators, judges and prison staff seek to give the victim a break.

This management group, in its submission to the British Columbia Ministry of the Attorney General, requesting permission to establish the project, made the following statement:

> It is our belief that the existing role of justice services ought to focus on the *consequences* of crime. In order that such a focus have meaning, we have adopted the goal, "to avail the victims of crime to reparation, restitution and compensation from offenders."
>
> The rationale for adopting this goal begins with our perception that present justice services do not identify a common purpose and are occasionally conflicting in goals or competing for resources of other agencies. This is demonstrated by staff confusion regarding their role, organizational difficulty in formulating measurable objectives, organizational resistance to forms of integration, feelings of frustration and disappointment when offenders repeat their crime and, seemingly, little or no long-term tangible results from either organizational or

personal effort. It is our opinion that most of our current difficulties are a result of an imbalance in the administration of justice. This imbalance is due to the State's inability or unwillingness to provide for the needs of the victim while accepting responsibility for policing, courts and offenders' needs. This imbalance has created a void that makes it difficult for the general public, victims, offenders and staff to perceive that justice is being done (Stelmaschuk 1982, 1).

In part, Project Restore was intended to result in a reorganization of correctional programs in order to more effectively support the needs of victims and to provide them with services. For example, the project called for adjustments in pre-sentence reporting procedures to include information about victim circumstances and information relating to the offender's ability to pay court-ordered sanctions. It also proposed that family counselling services should be introduced into prisons and that emphasis should be placed on providing for the administration of family maintenance or child support payments by offenders. Additionally, the program included a provision for the development of a community-employment resource program to provide employment options for offenders, with the intent that it would allow them to earn sufficient income to provide direct dollar benefits to the victim.

Programs such as Project Restore illustrate how the emphasis on services to victims can have an effect on the reform of conventional correctional programs. As the focus of interest shifts within the broader criminal justice system, the corrections component is both pushed and pulled to rethink its approach to correctional programming.

Similar effects occur among those private sector agencies which have traditionally played a role in the promotion of correctional reform. In the Province of British Columbia, a number of private agency victim assistance programs have been initiated. In March, 1981, the John Howard Society in Vancouver established a victim assistance program. According to the Coordinator, "our volunteers will do everything from helping clean up an apartment after a break-in to going with victims to the police or to court." During the first two years of operation, this program helped 363 victims of criminal acts, including 182 requests for assistance related to violent crimes, 133 requests related to property damage, and 48 requests for assistance related to combinations of other criminal acts (press release, John Howard Society of B.C., April, 1983).

The St. Leonard's Society of British Columbia also has established a Victim-Offender Reconciliation Services Program. In this program, a third-party mediator is provided to assist the offender and victim to work out a voluntary agreement for restitution or community work service. The agreement is then presented to the court as an alternative to the traditional sentence. If the court accepts the terms contained in the agreement, they can become part of the court's probation order.

The effects of these experiments, and the sentiments underlying them, influence correctional reform in two ways. First, they add to the language and repertoire of the correctional system and allow it to adopt new emphases, even within traditional programs. This is important, since it is one thing to establish reparation as a goal of correctional programs but quite another to visualize the practical methods which might be used to realize this goal. Furthermore, the criminal justice and corrections systems are being forced to define new terms or to re-define old terms in new ways. As this is done, new perceptions of program possibilities emerge. An example of this process of definition is provided by Thorvaldson (1981, 120) as he attempts to clarify the concept of reparation:

> "Reparation" or "redress" means the *general* principle of making up for harm done or restoring the balance between the wrongdoer and the victim — "victim" includes the individual citizen, the community, or both. Offenders can repay for the harm they do in several ways — *compensation* (paying money in lieu of harm) *restitution* (restoring property) *community service* (unpaid labour or service for the benefit of the State) and *victim service* (unpaid labour or service for any specific citizen or citizens harmed as a result of an offence).

The second and equally important influence that experimental projects have on correctional reform concerns the stimulus they give to the socio-political dialogue associated with the reform interest. Such a dialogue eventually will produce a requirement for legislative review, and it has already been pointed out that any legislative review related to criminal justice forces the corrections system to examine its policies and programs. This situation has developed in Canada with regard to victim services. As Thorvaldson (1981, 120) comments:

> How far can we go with such sanctions and what sort of provision should be made for them in the law? . . . There has already been a great deal of practical development of community and victim service programs and considerable expansion of compensation by offenders in the last ten years and the federal planners have gone to great lengths to determine current opinion and propose legislation which includes what they regard as appropriate and which strongly encourages the greater use of service and compensation.

Once again the issue of services to victims illustrates the cyclical nature of correctional reform: social interests stimulate a review and restatement of criminal justice objectives; the statement of these objectives stimulates a review of practices within all components of the criminal justice system, including corrections; program experiments contribute to the refinement of the objectives in practical terms; the expansion of program experiments and the clarification of operational objectives creates further social dialogue and a requirement for legislative review; and legislative change results in a requirement for the review of correctional programs in order to assure that they meet legislative intent.

The answer to Thorvaldson's question "how far can we go. . .?" has yet to be found. However, the influence on correctional reform arising from the interest in victim services is already evident.[16]

SUMMARY AND CONCLUSION

Correctional reform is more than prison reform, although the prison dominates the practical interests of the public, professionals and correctional administrators. In recent history, the prison has usually been seen as the thing which needs to be changed, either by making adjustments to it or by creating alternatives which will eliminate or reduce its use.

Correctional reform can be assessed both in terms of its process and its results. Correctional programs must be viewed within the broader context of the principles and practices established in the criminal system to respond to persons accused and to persons convicted of committing criminal offences. Corrections, as a part of this process, is subject to the social, economic and political influences which are brought to bear on the society as a whole. Initiatives in correctional reform and assessments of correctional reform must take into account the position of corrections as a government service which reflects a social purpose. Consequently, the attempt has been made throughout this chapter to show how initiatives which might not be viewed as strictly "correctional" do have an influence on correctional reform, both in terms of practice and in terms of the way corrections views itself as an expression of public and private interest.

In this regard, it is interesting to note that many reform initiatives have emerged as a result of frustration with the very idea of using traditional "correctional" responses to deal with offenders. As Geis (1975, 247-48) states:

Certainly, a considerable portion of the appeal of restitution programs for dealing with criminal offenders lies in what is now generally regarded as the almost-total bankruptcy of current correctional approaches. Imprisonment, in particular, has come to be seen as a counterproductive process, unable in general to deter subsequent criminal acts either in regard to the offender himself or those for whom he might serve as an object-lesson . . . In the face of what now is regarded as correctional failure, the way lies open for inauguration of different approaches to dealing with criminal offenders. Besides programs of restitution, ideas that have been put forward include the abolition of insanity pleas, swifter and surer sentencing, elimination of plea bargaining, reintroduction of capital punishment, decriminalization of so-called "victimless crimes", diversion of offenders from incarceration into community treatment programs, and the ending of the indeterminate sentence. Advocates of each of these positions see them as contributing to an alleviation of what is commonly regarded . . . as an epidemic condition of criminal behaviour.

Nevertheless, the corrections system and its prisons remain with us. Very few commentators argue that prisons can be totally abolished or that no circumstances exist where imprisonment can be justified. In fact, both in Canada and the United States, social, economic, and political pressures are resulting in the increased use of imprisonment as a disposition for offenders. Some argue that this development is the most important and pressing problem facing corrections today. As Friel (1982, 1) notes:

Few would dispute the claim that prison overcrowding is the primary issue facing Corrections today. Some may suggest that judicial intervention, inmate gangs and diminishing inmate-to-staff ratios are more important, but most of these problems are either the direct or indirect result of overcrowding.

Accordingly, while a variety of reform initiatives to create correctional alternatives (either within the system or in opposition to it), appear to be taking place, the prison continues to exist as the central problem and the dimensions of that problem are increasing.

Friel (1982) contends that another element of correctional reform is required if the current cycle of frustration is to be addressed. He suggests that the ability of the correctional system to forecast its requirements must be improved if it is to avoid the continuous repetition of "crisis" responses in correctional management and if any of the reform initiatives are going to have a chance to succeed in their attempt to address correctional problems. In the preface to the *Proceedings of the National Workshop on Prison Population Forecasting,* Friel (1982, i) states:

Since the early 1970's, prison populations have grown faster than the nation's prison capacity. By 1980, overcrowding reached crisis proportions precipitating numerous suits which claimed that imprisonment under such conditions constituted cruel and unusual punishment. Some argue that the only solution is an aggressive program of prison construction. Dissenters counter that there are too many prisons now, and what is needed is a massive expansion of diversionary programs.

Regardless of the position one takes, it is evident that there is a critical need for correctional forecasting technology. Planning for the future, whether it concerns prison construction, or the development of diversionary programs, requires reasonably accurate forecasts of what the likely future correctional population might be over the next 10 years. It is surprising, however, that while most correctional institutions are overcrowded, correctional forecasting technology is poorly developed, and not well understood by the correctional community.

Finally, regardless of its intent or the circumstances out of which it arises, reform requires committed and informed leadership. It has already been noted that corrections is an excellent example of the type of human enterprise where the ability to initiate and sustain reform initiatives is dependent on the commitment and effectiveness of individuals. As Levine et al. (1980, 578-79) point out:

How do we realistically expect these reforms to be successfully implemented? All reforms require bold leadership in which some individuals demonstrate the skill, sensitivity, and personal motivation to put the public interest in front of narrow self-interest. . . .

Making reform efforts last requires that leaders gain the support both of important clienteles within their organization and groups outside of the organization that can influence a leader's reform efforts. Thus, for example, prison reform requires the cooperation of inmates as well as staff members within the institution. In addition, a leader must gain the endorsement of some important political officials . . . The extent to which leaders can acquire broad-based internal and external support for their reforms determines how much change will be retained and made a lasting component of the criminal justice system. Ultimately, then, an effective leader uses the "power of persuasion" to mobilize groups to look a bit beyond the status quo and recognize that they can gain something by supporting a particular reform. (From *Criminal Justice* by James P. Levine et al., copyright © 1980 by Harcourt Brace Jovanovich, Inc. Reprinted by permission of the publisher.)

Most reform initiatives pose threats to some form of traditional or vested interest. Social institutions, by their very nature, are constantly pressed to maintain equilibrium through attempts to provide consistency in practice and through the desire to achieve a reasonable degree of comfort and predictability in day-to-day operations. Reform initiatives threaten this equilibrium and are naturally resisted.

Due to the lack of consistent objectives and the frustrations experienced in the attempt to achieve approval for what it does, the correctional enterprise has been subjected to a host of programming experiments, many of which have not been carefully thought out nor supported by effective leadership. Furthermore, because of its controlled and contained population and the social stigma generally attached to it, corrections has been regarded as a testing ground for a variety of theories and experiments in the social and behavioural sciences. Interventions of this kind are often made without any clear reform intent.

In spite of the resistance and frustration these initiatives have created, corrections remains a human enterprise. The correctional enterprise represents the worst and the best that is in all of us. If there is hope for the advancement and improvement of the human condition, there is justification for a continuing commitment to the resolution of problems associated with correctional reform.

Notes

1. The Canadian Criminal Justice Association (formerly the Canadian Association for the Prevention of Crime) is a national voluntary organization concerned with social welfare and criminal justice issues. The Association receives grants from the federal and provincial governments and fees from its members. These funds assist in maintaining a full-time executive and a support group located in Ottawa. The Association produces a monthly bulletin and a scholarly quarterly called the *Canadian Journal of Criminology*. The membership of the Association for the period April 1, 1981 to March 31, 1982 was 1,160 persons.

Each of the provinces also has similar associations (usually called Criminology and Corrections Associations). The Canadian Criminal Justice Association tends to act as an umbrella organization providing support for these provincial associations. Additionally, the provincial associations assist in fostering membership for the Canadian Association and members from the provincial associations sit on the Board of the Canadian Association. Six of the provincial associations (Alberta, Manitoba, New Brunswick, Nova Scotia, Ontario, and Saskatchewan) are in a joint membership arrangement with the Canadian Criminal Justice Association. Four provinces (British Columbia, Newfoundland, Prince Edward Island, and Quebec) do not have a formal association with the national body. However, regardless of the formality of the relationship, the national association works with all of the provincial associations to organize conferences, public education activities, and the presentation of briefs to government on a variety of criminal justice matters.

2. In 1978, the Continuing Committee of Deputy Ministers Responsible for Corrections and Deputy Attorneys General created a Steering Committee of

Deputy Ministers "responsible for the review of duplication and overlap in the administration of justice and corrections" (*Agenda,* Continuing Committee, First Meeting, Royal York Hotel, Toronto — December 13, 1978). With regard to corrections this Committee established two supplementary agenda items: *(1)* planning and operational issues in corrections, and *(2)* split in jurisdiction in corrections. From 1978 through 1980, the Continuing Committee addressed these two issues conjointly. The decision to do so was based on the assumption that the question of jurisdictional arrangement would require long-term effort but that, in the interim, improvements in the coordination of activities under the present jurisdictional arrangement could be made.

3. According to the report of the Task Force on the Role of the Private Sector in Criminal Justice (1977), private agency involvement in penal reform, while in evidence as early as 1878 through the work of the Prisoner's Aid Association of Toronto, really became a factor in Canadian corrections just after the end of World War II. Some of the important private agencies formed prior to the end of World War II were: The Canadian Prisoners Welfare Association (1919); The Citizens Service Association (1929); The John Howard Society of B.C. (1931); The First Elizabeth Fry Society (Vancouver, 1940); and, The Crime and Delinquency Division of the Canadian Welfare Council (1944). However, the years after 1946 saw a tremendous expansion of private agency interest. John Howard societies were established in all Canadian provinces and the first efforts were made to begin coordinating private agency interest through national conferences.

4. Perhaps the most important recent initiative in Canada to clarify the relationship between private sector agencies and government in the delivery of criminal justice services was the creation of the Task Force on the Role of the Private Sector in Criminal Justice by the Ministry of the Solicitor General in 1976. This Task Force held a variety of meetings across Canada and received briefs from numerous private sector agencies. Its report, in three volumes, was submitted to the Solicitor General in April, 1977.

5. The first joint session of Deputy Attorneys General and Deputy Ministers Responsible for Corrections to address issues in corrections was held on November 29, 1978.

6. The Task Force on the Creation of an Integrated Canadian Corrections Service (1977, 24-28) argued quite strongly that the rehabilitative ideal needed to be abandoned — or at least modified. Thus, the "statement of basic principles and objectives for Federal Corrections," contained within this document, avoided all reference to the term "rehabilitation" and concentrated instead on the terms "reintegration" and "opportunities."

The *Statement of Goals, Strategies and Beliefs* (1978c), developed by the Corrections Branch of the Province of British Columbia, also avoided the use of the term "rehabilitation" and concentrated on defining the services of the correctional system which provide for the protection of the public and the presentation of opportunities for the offender to make reparation. This document attempted to establish a balance between two ideals: "offenders must be held accountable for their acts" and "offenders should not be subjected to cruel and unusual forms of treatment."

7. In *The Criminal Law in Canadian Society: Highlighted* (Government of Canada 1982, 25), the prpoosed principles to be applied in achieving the purpose

of criminal law are presented. While the concept of rehabilitation is not dismissed, it is clear that the emphasis has shifted away from the rehabilitation model. for instance, the following principle is enunciated.

Wherever possible and appropriate, the criminal law and criminal justice systems should also promote and provide for:
(i) opportunities for the reconciliation of the victim, community and offender;
(ii) redress or recompense for the harm done to the victim of the offense;
(iii) opportunities aimed at the personal reformation of the offender and his reintegration into the community.

8. In *The Role of Federal Corrections in Canada* (1977,57) the following statement is made:

The "opportunities" principle is based on the assumption that the offender has the capacity to make choices — whether to engage in responsible conduct or irresponsible conduct perhaps leading to criminal activity ... The focus of the opportunities approach is to provide the offender with choices and to hold him accountable for those choices. This is preferable to making choices for the offender and, thereby, permitting him to escape his obligations and responsibilities.

9. In a review of figures on the incarceration of native Indians in Ontario, Jolly (1982a, 2) notes that "native men and women are continuing to be incarcerated at a level which is three to forty times the rate that their share of total population would seem to warrant — depending on the length of sentence, type of crime and age category." Of particular concern is the admission of native Indians to the Kenora Jail in Northwestern Ontario (Jolly 1982a, 3), where native Indians comprise 25-30 percent of the total population: "In 1981-82, Natives accounted for 78 percent of the total male admissions and 97 percent of the total female admissions to the Kenora Jail" (Jolly 1982a, 3). Further, Jolly (1982a, 4) reports that "while Native citizens in Ontario were disproportionately over-represented in 1981-82 admissions to the correctional system, they were less likely to be released on bail or on parole and were more likely to be incarcerated until the end of their sentence than non-native inmates."

10. On April 11, 1983, the *Province*, a Vancouver daily newspaper, printed a front-page lead article by B. McLintock titled "Jail Time May Need Reservation." The same issue also printed a companion article entitled "Officials Worried." During this week, a number of articles appeared in provincial newspapers reporting the comments of the Commissioner of Corrections and other corrections officials on the problems of prison overcrowding. These articles were clear evidence of the correction system's public attempt to communicate its concerns about prison overcrowding. In the *Province* article, the following comments were made:

Already B.C.'s adult prison population is stretching jail facilities to the limit, says Commissioner of Corrections Bernard Robinson, but the number of prisoners coming to jail is expected to continue and to increase during the next months and years. . . .

A key factor is the increasing number of people being sentenced to jail for drunk driving and other Motor Vehicle Act offences. These people, almost all of them on short-term sentences (less than 90 days), now make up about 40% of the total prison population. . . .

11. One of the unique and most promising initiatives to result from the 1975 Federal-Provincial Conference on Native Peoples and the Criminal Justice System was the Ontario Native Council on Justice. This organization evolved from the Ontario Native Advisory Committee to the Criminal Justice System which was established following the 1975 conference. Membership in the Council is composed of eight native organizations including the Association of Iroquois and Allied Indians, Grand Council Treaty #9, Grand Council Treaty #4, the Ontario Federation of Indian Friendship Centres, the Ontario Metis and Non-Status Indian Association, the Ontario Native Women's Association, the Union of Ontario Indians, and the Native Law Students' Association.

Among the objectives of the Ontario Native Council on Justice (cited in Jolly 1982a, 10-11) are the following:

1. To act in the development of justice policy pertaining to Native people and in so doing to identify problems and propose solutions.

2. To encourage and facilitate the initiation, development and funding of justice-related programs which are designed and operated by and for Native people.

3. To conduct and publish research on justice-related areas of concern to Native people.

4. To make recommendations and presentations to individual Ministries in the Justice Policy Field, the Cabinet Committee on Justice and any other provincial and federal ministries or departments or organizations on justice-related issues.

The Activities of the Council have included publication of *The Native Inmate in Ontario* (Birkenmayer and Jolly 1981), which reported on in-depth interviews with 513 native inmates in Ontario Institutions, the development of Liaison projects designed to assist native inmates through cultural and spiritual activities, pre-release planning, community service order projects for natives, and involvement in the development of a Fine Option program for Ontario. (For a detailed description of the structure and activities of the Ontario Native Council on Justice, see Jolly 1982a and 1982b.)

Another organization that has been extremely active in the area of native Indians and the criminal justice system is the Native Counselling Services of Alberta. The Native Counselling Services of Alberta began operation in 1970, providing assistance to native people involved with the criminal law. According to an Information Package produced by N.C.S.A., the primary objective of the organization is "to gain fair and equitable treatment for Native people involved in the Legal system." In addition to providing assistance for native persons during and after their appearance in criminal court, the organization provides services in corrections, probation and parole supervision, impaired driving education and suicide prevention (see Native Counselling Services of Alberta, *Annual Report* 1982).

12. Hogarth (1978, 4) in the discussion paper, "Tentative Policy Proposals on Diversion," makes the following statement:

Diversion does not seek to treat or rehabilitate, to deter or to punish. It does, however, meet the goals of reparation and reconciliation and in the course of that other things may happen. Individuals may be deterred, they may undergo attitude change, they may feel they have corrected the balance in the sense of just retribution. But these are *consequences* and not *purposes* of diversion. . . .

Ekstedt (1979, 2) in a report to the Executive Committee of the Ministry of the Attorney General (B.C.), entitled *Proposed Diversion Policy* states:

Diversion programs should not be established to realize the goals of the formal criminal justice system (i.e. rehabilitation, deterrence and retribution). If it is viewed that any of these goals apply to a case being considered for diversion, then that case ought not be diverted.

13. While there continues to be concern and uncertainty related to division programs for adults in Canada, the influence of attitudes about juvenile diversion are probably quite different in Canada than in the United States. The passage of the *Young Offenders Act* (1983) confirms diversion as an approved and legislatively supported principle with regard to the disposition of juveniles. Judge Omer Archambault, who was responsible for coordinating the drafting of the legislation, stated:

In appropriate cases, alternative measures to the formal court process may be used, particularly in those cases involving less serious offences. To this end the proposed legislation contains provisions that will sanction screening and diversion. Although it will provide provinces considerable flexibility in implementing such program measures, the Act does nevertheless contain a number of basic protections and safeguards for young persons who might become involved in the diversion process (*Liaison* 1981, 18).

14. Whitson (1979, 69) in an unpublished paper, "A Policy Oriented Legal Analysis of Adult Pre-Trial Diversion in the Canadian Context," dealt with the problem of "double-jeopardy" at some length and documented court cases addressing this phenomenon as it applies to diversion. As a result, in his synopsis of policy issues, he made the following statement:

The execution of a criminal diversion agreement by the alleged offender becomes somewhat analogous to a guilty plea. As long as the possibility of a return to the public criminal trial process exists, requirements would necessitate some legislative safeguards to provide protection to the alleged offender against the use of any incriminating disclosure related to the diversion negotiation in a subsequent criminal trial. . . .

15. In December, 1981, the federal and provincial Ministers responsible for Criminal Justice established a task force to investigate the needs of crime victims. In 1983, the task force forwarded 73 recommendations to the Ministers. To date, the task force has published at least twelve working papers, which focus specifically on crime victims. While the task force focused on street crime, it was recommended that inquiries be made into such areas as white collar and corporate crime, racially motivated crime, and environmental crime.

16. Despite the increased focus on the victims of crime and the payment of restitution by offenders, there is considerable debate over the concept of restitution and its use as a sanction of the criminal court. Specifically, observers have raised concerns over the role of the criminal court in levying and enforcing restitution orders, assessing victim culpability in determining restitution, and in ascertaining what constitutes "fair" restitution. Klein (1978), a critic of restitution, has argued that the criminal courts should not be involved in creating restitution schemes as they do not have the appropriate mechanisms that the civil courts possess to assist them in assessing losses and damages.

While Klein (1978) and others have assailed restitution programs, there is widespread support throughout the correctional system for such initiatives (see Hudson and Galaway 1974, 1975; Galaway 1977, 1980; Hudson et al. 1977).

References

Archambault, J. (Chairman). 1938. *Report of the Royal Commission to Investigate the Penal System of Canada.* Ottawa: King's Printer.

Baker, S.H. and S. Sadd. 1981. *Diversion of Felony Arrests: An Experiment in Pretrial Intervention.* Washington, D.C.: U.S. Department of Justice.

Bartollas, C. and S.J. Miller. 1978. *Correctional Administration: Theory and Practice.* New York: McGraw-Hill.

Berzins, L. (April) 1977. "What Next for the Female Offender?" 3 *Liaison.* 6-10.

Berzins, L. and S. Cooper. (October) 1982. "Political Economy of Correctional Planning for Women." 24 *Canadian Journal of Criminology.* 399-416.

Birkenmayer, A.C. and S. Jolly. 1981. *The Native Inmate in Ontario.* Toronto: Ontario Ministry of Correctional Services and Ontario Native Council on Justice.

Blomberg, T.G. 1980. "Widening the Net: An Anomaly in the Evaluation of Diversion Programs." In M.W. Klein and K.S. Teilman (eds.) *Handbook of Criminal Justice Evaluation.* Beverly Hills, California: Sage Publications. 571-92.

Bowker, L.H. (Spring-Summer) 1979. "The Maximum Security Prison and Its Transformation." 59 *The Prison Journal.* 24-33.

British Columbia Ministry of the Attorney General. (January) 1978a. 2 *Corrections Branch Newsletter.*

_____. 1978b. *Incarcerated Women in British Columbia Provincial Institutions.* Victoria: Corrections Branch.

_____. 1978c. *Statement of Goals, Strategies and Beliefs.* Victoria: Corrections Branch.

Canadian Sentencing Commission. 1987. *Sentencing Reform: A Canadian Approach.* Ottawa: Supply and Services Canada.

Carson, J.J. (Chairman). 1984. *Report of the Advisory Committee to the Solicitor General of Canada on the Management of Correctional Institutions.* Ottawa: Supply and Services Canada.

Chesney-Lind, M. 1980. "Re-Discovering Lilith: Misogny and the 'New' Female Criminal." In C.T. Griffiths and M. Nance (eds.) *The Female Offender: Selected Papers from an International Symposium.* Burnaby, B.C.: Criminology Research Centre, Simon Fraser University. 1-35.

Chinnery, D. 1980. "Managing the Female Offender: Some Observations." In C.T. Griffiths and M. Nance (eds.) *The Female Offender: Selected Papers from an International Symposium.* Burnaby, B.C.: Criminology Research Centre, Simon Fraser University. 221-27.

Coffey, A.R. 1975. *Correctional Administration: The Management of Institutions, Probation and Parole.* Englewood Cliffs, N.J.: Prentice-Hall.

Couture, J. 1983. "Traditional Aboriginal Spirituality and Religious Practice in Federal Prisons: An Interim Statement on Policy and Procedures." Unpublished paper. Edmonton: Correctional Service of Canada.

Culbertson, R.G. 1981. "Achieving Correctional Reform." In R.R. Roberg and V.J. Webb, (eds.) *Critical Issues in Corrections: Problems, Trends, and Prospects.* St. Paul, Minnesota: West Publishing Co. 308-45.

Ekstedt, J.W. 1979. *Proposed Diversion Policy.* Unpublished paper. Victoria: Ministry of the Attorney General of British Columbia.

Ekstedt, J.W. and T. Harrison. 1974. *Diversion: A Federal-Provincial Approach.* Unpublished paper. Ottawa: Continuing Committee of Deputy Ministers Responsible for Corrections.

Faguy, P.A. (January) 1973. "The Canadian Penal system of the 70's." 15 *Canadian Journal of Criminology and Corrections.* 7-12.

Farris, J.L. (Chairman). 1976. *Report of the Commission of Inquiry into Events at the British Columbia Penitentiary: June 8 to 11, 1975.* Ottawa: Solicitor General of Canada.

Fauteux, G. (Chairman). 1956. *Report of a Committee Appointed to Inquire into the Principles and Procedures Followed in the Remission Service of the Department of Justice of Canada.* Ottawa: Queen's Printer.

Friel, C.M. 1982. "Administrative and Policy Issues in Prison Population Forecasting." In *Proceedings of the National Workshop on Prison Population Forecasting.* Washington, D.C.: U.S. Department of Justice. 1-21.

Galaway, B. (January) 1977. "The Use of Restitution." 23 *Crime and Delinquency.* 57-67.

_____. 1980. "Is Restitution Practical?" In M.D. Schwartz, L.F. Travis and T.R. Clear (eds.) *Corrections: An Issues Approach.* 2d Edition. Cincinnati, Ohio: Anderson Publishing Co. 271-79.

Geis, G. 1975. "Restitution by Criminal Offenders: A Summary and Overview." In *Restitution in Criminal Justice: Papers Presented at the First International Symposium on Restitution.* Minneapolis, Minnesota: Minnesota Department of Corrections. 246-63.

Gosselin, L. 1982. *Prisons in Canada.* Montreal: Black Rose Books.

Government of Canada. 1978. *A Time for Action: Toward the Renewal of the Canadian Federation.* Ottawa: Supply and Services Canada.

_____. *The Criminal Law in Canadian Society.* Ottawa: Ministry of Justice.

_____. 1982. *The Criminal Law in Canadian Society: Highlights.* Ottawa: Ministry of Justice.

Griffiths, C.T. and L.F. Weafer: 1984. *Native North Americans: Crime, Conflict and Criminal Justice—A Research Bibliography.* 2d Edition. Burnaby, B.C.: Criminology Research Centre, Simon Fraser University.

Griffiths, C.T. and J.C. Yerbury. 1982. "The Delivery of Criminal Justice Services to Native Indians: Reconsidering the Issues." Unpublished paper. Burnaby, B.C.: Department of Criminology, Simon Fraser University.

_____. 1984. "Natives and Criminal Justice Policy: The Case of Native Policing." *Canadian Journal of Criminology.* Forthcoming.

Hagan, J. (August) 1974. "Criminal Justice and Native People: A Study of Incarceration in a Canadian Province." (Special Issue) *Canadian Journal of Sociology and Anthropology.* 220-36.

Haveman, P., K. Crouse, L. Foster and R. Matonovich. 1984. *Law and Order for Canada's Indigenous People.* Ottawa: Solicitor General of Canada.

Heijder, A. (January) 1980. "Can We Cope with Alternatives?" 26 *Crime and Delinquency.* 1-9.

Hogarth, J. 1978. "Tentative Policy Proposals on Diversion." Unpublished paper. Victoria: Ministry of the Attorney General.

Hudson, J. and B. Galaway (May) 1974. "Undoing the Wrong: The Minnesota Restitution Centre." 19 *Social Work.* 151-76.

_____. 1975. *Considering the Victim: Readings in Restitution and Victim Compensation.* Springfield, Illinois: Charles C. Thomas.

Hudson, J., B. Galaway and S. Chesney. (February). 1977. "When Criminals Repay Their Victims." 60 *Judicature.* 312-21.

Hugessen, J.K. (Chairman). 1972. *Report of the Task Force on Release of Inmates.* Ottawa: Solicitor General of Canada.

Hylton, J. (April) 1982. "The Native Offender in Saskatchewan: Some Implications for Crime Prevention Programming." 24 *Canadian Journal of Criminology.* 121-31.

Johnson, S.M. 1980. "Beyond Incarceration: A Woman's Alternative." In C.T. Griffiths and M. Nance (eds.) *The Female Offender: Selected Papers from an International Symposium.* Burnaby, B.C.: Criminology Research Centre, Simon Fraser University. 213-20.

Jolly, S. 1982a. "Native People in Conflict with the Criminal Justice System: The Impact of the Ontario Native Council on Justice." Unpublished paper. Toronto: Ontario Native Council on Justice.

_____. (April-July) 1982b. "The Ontario Native Council on Justice: A Unique Offspring of a Federal Provincial Conference." 5 *Canadian Legal Aid Bulletin.* 17-33.

_____. 1983. *Warehousing Indians: Fact Sheet on the Disproportionate Imprisonment of Native People in Ontario.* Toronto: Ontario Native Council on Justice.

Jolly, S., C. Peters and S. Spiegel. 1979. *Progress Report on Government Action Taken Since the 1975 Federal-Provincial Conference on Native Peoples and the Criminal Justice System.* Ottawa and Toronto: Solicitor General of Canada and Ontario Native Council on Justice.

Jolly, S. and J.P. Seymour. 1983. *Anicinabe Debtors' Prison: Survey of Fine Defaulters and Sentenced Offenders Incarcerated in the Kenora District Jail for Provincial Offences.* Toronto: Ontario Native Council on Justice.

Keon-Cohen, B.A. (April-July) 1982. "Native Justice in Australia, Canada and the U.S.A.: A Comparative Analysis." 5 *Canadian Legal Aid Bulletin.* 187-258.

Kirkpatrick, A.M. (July) 1962. "Prisons and Their Products." 4 *Canadian Journal of Corrections.* 160-78.

_____. (October) 1964. "Jails in Historical Perspective." 6 *Canadian Journal of Corrections.* 405-18.

Klein, J.F. (June) 1978. "Revitalizing Restitution: Flogging a Horse That May Have Been Killed for Just Cause." 20 *Criminal Law Quarterly.* 383-408.

Law Reform Commission of Canada. 1975a. *Working Paper 11: Imprisonment and Release.* Ottawa: Information Canada.

_____. 1975b. *Working Paper 7: Studies on Diversion*. Ottawa: Information Canada.

_____. 1976. *Report: Dispositions and Sentences in the Criminal Process*. Ottawa: Information Canada.

LeDain, G. (Chairman). 1973. *Commission of Inquiry into the Non-Medical Use of Drugs — Final Report*. Ottawa: Information Canada.

Letkemann, Peter. 1981. "Beyond Restitution: Reconciliation Between Victims and Offenders." In *Selected Papers of the Canadian Congress for the Prevention of Crime*. Ottawa: Canadian Association for the Prevention of Crime. 58-72.

Levine, J.P., M.C. Musheno and D.J. Palumbo. 1980. *Criminal Justice: A Public Policy Approach*. New York: Harcourt, Brace and Jovanovich.

Macdonald, Hon. A. 1975. "Introductory Statement by the Hon. Alex Macdonald, Attorney General of British Columbia." Federal-Provincial Conference on Corrections. Victoria, B.C. May 22-23.

MacGuigan, M. (Chairman). 1977. *Report to Parliament by the Sub-Committee on the Penitentiary System in Canada*. Ottawa: Supply and Services Canada.

McCaskill, D. 1985. *Patterns of Criminality and Correction Among Native Offenders in Manitoba: A Longitudinal Analysis*. Saskatoon: Prairie Region, Correctional Service of Canada.

Mikel, D. 1979/80. "Native Society in Crisis." 6/7 *Crime et/and Justice*. 32-41.

Ministry of Justice and Ministry of the Solicitor General. (May) 1979. *Federal Discussion Paper on Post-Arrest/Charge — PreCourt Adult Diversion*. Ottawa.

Mohr, H. (Chairman). 1971. *Report of the Working Group on Federal Maximum Security Institution Design: Design of Maximum Security Institutions*. Ottawa: Solicitor General of Canada.

Moyer, S., F. Kopelman, C. LaPrairie, and B. Billingsley. 1985. *Native and Non-Native Admissions to Provincial and Territorial Correctional Institutions*. Ottawa: Solicitor General of Canada.

Muirhead, G., and D. Hartman. 1980. *Native Indians in the B.C. Corrections System*. Victoria: Corrections Branch, Ministry of the Attorney General.

Murton, T.O. 1976. *The Dilemma of Prison Reform*. New York: Holt, Rinehart and Winston.

Murton, T.O. and J. Hyams. 1969. *Accomplices to the Crime*. New York: Grove Press.

National Advisory Commission on Criminal Justice Standards and Goals. 1973. *Corrections*. Washington D.C.: U.S. Government Printing Office.

Native Counselling Services of Alberta. 1982. *Annual Report*. Edmonton.

Newby, L. 1981. *Native People of Canada and the Federal Corrections System — Development of a National Policy: Preliminary Issues Report*. Ottawa: Correctional Services of Canada.

Norquay, G. and R. Weiler. 1981. *Services to Victims and Witnesses of Crime in Canada*. Ottawa: Solicitor General of Canada.

Ontario Ministry of Correctional Services. 1975a. "Long Term Objectives for Corrections — Statement by the Minister for Correctional Services, Ontario." Federal-Provincial Conference on Corrections. Victoria, B.C. May 22-23.

_____. 1975b. "Preliminary Draft of a Discussion Paper — Ontario Ministry of Correctional Services." Federal-Provincial Conference on Corrections. Victoria, B.C. May 22-23.

Ouimet, R. (Chairman). 1969. *Report of the Canadian Committee on Corrections — Toward Unity: Criminal Justice and Corrections.* Ottawa: Information Canada.

Outerbridge, W.R. (Chairman). 1972. *Report of the Task Force on Community-Based Residential Centres.* Ottawa: Information Canada.

Prevost, G. 1968. *Crime, Justice and Society: Commission of Enquiry into the Administration of Justice on Criminal and Penal Matters in Quebec.* Quebec City: Roch Lefebvre.

Proudfoot, P.M. (Chairman) 1978. *Report of the British Columbia Royal Commission on the Incarceration of Female Offenders.* Victoria: Ministry of the Attorney General.

Reasons C.E. 1975. "Native Offenders and Correctional Policy." 4 *Crime et/and Justice.* 255-67.

Reid, S.T. 1981. *The Correctional System: An Introduction.* New York: Holt, Rinehart and Winston.

Renner, K.E. 1979. "The Two Faces of Diversion: Reform Versus a Conceptual Alternative as the Choice Between Broadening the Net and Avoiding the System." Unpublished paper. Halifax, Nova Scotia: Department of Psychology, Dalhousie University.

Roesch, R. (January) 1978. "Does Adult Diversion Work? The Failure of Research in Criminal Justice." 24 *Crime and Delinquency.* 72-80.

Roesch, R. and R.R. Corrado. 1983. "Criminal Justice System Interventions." In E. Seidman (ed.). *Handbook of Social Intervention.* Beverly Hills. California: Sage Publications. 385-407.

Royal Commission on the Status of Women. 1970. "Criminal Law and Women Offenders." In *Report of the Royal Commission on the Status of Women.* Ottawa: Information Canada. 365-85.

Schmeiser, D.A. 1974. *The Native Offender and the Law.* Ottawa: Law Reform Commission of Canada.

Solicitor General of Canada. 1973. *The Criminal in Canadian Society: A Perspective.* Ottawa: Supply and Services Canada.

_____. 1975. *Native Peoples and Justice. Reports on the National Conference and the Federal-Provincial Conference on Native Peoples and the Criminal Justice System, Edmonton, February 3-5.* Ottawa: Communication Division.

_____. 1977a. *National Inventory of Diversion Projects.* Ottawa. Supply and Services Canada.

_____. 1977b. *Response of the Solicitor-General to the Parliamentary Sub-Committee Report on the Penitentiary System in Canada.* Ottawa: Supply and Services Canada.

_____. 1977c. *A Summary and Analysis of Some Major Inquiries of Corrections: 1938 to 1977.* Ottawa.

_____. 1978a. *Diversion: A Canadian Concept and Practice.* Ottawa: Communication Division.

_____. 1978b. *National Advisory Committee on the Female Offender: Report.* Ottawa.

_____. 1978c. *National Planning Committee on the Female Offender: Report.* Ottawa.

_____. 1978d. *Report of the Joint Committee to Study Alternatives for the Housing of the Federal Female Offender.* Ottawa: Correctional Service of Canada.

_____. 1981a. National Workshop on Services to Crime Victims: *Report of the Proceedings March 23-25, 1980.* Ottawa: Research Division.

_____. (March) 1981b. "Young Offenders Act Introduced." 7 *Liaison.* 17-20.

_____. (March) 1982. "Women in Prison: The Human Rights Connection." 8 *Liaison.* 16-21.

_____. 1983. Canadian Federal-Provincial Task Force. *Justice for Victims of Crime.* Ottawa: Supply and Services Canada.

_____. 1984. Report of the Advisory Committee to the Solicitor General of Canada on the Management of Correctional Institutions. Ottawa: Supply and Services Canada.

_____. 1986. Correctional Law Review Working Paper No. 1. *Correctional Philosophy.* Ottawa: Solicitor General of Canada.

_____. 1986. Correctional Law Review Working Paper No. 2. *A Framework for the Correctional Law Review.* Ottawa: Solicitor General of Canada.

Statistics Canada. 1982. *Correctional Services in Canada, 1980/81.* Ottawa: Canadian Centre for Justice Statistics.

Stelmaschuk, W.J. (March) 1982. "South Fraser Regional Justice Managers Group, *Project Restore.*" Unpublished paper. Victoria: Ministry of the Attorney General.

Stookey, J.A. 1975. "The Victim's Perspective on American Criminal Justice." In *Restitution in Criminal Justice: Papers Presented at the First International Symposium on Restitution.* Minneapolis, Minnesota: Minnesota Department of Corrections. 4-12.

Swackhamer, J.W. (Chairman). 1972. *Report of the Commission of Inquiry into Certain Disturbances at Kingston Penitentiary During April, 1971.* Ottawa: Information Canada.

Task Force on the Creation of an Integrated Canadian Corrections Service. 1977. *The Role of Federal Corrections in Canada.* Ottawa: Supply and Services Canada.

Task Force on the Role of the Private Sector in Criminal Justice. 1977. *Report: Community Involvement in Criminal Justice, Vol. 1.* Ottawa: Supply and Services Canada.

Thorvaldson, S.A. 1981. "Reparation by Offenders: How Far Can We Go?" In *Selected Papers of the Canadian Congress for the Prevention of Crime.* Ottawa: Canadian Association for the Prevention of Crime. 119-28.

U.S. Department of Justice. (November) 1981. *Bulletin — Victims of Crime.* Washington, D.C.: U.S. Department of Justice.

The Vancouver *Sun.* 1983. "Prison Fast Day 14." April 12, section B, p. 10.

Vantour, J. (Chairman). 1975. *Report of the Study Group on Dissociation.* Ottawa: Solicitor General of Canada.

Verdun-Jones, S.N. and G. Muirhead. 1979/80. "Natives in the Canadian Criminal Justice System: An Overview." 7/8 *Crime et/and Justice.* 3-21.

Western Premiers' Conference. 1977. *Report of the Western Premiers' Task Force on Constitutional Trends.* Presented at the Western Premiers' Conference meeting, May 5-6, 1977. Brandon, Manitoba.

_____. 1978. *Western Premiers' Task Force on Constitutional Trends, 2nd Report.* Presented at the Western Premiers' Conference meeting. April 13-14, 1978. Yorkton, Saskatchewan.

Whitson, D. 1979. "A Policy Oriented Legal Analysis of Adult Pre-Trial Diversion in the Canadian Context." Unpublished paper. Ottawa: Solicitor General of Canada.

Woods, G. and H. Sim. 1981. *Highlights of Federal Initiatives in Criminal Justice: 1966-1980.* Ottawa: Solicitor General of Canada.

ADDENDUM TO CHAPTER 10

THE PROUDFOOT COMMISSION — REACTION AND RESPONSE TO CORRECTIONAL REFORM

As discussed in Chapter 10 and throughout the text, correctional reform must be assessed from an integrated view of policy, process, and specific program results. The following history is provided as an example which illustrates this point.

Dr. J.W. Ekstedt, one of the authors of this text, was Commissioner of Corrections in the Province of British Columbia when the Royal Commission on the Incarceration of Female Offenders (Proudfoot 1978) was established. This Commission was created by Order in Council on December 5, 1977, and Madam Justice Patricia Proudfoot of the B.C. Supreme Court was appointed as its sole Commissioner.

According to the Commission Report (Proudfoot 1978, 1):

> The appointment of the Commission resulted from various allegations made public by the media. The allegations were of irregularities in the operation of the Oakalla Women's Correctional Centre, including sexual misconduct between male staff and female inmates. The Royal Canadian Mounted Police were called in to investigate matters. Subsequent to their confidential report to the Attorney General of British Columbia, this Commission was born.

The Proudfoot Commission was established as a direct result of Dr. Ekstedt's intervention within the Ministry of the Attorney General and, with the Attorney General, before Cabinet. His motives for the establishment of the Commission were several. First, he wished to assure that the serious allegations were not left unresolved as a result of the process of internal investigation or as a result of the Ministry's response to the investigation report of the Royal Canadian Mounted Police. Additionally, it was Dr. Ekstedt's concern that this occasion should be used to address a broader series of fundamental questions related to the incarceration of female offenders.

The Attorney General and Cabinet agreed with this position. As a result, the Commission's mandate extended beyond the simple investigation of allegations related to the operation of the Oakalla Women's Correctional Centre. The following terms of reference for the Commission were established through Order in Council (Proudfoot 1978, 2):

> A Commissioner be appointed to make inquiry into and concerning all aspects of the management and operation of programs and facilities related to the disposition and incarceration of female offenders whether under sentence or on remand in British Columbia and without restricting the generality of the aforesaid concerning any misconduct arising out of the same in so doing to inquire particularly into
> a) whether or not correctional management policies and practice are in accordance with proper standards within the administration of justice, reflect public attitudes and ideals, and provide for the proper incarceration of female offenders;
> b) whether or not the programs, equipment and facilities provided in the Province by the Corrections system for the disposition and incarceration of female offenders, are conducive to good correctional practice;
> c) whether the employment, promotion or placement of Corrections staff in women's correctional programs is in any way discriminatory as to sex;
> d) whether there are proper methods and procedures for the training of staff employed in correctional programs and facilities for women;
> e) whether or not the discipline within provincial facilities for female offenders is proper and effective and in compliance with Corrections Act regulations and management policy.

After the Commission was appointed, Dr. Ekstedt expressed his views regarding the attitude which he hoped would be taken by the Corrections Branch in relation to the Commission. In the January, 1978 issue of the *B.C. Corrections Newsletter* (B.C. Ministry of the Attorney General 1978a, 1), he stated:

> It is my hope that, as a Branch, we can take a positive and nondefensive stance in relation to this inquiry. We should see this as an opportunity to learn from our mistakes where they are shown to exist, address grievances where they are shown to be valid and build better programs for the present and future.

The Commission, and some of its recommendations, have been discussed in this chapter. It is the intention here to present some of the circumstances that applied at the time of the Commission's work and to illustrate how they are indicative of the difficulties encountered when attempts are made to achieve correctional reform. It also must be stated in a forthright fashion that Dr. Ekstedt was severely criticized by the Proudfoot Commission and his dismissal was recommended by the Commissioner herself. Neither this recommendation nor any of the other recommendations of the Proudfoot Commission is at issue here. Indeed, many of the criticisms and recommendations have been accepted by everyone who was subject to the Report or who was familiar with the issues it addressed. Most of these recommendations and criticisms would have been made regardless of whether the investigation took the form of a judicial inquiry or an "in-house" process.

Many of the criticisms and recommendations related to the incarceration of female offenders had been identified by the Corrections Branch and submitted by Dr. Ekstedt to the Attorney General prior to the Report of the Proudfoot Commission and even prior to the media allegations of misconduct at the Oakalla Women's Correctional Centre. Additionally, the Director of the Vancouver Region (within which the Oakalla Women's Correctional Centre was located) had made numerous submissions recommending structural improvements and reforms in practice, many of which were eventually contained in the recommendations of the Proudfoot Commission.

It had not been possible for the management of the B.C. Corrections Branch to acquire the resources necessary to effect even superficial improvements at the Oakalla Women's Correctional Centre. It was Dr. Ekstedt's original hope that the Commission's report would add support to the efforts being made by the Corrections Branch to acquire resources both for upgrading the facility and for more significant purposes. Dr. Ekstedt believed that the only way to add legitimacy to the long-standing concerns surrounding the incarceration of female offenders — expressed by the Corrections Branch and by others — was to have an independent judicial inquiry which would force a political and public response to these issues. Whether or not the Commission's work actually achieved the desired objectives will be shown only if empirical information is gathered on this matter. However, the lessons learned from initiating and participating in an examination of this aspect of B.C. Corrections have relevance to understanding the process of correctional reform and the role of judicial inquiries as reform instruments.

The conditions which pre-dated, surrounded and influenced

the work of the Proudfoot Commission are of considerable interest. They illustrate that the Proudfoot Commission represented reaction to the general emphasis on correctional reform which prevailed in the province, to a degree at least proportionate to the Commission's interest in the specific problems within the Oakalla Women's Correctional Centre. The Commission's work also illustrates that a judicial inquiry probably cannot be expected to comment effectively on the *process* of correctional reform, because it is limited to an assessment of results and conditions at a particular time. While the recommendations of such an inquiry may be effective in addressing particular conditions and abuses, this type of inquiry may be less effective in understanding and dealing with the assessment of general objectives in correctional reform and in appraising the conditions which need to be established or supported in order to realize those objectives.

For five years prior to the appointment of the Proudfoot Commission, the B.C. government had been engaging in intensive efforts at correctional reform. The reform movement began in earnest during 1972 with the election of the New Democratic Party (NDP) to form the Government of British Columbia. Mr. David Barrett, party leader and Premier of the province, had long expressed an interest in correctional reform, particularly with regard to prisons. Accordingly, the new government began to take initiatives in this area. A five-year plan for corrections was requested by the Attorney General with an emphasis on decentralizing the administration and creating alternatives to the institutions then existing in the province. Concurrently, the Corrections Branch became part of an overall planning initiative which brought together operational leadership from the major divisions of government service in the administration of justice — including police, courts, corrections and legal services.

Reform initiatives were planned for the administration of justice as a whole and a "systems approach" to planning was established. This approach to criminal justice reform was supported through legislation (*Administration of Justice Act, 1974*) which provided the authority for decision making to involve participation by all components of the criminal justice system; established the means for employing key personnel in the research, planning and implementation of new projects; and established the criteria for the release of funds to support various reform initiatives.

Consequently, by 1974 the Corrections Branch was not only engaged in a process of reform supported politically and legislatively; it also was involved in addressing reform questions in the context of the criminal justice system as a whole. It is accurate to state that from the beginning of 1973 to the end of 1975, the criminal justice system in B.C. was subject to more initiatives directed to substantive change than had ever been previously experienced in a comparable time period. In corrections, the dominant reform interest was the de-emphasis of prison as a place of rehabilitation and there was agitation against the use of prison as the primary disposition within corrections.

Due to the rapidity and substantiveness of change, which personnel had not been trained to deal with, there was severe reaction to these initiatives. Generally, personnel in the criminal justice system were divided into two groups: those who were excited by and who supported the changes and those who were opposed to them. Personnel were being disrupted, new personalities were constantly being introduced and "competition" (though this was not the intent of reform) was created between the traditional programs and the new programs. The emphasis on alternatives to imprisonment created a situation where programs of imprisonment were de-emphasized and devalued. Accordingly, existing prison programs began to suffer in the transition. Prisons, even more so than in the past, became locations of low-status employment. It was evident, and not surprising, in light of contemporary theories of organizational change, that competition by personnel to acquire placement in the new high-status programs increased.

It is also important to remember that these changes were initiated at a time of economic growth in the province. However, as was true across all of Canada, the economic situation abruptly changed beginning in 1975. Consequently, confusion and uncertainty resulted as programs which had been initiated during the period of prosperity began to suffer from lack of resource support.

Among the disruptive influences on correctional reform which preceded the work of the Proudfoot Commission was a change in government in 1975. It was during this year that the New Democratic Party was defeated by the Social Credit Party. The new regime not only began to establish its own priorities but also attempted to remove many of the influences on government services that had resulted from initiatives of the previous government. Indeed, the Social Credit Party was aided in its election victory by the apparent public perception that the New Democratic Party had gone too far with some of its reforms and had failed to demonstrate good stewardship over public funds and the public trust. Among other things, this perception lent force to a review of programs and the status of persons identified with the previous administration. Naturally, the administration of justice, which had received a great deal of attention by the New Democratic Party while in power, became subject to this type of review. In turn, the review created further uncertainty and confusion with regard to the various reform initiatives that had been taken.

Two years after the change in government, the Proudfoot Commission was appointed to inquire into an area which had been subject to and affected by the broader reform initiatives of the NDP administration. Moreover, as a result of the sequence of events described above, the confusion and uncertainty among correctional personnel was quite high. And finally, there is no doubt that Dr. Ekstedt himself was identified with the emphases which resulted from NDP policy — an identification which clearly had an effect on the work of the Proudfoot Commission.

This is not to say that the Proudfoot Commission was established by the Social Credit government in order to assist in discrediting NDP program initiatives. This was not the case. Nor is it in any way fair to suggest that Madam Justice Proudfoot had any political interest whatsoever in the evolution of correctional practice in the years which preceded the Commission's inquiry. What is suggested is that the Commission became one of the few means available, to a wide range of persons who had been seriously affected by the reform process, for redress of personal and professional grievances. Thus, the recent history of reform initiatives influenced practically every submission that was made. As a result, the Commission experienced difficulty in understanding whether or not it was dealing with concerns pertinent to its mandate, or whether it was being subjected to a series of strategies which were intended to discredit both the process of correctional reform in British Columbia and the reformers themselves.

This is not a new or unusual phenomenon and it has been reported by others. It exemplifies what Levine et al. (1980, 579) refer to as "the potential costs of promoting organizational change." Similarly, Tom Murton's works *Accomplices to the Crime* (with co-author J. Hyams) (1969) and *The Dilemma of Prison Reform* (1976) are important for their discussion of the complexities surrounding correctional reform and for their description of the types of circumstances which can inhibit it.

As Murton and Hyams (1969, 236-37) state:

> The model of reform viewed from the perspective of time can be represented as a spiral. At the low point there is a scandal which sparks the demand for drastic reform measures. The reforms are implemented. The curve of progress arcs upward toward the apex of achievement.

Just short of consolidating the gains, the reformer is removed. The process is reversed and the arc curves downward until it approaches the point of origin.

The lineal difference between the beginning point of the spiral and the new low indicates the net gain (or loss) that has been accomplished. The reformer must be willing to scale a mountain of obstacles and fall short of the pinnacle of "success" to attain the foothills of reform.

While the initiative for reform from 1973 to 1978 in British Columbia might not be described as a "scandal" but as a peculiar political initiative, all the other factors in Murton's "spiral" apply. It is unclear whether or not the Proudfoot Commission symbolized a "new low" in British Columbia. If so, the question is whether or not there was any "lineal difference" between the beginning point of the spiral of reform and the point reached following the Proudfoot Commission.

Such questions are difficult to assess. However, there are indications that some gains were made by the reform initiatives taken prior to the Proudfoot Commission. It is worth remembering that the Proudfoot Commission was established in response to media reports claiming irregularities at the Oakalla Women's Correctional Centre. It is therefore interesting that excerpts from media responses to the report of the Proudfoot Commission indicate that there may have been a general increase in the public understanding of the fundamental issues which were involved in correctional reform in the province. A similar increase in sophistication was also evident in the political response to the Report. For instance, the Vancouver *Province* (May 17, 1978; p. A11), published an article entitled "Ex-Jail's Chief Caught in Cross-Fire." In this article, the following comments were made:

(Attorney General Garde) Gardom rose to Ekstedt's defence when he released the report, saying Ekstedt had created changes in B.C. that the federal government is just waking up to. . . .

An entrenched government system slow to change had much to do with his fate. So did inadequate public interest and debate on the kind of prison system government wanted. . . .

The fact is, Ekstedt was put in charge of a system the government wanted improved and for which some changes were already underway. But as the man in charge, he took the blame for ills that had been contracted in the past and left untreated. (Reprinted with permission of *The Province*.)

Additionally, an article in the *Victoria Times* (May 15, 1978; p. 2), entitled "Keep John Ekstedt," made the following comment:

It would have been easy for Ekstedt, or any other Commissioner of Corrections, to implement a single philosophy for the whole Branch: the "lock'em all up and throw away the key" school was popular for years, and would probably still be quite politically popular. It undoubtedly led to fewer morale problems among staff; everyone knew exactly what he was supposed to be doing.

In fact, there was only one thing wrong with it — it didn't work.

Ekstedt, therefore, stepped into a situation in which it was becoming increasingly evident that it didn't much matter what went on in jails because no programs for them seemed to do any good. He did not try to evade that situation by imposing a simplistic philosophy, and that should go to his credit, not his debit.

Among the many newspaper articles and other media responses to the report of the Proudfoot Commission, one other is worth mentioning here. An editorial in the *Victoria Times* (March 18, 1978) discussed the issue of the use of judicial inquiries to address matters which must be politically resolved:

What remains is a question that has been arising from several recent Royal Commissions, not just from the Proudfoot report: a question of the role of the judiciary in conducting public inquiries of this type. . . .

What must be questioned . . . is whether the position into which judges are put in many Royal Commissions does not force some compromise of those very virtues for which they were appointed. It seems that in many cases now, judges must make recommendations which are, in essence, political.

Let one point be very clear: political, as used here, does not refer to partisan politics. It is much broader in scope than that, referring to decisions that cannot help but be based on an individual judge's philosophic perceptions — on his views, not only of what our society is like, but of what it *should be* like. . . .

The Proudfoot Commission is one example of this: Madam Justice Proudfoot undoubtedly did a thorough and conscientious job of collecting evidence on the topic of corrections, especially corrections for women in B.C. But to make her recommendations, she had to apply that evidence to some framework, and in such situations the only useful framework available is not that of existing law, but that of her own assumptions, perceptions and beliefs about what the direction and role of the corrections system ought to be. And decisions about the direction and role of the corrections system are essentially political decisions.

The Proudfoot Commission is an excellent example of the difficulty faced by an observer who attempts to assess correctional reform through investigation of specific program results, without attention to the process of reform which is in place and the reform intent which is being expressed.

Chapter 11

The Future of Corrections in Canada

Throughout North America, there is a growing interest in the development of techniques to plan for change and to improve the ability of social institutions to predict future needs and circumstances. As a result, there has evolved a series of activities and study specialties which concentrate on assessing the future of social institutions, including criminal justice and corrections. Futures conferences have begun to proliferate and "futures societies" are being formed. For example, an International Futures Conference was held in Toronto during July, 1980. A portion of the conference agenda provided for discussions on the future of criminal justice. A Futures Workshop also was held in Vancouver in May, 1982. This conference enjoyed national participation from the academic community, the private sector, and from criminal justice agency personnel who met to discuss the subject "Corrections in British Columbia: The Next Ten Years." Additionally, in recent years there has been a trend within government to project program and budget requirements over extended periods of time, which has resulted in the production of planning documents that project goals, strategies and resource needs within designated timeframes. In 1974, for instance, a "Five-year Plan" for the B.C. Corrections Branch was developed and was included in a document entitled "Corrections Planning — An Overview" (see Ekstedt and Montz 1974).

While the growing awareness of diminishing resources has stimulated much of the emphasis on future planning, further impetus has been given to criminal justice planning by the growing perception that advances in crime are outstripping advances in the criminal justice system. In a recent article in the *Australian Institute of Criminology Quarterly,* Clifford (1982, 7) observes: "The criminal justice system is not working because it does not get the community support which it needs, and because it has been significantly outpaced by advances in crime both national and international." Clifford (1982, 7) further notes that "the criminal justice system had difficulty detecting crime and obtaining evidence, and that courts and corrections were not equipped to deal with the problems of modern sophisticated crime."

Commenting on the future of criminal justice and corrections is fairly common in modern textbooks and other publications (see, for example, Bartollas and Miller 1978; Levine et al. 1980; Fox 1983). With regard to the issues identified above, it is the intent of this chapter to add to the futures dialogue and to provide a brief comment on the future of corrections in Canada.

One way to approach a discussion on the future of corrections is to attempt to predict the types of programs and the changes in structure which are likely to emerge. To an extent, this attempt has already been made in the chapter on Correctional Reform. Another possible approach is to invent a "futuristic" correctional system by imagining what an ideal system might be in terms of its programs and mechanisms for admission and release. However, in keeping with the theme of this text, it has been decided to concentrate on those factors which are likely to have the most influence on the development of correctional policy.

In previous chapters we have attempted to show that correctional practice flows from policy. And because an appreciation of the factors which influence correctional policy is necessary in order to understand the correctional enterprise — both today and in the past — then it is proper to assume that they also must be understood in order to assess the future. The future, however, will likely give new shape to the factors which influence correctional policy. With this proviso in mind, the future of corrections is discussed by addressing the following topics: *(1)* perspectives on the future of corrections policy and practice; *(2)* the influence of social and economic restraint; *(3)* social policy and criminal law reform; and *(4)* planning and research.

PERSPECTIVES ON THE FUTURE OF CORRECTIONS POLICY AND PRACTICE

It is a perilous undertaking to speculate about the future. As Ekstedt (1980, 7) states:

The interest in the future is, at least partially, an attempt to grapple with the speed and intensity of change in our modern world with the realization that change can be devastating or fulfilling depending on the capacity of human beings to understand its substance and control its direction . . . human beings find it difficult to understand the past, more difficult to make meaning of the present and nearly impossible to speculate accurately about the future. The future is particularly a problem the more we are (or believe ourselves to be) unable to control the various factors which determine its direction. . . .

If there is any theme which has been consistently illustrated in this book, it is that the correctional enterprise has difficulty in learning from its past, in acting consistently and with common purpose in its present, and in making reasonable projections about its future.

We are constantly reminded that the correctional enterprise is "unable to control the various factors which determine its direction." Corrections is viewed, and perceives itself, as the "tail-end" of the criminal justice system — corrections becomes the "catch point" for persons whose status and circumstances have been determined by the decisions of others. Additionally, we see that the criminal justice system establishes its priorities and exercises its mandate as a reflection of broader social, economic, and political conditions. Thus, predicting the future of corrections is hazardous at best since it is the future of society's response to criminality that is at issue.

As noted in the previous chapter, there are those who argue that corrections cannot adequately project its prison populations, even when the assumption is made that there will be no change in past or current practice. As Elias (1982, 89) points out:

As traditionally applied to the criminal justice system, population forecasting methodologies operate on the assumption that future practices will replicate the past. In other words, these methodologies assume that the criminal justice system will continue to operate in essentially the same manner as it has in the past. The fact of the matter is that this is an extremely "shaky" assumption, given the mechanisms by which jail population levels are established.

One of the purposes in writing this book has been to illustrate that corrections in Canada (and elsewhere) is an activity which both results from policy and is dependent upon it. Attempts have been made to show that correctional practices are determined by policy and that the policy-making process can only be understood and influenced by accounting for all of the factors which contribute to it. Accordingly, the key to the future of corrections resides in the policy domain. And it is not enough to assess efficacy on theoretical or even empirical grounds. Instead, information and ideas arising from an assessment of practice must be dealt with in the clear understanding that policy making is an exercise in social and political will.

In discussing the limited task of prison population forecasting, Elias (1982, 91-92) observes:

> In addition to the technical problems associated with population forecasting methodologies, there are significant difficulties associated with applying the technique to the criminal justice system, an interdependent system of actors with different and competing roles and responsibilities, whose sometimes disjointed decisions result in the phenomenon the planner or analyst is trying to measure. Furthermore, change in other social systems and in other levels of government can have unanticipated and dramatic effects on jail and prison populations. Finally, the social and economic environment may change drastically, thus invalidating even the most technically correct applications of this technique.
>
> The crux of the problem for criminal justice planners and analysts lies in the fact that the jail population is policy-dependent — and the methods that in most cases are being used to predict future needs are policy-blind. And until these methods are linked with policy decision-making, population forecasting in the criminal justice system is a lot like shooting craps.

As we have learned from previous chapters, prisons and their populations are likely to remain the major concern in both policy and practice. However, any discussion of the future must take into account the other correctional interests which have either evolved as alternatives to imprisonment or as dispositions in their own right. Coupled with this understanding is an appreciation of the variety of non-correctional initiatives which have been developed as alternative forms of conflict resolution. In this context, some major problems for the future of corrections are presented. Heijder (1980, 6-7) outlines them as follows:

> A realistic approach would be never to propose an alternative to the prison unless one specifically indicated for which of the present functions of the prison it was meant to be a functional equivalent and how the other functions of the prison were to be dealt with. To neglect this is to risk falsifying the role of the prison in the scheme of penal justice, to risk presenting an alternative that after some time turns out to be not a substitute for prison but an alternative to already existing noncustodial sanctions . . . several clusters of problems present themselves when we think of alternatives. First, there is the rather commonplace observation that, while it is relatively easy to incorporate new sanctions in the statute, such legislation in itself does not change correctional reality. Measures like supervision and control orders or the community service order are not so difficult to put down in legal provisions. But it is a sobering thought to realize that they require a tight network of skilled and highly motivated professional social workers and other behavioral experts, each with a

caseload small enough to prevent the alternative from becoming a farce. It can be argued that, unless the requirement of a well-organized and well-equipped infrastructure is met, we cannot expect too much of any new device. This leads us right into a second cluster of problems. Where is the political will and energy, not only to enact new alternatives, but also to provide the necessary conditions for their success? (A Heijder, "Can We Cope with Alternatives?" *Crime and Delinquency,* vol. 26 (Jan. 1980), p. 6-7. Copyright © 1980 by the National Council on Crime and Delinquency. Reprinted by permission of Sage Publications, Inc.)

The future of any social institution can be addressed from one or both of two related perspectives: first, "given what we know now, what is likely to happen in the future?" and, second, "given what we know now, what *should* happen in the future?" The first approach uses *techniques* to analyze and assess current trends in order to determine future possibilities, should those trends continue. The second deliberately adds an assessment of values. The result is not merely an attempt to predict the future, but to influence and direct it. Clearly then, in commenting on the future of corrections, both approaches are needed.

Because these two perspectives go hand in hand, in this chapter we shall attempt to apply each of them. There is some evidence, much of which has already been stated, that decisions are being taken and practices are evolving in ways which are quite likely to shape the future of corrections (regardless of agreements or disagreements about their value). Moreover, there are issues related to the correctional enterprise whose future import remains undecided and where the future will clearly be influenced by the values that are brought to bear on policy making (see Epstein 1982; Tarnopolsky 1982). As Elias (1982, 97) states:

Criminal justice system analysts and planners must realize that they are dealing with a classical problem in policy analysis; they are using a rational technique in a value-laden environment. As a result, they must deal with issues of implementation and political values if their analysis is to be lasting and useful. The strength of population forecasting methodologies is that they can provide a framework within which informed choice, based on value preference, can occur. Criminal justice planners and analysts can clearly lay out for policy-makers the consequences of their policy decisions. The art in their analysis is to relate their findings to the policy-making process. Then, and only then, do their results have the potential to stand the test of time.

The following comments on the future of corrections are made with the understanding that in a free and democratic society, regardless of the form of political organization, the citizens must finally decide what they want from their government in terms of legislation and services. Additionally, as we have already stated in previous chapters, planning for the future relies upon the best possible understanding of the past and the present. We have already identified many of the problems which any human enterprise encounters when assessing its history or present practice. Finally, we have seen that many of the reform initiatives on which judgements of the future might be based have occurred only recently and, if for no other reason, their immediacy presents problems of interpretation. As stated in *The Role of Federal Corrections in Canada* (Task Force on the Creation of an Integrated Canadian Corrections Service 1977, 1-2):

> Federal Corrections is responsible for providing a service to the Canadian public and the offender. As a means of determining the quality of this service and with a view to improving the delivery of service to the public and the offender, attempts must be made to assess the attitudes and concerns expressed by the Canadian public. We are acutely aware of the hazards of attempting to read the mood of the public at any given period of time, mindful of Sir Walter Raleigh's warning that if someone tries to write an interpretation of historical events close on the heels of their occurrence, "the truth . . . may haply strike out his teeth". . . .

THE INFLUENCE OF SOCIAL AND ECONOMIC RESTRAINT

There is no doubt that the economic restraint which is affecting all social institutions will also have a continuing effect on Canadian corrections. As Evans (1981, 7-8) points out:

> The fact is, however, we are not in a temporary period of restraint but are entering a period of economic slow-down that may well become the norm. There will be no more large increases in staff or budget; if anything, there will be further retrenchment. . . .

It is common to equate the term restraint with the limitations imposed by "economic slowdown." Professional management consultants now find it useful to develop education and training programs which are marketable because they propose to assist managers in developing the style and technique of managing with fewer resources. It is true that the economy has changed in recent years in ways which present serious difficulties for managers who are used to managing in periods of growth. This problem has been aggravated in North America by the speed with which unusual economic growth was followed by severe recession. As Ekstedt (1979, 37) states:

Canadians experienced, during the early and middle part of this decade, a level of economic viability which was probably unique to the Canadian experience. This resulted in the release of significant funds at all levels of government for the development of new programs and projects in many fields including criminal justice. While this newfound "economic freedom" may have turned out to be more apparent than real, it did result in a few years of increased program experimentation in the justice field . . . It should be noted that the sharp economic downturn which occurred in the latter part of this decade did create a number of serious problems for programs which had been initiated only a year or two previously. Serious economic restrictions were placed on operating government branches which resulted in shifts in manpower and priorities before some programs were able to be stabilized. . . .

However, the modern concept of restraint management involves more than economic restrictions. It is arguable that in Canada restraint management evolved as a factor in correctional practice prior to the dramatic downturn in the economy. While it is true that restraint management always involves a demand for increased care in the stewardship of available resources, it is a mistake to assume that the cause of this demand is economic recession alone. If this were true, then we could predict that restraint management would not be a factor in corrections once the economy improves. On the contrary, it is more than likely that restraint management will continue as a major factor influencing correctional practice whether or not the economy improves.

The reason for this likelihood is that there are factors, other than the economy, which in recent history have imposed restraint on the management practices of the correctional enterprise. Restraint management really means that managers are required to perform in a highly competitive environment. They cannot assume that material and manpower resources will be forthcoming even if the economy is viable enough to support the acquisition of additional resources. Indeed, it is the atmosphere of competition itself which creates the condition now being referred to as restraint management. A competitive atmosphere may be generated, either as a result of the social and political conditions which have economic effect in the management of resources, or as a result of economic conditions which have social and political implications for the management of resources.

In Canada, as a factor in correctional practice, restraint management first emerged as a result of social and political conditions which forced corrections into an increasingly competitive environment and which required it to justify priorities in practice (and related expenditures) in ways which had not occurred before. Even if the economy improves, it is likely that the factors which first stimulated the requirement for competitive management in the delivery of criminal justice services will continue. Therefore, it is predictable that restraint management will be a factor in corrections practice for the foreseeable future.

The factors which have created the competitive environment resulting in the requirement for restraint management have been documented in a variety of ways earlier in this text. They include: the increasing criticism of the use of prisons as a form of disposition; the demand on both politicians and bureaucrats for higher levels of public accountability in the delivery of services; the demand for clarity of objectives in correctional practice; the trend towards "systems" management which places corrections in competition with other components of the criminal justice system; the movement toward non-correctional forms of conflict resolution; the intervention of the courts in correctional administration; and inter-governmental tension resulting from the split in jurisdiction. All of these factors create a competitive environment regardless of the state of the economy. The economy in recession only exacerbates their influence on corrections management. It seems apparent these conditions will force the correctional enterprise to continue its concentration on problems of management and will result in an increased emphasis being placed on the ability of the system to plan effectively and to budget competitively. Cost effectiveness and cost efficiency will remain the centre of interest at the political and bureaucratic levels of negotiation on correctional matters.

While the economy may not have a direct influence on the character of management practice, it will play a major role in determining program emphasis. As economic recession contributes to a hardening of attitudes on the part of the general public with regard to crime and punishment, the program emphasis in the context of competitive management will centre on prison programs. As the economy improves, resulting in a "softening" of social attitudes related to crime and punishment, the program emphasis will shift away from prison program concerns to a concentration on non-penal sanctions. This is the cycle of corrections practice that has been consistent throughout modern history. What has changed is the environment within which the cycle occurs. The key to the future of corrections will be the ability of persons engaged in the correctional enterprise to understand the new character of "restraint," and to use it effectively to accomplish legitimate correctional reforms.

SOCIAL POLICY AND CRIMINAL LAW REFORM

As stated above, the future of corrections is fundamentally dependent on the future of society's response to criminality. Society's response to criminality is centred in its system of criminal justice, of which corrections is a part. The criminal justice system is a reflection of social policy. The formal expression of social policy in relation to criminality is the criminal law.

Thus, when speculating about the future of corrections, it is necessary to comment on the conditions which will likely influence criminal behaviour in the future and which result in social policy, as it finds expression in the criminal law. While such a subject is massive and beyond the scope of the present work, nonetheless, it is important to introduce the subject here since the future of corrections is so closely dependent on the evolution of law and social policy. Additionally, trends which give evidence to the possible future of criminality must be assessed if planning to develop a criminal law and a correctional response to crime is going to have any possibility of serving the interest of society under conditions of "restraint."

The interest in the future, as we have already noted, is directly related to the speed and intensity of social change in modern society. It is this phenomenon which has created the emphasis on planning which has shifted the current correctional focus from operational, client-centred issues to management, systems-centred issues. As we have seen, this trend has had considerable effect on the evolution of management practice in Canadian corrections, including the increased demand for information which can be gathered and collated for planning purposes.

However, these trends also are influencing the way in which criminal law is viewed as an expression of Canadian social policy. A major review of the criminal law has been initiated by the federal government of Canada. This review is likely to continue as a priority activity associated with Canadian criminal justice throughout the decade of the 80s. The definition of criminal acts, the establishment of sentencing policy, the refinement of criminal law procedure, and the review of dispositions available in sentencing, all are subjects encompassed in the review.

The relationship between the review activity and the future of corrections in Canada is clear. The Canadian commitment to reappraise its criminal law is an indication that there is a recognition that social conditions require re-evaluation of the very purpose of criminal law as an expression of social policy. As stated in *The Criminal Law in Canadian Society: Highlights* (Government of Canada 1982, 9):

Will crime in the year 2001 resemble crime as we knew it in 1901? While it is always perilous to attempt to predict the future, it does seem likely that many of the factors that contributed to our current situation will continue to influence the general shape of future events. In formulating a criminal law policy, however, we must take into account the fact that crime is not static — it evolves as society evolves. We must also bear in mind that resources are becoming less abundant, and attitudes are changing. What are the implications of this process of evolution for criminal law policy?

Further, the document (1982, 19) states:

The basic problem confronting criminal law and the criminal justice system is a confusion, at the most basic level, about what it is the criminal law ought to be doing. There has never been an explicit policy to assist legislators in the amendment or creation of criminal laws in the Criminal Code and other statutes. The time has arrived to consider just what conduct the criminal law should deal with, and to whom criminal penalties should be applied.

It has been pointed out previously that any review of correctional law forces the correctional enterprise to review its policies and practices. The Canadian Criminal Law Review also has had this effect. The Directors, Commissioners and Deputy Ministers, as senior civil servants responsible for the delivery of correctional services at both the federal and provincial levels of government, have been meeting regularly since 1973. Moreover, this Continuing Committee of "Heads of Corrections" recently developed a Joint Submission on the Criminal Law Review (Heads of Corrections 1982). In this Joint Submission (1982, 1-2) it was stated:

Two matters have recently appeared on the agenda of the Heads of Corrections which have resulted in joint agreement. The first results from the desire to establish a common position on the "principles of corrections" which can serve as a guide in the development of correctional policy and practice in Canada. The second results from the work of the Law Reform Commission of Canada and the initiative of the Ministries of Justice and Solicitor General (Canada) to proceed with a major review of Canadian criminal law.

As a consequence of deliberations on these items, the Heads of Corrections have developed a common statement of "principles of corrections" and have agreed that a joint statement of correctional opinion on matters associated with the Criminal Law Review could assist individual jurisdictions in their consideration of these matters and provide additional data for those persons and agencies ultimately responsible for the criminal law review process.

It can be seen, therefore, that the Criminal Law Review is already having an influence on the future of Canadian corrections. The conclusion that will be reached in Canada with regard to the purpose and scope of its criminal law is fundamental to the future of correctional policy and practice.

The review movement in Canada also reflects a concern which is international in scope and which holds global implications for the purpose of law as an instrument of social policy, including the way in which both academics and criminal justice practitioners pursue the study of crime and the social responses to it. For example, Chappell (1981, 2-3) makes the following assertion:

> Apart from some speculation about the impact of population trends and new technologies, like the computer, upon patterns of criminal behaviour, criminologists have been largely occupied with immediate and contemporary problems. This apparent lack of interest in the future is perhaps partly explained by the close association between criminology and the law. As a major instrument of social control, the law has traditionally been concerned with the protection of existing institutions and values, relying heavily upon past experience to provide guidance in reaching decisions about how to behave in the present.
>
> Such a conservative legal and criminological approach may be suitable for societies which are not undergoing rapid change. However, during the twentieth century, and particularly the latter part, many nations have witnessed radical change in almost every aspect of life ranging from such fundamental institutions as the family to the use of nuclear energy. The pace of this change has frequently left the law, and the institutions and values it seeks to protect, in a bewildered and discredited condition. . . .

But if there is a general acknowledgement that the law, as an instrument of social policy, is inadequate to address the criminality resulting from changing social conditions, and if the adequacy of law in defining crime, and the social response to it, is central to the future of corrections, then what must be addressed in the reform of criminal law which will give positive direction to criminal justice and correctional practice? This, of course, is the question which is central to the review of criminal law in Canada. As stated in *The Criminal Law in Canadian Society: Highlights* (Government of Canada 1982, 8): "At the heart of this criminal law review process is the need to rethink and reshape the criminal law so that it effectively responds to 'crime', however we define it, in our society."

Regardless of how this matter is eventually resolved, there are some trends which must be acknowledged and which will undoubtedly have an influence on the future of criminal justice and corrections. It is obvious, for instance, that society cannot continue to bear the cost of a burgeoning criminal justice system. The climate of fiscal restraint will not only press for a reduction in the use of imprisonment as a disposition available to the court in sentencing but will also serve to limit the use of the criminal justice system as an agent of social control. Thus, the Criminal Law Review in Canada will result in narrowing the scope of criminal law and will correspondingly reduce the number of offences for which there is a penal sanction. As *The Criminal Law in Canadian Society: Highlights* (Government of Canada 1982, 10) points out:

> Planning for a less abundant future involves the use of more innovative and cost effective approaches to crime, which will limit the role of government, restrict the use of costly imprisonment as a sanction, and increase reliance on community-based, victim-oriented restitution and reparative sanctions.

Regardless of the current trend toward a "hard-line" response to those offences which society currently regards as criminal, society simply cannot afford to use the penal sanction for any but the most hard-core, dangerous offenders. A reassessment, therefore, will be required of those offences which society considers to be the most serious; there will be a reassessment of the concept of punishment itself. It will be determined, for instance, that for some offences, the use of non-penal sanctions is much more "punitive" than imprisonment. Rather than increasing the danger to society by overcrowding prisons with persons convicted of drinking-driving offences, it will be determined that confiscation of the offenders' automobiles is a much more effective punishment in many cases.

Similarly, imprisonment for default of fines will be increasingly seen to be a less effective punishment than other civil and criminal sanctions which might be made to apply. This trend is already occurring in Canada, and changes in the sanctioning process related to these two categories of offences alone will considerably reduce the pressure on provincial prison populations. The key to changes of this nature is the need to increase the sanctioning power of the court with regard to non-penal options, and to put an end to the idea of imprisonment as the punishment which is likely to have the most deterrent effect — particularly in those cases where enforced social and economic disability are likely to have a much more profound effect on the offender.

It is this type of reassessment of penal philosophy which is at the heart of the current Canadian Criminal Law Review. The philosophical realignment is emerging not only as a result of the demand for improved cost effectiveness in the provision of dispositions for offenders, but also as a result of the increasing realization that the use of prison sanctions must be limited if they are to serve the purpose of deterring crime and protecting the public. As van den Haag (1982, 202-03) states:

> A uniform threat weakens moral distinctions, while eliminating the fear of greater punishments to follow greater crimes. Laws threatening additional punishment when crimes are committed with guns imply that additional deterrence is produced when threats are not uniform and can be increased. Proportioning punishments in accordance with the harm done by offences — in accordance with the felt need for deterrence — is essential to the effectiveness of the penal system.
>
> The more penalities can be proportioned to harm, the more deterrent the penal system. Hence, the wider the range of possible penalities, the better. . . .

It is interesting that the Heads of Corrections (1982, 4-5), in their Joint Submission, consistently supported this principle. Included in their statement of "principles of corrections" are the following:

> The primary responsibility of correctional services is to contribute to the protection of society in accordance with the orders of the court.
>
> With due regard to their primary responsibility, correctional services shall provide a wide range of program and service opportunities to offenders.

When addressing the "purposes and principles of criminal law," the following statement was made (Heads of Corrections 1982,7):

> The general purpose of the criminal law is to contribute to the maintenance of a just, peaceful and safe society through the establishment of a system of prohibitions, sanctions and procedures to deal fairly, and in accordance with the principle of minimum necessary intervention, with culpable conduct that causes or threatens serious harm to individual or public interests and values.

The Heads of Corrections (1982, 8) went on to recommend that among the objectives and principles used to guide their review of criminal law in Canada, the following should be considered:

Prescribing sanctions that take into account the culpability of the offender and the seriousness of the harm involved. . . .

Finally, when commenting on "the function and scope of criminal law," the Heads of Corrections (1982, 11) state:

It is recommended that imprisonment be regarded as a sanction of last resort in the criminal law and specific criteria be established for its use.

The recent commitment of the Heads of Corrections to establish an agreement on common principles for the delivery of correctional services in Canada offers hope that the future development of correctional services might be better coordinated and less subject to jurisdictional fragmentation. This activity has been partially stimulated by: the Criminal Law Review; the conditions associated with restraint management; the recent interest in resolving jurisdictional conflict; the implications for corrections of the Charter of Rights and Freedoms; and the growing demand for increased public accountability in the delivery of government services.

The statement of the Heads of Corrections supports the proposition that all of these factors will continue to influence the future of the correctional enterprise. Additionally, we see in this activity a merger between "what is likely to happen" and "what should happen." It is clear that the Heads of Corrections perceive that the correctional enterprise is being shaped by factors beyond their control. However, it is also of interest that the Heads of Corrections assume a proactive stance in the face of changing conditions and that, on the basis of their experience and collective value judgements, they attempt to influence the direction that change will take.

PLANNING AND RESEARCH

In our discussion of correctional policy making in Chapter 4, academic research was identified as one potential source of influence on the formulation of correctional policy. A close examination of the interface between evaluation research and correctional policy, however, suggests that the correctional enterprise has often been less than receptive to research, particularly in those instances where evaluations have identified the need for substantial changes in the structures by which correctional services are delivered (see Garabedian 1971; Glaser

1975). Despite this traditional resistance, Waldo (1973, 365-66) argues that there is a critical need for research to inform correctional policy:

> It has been said that "research is the bookkeeping of corrections". It is indeed unfortunate that most correctional systems continue to operate without the advantage of such a bookkeeping system. If we were operating a commercial business and selling our products to the public, we would be bankrupt in a short time if our bookkeeping system was as poor as the one used in evaluating correctional programs.

In his discussion of evaluative research and the role of research findings in correctional policy, Shover (1979) identifies two opposing perspectives on the relationship between research and practice: the objectivist, and the critical. According to Shover (1979, 299), objectivists view the process of social research as a technical, rational activity: "Regardless of an individual's personal or organizational commitments, they can evaluate the same correctional program or research findings and arrive at the same conclusions about the program's efficacy. Having done so, they then would be willing and ready to modify their own commitments." Shover (1979, 300) notes that observers adopting the critical perspective, on the other hand, are more pessimistic about both the ability to conduct "objective" research and the probability that research findings will be translated into policy: "What is considered to be good research, reliable research findings, or reasonable inferences from research varies with the evaluators' backgrounds, social contexts, and organizational affiliations . . . individuals conceive, conduct, and interpret research as members of groups or communities whose collective standards and perspectives are employed in the process." From the critical perspective, the entire process of correctional evaluation is "socially negotiated and constructed" (Shover 1979, 301).

Shover (1979, 301, 302) goes on to argue that while the prevailing view of correctional research is the objectivist position that "research results speak unambiguously and that researchers and administrators will modify their beliefs and programs on the basis of research findings," the critical perspective reflects the reality of evaluative research in corrections:

> Evaluative research seems incapable of generating proposals or programs that represent truly fundamental or radical alternatives to existing correctional arrangements . . . the prevailing tendency is for evaluative research to examine or propose programs that are only incrementally different from existing ones and that do not fundamentally contradict them.

The arguments of observers adopting a critical perspective receive additional support from correctional observers such as Cohn (1970, 20-21), who concluded: "Scientific activity in corrections does occur, but the extent to which the results are shared, understood, and implemented by correctional authorities, and the extent to which their impact on institutionalized services is measurable, can only be speculated to be minimal." Similarly, Garabedian (1971, 43) has argued that the sum total of evaluative research has had little impact on the operations of the correctional enterprise. "Although most research has played a role in changing the *face* of corrections, to date it has failed to have any substantial impact on changing its underlying *structure*. . . Most correctional research has had the latent function of perpetuating the existing system."

A primary reason for the apparent resistance of the correctional enterprise to evaluative research findings, is the traditional lack of accountability in corrections. As Thomas and Peterson (1977, 14) contend: "Seldom, if ever, are criminal justice agencies required to show that their procedures, policies, programs, and expenditures serve the functions for which they were presumably designed or that they do so more efficiently than available alternatives." Our discussion of the activities of individuals involved in the management and planning of correctional services has indicated that while decision makers are accountable to the organizational structure within which they make decisions, they are generally not accountable to the clients (inmates) who are often the ultimate recipients of such decisions.

A related difficulty in informing correctional policy through evaluative research is the vagueness of the objectives of specific programs and policies. As we have seen in our discussion of correctional treatment in Chapters 7 and 8, not only does the prison operate under a conflicting mandate of custody and treatment, but there is often considerable confusion as to the best way to measure the success of treatment initiatives. The consequences of the problem of the correctional enterprise in assessing "outcome" is noted by Manning (1979, 714):

> One of the most common modes of adjustment of the evaluation and productivity problem has been to use efficiency measures of the allocation of resources (i.e. the costs of engaging in a particular line of action, given . . . budgetary limits or obligations).

It might be argued that the concern with the cost effectiveness of a particular policy may be only peripherally related to the ultimate benefit of the policy for the protection of society and/or the reintegration of the offender into the community.

Here again we see how important it is that those who would wish to influence the future of correctional policy and practice, either through independent research or through policy analysis, understand how to make their findings known to those who occupy responsible positions in the policy-making process. This is not an easy task. While it is evident that the Heads of Corrections have a stake in the future of correctional policy and practice and are actively pursuing their interests, it is not so clearly evident that they have the means to acquire and interpret the type of information which can assist them to make the best possible decisions for the future. As Chappell (1981) has pointed out, criminologists and others who seek to make independent inquiries into criminal justice issues must also take an interest in the future and must be willing to assess and to comment on the ways in which institutions can be reformed in order to reflect important social values.

The future of corrections in Canada is at least partially dependent on the ability to assess values in the context of a rational planning process which is based upon systematically acquired information.

Policy making is not rational where it excludes values or reaches conclusions only as a result of a dispassionate assessment of the evidence. However, one of the important attributes of independent research is that it can seek to provide a systematically acquired information base. And when such an information base is employed by decision makers, it can assist in the assessment of values and in the determination of those consequences which will likely result from the possible decision-making options.

Also important is that social conditions are now changing too rapidly to allow for policy decisions to be made "by the seat of the pants." It is precisely in periods of dramatic change that solid information is needed if the public is to be properly served. Many commentators argue that adequate planning and the development of information systems that can support it are primary requirements in addressing the future of criminal justice (see Bartollas and Miller 1978; Levine et al. 1980; Elliston and Bowie 1982; Fox 1983). And without doubt, criminologists and other social science researchers can play a role in promoting this development. The acceptance of rational planning techniques in itself reflects a value judgement related to the way in which social institutions can best serve the needs of the public. The degree to which institutions can be reformed to promote the use of rational techniques in value-laden environments is directly proportional to their ability to influence and direct the future. As Waller (1982,

363-64) states:

> How should public needs be assessed? Often government operates with methods that predate the social sciences and the computer. However, we live today at a time when these tools can make much more relevant information available. These tools are not necessarily perfect, but they are a significant improvement over nineteenth century methods. The social sciences can provide some reliable and valid information to assess what the individual citizen needs, and why, as well as what the society needs, and why. . . .
>
> To meet public needs, rational planning based upon systematically acquired information must become the norm. . . . Incrementalism and syndicalism have allowed a system to grow that does not focus on public needs or deliver effective programs to meet these needs. If the public wants protection, then research and development should be undertaken to identify programs that will give some protection. Once alternative programs have been identified, they must be implemented and evaluated. Most important, however, is the commitment of political officials to goals such as these. If the attorneys general want to meet noble constitutional objectives, then they must be aggressive in assuring planning, research and development, implementation, and evaluation. The assessment of needs and the evaluation of results must become the subject of discussion by political leaders, whose responsibility it must remain to make the final decisions.

INDICATORS OF CHANGE: PORTENTS FOR THE FUTURE

Throughout this book, various trends and movements have been discussed which have implications for the future of corrections. It is difficult to present and discuss, in one textbook, all the factors, or even most of the factors, which are influencing change and decision making in the life of any social institution at any particular moment. Consequently, the tendency is to discuss these factors in a general way, while trying to describe the analytical tools and models which might be employed to assess them. However, to illustrate, it might be useful to discuss briefly some current indicators of change which seem likely to occupy the attention of correctional observers, practitioners, and "clients" in the future. Four categories will be briefly discussed. They are: *(1)* privatization; *(2)* technological innovations; *(3)* the capital punishment debate; and *(4)* sexually transmitted diseases.

Privatization

Throughout the text, the relationship between corrections as an activity of government and corrections as an activity of the private sector has been discussed. The private sector has been involved in correctional work, in a variety of ways, throughout Canadian correctional history. Thus, the concept of "privatization" is not new to corrections. (For an interesting discussion of the historical development of private-sector involvement in prison industries, see Gandy and Hurl 1987.) For example, during the late 1800s, private entrepreneurs in Canada used cheap, inmate labour to produce goods for the open market (Lightman 1982). Various forms of prison industry emerged from this practice, until the organized labour movement began to express concern, and a decline occurred in the use of prisoners as cheap labour in the private sector.

Today, privatization in the corrections context usually involves the contracting out, by government, of various correctional programs. Such programs cover the gamut from non-profit halfway houses and parole supervision to medical and dental services, educational and counselling programs, chaplaincy programs, and food services in institutions. In 1983/84, the Correctional Service of Canada held contracts with 175 privately owned, non-profit halfway houses and aftercare agencies, at a cost of $10.5 million (Solicitor General of Canada 1985).

While various kinds of privatization occurred within the corrections context historically, the practice today has become the focus of considerable controversy. It has been defined as ". . . a new practice in which government gives up its traditional role in the construction and routine management of prisons and jails, and relies instead upon private corporations to do the job for an agreed upon fee" (National Council on Crime and Delinquency 1985a, 1).

This new trend is of course associated with the general desire throughout the western world to reduce the cost of government, by placing as many programs as possible in the hands of the private sector. It is argued that programs relocated in this manner will be operated more efficiently, given the competitive demands of the private sector and the stimulation provided by the profit motive.

In the context of corrections, it has been argued that the interest in privatization stems from a variety of factors. These include the public demand for harsher sanctioning practices, the apparent failure of the State to run the prison system, soaring costs, diminishing resources, dismal conditions (including overcrowding) within the institutions, the inefficiencies of bureaucracy, demands for accountability and cost effectiveness, and the intervention of the courts in correctional practices (Robbins 1986, Camp and Camp 1985, Elvin 1985).

While the trend toward privatization in corrections is not, as this book is being written, as advanced in Canada as in the United States, the evidence indicates that it will become an important issue in Canadian corrections. The new practices of privatization that appear to be emerging in North America raise a number of policy questions:

1. Would privatization lead to an expansion of the prison system and a consequent increase in the use of incarceration for persons convicted of offences?
2. Would the profit motive conflict with the provision of adequate conditions within the institutions? Would cost-cutting measures mean that only the minimum legal standards would be met? Would these measures mean higher staff/inmate ratios?
3. To what extent could private employees use force? Would there be an increase in violence and vindictiveness within institutions?
4. What role would private organizations play in quasi-judicial matters involving the legal status of inmates, e.g. parole, recommendations for disciplinary actions, transfers, etc.?
5. Would privatization lead to further dispersion of accountability, or decreased opportunity for public scrutiny of the correctional system?
6. What options would remain if the government became dependent on private organizations and these organizations, substantially raised their prices, went bankrupt, closed their doors because of insufficient profit, or experienced a strike by employees?
7. Who would ultimately be responsible for the safety of staff, inmates, and the public in the event of escapes, riots, or actions that violated offender rights as established by the Charter of Rights and Freedoms?
8. Would powerful lobbyists come to influence policy within corrections?

A fundamental political issue in relation to privatizing trends is whether any part of the administration of justice is an appropriate market for economic enterprise (Solicitor General of Canada 1985). A related question that will need to be resolved is "To what extent is corrections part of the administration of justice?" For example, should the administration of sentences by a prison system conform to the same principles of neutrality, lack of vested interest and fairness as used by the courts in deciding what the sentence should be? The answer to these and similar questions will have much to do with how the privatization trend influences correctional practice in Canada.

Technological Innovations

"High-Tech" applications are becoming more prevalent in correctional practice. Elsewhere in this text we have discussed the various ways that computers and other forms of automation may be used to improve information systems, set up simulations to help determine the effect of decisions, and generally improve administrative efficiency in the processing of human beings in correctional programs. In Canada, there have been several recent developments that have considerable potential to improve the planning capacities and capabilities of correctional decision makers, both regionally and nationally. For example, a joint project was sponsored by the Ministry of Attorney General for British Columbia and the Canadian Centre for Justice Statistics in 1986 to develop a Justice Planning Model, called JUSTPLAN.

However, the application of technology to correctional practice in the future will probably evolve far beyond these types of applications. By way of illustration, two other types of technological applications will be briefly discussed. They are electronic monitoring and expert systems.

Electronic Monitoring

The Correctional Service of Canada has recently considered the possibility of employing electronic surveillance technologies in the supervision of offenders. Two applications have been studied: the first involves monitoring devices used to supervise offenders under conditions of house arrest, while the second involves the employment of monitoring devices in halfway houses (National Joint Committee of the CACP and FCS 1986).

While the federal corrections service has decided not to employ these techniques at this time, the provincial system in British Columbia has. As of June 1, 1987, $140,000 have been allocated for a nine-month pilot project utilizing electronic monitoring for non-violent offenders serving intermittent sentences (Mason and Hall 1987). Advocacy for the system stems from the United States. (For a more detailed discussion on the evolution of this technique, see Griffiths 1987.) Electronic monitoring was first employed in Florida in 1983. As of this writing, there are 44 programs operating in twenty different states and, since implementation, U.S. programs have reported a 98 percent compliance rate (Vancouver *Sun,* March 25, 1987).

Presently, electronic monitoring involves the use of an electronic bracelet which is placed on the offender. The bracelet transmits a weak radio signal to a receiver plugged into the telephone. The receiver has a range of approximately 200 feet, and if the offender goes outside this range, breaks a curfew, or tampers with the system in any manner, an alarm is triggered, notifying the probation officer or agency (National Council on Crime and Delinquency 1985c).

It has been suggested that electronic monitoring may be a less costly, less intrusive, and more humane means of monitoring offenders, when the alternative is incarceration. If, on the other hand, this type of monitoring is employed with offenders who would normally receive a probation order, it could prove to be more costly and could serve to widen the social control net.

Not surprisingly, initial reaction to electronic monitoring has included warnings concerning possible infringements of civil liberties and the dangers of a subtle advancement in the powers of social control agents possibly leading to a "police state".

While the system is far too new to have been challenged in the courts, there is general consensus thus far that it will not contravene the Charter of Rights and Freedoms as long as it remains a sentencing alternative or option for offenders who would otherwise face a prison sentence (National Joint Committee of the CACP and FCS 1986).

Expert Systems

A number of the difficulties associated with management decision making in a corrections system have been described earlier in this text. Problems of resource management, population forecasting, integrated planning with other components in criminal justice, and persistent demands for policy reviews place significant stress on the political and bureaucratic systems responsible for the delivery of correctional services. Recent technological innovations have improved the capacity of corrections to maintain reasonably up-to-date information systems, which can be used for both management and planning purposes. The weaknesses of these systems are related to their capacity to integrate research findings, political objectives, public interests, and professional interests. The limitations imposed by an inadequate or uneven resource base have also been noted.

However, there are emerging technological innovations which are likely to improve the capacity of correctional organizations to develop decision-making processes that can effectively account for all or most of these variables. One such development in the computer sciences is the so-called Expert System.

The Expert System is a product of a new discipline in computer science called Artificial Intelligence. After 30 years of research, it is now possible to endow computers with traits involved in human thought processes (Roberts and Ryder 1987). Scientists have made significant progress in emulating human thought, and Artificial Intelligence may prove to be an invaluable tool within the criminal justice system. Roberts and Ryder (1987) maintain that expert systems are one of the leading applications of Artificial Intelligence. They describe the programs in the following manner:

> Expert Systems are computer programs that embody human expertise in a particular domain (area of expertise) of knowledge. They are, in a figurative sense, the cloning of an expert's method of problem solving.

An Expert System begins with the development of a knowledge base, which consists of the expert's knowledge and the methods employed for problem solving. To this knowledge base is added an element referred to as the "inference engine." This component decides which rules to use, applies the rules, and determines when the problem has been solved. The inference engine is the reasoning element of the system. Finally, a further component is introduced to allow communication between the system and its user. If necessary, it provides an analysis of the processes used to reach a given solution.

In the criminal justice field, Expert Systems are under development for use in such areas as counter-terrorism, organized crime and labour racketeering, narcotics, and criminal profiling for serial murder and rape (Roberts and Ryder 1987). While Expert Systems are not yet available for correctional decision making, there have been other technological changes. For example, the data base which might eventually support an Expert System is being developed and, in the process, the capacity of human beings to make better decisions is being improved. As correctional managers increasingly use the data base for decision making, they will be able to devise models for problem solving which, in turn, can become part of the data base for the Expert Systems.

It is now conceivable that a correctional system (or any other organization) may retain, rather than lose, the knowledge *and* experience which individuals in the system have accumulated over long periods of time. The capacity to store and retrieve expertise will soon improve significantly, and will change the face of management practice even in a system as conservative and tradition-bound as corrections. It is now evident that everything from law enforcement targeting strategies to sentencing decisions to conditional release decisions will be influenced by the evolution of Expert Systems.

The Capital Punishment Debate

The Parliament of Canada recently considered a motion to give approval in principle to restoring the death penalty (June 1987). (Parliament had previously abolished the death penalty in 1976. The last time a death penalty was carried out in Canada was 1962.) While this motion was defeated, the issue of capital punishment will continue to be part of the rhetoric on criminal justice matters and will continue to have an influence on the tone and temper of correctional practice.

Like so many other issues which influence correctional policy and practice, this one is subject to the cycles of public perception concerning personal safety and well-being, which themselves are triggered by cycles in the economy and the socio-political environment. The hardening of public and political attitudes, which is related to unmet expectations and broken promises resulting from the crisis of the world economy, has been discussed repeatedly in this text.

The capital punishment debate, however, is fundamental to our perceptions of crime and punishment. It has to do with whether socio-economic variables are so determining as to render our justice "situational" (i.e., reactionary), and without a declared and consistent moral foundation, or, on the other hand, whether we are able to uphold basic notions of justice, regardless of the economic or political climate.

The confusion about society's stand on this issue renders criminal justice inefficient and, in some cases, incompetent in the control of criminal populations. Simply stated, the abolition of capital punishment resulted in a political requirement to reassure the public by augmenting the severity of punishments for persons committing serious offences. Consequently, there was an increase in the minimum time required to be served prior to consideration for parole for persons serving a life sentence.

The existence of the death penalty, perhaps ironically, tended to influence the justice system to seek avoidance of the death penalty. However, with the death penalty unavailable, the psychology of decision making tends to press for the use of the life sentence in a disproportionate way, so that there is an increase in the numbers of persons serving life sentences. Part of the capital punishment debate, of course, is to find a reason for what appears to be a disproportionate increase in life sentences. Thus, some argue that more persons are committing the type of crime for which a death sentence might be given. Others argue either that there is not a disproportionate increase in life sentences, or that the increase is the result of an overreaction on the part of the judiciary to the need for visible examples of severity, in the absence of the death penalty.

Regardless of these arguments, the correctional system in Canada is convinced that serious problems are emerging because of the increase in persons serving long-term and life sentences. According to Zubrycki (1984), this concern focuses mainly on the effects that life sentences have on the system as well as the inmate. It is generally believed that there is a growing core of inmates who feel hopeless and desperate, and who have nothing to lose by using violence or even murdering again in attempts to escape. It is feared that, as this population increases, violence will become more frequent, and special measures will be needed to maintain control, so that a harsher and more vindictive environment will result.

Flanagan (1982) points out two principal characteristics of this inmate population that pose considerable challenges to corrections and correctional policy. The first characteristic has to do with the extremely diverse character of long-term inmates. They range from career criminals whose lives have revolved around the commission of criminal acts to persons who are not likely ever again to be involved in a serious criminal act. Second, the heinous nature of the crimes committed by this population group makes these inmates a highly controversial public concern. Flanagan suggests that the public is unlikely to approve of programs that appear to take a lenient stance or to put the public further at risk.

These characteristics, the diversity of the population and the nature of their crimes, will tax the imagination and resources of the correctional system, according to Flanagan (1982). They pose the greatest need for variety and diversity in policy making and programming, yet they are the least desirable beneficiaries of flexibility, from a political or public perspective.

Many issues emerge from the dilemma created by the long-term offender. Some of these have to do with the fundamental philosophy of imprisonment. For instance, Haley (1984) suggests that Canadian legislation generally construes imprisonment as a loss of liberty for a specified period of time. In other words, the punitiveness of a sentence has generally been gauged by its length and not by the effects, intended or unintended, of being in a prison. The emphasis on the time dimension means that little direction is given as to what is to be done to offenders within the prison environment. In situations where the term of imprisonment is literally not known, the problem of what to do is even more difficult.

Even when the length of an imposed sentence is known, it is clear that the sentence involves more than simply a loss of liberty for that specified period of time. A prison is an environment which contributes to the punishment. Thus authorities like Flanagan (1982) and Cheatwood (1985) suggest that the psychological effect of endless punishment, for both the offender and prison personnel, becomes more problematic as the long-term population group increases.

It is worth noting here that, while this discussion has linked the problem of the long-term offender with the issue of capital punishment, there is a growing body of literature which explores this problem from a variety of perspectives. For a sample of recent Canadian literature, see Gendreau and Bonta 1984 and 1985; Mohr 1985; Palmer 1984; Suedfeld et al. 1982; and Wormith 1985a and 1985b.

The cycles of decisions within the capital punishment debate will continue to create problems for corrections. As the right of the state to take a life is affirmed and then denied, the population base of correctional systems changes in a way that is extremely destabilizing. The effects of this debate on correctional operations in Canada will be quite important in the near future, as well as in the long term.

Sexually Transmitted Diseases

The management of persons who are segregated by sex in closed institutions has, as noted earlier, presented persistent problems. These problems are exacerbated to the degree that the environment promotes homosexual behaviour, either because of the unusual or unnatural pressures created by these types of institutions, or because these institutions include disproportionate numbers of persons whose lifestyle is either homosexually or bisexually oriented, or which is or has been conducive to acquiring and transmitting sexually transmitted diseases.

These issues and related problems have become more significant and pressing since 1980. The spiralling incidence of a sexually transmitted disease known ˙as Acquired Immune Deficiency Syndrome (AIDS) has created demands for a review of policy and practice not only within prisons, but within all types of closed institutions, as well as medical and dental facilities, law enforcement agencies, and para-medical units. This disease is having the effect of reorienting social attitudes about sexuality and sexual behaviour, and is generally regarded as being an important factor in both immediate and long-term social and institutional changes. The correctional system, as is usually the case, has become a microcosm of our society, in its response to this disease.

The correctional literature addressing the problem of AIDS has increased significantly since 1983. Correctional organizations have been responding to the demands for policy on AIDS-related issues in a variety of ways. For example, the state of California has established a policy of placing all persons under its jurisdiction who are diagnosed as having AIDS in a single medical facility (National Council on Crime and Delinquency 1985b). In Canada, the Ontario Ministry of Correctional Services has produced a handbook entitled "AIDS — Information and Guidelines for Correctional Employees" (Ministry of Correctional Services 1986).

Generally, the literature addresses the subject of AIDS in the correctional context as follows:

1. Some attempt has been made to describe the rate of incidence. For instance, the Ministry of Correctional Services in Ontario reported that, in 1986, there were 16 suspected cases of AIDS within the Ministry's prisons. In the United States, the confirmed cumulative total of AIDS cases in federal, state and local prisons and jails in March 1987 was 1,232 (National Council on Crime and Delinquency 1987a).

   A study by the National Institute for Justice in 1986 stated that the rate of increase of AIDs within the prison system was somewhat less than in the nation's population as a whole. This study indicated that 254 people had died of AIDS in federal, state or local institutions during the eleven months of the study. It found that most inmates had acquired the disease before entering the system, and the authors speculated that the disease was passed between inmates in the institutions only infrequently.

2. Much of the current literature concentrates on the fears

expressed by correctional staff about handling inmates with AIDS. These fears have become extreme in some cases, with line officers refusing to conduct body searches or otherwise participate in activities involving intimate contact. Many correctional facilities in the United States and Canada are now conducting educational programs on AIDS for both employees and inmates.

3. There is considerable discussion on the policy questions being generated by the increasing incidence of this disease. The study by the National Institute for Justice did identify a trend toward selective screening of homosexuals, intravenous drug users, and prostitutes.

Homosexual activity and intravenous drug use are means by which AIDS is spread. Both of these activities are contrary to regulations in correctional systems, so that there is considerable discussion about the means by which AIDS may be prevented. The distribution of condoms and even sterile intravenous needles in correctional institutions has been discussed. At the time of this writing, New York and Vermont had policies to allow inmates access to condoms through consultation with medical personnel. It was decided to handle these consultations confidentially, in the belief that "the safety and security of the institution is not threatened by such a policy" (National Council on Crime and Delinquency 1987b). These and other policy matters will continue to occupy the attention of correctional administrators in the near future.

According to an article by Ann Mullens (Vancouver *Sun*, June 13, 1987), AIDS "will be the most significant health factor in modern times, changing not only the way that people relate to each other sexually, but having both subtle and outright effects on art, literature, film, fashion, music, commerce and all other aspects of society and popular culture." If correctional programs are reflective of society's larger concerns about public safety and social welfare, then some serious questions emerge about the role of correctional institutions in relation to the AIDS phenomenon. To what degree should prisons be used to assist in the prevention and control of AIDS? Should prisons be used as sites for compulsory testing? If inmates are identified as having been exposed to the AIDS virus, should they be classified to separate institutions? If persons are diagnosed as having the disease, either on admission or prior to release, should they be released into the community at the expiration of their sentence without further restrictions?

As stated earlier in Chapter 1, the criminal justice system is intended to achieve a fair dispensation of justice by preventing the arbitrary application of group power. The AIDS phenomenon is one more example of a social factor which forces the system to make difficult decisions, while at the same time attempting to remain fair and non-arbitrary. It would appear that Ann Mullens' prediction about the significance of AIDS to society in general will apply specifically to corrections as well.

CONCLUSION

If we were to imagine an ideal Canadian correctional system for the future, it would be based on a criminal law which was "reflective of and responsive to evolving public attitudes and values" (Government of Canada 1982, 10). An act of commission or omission would only be regarded as criminal if it involved "culpable conduct that causes or threatens serious harm." Within the dispositions available to the court in sentencing on criminal matters, a range of options would be available to proportion punishment in accordance with the *degree* of harm done. And sentencing would be standardized to the degree that courts would be provided with guidelines for the purpose of

> Assuring fairness and predictability in sentencing while maintaining the flexibility needed to take into account certain aggravating and mitigating factors. . .
>
> Establishing means of evaluating the effectiveness of sentencing policy. . .
>
> Preventing increased demand on prison capacity or increased average time served in prison as a result of the use of such policies . . . (Heads of Corrections 1982, 17).

It is to be hoped that the Canadian correctional system of the future will seek to improve its capacity to acquire information both internally and through association with independent investigators. Moreover, it is to be desired that corrections will seek to apply this information to policy making in a way consistent with the requirement for public accountability and efficiency in the delivery of correctional services.

Additionally, administrative and managerial responsibility for corrections will evolve toward a unified, provincially based system of operational control, with a clearer distinction between the federal responsibility for the development of standards in operational practice and the provincial responsibility for the provision of programs and services.

Finally, the trends discussed in the previous chapters will

continue to have an influence on corrections programs. The current overcrowding of Canadian prisons, resulting in part from the economy and related social conditions, will primarily serve to revitalize and expedite the drive to establish alternatives based on reparative principles, including changes in law which make alternative dispositions available to the court (see, for example, *Sentencing Reform: A Canadian Approach,* Report of the Canadian Sentencing Commission 1987). Where new prisons are developed, there is likely to be careful consideration of questions of purpose and utility in both size and design.

These are relatively safe predictions for the future of Canadian corrections and they represent a logical progression of trends already underway. While it may be predicted that these trends will continue, it is more difficult to anticipate the cycle of reactions which will undoubtedly have an effect on both the timing related to the achievement of their results and the changes in emphasis which the trends can be expected to experience. With regard to the American context, Thomas Murton (cited in Levine et al. 1980, 341) stated in 1978:

> Prison reform across the country is dead . . . The law-and-order folks have spawned a new breed of writers who have rushed into print acknowledging the futility of reform and, instead, have advocated a return to longer sentences, more punishment—consequently, less humanization of the confined. And they shall prevail for a time. Prevail until the cost of new prisons becomes prohibitive, the harshness of the law once again becomes self-defeating, and the cycle of change is complete.

Murton's comment reminds us that there are cycles of action and reaction through which trends in correctional policy and practice move. Correctional history teaches us that rarely, if ever, is a trend totally nullified by reactions to it or by social and economic conditions which run counter to it. However, the cycles of action and reaction do have the effect of modifying trends and often delaying the implementation of programs which support them. This situation is particularly frustrating to correctional reformers. Furthermore, it explains why the previous chapters in this book have distinguished between the process of reform and its results. Nonetheless, there have been changes in Canadian corrections with regard to both policy and practice; as with any social institution, change is inexorable and will continue. But questions remain: how do we perceive the changes which are occurring? and, having perceived them, how do we value them? and, having evaluated them, how do we influence their direction?

Perhaps the most difficult factors to predict in relation to the future of corrections and criminal justice in general are those factors which will contribute to the nature of crime in the future. Chappell (1981, 3-4) makes the following assertion:

> No criminologist can reasonably assert that the next century will be crime free. Such a utopian state is simply inconceivable — every society requires some form of regulation to control the conduct of its members and sanctions for those who breach the prescribed rules. Crime, as the sociologist Emile Durkheim has asserted, is a "social fact" which is present to a greater or lesser degree in any community. The nature and extent of crime in the next century is likely to depend on a combination of the following factors: population growth and density; political and cultural stability; moral, religious and allied values; and, technology developments.

Many commentators have speculated about the factors which will influence crime in the future: demographic changes, increased urbanization, advancing technology, changes in family life, changes in the role of women in society, and crises in government. Added to this list (or perhaps resulting from it) are trends in white-collar crime, computer crime, environmental crime, and political terrorism. The ability to assess these trends, and to develop criminal justice and correctional responses to them will be critical to the future of corrections both in Canada and elsewhere. Canada and elsewhere.

What is probably most important is the attitude and perspective which is taken with regard to the future. Charles Friel (1980, 16-17), in a paper titled "The Lessons of Corinth, Sparta, and Athens: Thoughts on the Future of Justice," offers the following observations:

> There are many other forecasts that might be made about problems which will encroach upon the justice community in the future. Whether these forecasts are correct is secondary to whether they evoke in the reader some sense of the changing times and the realization that the odds of tomorrow being like yesterday are approaching zero.
>
> How should the justice community prepare for this evolving future? Should we follow Corinthian leaders who say that crime is crime and what works now is OK for the future? Can we afford to remain content with current laws, policies and procedures moving into a capricious future like a bubble borne on the wind? If the times don't change, then the Corinthian solution is efficient. If they do change, the solution of Corinth will lead us to obsolescence without ever knowing that the bubble has burst.
>
> The Spartan solution is most appealing when the future seems menacing, as evidenced by the flourishing of European fascism in the uncertainty of the great depression. As energy and inflation supersede crime as major political issues it is natural for those in the justice

community to rattle sabers and bicker over diminishing public support and sparse resources. Spartans decry the movement of national interest away from crime, feeling isolated by the lack of attention. They call for a return to the basics, agitate Congress and the statehouses for more money to make things like they used to be. The Spartan solution does not lead, it takes away, coveting political and financial turf in a zero-sum game of dwindling proportions.

What remains is the Athenian solution. It begins with the recognition that progress, invention, and creativity are the products of external adversity and that within limits, the greater the adversity, the greater the opportunity for hellenization. Like the two-faced god Janus who could see both past and future, the Athenian senses when the times change and has the humility and vision to see the alternative futures ahead. When beset by the fears of an unknown future, he does not buy his head like the Corinthian, but sets aside the technologies, laws, and practices of today for those befitting a new and different future. Unlike the spartan, he doesn't argue over his share of the pie, but asks why the pie can't be made bigger or if eating pie is even relevant.

As Winston Churchill once noted, the measure of a civilization is seen in its response to crime and offenders. It is probably fair to argue that the correctional enterprise of the future will be a measure of the degree to which Canadian society has progressed in its pursuit of a free and just society that provides equality before the law for all of its members.

References

Bartollas, C. and S.J. Miller. 1978. *Correctional Administration: Theory and Practice.* New York: McGraw-Hill.

Camp, Camille and George Camp. 1985. "Correctional Privatization in Perspective." 62 *The Prison Journal. 14-31.*

Canadian Sentencing Commission. 1987. *Sentencing Reform: A Canadian Approach.* Ottawa: Minister of Supply and Services.

Chappell, D. 1981. "Crime in the Twenty-First Century." Unpublished paper. Burnaby, B.C.: Department of Criminology, Simon Fraser University.

Cheatwood, Derral. 1985. "Capital Punishment and Corrections: Is There an Impending Crisis?" 28 *Crime and Delinquency.* 82-95.

Clifford, W. (June) 1982. "Criminal Justice System Outmoded." 3 *Australian Institute of Criminology Quarterly.* 7.

Cohn, A.W. (September) 1970. "Contemporary Correctional Practice: Science or Art?" 34 *Federal Probation* 20-23.

Ekstedt, J.W. and R. Montz. 1974. *Corrections Planning — An Overview.* Victoria: Ministry of the Attorney General.

Ekstedt, J.W. 1979. "New Directions in the Administration of Justice and Corrections, Province of British Columbia, Canada." In *Proceedings of the Fourth International SEARCH Symposium.* Sacramento, California. SEARCH Group Inc. 37-40.

_____. (Summer) 1980. "Policing in the Twenty-First Century." 2 *British Columbia Police Journal.* 7-10.

Elias, G.L. 1982. "A Policy-Oriented Approach to Forecasting Jail Populations." In *Proceedings of the National Workshop on Prison Population Forecasting.* Washington, D.C.: U.S. Department of Justice. 61-106.

Elliston, F. and N. Bowie. 1982. *Ethics, Public Policy, and Criminal Justice.* Cambridge, Mass.: Oelgeschlager, Gunn and Hain.

Elvin, Jan. 1985. "A Civil Liberties View of Private Persons." 65 *Prison Journal.* 48-52.

Epstein, H. 1982. "The Anticipated Effect of the Canadian Charter of Rights and Freedoms on Discretion in Corrections." In *The National Parole Board Report on the Conference on Discretion in the Correctional System.* Ottawa: National Parole Board.

Evans, D.G. (Fall) 1981. "Management: A Lesson Learned." 1 *Corrections Options.* 7-11.

Flanagan, Timothy J. 1982. "Correctional Policy and The Long Term Prisoner." 28 *Crime and Delinquency.* 82-95.

Fox, V. 1983. *Correctional Institutions.* Englewood Cliffs, N.J.: Prentice-Hall.

Friel, C.M. 1980. "The Lessons of Corinth, Sparta and Athens: Thoughts on the Future of Justice." In *Proceedings of the Fourth International SEARCH Symposium.* Sacramento, California, May, 1979. SEARCH Group Inc.

Gandy, John and Lorna Hurl. 1987. "Private Sector Involvement in Prison Industries: Options and Issues." 29 *Canadian Journal of Criminology.* 185-204.

Garabedian, P.G. (January) 1971. "Research and Practice in Planning Correctional Change." 17 *Crime and Delinquency.* 41-55.

Gendreau, Paul and James Bonta. 1984. "Solitary Confinement is Not Cruel and Unusual Punishment: People Sometimes Are." 26 *Canadian Journal of Criminology.* 467-478.

_____. 1985. "The Cruel and Unusual Punishment of Solitary Confinement: A Challenge for Liberal Ideology." 27 *Canadian Journal of Criminology.* 369-371.

Glaser, D. (September) 1975. "Achieving Better Questions: A Half-Century's Progress in Correctional Research." 39 *Federal Probation.* 3-9.

Government of Canada. 1982. *The Criminal Law in Canadian Society: Highlights.* Ottawa: Supply and Services Canada.

Griffiths, C.T. 1987. *Electronic Monitoring of Offenders: The Application of High Technology In Corrections.* Tokyo: United Nations and Far East Institute for the Prevention of Crime and the Treatment of Offenders.

Haley, Hugh J. 1984. "Does the Law Need to Know the Effects of Imprisonment?" 26 *Canadian Journal of Criminology.* 479-491.

Heads of Corrections (Canada). 1982. "Criminal Law Review: Joint Submission of Heads of Corrections." Unpublished paper. Ottawa.

Heijder, A. (January) 1980. "Can We Cope With Alternatives?" 26 *Crime and Delinquency.* 1-9.

Levine, J.P., M.C. Musheno and D.J. Palumbo. 1980. *Criminal Justice: A Public Policy Approach.* New York: Harcourt, Brace and Jovanovich.

Lightman, Ernie S. 1982. "The Private Employer and the Prison Industry." 22 *The British Journal of Criminology.* 36-47.

Manning, P.K. (July-August) 1979. "The Reflexivity and Facticity of Knowledge: Criminal Justice Research in the 1970s." 22 *American Behavioral Scientist*. 697-732.

Mason, Gary and Neal Hall. (March 25) 1987. "Electronic Shackle called Big Brother." Vancouver *Sun*.

Ministry of Correctional Services. (Jan.) 1986. "Guidelines on AIDS available to staff." 14 *Correctional Up-date*. 1.

Mohr, J.W. 1985. "Long-Term Incarceration." 27 *Canadian Journal of Criminology*. 497-501.

Mullens, Anne. (June 13) 1987. "Everything from culture to commerce will change." Vancouver *Sun*.

National Council on Crime and Delinquency. (March) 1987a. "254 Prison and Jail Inmates Died of AIDS in 11-Month Period." 18 *Criminal Justice Newsletter*. 7-8.

_____. (May) 1987b. "Vermont, New York City to Provide Inmates with Condoms." 18 *Criminal Justice Newsletter*. 4-5.

_____ (Feb.) 1985a. "Controversial ACA Policy Calls for Further 'Privatization'." 16 *Criminal Justice Newsletter*. 1-3.

_____. (Oct.) 1985b. "Tough New Problem for Institutions: Inmates with AIDS." 16 *Criminal Justice Newsletter*. 1-2.

_____. (Oct.) 1985c. "Electronic Monitoring of Probationers on the Increase." 16 *Criminal Justice Newsletter*. 1-3.

National Joint Committee of the CACP and FCS. (Fall) 1986. "Electronic Monitoring as a Tool for Community Supervision." 5 *Contact* (no. 1). Ottawa: Ministry of the Solicitor General.

Palmer, William R.T. 1984. "Programming for Long-Term Inmates: A New Perspective." 26 *Canadian Journal of Criminology*. 439-457.

Robbins, Ira P. 1986. "Privatization of Corrections: Defining the Issues." 69 *Judicature*. 324-331.

Roberts, David J. and Judith A. Ryder. 1987. *New Technologies in Criminal Justice: An Appraisal*. California: Search Group Inc.

Shover, N. 1979. *A Sociology of American Corrections*. Homewood, Illinois: The Dorsey Press.

Solicitor General of Canada. (March) 1985. "Prisons for Profit." 11 *Liaison*. 11-19.

Suedfeld, Peter, Carmenza Ramirez, John Deaton, and Gloria Baker-Brown. 1982. "Reactions and Attributes of Prisoners in Solitary Confinement." 9 *Criminal Justice and Behavior*. 303-340.

Tarnopolsky, W. 1982. "The Anticipated Effect of The Canadian Charter of Rights and Freedoms on Discretion in Corrections." In *The National Parole Board Report on the Conference on Discretion in the Correctional System*. Ottawa: National Parole Board.

Task Force on the Creation of an Integrated Canadian Corrections Service. 1977. *The Role of Federal Corrections in Canada*. Ottawa: Supply and Services Canada.

Thomas, C.W. and D.M. Peterson. 1977. *Prison Organization and Inmate Subcultures*. Indianapolis, Indiana: Bobbs-Merrill.

van den Haag, E. 1982. "Punishment as a Device for Control in the Crime Rate." In F. Elliston and N. Bowie (eds.) *Ethics, Public Policy, and Criminal Justice.* Cambridge, Mass: Oelgeschlager, Gunn and Hain. 195-218.

Waldo, G.P. 1973. "Research in Correctional Education." In A.R. Roberts (ed.) *Readings in Prison Education.* Springfield, Illinois: Charles C. Thomas. 364-76.

Waller, I. 1982. "Public Policy on Crime and Criminal Justice: Who Does and Who Should Determine It." In F. Elliston and N. Bowie (eds.) *Ethics, Public Policy, and Criminal Justice.* Cambridge, Mass: Oelgeschlager, Gunn and Hain. 353-69.

Wormith, J.S. 1985a. "Long-Term Prison Impact in Canadian Penitentiaries." Paper presented at the American Society of Criminology, 37th Annual Meeting, San Diego, California. November 13-17.

_____. 1985b. "Long-Term Incarceration — Data and Reason Meet Ideology and Rhetoric." 27 *Canadian Journal of Criminology.* 349-357.

Zubrycki, Richard M. 1984. "Long-Term Incarceration in Canada." 26 *Canadian Journal of Criminology.* 397-402.

Appendix A

Chronology of Events in Canadian Corrections

1754 to 1867

1754   The first Canadian workhouse constructed in Nova Scotia

1791   *Constitutional Act* passed, dividing country into the provinces of Upper and Lower Canada, both of which utilize the English criminal law

1792   First Parliament of Upper Canada passes an Act providing for the construction of a courthouse and a gaol in each district of the province

1800   Passage of the *Act of 1800,* lessening the severity of punishments for many criminal offences

1826   Proposal to construct a penitentiary in Canada first presented in the House of Assembly in Upper Canada

1831   Report of H.C. Thomson documenting the need for a penitentiary accepted by the House of Assembly

1832   Report of the Commissioners on Penitentiaries, issued by H.C. Thomson and J. Macauly, recommends construction of a penitentiary premised on the Auburn model

1834   Recommendations of Thomson and Macauly embodied in the *Penitentiary Act of 1834*

1835   First Canadian Penitentiary opens at Kingston, Ontario

1838   *Act of 1838,* passed by Parliament of Upper Canada, is first attempt to legislate control over the local goals

1848   Appointment of a Royal Commission of Inquiry to investigate charges of corruption at Kingston (Brown)

1851   *Penitentiary Act* enacted providing for reforms within the Kingston penitentiary, including an end to practice of allowing the public to buy admittance to view the inmates

1857   *Prison Inspection Act* passed providing for the construction of a separate facility for insane convicts and the building of a reformatory for young offenders

1867 to 1900

1867   Passage of the *British North America Act*

1868   Department of Justice created and given responsibility for federal penitentiaries

        Penitentiary Act passed, bringing the pre-Confederation prisons in Kingston, Halifax, and St. John under federal jurisdiction, thereby creating the federal penitentiary system

        Province of Ontario passes *Prison and Asylum Inspection Act* providing for the inspection of provincial gaols; this is one of the first attempts by a province following Confederation to reform local gaols

1875   Supreme Court of Canada created

1880   Completion of the first federal penitentiary construction program: St. Vincent de Paul (1873), Stony Mountain (1876), and the B.C. Penitentiary (1878)

1886   An *Act Respecting Public and Reformatory Prisons* is passed which provides for the operation of provincial correctional facilities

        Penitentiary Act passed providing for federal-provincial agreements relating to the transfer of prisoners and giving provinces the authority to establish prisons for offenders under provincial jurisdiction

1889   *Act to Permit the Conditional Release of First Offenders in Certain Cases* provides for the release of offenders on their own recognizance on "probation of good conduct"

1891   The *Report of the Commissioners Appointed to Enquire into the Prison and Reformatory System of the Province of Ontario* under the Chairmanship of J.W. Langmuir documents the continuing problems of provincial and local institutions, including the lack of classification, poor physical facilities, and inadequate management

1892   First Canadian *Criminal Code* enacted

1898   *Act to Provide for the Conditional Liberation of Penitentiary Convicts (Ticket of Leave Act)* establishes parole

1900 to 1960

1905   First Dominion Parole Officer appointed

1906   Passage of the *Penitentiary Act* includes provisions for appointment of a parole officer, conditions for earned remission, and outlines the powers of prison inspectors

1934   Kingston Penitentiary for Women opens

1936   Royal Commission on the Penal System of Canada (Archambault) is appointed to investigate federal prisons

1938   Report of the Archambault Commission recommends reform of the federal prison system

1945   "Rule of Silence" abolished in federal institutions

1955   Federal *Criminal Code* is entirely revised

1956   *Report on a Commission Appointed to Inquire into the Principles and Procedures Followed in the Remission Service of the Department of Justice of Canada* (Fauteux) recommends adoption of philosophy of rehabilitation

1958   The *Parole Act,* replacing the *Ticket of Leave Act,* establishes the National Parole Board. The *Act* gives the Board exclusive jurisdiction to grant, refuse, or revoke parole. The authority of the NPB extends to all federal inmates and to provincial inmates in provinces that do not subsequently create their own parole boards

1960 to Present

1961   A new *Penitentiary Act* is passed, establishing procedures for the operation of penitentiaries, authorizing statutory remission and the granting of temporary absences, and permitting the transfer of inmates

1963   "Ten-Year Plan" for penitentiary construction is initiated and ten new prisons of varying size and security classifications are subsequently built

1966   The *Government Organization Act* is passed, creating the Ministry of the Solicitor General of Canada, responsible for federal police, penitentiaries, and parole

1968   First Community Correctional Centre opens in Montreal, accommodating a small number of inmates on day parole

1969   Canadian Committee on corrections (Ouimet) presents recommendations for the development of a unified federal justice system

        Day Parole is created through an amendment to the *Parole Act*

        The Living Unit concept, based on a therapeutic community model, is initiated on an experimental basis and subsequently adopted in federal penitentiaries

1970   Amendments to the *Parole Act* provide mandatory supervision for inmates released prior to the completion of their sentence under earned remission and who were not granted a parole

1971   Bail reform legislation enacted which is designed to reduce the interference with freedom of persons awaiting trial and to encourage the use of summonses in place of incarceration

Working Group on Federal Maximum Security Institutions (Mohr), a joint effort of the Canadian Criminology and Corrections Association and the Canadian Penitentiary Service, is established to make recommendations to the Solicitor General concerning accommodation for federal maximum security inmates

Restrictions and censorship of inmate correspondence is reduced and provision is made for inmates to correspond with a wide range of individuals outside the prison

Program to expand inmate visiting rights initiated and the restrictions surrounding family visits are reduced

Solicitor General initiates contracts with private, non-profit organizations to operate Community-Based Residential Centres (CRC's or CBRC's) to accommodate federal offenders. By 1980, there are 123 CRC's operating

1972   Corporal punishment (whipping) as a punishment for disciplinary offences in federal penitentiaries is abolished

Absolute and conditional discharge and the intermittent sentence (less than 90 days) are introduced as sentencing options

Treasury Board authorizes the Solicitor General to enter into agreements with provincial and after-care agencies for federal case preparation and parole supervision services. Under these agreements, provincial correctional agencies and private sector organizations conduct community assessments and supervise inmates released on full parole, day parole, mandatory supervision, or unescorted temporary absences

Advisory Board of Psychiatric Consultants (Chalke) is appointed to advise the Solicitor General on treatment of mentally ill offenders; Board recommends the establishment of Regional Psychiatric Centres and provides a policy on psychiatric care for federal inmates

First Regional Psychiatric Centre opens to provide treatment for federal offenders who are mentally ill and/or emotionally disturbed

Task Force on Community-Based Residential Centres (Outerbridge) recommends that the federal and provincial governments encourage the development of CRC's

1973   Task Force on the Release of Inmates (Hugessen) examines the procedures for the release of offenders from institutions prior to the completion of their sentence. Recommendations create five regional parole boards at the federal level and provide for the appointment of part-time board members

First federal Correctional Investigator is appointed to act as a "prison ombudsman" and make recommendations on prisoner's complaints

Federal-Provincial Conference on Corrections develops mechanisms for a coordinated approach to correctional issues including the creation of the Continuing Committee of Deputy Ministers Responsible for Corrections

1974   The Continuing Committee of Deputy Ministers Responsible for Corrections creates a special Federal-Provincial Steering Committee on Inmates' Rights and Responsibilities and establishes the National Advisory Network on Correctional Manpower Training

Creation of five regional districts of federal parole system

National Consultation Team (Sheppard) examines the feasibility of employing offenders in the criminal justice system

1975   The National Conference and the Federal-Provincial Conference on Native Peoples and the Criminal Justice System recommends more involvement of native Indians in the delivery of justice services to native people

Continuing Committee of Deputy Ministers Responsible for Corrections establishes the Federal-Provincial Task Force on Long-Term Objectives for Corrections in Canada

The Study Group on Dissociation (Vantour) examines the use of three types of dissociation: protective custody, punitive dissociation, and administrative segregation, and recommends the creation of guidelines for the use of each

1976   Creation of the position of National Consultant on Natives and the Criminal Justice System in the Ministry of the Solicitor General

Capital punishment is abolished by a free vote in Parliament and is replaced by a mandatory sentence of life imprisonment. Mandatory sentences of 25 years minimum are introduced for certain types of crimes

Bill C-51, the Peace and Security Bill, is enacted in an attempt to reduce violent crime and creates the category of "dangerous offenders" who could be subjected to indeterminate prison sentences

1977   Amendment to the *Parole Act* allows provinces to create their own parole boards with jurisdiction over most provincial inmates

The Temporary Absence program is expanded to include both escorted and unescorted TA's

Statutory remission, under which an offender automatically received a remission of one-quarter of the sentence, is abolished and replaced by a system of earned remission through "good time" which is earned by good conduct and which may be forfeited by misconduct

The Metis and Non-Status Indian Crime and Justice Commission reports on the over-representation of native offenders in federal and provincial institutions and recommends the involvement of natives in the development of correctional policy

Task Force on the Role of the Private Sector in Criminal Justice (Sauvé) recommends that government involve the private sector in program planning, policy development, and in the legislative process

Parliamentary Sub-Committee on the Penitentiary

System in Canada (MacGuigan) inquires into the operation of federal maximum security institutions making 65 recommendations for reform

Response of the Solicitor General to the Parliamentary Sub-Committee Report on the Penitentiary System in Canada endorses the principles of the MacGuigan report and accepts the majority of the recommendations

Task Force on the Creation of an Integrated Canadian Corrections Service recommends the merger of the National Parole Service with the Canadian Penitentiary Service into an organization called the Correctional Service of Canada. The Task Force also concludes that rehabilitation is an unrealistic goal of incarceration and that incarceration *per se* should constitute the sole punishment for offenders sentenced to prison. Calls for the development of an "opportunities model"

First Special Handling Unit, designed to hold inmates with a history of violence, opens at Millhaven Penitentiary in Kingston, Ontario

Criminal Law Amendment Act provides for *(1)* the appointment of regional community members to the National Parole Board, *(2)* the appointment of temporary board members, and *(3)* clarifying the guidelines for granting of unescorted temporary absences

National Advisory Committee on the Female Offender (Clark) emphasizes the need for more community-based residences, recommends the closing of the Kingston Prison for Women and proposes that the federal government construct small facilities for female offenders in each region of the country or grant authority for housing federal female offenders to the provinces

The Canadian Association for the Prevention of Crime (formerly the Canadian Criminology and Corrections Association) is established as a liaison between federal corrections and the private sector

1978   Inmate committees are established in federal institutions

The National Planning Committee on the Female

Offender is created by the Continuing Committee of Deputy Ministers Responsible for Corrections to assess the Clark (1977) report. Planning Committee's report supports the closure of Kingston Prison for Women and creation of regional facilities

The Joint Committee to Study Alternatives for the Housing of the Federal Female Offender recommends that the federal government purchase the Vanier institution for use as a central facility for housing federal female offenders and that a co-correctional facility be created at Mission Institution in British Columbia

Transfer of Offenders Act permits Canadian offenders confined in other countries to be transferred back to Canada and foreign offenders to be transferred from Canadian jurisdiction to their native country

The National Associations Active in Criminal Justice becomes a major channel of communication between the federal government and non-government organizations on corrections issues

1979   An independent role is established for the Citizen Advisory Committees attached to federal correctional institutions

The position of National Coordinator for Native Offender Programs is created to develop national policy on native inmates and parolees

1980   Introduction of a 12-week, full-time training course with a 24-month probationary period for all correctional officer recruits

Family visiting program is initiated at Millhaven Maximum Security prison under which inmates with long sentences can spend up to three days with family members in home-like setting

Working Group on Conditional Release examines temporary absences, day parole, full parole, earned remission, and mandatory supervision and makes specific recommendations

1982   Bill S-32 is introduced by the Solicitor General of Canada, proposing amendments to provisions governing mandatory supervision

1983   The Solicitor General of Canada places before the Senate Committee on Legal and Constitutional Affairs draft legislation to create a specific power to "gate" federal offenders

1984   The Royal Prerogative of Mercy is extended to remove the habitual criminal status of individuals sentenced before the law was repealed in 1977. Habitual criminal legislation was enacted by Parliament in 1947 through amendments to the *Criminal Code*. A person found to be a habitual criminal could be sentenced to preventive detention (an indeterminate sentence), and thus could be imprisoned for life

1984   The report from the Correctional Investigator on his inquiry into allegations of mistreatment of inmates at Archambault Institution is published by the Solicitor General of Canada

1984   The National Victims Resource Centre is officially opened. The Centre was established in response to recommendations of the Federal-Provincial Task Force on Justice for Victims of Crime

1984   The Solicitor General of Canada releases the *Report of the Advisory Committee on the Management of Correctional Institutions in Canada* (Carson)

1984   The *Criminal Law Reform Act, 1984* (Bill C-19) brings forward important proposals for legislative reform in Canadian sentencing and a recommendation for a commission of inquiry to conduct an in-depth investigation of issues which could not be addressed by immediate legislative change. While Bill C-19 dies on the order paper in July, 1984, the Canadian Sentencing Commission is created in May, 1984. The Commission completes its inquiry and submits its proposals in February, 1987

1985 The Canadian Criminal Justice Association (formerly the Canadian Association for the Prevention of Crime) develops a set of standards for corrections in Canada. The standards are based on Canadian jurisprudence, and replace the standards, developed by the American Correctional Association, that were previously used by both federal and provincial correctional systems

1985 The Solicitor General of Canada introduces two new bills in the House of Commons. The bills give the National Parole Board the power to alter conditions of mandatory release and to make technical changes to the *Parole Act,* the *Penitentiary Act,* and the *Prisons and Reformatories Act.* Under the Conditional Release Bill, the National Parole Board has the authority to prevent the mandatory release of inmates believed to be dangerous

1986 The Correctional Service of Canada introduces the concept of Functional Unit Management, substantially altering the Living Unit Concept

1986 A five-level pay system for federal inmates is introduced. The daily wage earned is dependent upon the security level of the institution in which the inmate resides, as well as work performance

1987 A motion to reinstate the death penalty is defeated in a free vote in Parliament

1987 Following the conclusions of the Ministerial Task Force on Program Review, the responsibility for young offenders and firearms programs and policies is transferred from the Solicitor General of Canada to Justice Canada. The Solicitor General of Canada retains responsibility for federal policing, adult corrections, and parole

NOTE: Some of these events were excerpted from G. Woods and H. Sim. 1981. *Highlights of Federal Initiatives in Criminal Justice: 1966-1980.* Ottawa: Solicitor General of Canada. For an overview of recent events in corrections at the provincial level, see Canadian Centre for Justice Statistics 1966. *Correctional Services in Canada, 1985/86.* Ottawa: Supply and Services Canada.

Index

Royal Commission on the Penal
System of Canada (1938), *see*
Archambault
Royal Commission on the Status of
Women (1970, B.C.), 337
Royal Commission to Investigate the
State and Management of
Kingston Penitentiary (1914),
48-49
Ryerson, G., 44

S

St. Leonards Society of British
Columbia, 355-356
Salvation Army, 59, 60
San Francisco Project (parole study),
267
Schwartz, M.D., *see* Travis, L.F., et al.
Scott, F., 51-52
Scull, A.T., 25-26, 27-29, 31, 60-61,
257
Sechrest, L., et al., 248
security classifications (federal
institutions), 191
Seiter, R.P., 279
sentencing, 6-7
indeterminate, 243
objectives of, 71
Sexually Transmitted Diseases,
404-407
Sheridan, A.K.B., 57-58
Shoom, S., 35, 36, 38
Shover, N., 16, 18, 27, 112, 118,
119-120, 242, 289, 393
Silverstone, S., 285-286, 287, 288
Sim, H., 331
Singer, L.R., 6
Skinner, S., et al., 16, 23, 24, 45, 50
Smandych, R.C., 31-32
Smith, H., 37
social policy, 387-388
social science research, 119
special interest groups, 328-329
Splane, R.B., 22, 40
staff, correctional, *see* personnel,
correctional
Stony Mountain Institution (Man.),
41
Stookey, J.A., 352
Strong, M.K., 22
summary offences, 5
Swackhamer Commission (1972),
317

Sykes, G.M., 232
systems analysis, 151

T

Takagi, P., 25, 27
Task Force on Community-Based
Residential Centres
(Outerbridge, 1973), 256, 276
Task Force on Corrections (1976), 47
Task Force on the Creation of an
Integrated Canadian
Corrections Service (1977), 56,
322-323, 326, 327, 384
Task Force on the Release of Inmates
(Hugessen, 1981), 285, 288-289
Task Force on the Role of the Private
Sector in Criminal Justice
(1977), 259, 276, 322
Taylor, C.J., 30-31, 33, 34
Technological Innovations, 399-402
temporary absence programs, 83-84,
255, 268-271, 272
temporary absences, 269, 271
Theory X and Theory Y, 170, 174
therapeutic community, 204, 208-209
Thomas, C.W., 230-231, 236, 245, 394
Thomson, H.C., 32-33
Thorvaldson, S.A., 356-357
Ticket of Leave Act (1899), 59, 60, 320
Tittle, C.R., 242
training, *see* education; vocational
training programs
transition homes, *see*
community-based correctional
centres
Travis, L.F., et al., 237-238, 246, 248
treatment, correctional
appropriateness of, 246-247
as punishment, 247-248
delivery of, 229
differential, 221
ethics of, 247-249
modalities, 203-209
organizational context of, 229-241
programs, 189-228
criticism of, 238
evaluation of, 216-221
integrity of, 241-247
staff, 234-235
"two-year rule", 71-72
see also jurisdictional
responsibility